STEINER AND KINDRED SPIRITS

For Joseph,
philosopher,
spiritual seeker
and dear friend,

Affectionately,
Robert

STEINER and KINDRED SPIRITS

Robert McDermott

SteinerBooks | 2015

2015 | SteinerBooks

An imprint of Anthroposophic Press, Inc.

610 Main Street, Great Barrington, MA 01230

www.steinerbooks.org

Cover image: *Kindred Spirits* (1849) by Asher Brown Durand of the Hudson
River School. It depicts Thomas Cole with the poet William Cullen Bryant in
the Catskill Mountains. Book & cover design: William Jens Jensen

LIBRARY OF CONGRESS CONTROL NUMBER: 2015943252

ISBN: 978-1-62148-136-2 (paperback)
ISBN: 978-162148-137-9 (eBook)

Contents

Dedicated with gratitude to two communities—

friends devoted to Anthroposophy

and

faculty, students, and alumni of the

Philosophy, Cosmology, and Consciousness Program,

at the California Institute of Integral Studies

Preface

This preface and the first two chapters are intended as an introduction to the subsequent ten comparative chapters (3 to 12), which can then be read in any order. I have written all twelve chapters in an effort to convince students of Steiner that they benefit by gaining knowledge and appreciation of the "kindred spirits" with whom Steiner can be compared. I have written equally in an effort to convince readers of one or more of those kindred spirits that Steiner is worthy of their attention. Kindred spirits in this book include His Holiness the Dalai Lama, C. G. Jung, Teilhard de Chardin, Martin Buber, Sri Aurobindo, Rabindranath Tagore, Gandhians, feminists, and ecologists.

While thinking about this book before I began writing in January 2014, I used the title "Unique Not Alone: Steiner and Others." I recognized that, strictly speaking, the word *unique* does not permit a modifier—something is either unique or not—but among billions of unique persons, some have capacities shared by very few others and so are unique in some important ways. Because Steiner seems to anthroposophists to be extremely (uniquely) incomparable, there has been a tendency to keep him apart from comparisons, to keep him too much alone, a little too unique. Some of the thinkers in this book resist comparison with billions of other people but not with one another, and as this book tries to show, not entirely with Steiner. Just before publication, in consultation with the colleagues to whom this book is dedicated, I abandoned *unique* and replaced the generic word *others* with the more positive term, *kindred spirits*.

Throughout this book, I compare the life and ideas of Steiner with the lives and ideas of the "kindred spirits." They are the thinkers whom I imagine could have been his companions on the way to spiritual insight. I have never wanted to be someone who participates in every conversation by quoting and recommending Rudolf Steiner. Rather, I want to be—as I want this book to be—one who puts Steiner in relation to other major spiritual thinkers important for contemporary culture and for our individual spiritual seeking. Some chapters (especially those on social justice, feminism, and ecology) discuss groups of spiritual thinkers. The six primary figures with whom I am eager to compare Steiner—Sri Aurobindo, Teilhard de Chardin, the Dalai Lama, Martin Buber, C. G. Jung, and Rabindranath Tagore—did not contribute to as many fields as Steiner did. We should not look to Sri Aurobindo, Teilhard, or C. G. Jung for significant contributions to social justice, education, or ecology. For those chapters for which these six do not offer substantial comparisons, I have introduced other thinkers.

After the two introductory chapters ("Kindred Spirits" and "Steiner Alone") the remaining ten chapters present the thinking of twentieth- and twenty-first-century thinkers, followed by a discussion of Steiner. Each of these comparisons is intended to be free of "one-upmanship" and the kind of discipleship that pits one spiritual teacher, religious tradition, worldview, paradigm, or spiritual perspective against another. The entire book is an attempt to honor the conviction that love, truth, beauty, and justice (as well as their opposites) are to be found throughout the human community. No one individual and no one perspective— even Steiner's—can offer an adequate description of the human condition in its manifold expression. No matter how deep, vast, and trustworthy, no thinker, including Steiner, can be an adequate source of all the ideas, insights, inspiration, and solutions needed at any given time.

If this is so, why should anyone today take up the study of Anthroposophy in addition to, or instead of, one of many available old or new philosophies, religious traditions, or spiritual practices? Steiner is thought by anthroposophists to be a scientist and a philosopher, as well as an interpreter of events depicted in Christian scriptures, yet he is generally ignored by scientists and philosophers, as well as by both liberal and fundamentalist scriptural scholars and theologians.

Waldorf schools and biodynamic agriculture, both of which arose directly from Steiner's esoteric research and lectures, are increasingly admired but have not led to a widespread interest in the individual who generated them. Perhaps Steiner has been neglected because he knows (or claims to know) too much, and some of his claims are "too far out."

In reply, there is a mountain of evidence that the seemingly impossible does happen.[1] Individuals with serious illnesses have reportedly been cured directly by the intervention of Peruvian shamans, Hindu saints, and the waters at Lourdes. When faced with such evidence, some of us are interested in the event (What really happened?), some in the biographies (Who was cured and by whom?), and some in the source of the cure (What enabled this to happen?). Steiner spoke in detail about all three aspects of non-ordinary events, as well as seemingly ordinary events that he knew in non-ordinary ways. He focused on the places and points at which something or someone numinous (spiritual, awesome, and mysterious) affected, and continues to affect, seemingly ordinary reality.

Though he is comparable to great thinkers in their specialized areas, Steiner is singular in the depth and extent to which his thought is the result of an esoteric capability. He was apparently able to research beings, topics, and ideas ordinarily not available even to the "kindred spirits" in this book. Because of this capacity, whether referred to as *esoteric* (ordinarily inaccessible) or *clairvoyant* ("clear seeing"), Steiner is typically kept apart from these and other important spiritual and cultural thinkers, and to some extent he kept himself apart. Because he offers so many unusual ideas that have practical consequences and recommends so many spiritual practices that many experience as efficacious, followers of Steiner tend to think of him exclusively in terms of his uniqueness and not in terms of his similarities with other thinkers. As a result, Steiner and Anthroposophy tend to be kept in a box or silo or some similar metaphor, stressing his singularity and incomparability. This

---

1. See Stanislav Grof, *When the Impossible Happens: Adventures in Non-ordinary Realities.*

book is an attempt to explain ideas that show Steiner to be on his own as well as ideas that show him to share perspectives with "kindred spirits."

Each chapter assumes the ontology (real existence) of the heights and depths of consciousness described by religious and spiritual thinkers during the past one hundred years or so. Unavoidably personal and subjective, these chapters present multi-perspective claims from mountaintops of spiritual life down to the rest of us, as though at base camp. Unlike the skeptics who spend no time in a religious or spiritual base camp, I, and pre-sumably you, do spend time trying to understand messages from heights and depths, and occasionally, or perhaps habitually, we attempt a spiritual ascent ourselves. In my view, Steiner went as far up the spiritual ladder as any modern person I have found through books. Unlike some enthusiasts for Steiner, however, I am also impressed by other religious thinkers and spiritual prac-titioners who have made progress that can be helpful to those of us in need of encouragement and guidance by those whose ascents and descents perhaps permit certain vistas and insights not researched or explained by Steiner.

Since 1964, when I was appointed a professor of philosophy at Manhattanville College, New York, I have been teaching about many of the thinkers and ideas discussed in this book. Most of what I know about these thinkers, including Steiner, was initially from books and, subsequently, from thinking, writing, lecturing, and discussion. I have written this book as I teach and lecture; each chapter could be a three-hour seminar. I have tried to com-municate what I think is intellectually and spiritually edifying, what I am most eager for you, the reader, to consider for your thinking and your spiritual life. I read in order to teach, lecture, and write. To almost all of the authors from whom I have learned, I have contributed what I hope are improvements (owing to my desire to communicate their ideas in sensible, contemporary lan-guage) as well as what I fear are distortions (owing to the limita-tions of my age, gender, ethnicity, and ego). Some of my opinions on these thinkers are descriptive and probably unobjectionable but others are quite personal and assertive.

Although I have been writing and lecturing on Steiner for almost forty years, very few of my relatives or friends have read a book by or about Steiner or Anthroposophy. One readily recalls Owen Barfield's frustration that C. S. Lewis, Barfield's closest friend and colleague for forty years, similarly never read a book by or about Steiner. But this neglect is not true of my five CIIS colleague-friends with whom I teach in Philosophy, Cosmology, and Consciousness (PCC), the CIIS graduate program founded in 1994 by Richard Tarnas. I have jointly taught graduate courses on Steiner with Rick Tarnas (author of *The Passion of the Western Mind* and *Cosmos and Psyche*), with Brian Swimme (coauthor with Thomas Berry of *The Universe Story* and author and narrator of *The Journey of the Universe*), and with Sean Kelly (author of *Individuation and the Absolute* and *Coming Home: The Birth and Transformation of the Planetary Era*). These courses have enabled me to deepen my knowledge of many of the thinkers and fields I discuss in this book.

I have also learned from Jacob Sherman (coeditor with Jorge Ferrer of *The Participatory Turn: Spirituality, Mysticism, and Religious Studies,* and author of *Partakers of the Divine: Contemplation and the Practice of Philosophy*), and Elizabeth Allison (author of essays on ecology and religion, especially in the Himalayas). The influence of these colleague-friends, as well as PCC students, especially Matthew David Segall and Aaron Weiss, is evident throughout this book and in almost all of my thinking, teaching, and writing. It is an honor to dedicate this volume to these PCC colleagues. In so doing, I also wish to express my gratitude to other learned and generous colleague-friends, faculty, administrators, and students at CIIS, a university dedicated to integrating the intellectual and academic and a variety of spiritual teachings and practices.

May 2015
San Francisco

Acknowledgment of Assistance

Elizabeth Jennings copyedited and Jens Jensen designed this volume.

This volume benefitted from expert feedback on individual chapters from the following colleagues, to all of whom I am grateful:

Elizabeth Allison (Integral Ecologies; Divine Feminine and Feminism)

Joan Almon (Education)

Frederick Amrine (Steiner Alone)

Debashish Bannerji (Tagore, Gandhi, Sri Aurobindo, The Mother)

Penelope Baring (Christ; Spiritual Practice)

Carol Cole (Social Justice; Education)

Brian Gray (Philosophy of Freedom; Evolution of Consciousness)

Robert and Louise Hill (Spiritual Practice)

Terry Hipolito (entire manuscript)

Timothy Hoffman (Waldorf Education)

Sean Kelly (Integral Ecology)

Ellen McDermott (proofed the first and final draft)

R. P. (Ray) McDermott (American Philosophy)

Martin Ping (entire manuscript)

Matthew David Segall (Kindred Spirits)

Jacob Sherman (Philosophy; Spiritual Practice)

Jeremy Strawn (Biodynamic Farming)

Brian Thomas Swimme (Evolution of Consciousness; Thomas Berry)

Richard Tarnas (Evolution of Consciousness; Jung)

Aaron Weiss (His Holiness the Dalai Lama)

Kindred Spirits

The Possibility of Spiritual Knowledge

Because I believe that Rudolf Steiner is neither the only word nor the last word, this book is about the worldviews and insights contributed both by Steiner and by other thinkers (some of whom are also activists) who seem to me in some respects as deep as Steiner in the same fields, as well as more contemporary. This book assumes that more than one spiritual thinker is needed for anyone searching for light in a dark spiritual environment. Steiner was expert not only on the nature and causes of this darkness but also on its causes and the methods for its cure. He is a supreme guide for the healing of our individual lives and modern Western culture. Along with Jung, Steiner is a healer of the *anima mundi*, the increasingly sick soul of the world. But more than Jung, and more than any other thinker who is or could be included in a book comparing spiritual worldviews, Steiner's contributions run from truly arcane insights on obscure topics to contemporary methods of education, agriculture, and medicine. To his great credit, but at high risk, Steiner institutionalized his teachings, thereby allowing both followers and casual observers to exploit his insights for less ideal purposes than the ones that he served throughout his life. Overall, Steiner's contributions are clearly positive, but because their implementation has depended on others, thus far the results have been inadequate, even tragic, relative to their potential.

With so many great figures to inspire us, why focus on Rudolf Steiner? Why attend to a still-peripheral European esoteric teacher who died several generations ago? What can Rudolf Steiner add to C. G. Jung's profound analysis of the unconscious, or Teilhard de Chardin's union of science and spirituality, or the exalted words and exemplary lives of Mahatma Gandhi, Martin Luther King, Jr., and His Holiness the Dalai Lama? Or the ideas of Thomas Berry, Wangari Maathai, Joanna Macy, and other prophetic voices awakening us to impending ecological catastrophe and its solutions? The wisdom of all of these individuals is needed as we confront unprecedented challenges. Rudolf Steiner's contributions are vast, deep, and timely. He is needed for his insights, his selfless service to humanity, and the practical import of his research and counsel. He merits our attention because his thought and spiritual practice are profound and comprehensive, and have not yet received the serious attention they deserve.

In this book I have concentrated on thinkers whom I have studied, taught, and written about for several decades. As a result, I am convinced that their methods and insights are in one or more respects comparable to Steiner's as well as worth recommending on their own terms. These comparisons do not include any substantive criticisms of these thinkers, though critiques have been published on all of them, as well as, of course, on Rudolf Steiner. Along with making the case for Steiner, I also recommend a variety of methods, worldviews, and individual ideas. I affirm Steiner's abilities and contributions while showing that he was not alone in some of the problems he tried to solve, in some of his methods, and in some of his insights.

Steiner worked on many of the same problems, and offered insights, however differently articulated, comparable to those of Rabindranath Tagore, Sri Aurobindo and the Mother, Teilhard de Chardin, C. G. Jung, and the Dalai Lama, as well as a spiritual basis for democracy, human rights and dignity crucially developed by the civil rights and feminist movements of the past fifty years in the West. Steiner's teachings should be significant for anyone committed to the work of M. K. (Mahatma) Gandhi and Rev. Martin Luther King, Jr., to the South African Truth and Reconciliation Commission, and to the single most important challenge facing humanity, the ecological sustainability of Gaia. These thinkers I wish to compare with Steiner include the following, some more prominently than others:

Ralph Waldo Emerson, William James, and Josiah Royce, American philosophers

Martin Buber, philosopher of an I–Thou way of life

C. G. Jung, archetypal psychologist

Sri Aurobindo, Hindu poet, philosopher, teacher of Integral Yoga

Pierre Teilhard de Chardin, mystical scientist

His Holiness the Dalai Lama, Tibetan Buddhist exemplar of compassion

Scholars and devotees of the goddess Sophia

Rabindranath Tagore, Bengali poet, musician, educator, internationalist

M. K. (Mahatma) Gandhi and other exemplars of nonviolence

John Dewey's and Maria Montessori's insights concerning education

Thomas Berry, prophetic exponent of "The New Story"

Most of the comparisons between Steiner and these others have some spiritual content, though not very much esoteric content. There would be not much point in comparing Steiner's view of the human soul, or of human afterlife, or of Buddha or Christ, with a thinker who flatly denies spiritual knowledge or spiritual realities. Consequently, with few exceptions (e.g., John Dewey) the twenty or so thinkers brought into conversation with Rudolf Steiner in this book all affirm a height or depth dimension, broadly categorizable by the Buddhist term "Mahayana," the more expansive path, or, in the felicitous phrase of William James, "Something More."

This book summarizes and recommends a wide variety of religious and spiritual individuals, practices, and worldviews, along with various conceptions of the divine, the sacred, and spiritual ideas. A synonym for these words is *numen*, which literally means "a bow of the head," and by application, bowing to what is perceived to be a manifestation of the divine. In *The Idea of the Holy* (1923) Rudolf Otto extended the noun *numen* to the adjective *numinous*, "something bearing the character of a '*numen*.'"[1] Like the words *sacred* and *spiritual*, the word *numinous* is most use-

---

1. Rudolf Otto, *The Idea of the Holy*, 11.

ful as an adjective, but in my opinion all of the terms just intro-duced—*sacred, spiritual, holy,* and *numinous,* or *numinal*—can also be used as a noun in an effort to render it an objective reality. This book affirms and tries to point the reader to Spirit as well as spiritual, to divinity as well as to holy, and to Numen, as well as to numinous experience. *Numen* and *numinous* are perhaps more useful words than *holy, spiritual,* or *sacred,* all of which have been overused, flattened, and somewhat drained of their spe-cial meanings. All of these words can be useful, however, in the attempt to describe and recommend lives characterized by spiri-tual capacities, places that enable us to glimpse depth and mystery, and ideas that encourage us to think at a higher level of creativity.

Among historical figures, Krishna, Buddha, Christ, and Mohammed are almost universally considered numinous. Among individuals presently living, the most obvious such person is His Holiness the Dalai Lama, as well as other recent Nobel Laureates such as Desmond Tutu, Wingari Maathai, and Aun Sang Suu Kyi—perhaps not coincidentally, all persons of color. "Numinous" justifiably can also modify certain places such as the birth and death places of Gautama Buddha, Jesus, and Mohammed; the Ajanta Caves and Dharamsala (both in India); the Dome of the Rock and Church of the Holy Sepulcher in Jerusalem; Chartres Cathedral and Lourdes in France; Mecca in Saudi Arabia; and the ashrams of Sri Aurobindo and Ramana Maharshi in India. In quite a different way, Gettysburg, Hiroshima, and Auschwitz are also at least sacred (they deserve to be visited and ought not be disturbed), and perhaps are numinous (they emit a sense of eternal, transcendent mystery). Yosemite and the Grand Canyon are obviously awe-inspiring, and they certainly make us feel one with nature, with the whole of creation.

I consider certain contemporary experiences, particularly with a spiritual person, to be numinous, for example, a hug by Amma or a meeting with the Dalai Lama. Experiential traces of such a per-son can be found at the ashram of Sri Aurobindo and the Mother, or the Goetheanum of Rudolf Steiner. Such experiences typically transcend our ordinary categories; they are not just interesting or impressive, but mysterious, incomparable, irreducible. Ideas can also be numinous, for example, the Christian Trinity, *Sunyata* (the Buddhist teaching of Emptiness), the Beloved Community according to Josiah Royce and Martin Luther King, Jr., Gandhi's *satyagraha*, Sri Aurobindo's idea of Supermind, Jung's archetypes, and perhaps the Ontological Argument (God understood as "that than which nothing greater can be conceived"). The arts offer excellent opportunities for numinous experience: The Bach Mass in B-minor, a cello concert by Yo-Yo Ma, a performance of *King Lear*, or eurythmy performance. A simple conversation can be sacred, full of grace, an opportunity for gratitude, transformation words, or an inspiring presence deeper than words. Steiner referred to such a conversation as a contemporary form of Eucharist. Consider numinous as well the seeming miracle of a child's first poem or mathematical answer.

The criteria for designating something or someone as numinous, sacred, spiritual, transpersonal, or divine are not at all objective, but neither are they entirely arbitrary. The criteria require a recursive loop or a relationship between a mysterious source and someone with capacity to appreciate that phenomenon. For a tree to be known to fall in the forest someone needs to know the concept "tree," the concept "forest," and the concept "fall." Similarly, to experience someone or something as numinous is to be capable of such an experience. Numinous objects, places and persons do not ray out uniformly. Because the effect of a numinous experience might be felt slowly and imperceptibly, I try not to judge any of these situations confidently. Some inspiring experiences might be powerful in the moment but not have a lasting impact. A numinous object that impacts one person or group can be lost on another. When I was in the presence of the Mother of the Sri Aurobindo Ashram, I felt that nothing happened to me while around me disciples swooned and cried. By contrast, when I met His Holiness the Dalai Lama in the penthouse of the Fairmont Hotel in 1992, I was overwhelmed and unable to look at him directly, yet I noticed that some others seemed to register only a slight impact. When a young chorister sings "Once in Royal David City" at Midnight Mass at Grace Cathedral, some seem not to notice. On average, however, these and similar events elicit an intense response, at least temporarily—and perhaps more than temporarily—transformative.

Here I have discussed more than a dozen thinkers and activists who seem to me likely to lead you, the reader, to a glimpse (or more) of the numinous dimension, to a connection with a deep transcendent reality, an experience of grace and an occasion for gratitude. This book consists of a series of pointers: "Look here, do you see what I see, what I hear; would you be willing to consider this worldview, these ideas, these practices?" I have written this book in the hope that you will think these same insights that I have learned from Steiner and others. Just for a minute consider the possibility that Buddha and Christ, while separated by language, geography, and five centuries, are nevertheless deeply connected in the spiritual world, and devoted collaboratively to the evolution of humanity. Or consider that human evolution is guided by higher beings, and that Sophia is again emerging in human consciousness in many forms and in many parts of the world.

Also consider the possibility that in the spiritual world after death some of the thinkers discussed in this book encountered each other. As my friend Becky Gould wrote an essay that imagined a conversation at Walden Pond between Steiner and Thoreau, we might similarly imagine Rudolf Steiner in conversation with Pierre Teilhard de Chardin, Sri Aurobindo, or His Holiness the Dalai Lama. This book does not recreate such conversations, but it does try to bring a dozen great religious and spiritual thinkers of the last one hundred years, approximately, into closer proximity than they themselves communicated during their lifetime—even though many of them could have done so. Steiner did not personally know any of his contemporaries discussed in this book; through their writings he knew only Rabindranath Tagore, who was born in 1861, the same year as Steiner, Gandhi, whom he referred to as "a great soul," and C. G. Jung, who lived in Zurich, a short train ride from Basel where Steiner lived for the last thirteen years of his life.

Among philosophers he would have benefitted from conversations with three representatives of the classical American philosophical tradition: Ralph Waldo Emerson, William James, and Josiah Royce, the latter two almost his exact contemporaries. Among religious thinkers, he would have learned about Indian arts from Rabindranath Tagore, about advanced yogic practices from Sri Aurobindo, paleontology and Jesuit spirituality from Teilhard de Chardin, the archetypes of the collective unconscious from C. G. Jung, and compassion from His Holiness the Dalai Lama. He could have learned contemporary feminism from Rosemary Ruether, Catherine Keller, and Charlene Spretnak, and ecology from Rachel Carson, Caroline Merchant, Wingari Maathai, and Mary Evelyn Tucker. He could have appreciated the great social justice activists influenced by Gandhi—Dorothy Day, Martin Luther King, Jr., Desmond Tutu, Aun Sung Sau Kyi, and Joanna Macy. Because of Steiner's intuitive power and dedication to high spiritual beings, each of these great thinkers, teachers, and activitsts would likely have benefitted from conversations and collaboration with him. This book is an attempt to make up for the conversations that did not take place during Steiner's lifetime.

This book is also a defense of spiritual genius, of charismatic (literally, gifted) individuals. A tour of the vast museums in Florence and Rome reveal the paintings, sculptures, and architecture of three astonishingly creative artists: Leonardo da Vinci, Michaelangelo, and Raphael. We do not compare to their genius but we do not therefore deny their genius. Our writings do not approach those of Plato or Aristotle, Dante or Shakespeare, Emerson or Whitehead. And then there are the three musical miracles, Bach, Mozart, and Beethoven. How was Mozart possible! In the late eighteenth and early nineteenth century Goethe not only wrote *Faust*, considered the greatest work of modern literature, but he also made important advances in optics and botany. Thomas Jefferson, primary author of the United States Declaration of Independence, designed the University of Virginia and made contributions to agriculture. As President John Kennedy said to a room of Nobel Laureates gathered at a dinner at the White House, "There has not been this much intelligence in this room since Thomas Jefferson dined alone." Though hyperbolic, this remark was not wild: Jefferson was an original genius. We do not say, "No, such genius is impossible. Since we do not have the level of knowledge and creativity of these great figures, then neither could they have had that level."

Opponents of religious and spiritual worldviews, however, not only deny the experiences and insights of religious and spiritual thinkers, but also insist that no such experiences and insights are possible. Such opponents who sell books in the millions and are in charge of university departments of science and philosophy insist that those who claim spiritual knowledge are delusional, because there is no spirit to be known. William James faced such opposition head-on in his brilliant set of lectures published as *Varieties of Religious Experience* (1902). At the end of the *Varieties*, James asserted that the accumulative evidence provided by those he called experts in religious experience—for example, Saint Paul and Saint John, Augustine and Aquinas, Whitman and Tolstoy—indicate that we are "continuous with 'Something More' through which saving experiences come."

In the spirit of Rudolf Otto and C. G. Jung, this book is about the numinous, the sense of the irreducibly mysterious and sacred. It is about Krishna, Buddha, Christ, and Sophia, all in the context of the evolution of consciousness. It is also about the "Thou" of daily life and relationships according to Martin Buber. Drawing on Sri Aurobindo, it describes several yogas, including knowledge, action, love, and contemplation. It recounts the Gandhian tradition of nonviolence. It is about Sophianic wisdom, thinking that is infused by the divine feminine. It portrays wisdom and compassion in the spirit of His Holiness the Dalai Lama. In addition to the chapter on Sophia, the entire book is an effort by a senior male professor to practice and present ideas in a way that might deserve to be considered feminine, a difficult word to characterize, but probably well understood as relational, affective, and nuanced rather than assertive, argumentative, and competitive.

Because the ecological situation must be addressed, this book surveys some of the most important books on ecology written in the past half century (from Rachel Carson to Joanna Macy and Elizabeth Kolbert), and offers a full discussion of the ecological

Teilhardian vision of Thomas Berry. The last chapter offers some spiritual practices of the Hindu, Buddhist, Christian, and anthroposophic traditions. The entire book aims to be pluralistic but not relativistic, positive but not preachy, and contemporary without being so recent as to be faddish. It focuses on twentieth-century thinkers who will, I believe, be important throughout the twenty-first century, and in the case of Steiner, Buber, Jung, Teilhard, Aurobindo, Gandhi, and Tagore, quite likely for many centuries to come.

Unlike some professors who insist that overviews should come before seminars, or others who insist that seminars should come before overviews, I think that whichever comes first can serve perfectly well as an introduction. I chose philosophy as the first comparative discipline simply because it is foundational and because it came first in Steiner's life. Topics such as social justice, education, or ecology would probably have served equally well. This is a book with two introductory chapters and ten comparative chapters, all of which are intended as entry points. All twelve chapters are summarized in the remainder of this chapter. After reading this chapter, Steiner's "Kindred Spirits," and the next, "Steiner Alone," both of which are summarized below, you should be well prepared to proceed to any of the ten comparative chapters.

CHAPTER ONE: KINDRED SPIRITS

Whether he was seeing into the etheric forces of plants, experiencing discarnate human souls, or reading the inner meaning of the sacrifice of Christ, Steiner knew in ways available to very few others—not to no one else, but to very few. Students of esotericism generally agree that any list of such individuals would include, in addition to Steiner, Pythagoras, Paracelsus, Ibn 'Arabi, Jakob Böhme, Immanuel Swedenborg, Goethe, Blake, H. P. Blavatsky, Gurdjieff, C. G. Jung, and Valentin Tomberg. This list could be extended to dozens and perhaps hundreds of Western esoteric teachers. Lists could also be developed for Asian traditions to include Hindus (Yogananda Paramahansa, Sri Aurobindo),

Buddhists (Lama Govinda, His Holiness the Dalai Lama), and Dàoists (John Blofeld), as well as countless ancient and contemporary practitioners of shamanism such as Black Elk.

By comparing Steiner's worldview to those of modern philosophers and spiritual teachers, this book makes a case for claims at once radical and practical. To the reductionist, scientistic "nothing but" worldview, the content of this book says essentially, "Maybe your skepticism is warranted, but consider the possibility that claims by and about Steiner might be true, that he exhibited the level of knowledge he recommends, and that such knowing might be possible for some individuals." If tried, some of Steiner's ideas might prove to be profoundly efficacious, even though seemingly, or initially, unlikely. Consider asking, what are the alternatives? Does reductionist science explain as well as Steiner does the mysteries of the cosmos, or birth and death? In the conclusion of his brief, significant book, *Mind and Cosmos*, Thomas Nagel, a philosopher of science and acknowledged atheist, recommends to his readers a definition of philosophy first offered by William James, namely, that it is a habit of seeing alternatives:

> Philosophy has to proceed comparatively. The best we can do is to develop the rival alternative conceptions in each important domain as fully and carefully as possible, depending on our antecedent sympathies, and see how they measure up. That is a more credible form of progress than decisive proof or refutation.[2]

Following Nagel's reminder, Steiner's thought would seem to be exemplary of a rival worldview and ideas "in each important domain" developed "as fully and carefully as possible." He understood "antecedent sympathies" as one's multi-lived karmic history. Some individuals, irrespective of their family of origin, come looking for spiritual ideas, practices, and communities, while others, again irrespective of their families of origin, cannot imagine the validity of any of these. John Dewey, entirely admirable and nonreligious (in traditional institutional terms) immediately comes to mind.

---

2. Thomas Nagel, *Mind and Cosmos*, 127.

In some respects, Steiner's worldview, specific ideas, and practical counsel are clearly singular, and in other respects they can be profitably compared with other spiritual and esoteric teachers. He drew from Goethe's "gentle empiricism" and understanding of metamorphosis, as well as the concept of the "I" or Self in the epistemological and metaphysical idealism of Fichte, Schelling, and Hegel. He also drew heavily from the insights and terminology first expressed by H. P. Blavatsky, the cofounder of the Theosophical Society and its primary teacher until her death in 1891.

Of the figures in this book, only Jung knew of Steiner and most of them did not know one another. Gandhi and Sri Aurobindo never met, although Gandhi, and subsequently his son, went to Puducherry with a message in an attempt to coax Aurobindo to join the campaign against the British colonization of India. Tagore visited Aurobindo in Puducherry and Jung and Buber met at an Eranos conference in Switzerland and engaged in a brief unsuccessful correspondence concerning their differing conceptions of God. Unlike philosophers and scientists, great spiritual thinkers, particularly those with followers, typically do not collaborate. They seem to have insufficient peripheral vision for seeing other great spiritual teachers. Aurobindo had many visitors, but he himself did not leave his apartment in Puducherry for the last twenty four years of his life. Steiner lectured on Jung's psychology but despite their living a few hours apart in Switzerland for thirteen years, they never met. Tagore and Teilhard were the most collaborative: Tagore visited more than a dozen countries and met the major thinkers and artists in every one. Teilhard had a copy of Aurobindo's *Life Divine* on his night table when he died, and Jung had a copy of Teilhard's *The Human Phenomenon* on his night table when he died.

Anyone interested in Sri Aurobindo's Integral Yoga is likely to appreciate his relationship with Mira Richard, the Mother of the Sri Aurobindo Ashram. Those interested in Jung's study of archetypes are likely to be interested in his approach to alchemy, his theory of individuation, and his analysis of contemporary consciousness. Those interested in Teilhard's understanding of evolution are likely to be interested in his experience of Christ. Finally, anyone interested in the Dalai Lama's Tibetan Buddhist teaching of compassion is likely to be interested in his understanding of Western science and the relationships among religions. We follow these great thinkers into several fields for the same reasons that they went into those fields: there are mysteries to be illumined, problems to be solved, and human communities in need of spiritual insight and inspiration. The rest of this chapter offers a brief introduction to the remaining chapters and the religious and spiritual thinkers who offer perspectives comparable to Steiner's.

CHAPTER TWO: STEINER ALONE

Since very few human beings—especially in contemporary society—can "see clearly" into the invisible, many consider Steiner's esoteric ability to be impossible. This book aims to show that Steiner did indeed have such an ability, that he used it wisely and selflessly to the advantage of anyone who would attend to the results of his research, and that disciplined effort makes it possible for individuals not born with this ability to develop some degree of it. As Saul Bellow noted in his foreword to *Boundaries of Natural Science,* a series of lectures Steiner delivered in 1920:

> I have thought it best not to interpose myself but to allow Steiner to speak for himself, for he is more than a thinker, he is an initiate and only he is able to communicate what he has experienced. The human mind, he tells us, must learn to will pure thinking, but it must learn also how to set conceptual thinking aside and to live within phenomena. "It is through phenomenology, and not abstract metaphysics, that we attain knowledge of the spirit by consciously observing, by raising to consciousness, what we would otherwise do unconsciously; by observing how through the sense world spiritual forces enter into our being and work formatively upon it."[3]

Steiner taught initiation in the Western esoteric tradition. In ancient cultures such as Egypt and Greece, a neophyte, or esoteric

---

3.　Saul Bellow, "Foreword,"Rudolf Steiner, *The Boundaries of Natural Science,* xxi.

student, would submit to the discipline of a spiritual master, and then undergo a kind of death, from which the master would call forth the disciple in a heightened state of awareness. An initiate would then be able to benefit fully from the teachings of the initiator, and could in turn develop into a teacher in his or her own right. Following in this tradition, Steiner encouraged them to develop their esoteric ability and to benefit from the influence of spiritual beings. Steiner's commitment to freedom of the individual in all religious and cultural endeavors encourages each person to approach esoteric ideas and practices as each thinks best for his or her individual capacities and aspirations. Steiner always had an eye on individual karma: He recognized that an idea or action that would be spiritually, morally, and culturally right for one person would not necessarily be right for another. He thought that Anthroposophy and Christianity were right for some persons and not others.

No doubt many in Steiner's audiences believed what he said simply because they believed in him and everything that he said. Audiences of several thousand (as were typical toward the end of his life) presumably included a range of responses from total affirmation to total skepticism. But Steiner himself was not arguing for anyone to believe his ideas. He considered individual freedom to follow from the replacement of belief by knowledge He calmly described what he was seeing and researching, and then asked his audiences to do their own research. Here is what he said and thought concerning acceptance of his clairvoyant research:

> Much that I have said today can be substantiated only by means of occult investigation. Yet I beg you not to give credence to these things because I say them, but to test them by everything known to you from history, and above all by what you can learn from your own experience. I am absolutely certain that the more closely you examine them, the more confirmation you will find. In this age of intellectualism, I do not appeal to your belief in authority but to your capacity for intelligent examination.[4]

---

4. Rudolf Steiner, "Bodhisattvas, Buddhas and Christ" in *From Buddha to Christ,* 91–92.

In his singularity, Steiner might prove important for each person's intellectual and spiritual life. For a start, considering these summaries of Steiner's ideas in comparison to the ideas of other twentieth- and twenty-first-century religious and spiritual thinkers might establish that there is at least one individual (and surely many others) who has attained important knowledge regarded by the dominant modern Western paradigm as impossible. You might decide that Steiner was a genuine clairvoyant, a clear seer concerning research on topics (such as karma, afterlife, and rebirth) widely regarded as unknowable. You might consider Steiner to be an example of the "one white crow" sought by William James.[5] Steiner was apparently able to see spiritual realities, including something about exalted spiritual beings such as Krishna, Buddha, Christ, and Sophia. He reported on individuals who had died as well as the causes and meanings of important events. He disclosed these findings in lectures to audiences familiar with his research.

In the same way that many Christians, Buddhists, Jungians, and followers of Aurobindo and the Mother tend to see the world and all of its particulars through the lens of their specific religious or spiritual commitment, devoted followers of Rudolf Steiner tend to see every topic, every event, every relationship, and in fact absolutely everything, through the lens of Steiner and Anthroposophy. Given the almost impossible range of Steiner's interests and insights, this exclusivist focus is understandable. It can also be regrettable: It can lead to arrogance, dogmatism, and fundamentalist literalism. I have met many individuals whose initial interest in Steiner and Anthroposophy was discouraged, and sometimes negated, by contact with a devoted anthroposophist. One does not meet followers of Teilhard de Chardin or His Holiness the Dalai Lama who make one want to avoid these teachers or their followers. This unfortunate phenomenon does, however, affect the communities around Steiner and Sri Aurobindo. One of the reasons for this cultic appearance, and to some extent cultic reality, probably is the attempt by both Steiner and Aurobindo to institutionalize their influence.

---

5. William James, *Essays in Psychical Research*, 13.

Beginning with the founding of the Anthroposophical Society in 1912, and then more systematically and decisively beginning in 1923 (for the last two and a half years of his life) Rudolf Steiner was the esoteric teacher not only of Anthroposophy, but of the Anthroposophical Society. Similarly, since 1926 Sri Aurobindo's and the Mother's teachings have been the guide of thought and practice at the Sri Aurobindo Ashram in Puducherry (formerly Pondicherry), and in ashrams throughout the world. Institutions bring the problems characteristic of religion—dogmas, regulations, hierarchy, politics, and intolerance of outsiders. There are many historically grounded reasons to oppose religion, not just a religion, but all religion. Hence, the contemporary mantra, "spiritual not religious." But spirituality disconnected from a religious institution can be elitist and invisible: No one has to show up to do the work, publish the books, give the lectures, lead the artistic experiences, and update the website. The ideal is for the spiritual and the religious to work complementarily without the elitism of spirituality and without the political, dogmatic, and cultic problems of religion.

Steiner also made significant contributions to fields not usually considered spiritual, that are regrettably neglected in this volume. However impossible it might seem to anyone not previously familiar with Steiner, in addition to the wide variety of his contributions explored in this book, there are other topics, fields, and achievements that would need to be addressed to treat Steiner's significance comprehensively. Among sciences, he contributed to an understanding of light, warmth, geometry, chemistry, occult physiology, bees, and medicine. Among social sciences he lectured extensively on money, community, historical patterns, the destinies of civilizations and nations, and the psychology of individuals and peoples. I have omitted some of these topics because I could not find an appropriate comparison for Steiner's contributions, and some quite simply because I do not feel competent to discuss them. The fields that would have been ideal for inclusion in this book but of which I am still regretfully ignorant include medicine, economics, evolutionary biology, contemporary Islamic thought, and recent European philosophy.

Steiner sought to show the inner realities of the natural world, the significance of the spiritual world, and the relationship between them. He sought to explain not only how he himself knew spiritual realities but also how others could do the same. In addition he also strove to expose and oppose all the negative, destructive, and alienating aspects of contemporary thought and culture. To a degree that appears to be unsurpassed by any other modern figure, almost nothing was foreign to Steiner. He described the inner realities of many physical and spiritual entities, complex processes, and specific phenomena.

Rudolf Steiner came into life with spiritual gifts that he further developed. He spent the last twenty-five years of his life helping others to develop spiritual insights and capacities. He is one of the truly great "experts" who experienced and explained James's "Something More." Unfortunately, James did not know of Steiner and so did not include his expertise in the Gifford Lectures that James delivered in 1901, the very year that Steiner began his career as an esoteric teacher. Steiner is more controversial than most (and perhaps all other) religious thinkers such as James himself, because he not only made important contributions in a dozen fields, far beyond the claims of James or any twentieth-century philosopher, but because he also exhibited and defended a depth and range of knowledge that challenges the dominant reductionist view of what is knowable.

Steiner's claims to the truth of his method and teaching are backed and tested by his willing sacrifice on behalf of his claims. He did not simply make claims; he reached important truths through strenuous and selfless effort, and then offered them freely to anyone who asked for them. All of his claims arose from experience won by diligent effort and held up against frequent intellectual opposition. Toward the end of his life this opposition became increasingly personal and violent. When a teacher or leader offers insights selflessly and peacefully that prove effective, and are backed by a demonstrated willingness to suffer on their behalf, such a person would seem to warrant a respectful hearing—certainly more than Steiner has received to date.

To appreciate Steiner and his contributions it is possible to focus on only one field—for example the Waldorf approach to education or biodynamic (BD) agriculture, two of his most prominent practical works—but it is important and rewarding to honor the unity of Steiner's thought by proceeding from Waldorf or BD back to his ideas on philosophy, evolution of consciousness, exalted beings, and esoteric cosmology. Perhaps the best reason for studying the results of his esoteric research is simply that they might lead one to engage with his spiritual practices either on their own or as a complement to those of another spiritual teacher such as Teilhard de Chardin or His Holiness the Dalai Lama, both of whom are included prominently in several chapters in this book, including the last chapter on spiritual practice.

CHAPTER THREE: PHILOSOPHY

The first of ten chapters that compare Rudolf Steiner with other important religious and spiritual thinkers summarizes the leading ideas of three classical American philosophers: Ralph Waldo Emerson (1803–1881), William James (1841–1910), and Josiah Royce (1855–1916). Before Steiner was an esoteric teacher—i.e., before he spoke from his clairvoyant experiences concerning the spiritual world—he wrote about Goethe, German Idealism, and Nietzsche as well as philosophized concerning knowledge, ethics, aesthetics, nature, culture, and history. At the end of his life he considered his *Philosophy of Freedom*, his first major work, to be the one most deserving to remain influential in future centuries. Consequently, it is appropriate that the first comparative chapter should explore similarities and differences between Steiner and three twentieth-century philosophers with whom his philosophy is most comparable.

These three philosophers share with Steiner the influence of the same nineteenth-century European thinkers, especially the German Idealists (Kant, Fichte, Schelling, and Hegel), a commitment to evolution, and a focus on the interpenetration of matter and spirit. They also share with Steiner a focus, variously developed, on the relationship between the individual and community.

They all drew deeply from the Christian tradition and they affirm broad religious ideals and perspectives. Of these three thinkers the one closest to Steiner is Josiah Royce, a philosopher with a profound sense of the long intelligible arc of history, including the incarnation of Christ, the efficacy of ideals, and the redemptive mission of sorrow.

CHAPTER FOUR: EVOLUTION OF CONSCIOUSNESS

Evolution of consciousness can be thought of as very deep history—the sources, inner processes, and implications of history that are not on the surface to see. Whereas history can be observed by intellect, evolution of consciousness needs to be observed by intuition. Henri Bergson's classic study, *Creative Evolution*, was one of the first and most influential accounts of natural evolution generated by a deep source that he called *elan vital*. Aurobindo, Teilhard, and Steiner, all of whom had read Bergson's *Creative Evolution*, offer the three most detailed and comprehensive accounts of evolution of consciousness.

All of Sri Aurobindo's major works—*Human Cycle, Savitri, The Life Divine, Synthesis of Yoga*—chronicle the subtle, invisible patterns of historical change. Teilhard de Chardin's major work, *The Human Phenomenon*, chronicles the four major phases of the evolution of consciousness: prelife, life, thought, super life. Sri Aurobindo describes four almost identical phases: matter, life, mind, and Supermind. Both Aurobindo and Teilhard are eager to show their readers that the present holds the possibility of the next great evolutionary leap, which Aurobindo refers to as the Supermind and Teilhard refers to as the Omega Point. According to Aurobindo, the descent of Supermind will facilitate the ideal synthesis of Western intellect and science and Indian spirituality. For Aurobindo, the next evolutionary stage, which he refers to as "the life divine on Earth" and "the coming of a spiritual age," will be realized when the West overcomes its "materialist denial" of spirit and the East (by which he means India) will overcome its "ascetic refusal," the denial of the individual and history characteristic of some forms of Indian monism, particularly *a-dvaita* (non-dual) Vedanta.

Teilhard, the most optimistic thinker discussed in this book, looks to the convergence of spirit and matter made possible by the guidance of Christ. The end point which he envisions is essentially the triumph of love, the energy of the entire evolutionary process. Profoundly Christian and mystical, Teilhard identifies love with Christ through whom, as in the Prologue to the Gospel of John, everything came to be.

CHAPTER FIVE: KRISHNA, BUDDHA, AND CHRIST

Whereas leaders and interpreters of religious traditions typically have a significant relationship to a specific divine source of their tradition—Hindus to Krishna (and other deities such as Shiva), Buddhists to Buddha, and Christians to Christ—a few advanced individuals such as Sri Ramakrishna, Yogananda Paramahansa, Bede Griffiths, and Rudolf Steiner have described their deep relationship to more than one of these figures. Some contemporary spiritual teachers and scholars are increasingly able to introduce these deities in ways that make them more accessible to adherents of other religious traditions. Such is the case with the way that Sri Aurobindo writes about Krishna, His Holiness the Dalai Lama writes about Buddha and Buddhanature, and Teilhard de Chardin writes about Christ.

In 1908 to 1909, while Aurobindo Ghose (as he was then known) was in jail for opposition to the British Government of India, he memorized the Bhagavad Gita in Sanskrit and recited it daily in his cell. He envisioned Krishna holding the murderers and jailers in one loving embrace. In 1926 he experienced the descent of Krishna entering his transformed subtle body and endowing him with a level of consciousness that he later described as "Overmental." His Holiness the Dalai Lama offers a view of Buddha as Buddhanature, or the infinite and eternal *Dharmakaya* or truth body of Buddha. Teilhard de Chardin offers a view of Christ that is cosmic, far transcending the conception of Christ as Jesus in traditional Christian theology.

Based on his esoteric research, especially during the years that he was inexorably moving away from the Theosophical Society, Steiner offered an interpretation of Krishna that resembles Aurobindo's interpretation, an interpretation of Buddha that resembles the Dalai Lama's, and an interpretation of Christ that resembles Teilhard's. In this book, the relations between Christ and other beings are explored in seven of twelve chapters:

> Chapter Five: In addition to describing complex esoteric relations among Krishna, Buddha, and Christ, Steiner discusses important figures in the New Testament.
> Chapter Six: Christ is discussed in relation to Sophia.
> Chapter Seven: Both Jung and Steiner see Christ as the great healer.
> Chapter Eight: Dorothy Day, Dietrich Bonhoffer, Rev. Martin Luther King, Jr., and Archbishop Desmond Tutu took their inspiration from the teachings and example of Jesus.
> Chapter Ten: Steiner presents Christ as the balance between matter and spirit (and in their distorted expressions, between the opposite tempters, Lucifer and Ahriman).
> Chapter 11: Steiner presents a picture of Christ surrounding Earth.
> Chapter 12: Jung, Teilhard, and Steiner affirm that Christ is spiritually active in the Consecration of the Mass.

This entire book recommends the reality and transformative influence of Krishna, Buddha, Christ, and Sophia, and all human consciousness that partakes of their influence, however unconsciously.

CHAPTER SIX: THE GODDESS SOPHIA

The core of the Christian faith that establishes its uniqueness in relation to all other religious traditions, and permeates the thought and culture of a large segment of the world's population, is the incarnation of a divine being, Jesus Christ, in a human body and in human history. This chapter adds to this standard theological conception of Jesus Christ an account of the Christian divine feminine, usually referred to as Sophia, active in history as well as in the spiritual world. Since the Council of Constantinople in 325 CE, Christian churches have affirmed the doctrine of the Holy Trinity consisting of Father (often depicted as the Creator, as in Michelangelo's ceiling in the Sistine Chapel), Son (Jesus Christ, in a wide variety of representations), and Holy Spirit (often depicted as a dove). Christians aware of the problem attending the unconscious assumption and ubiquitous influence of patriarchy, and the exclusive male gender language for the Christian conception of the Trinity will understand Mary Daly's angry dismissal: "Two men and a bird."

One attempt to solve the problem of this all-male language is to add Mother to Father and Hers to His in all references to the three Persons of the Trinity. Another solution is to retrieve the reality, and not merely the language, of the divine feminine. This solution is found in an expanding library of books and images that form an impressive movement aimed at retrieving the image of the goddess Sophia. The most convincing of these accounts, *Myth of the Goddess: Evolution of an Image*, is the foundational book for the Sophia component of this chapter.

As Christopher Bamford wrote in the introduction to a volume of Steiner's lectures on Sophia, "Over the past centuries, the being of Sophia, or feminine Divine Wisdom, has been emerging from the mists of ancient history, like Venus from the waters, to become a sign of our times."[6] This chapter traces some of the important contributions to this emergence: Sophia in world religions; in the history of Christianity; in the thought of Thomas Merton, Teilhard de Chardin, C. G. Jung; three anthroposophic sophiologists—Valentin Tomberg, Sergei Prokofieff, and Michael Debus; and Sophia and feminism, including the theology of Elizabeth Johnson. The chapter concludes with my "Invocation to Sophia."

CHAPTER SEVEN: GOD, EVIL, AND SUFFERING

Some of the best philosophizing has been done at the edge of the academy. Buber was more a public intellectual than a professor, and Jung was not a professor at all but a psychiatrist in private practice. Both were devoted to the restoration of religious and spiritual values to European individuals and cultures.

---

6. Christopher Bamford, ed., "Introduction," in Rudolf Steiner, *Isis Mary Sophia: Her Mission and Ours*, 7.

Using one of Buber's key terms, his defining task was to "Hallow Life." Buber drew from and advanced German intellectual culture and twentieth-century Jewish thought, specifically biblical faith, Zionism, and Hasidism. His most original and enduring contribution is *I and Thou* (1923), a poetic and inspiring text that combines the Jewish ideal of community and twentieth-century European existentialist radical individualism. This combination closely resembles Steiner's *Philosophy of Freedom*, a philosophy of ethical individualism—i.e., individuals ethically committed to community. Significantly, Buber, Jung, and Steiner all began their intellectual careers in response to Kant's unavoidable volume, *Critique of Pure Reason* (1781).

Buber, Jung, and Steiner broke through the limits set by Kant's first *Critique*, but to some extent Jung wrote as though he were observing the limitations Kant set to theoretical knowledge. In fact, Jung went much further than Buber (though not as far as Steiner) in his affirmation of knowledge above the line set by Kant—to knowledge of the divine, human freedom, and the enduring self. Beginning in 1913, immediately after his break with Freud, and even more dramatically in the 1940s and 1950s, Jung experienced the heights and depths of the personal and collective unconscious, including its myths, archetypes, symbols, and images. In all of his researches, Jung functioned as a physician for individuals and contemporary European culture, always in an effort to unite the individual ego with the wise and active unconscious.

Steiner wrote philosophy with an eye to the alienation profoundly affecting modern Western culture, and he offered an epistemology intended to help Western humanity think with feeling and will—i.e., freely and ethically. Steiner understood the individual person in terms of a lifelong struggle to realize authentic destiny: one's karma and ultimately one's identity with the spiritual world. Whereas Buber's terminology employs a highly original existentialist vocabulary, Steiner's is Idealist, Christian, and esoteric. Steiner characterizes Anthroposophy—his spiritual-esoteric research and discipline as a path of will and feeling-imbued knowing to lead the spiritual in the individual (Buber's potential "I") to the spiritual in the Universe (Buber's "Thou").

One of the important differences between Buber and both Jung and Steiner is Buber's strictly monotheistic Jewish, and specifically biblical, theology. Buber and Steiner agree on the personal character of God (as creator, revealer, and redeemer) but of course they diverge on the status of Christ. Whereas Buber regards Jesus as "his older brother," a rabbi of great historical significance, Steiner regards Jesus as the bearer of the Christ, the second Person of the Trinity. This theological difference, however, does not significantly detract from their philosophical conviction concerning the need of each person to realize his or her authentic self by dedicated effort, including person-to-person and person-to-universe dialogue.

C. G. Jung, a psychiatrist and gnostic scholar, shares with Steiner the conviction that modern Western consciousness is characterized by many problems and disabilities mostly having to do with what Jung calls the shadow (the forceful, usually negative dimension hidden in the unconscious). Jung was convinced that by embracing the Western scientific paradigm (a way of seeing, thinking, and behavior) exclusive of the unconscious, Western humanity had lost its soul. Jung sought to reconnect Western humanity to unconscious depth by showing the wise revelatory power of dreams, myths, symbols, and archetypes (psychic structures such as the Self, Christ, Divine Feminine, Senex, Puer, Shadow, and Mandala).

Jung's research into the unconscious was personal and experiential: He wrote from his own journey into his own unconscious. He also researched esoteric teachings and practices of entire cultures, past and present. He brought to the attention of secular Western readers the wisdom and transformative power of the Chinese *I Ching*, Tibetan mandalas, the spiritual significance of the Roman Catholic mass, medieval Christian alchemy, and worldwide shamanic traditions. This chapter's discussion of Jung's archetypal psychology concludes with an introduction to a scholarly and beautifully written case for astrological cosmology, *Cosmos and Psyche*, by Richard Tarnas who is also the author of an important study, *Passion of the Western Mind*.

CHAPTER EIGHT: SOCIAL JUSTICE

In a manifestly unjust world there is no shortage of theories and explanations (beginning with original sin) as well as recommendations, pleas, and exemplars, concerning social justice. Among twentieth-century exemplars, Gandhi would seem to be preeminent. On the occasion of Gandhi's seventieth birthday, Albert Einstein wrote: "Generations to come, it may well be, will scarce believe that such a man as this once ever in flesh and blood walked upon this Earth." Gandhi is the primary source of nonviolent theory and action subsequently advanced by Dorothy Day, the American pacifist; Thomas Merton, the Roman Catholic monk; Martin Luther King, Jr., the martyr and leader of the American Civil Rights movement; His Holiness the Dalai Lama, the spiritual and former political leader of the Tibetan people; Aun Sang Suu Kyi, the pro-democracy activist of Myanmar; and Desmond Tutu, the South African Episcopal Archbishop. Four of these individuals—King, Dalai Lama, Tutu, and Suu Kyi,—are Nobel Laureates and also people of color. Obviously, these are not the only exemplars of peace and justice, but there is a special power in the Gandhian tradition because it includes a commitment to the practice as well as the theory of nonviolence. To the extent that it is viable, Gandhian nonviolence is a direct challenge to the dominant paradigm that considers war to be inevitable. Despite the limitations of Gandhian nonviolent action—Gandhi's letters to Buber and Hitler concerning the Nazi holocaust of European Jews are uninformed, presumptuous, and naive—nonviolence as a way of life is clearly positive and necessary.

Steiner did not announce himself as a pacifist or practitioner of nonviolence, but his entire teaching and way of life are counters to egoism and selfishness, in favor of love and service. He considered violence to be an inevitable if indirect result of a faulty construction of society which allows the economic and rights spheres to overwhelm the cultural sphere—which absolutely should be free of such control.

CHAPTER NINE EDUCATION

Rudolf Steiner is perhaps best known for the Waldorf approach to education, which now consists of several thousand nursery, elementary, and high schools in more than one hundred countries. The teachers in Waldorf schools continue to draw guidance from the hundreds of lectures that Steiner delivered on child development, curriculum, and pedagogy, all made possible by his ability to see and to communicate the realities of the inner lives of children. This is one way in which Steiner contributes to the spiritual renewal of the individual and of Western culture in ways comparable to other important thinkers, but because he thinks more deeply and more widely than any of them, he can be shown to have established the truth of their contributions in addition to his own.

The chapter on education is an extension of the previous chapter on social justice. Because of an imbalance of power between children and adults who care for children, any thought or action that affects children is necessarily a matter of justice. In every society care for children should be a deep moral and spiritual as well as a cultural responsibility. John Dewey, a world-class philosopher, not only studied and wrote about child development and the education of the child, he also created and devoted a significant portion of his life to a school laboratory that he founded and directed with his wife Alice Chipman. Maria Montessori, an Italian physician, created a brilliant approach to education for children who had been left behind (literally left on the street) as a result of World War II. Rudolf Steiner developed an approach to education based on his spiritual understanding of the inner life of the child. While the differences in approach to education of these three great educators are significant, their similarities are important and generally not acknowledged.

CHAPTER TEN: ART AND AESTHETICS

All of the chapters in this book, and particularly this chapter on art and aesthetics, point from the visible to the spiritual. We might say that art, particularly as understood and practiced by Rabindranath Tagore and Rudolf Steiner, is a pointing. Tagore's poetry, songs, plays, short stories, and paintings all serve to point matter toward spirit, the finite toward the infinite, and the human toward the divine. While Tagore was religious, philosophical, and political, he was essentially an artist, a person whose entire life was devoted to releasing the encased spirit by activating the artistic imagination. The school that he founded and directed, Shantiniketan, is devoted to traditional Indian arts, all of which remain devoted to releasing and celebrating spirit.

Because Indian thought and culture has not experienced the separation of arts and spirit characteristic of the arts in the modern West, virtually all Indian arts, whether music, dance, painting, or literature, are suffused by the reality of spiritual experience and spiritual beings. In the modern West spirit is sustained in the arts by Dante, Shakespeare, Goethe, and Rilke, by Bach, Mozart, Beethoven, and Mahler, as well as Turner, Kandinsky, Marc Chagall, and Matisse. Rudolf Steiner is one of the few twentieth-century artists to have held spirit and matter together in several arts and in ways comparable to the painting, poetry, dramas, and songs of Tagore. Tagore's fabulous artistic creativity is thoroughly rooted in the Upanishads, classical Indian texts of the eighth to fifth centuries BCE. His art carries a deep revelation of the divinity in all creation, whether sound and sight, word and gesture. Steiner's conception of art, and practice of many arts, is revealed in two series of lectures: *Art as Seen in the Light of Mystery Wisdom* (1915) and *Arts and their Mission* (1923). Steiner's most important lectures on the particular arts to which he contributed by theory and practice—sculpture, architecture, music, poetry, mystery dramas, speech, and singing—are collected in a volume accurately entitled *Art as Spiritual Practice*. It is common for followers of Steiner to think of Anthroposophy in terms of a redeemed thinking, but anthroposophic practice is devoted very significantly to arts.

CHAPTER ELEVEN: ON BEHALF OF GAIA

The ecological movement, which is really the process of awakening to unimaginable devastation, was launched in popular consciousness in 1962, more than fifty years ago, by the publication of Rachel Carson's book, *Silent Spring*. The next major ecological event was Earth Day, 1971, followed by *An Inconvenient Truth* (2006), the bestselling book and widely viewed film by former Vice President Al Gore. In 1978 Thomas Berry published "The New Story," an essay that has served as a proclamation and plea for a vision of humans as Earth creatures. By a combination of his profound knowledge, his inspiring person, and his oracular writing, Thomas Berry has exercised a significant impact on several scholars of ecology and religion, including Matthew Fox, Brian Thomas Swimme, and most significantly the husband-and-wife team Mary Evelyn Tucker and John Grim.

In addition to the mystical ecology of Teilhard and the humanistic ecology of Thomas Berry, the impending ecological challenges have been met by a variety of charismatic ecological activists. As the work of Paul Hawken and Sean Esbjorn-Harkens has shown, there are many important approaches to ecological theory and activism, including Sean Kelly's five principles of an integral ecology. One of the tasks of this chapter is to try to discern, in William James's helpful phrase, "what difference will it make" if we approach the ecological crisis from a humanist, religious, spiritual, or esoteric worldview? The need for humanist and religious approaches ("where the people are") is obvious, whereas the need for a spiritual and esoteric approach is difficult to demonstrate. But it is one of the tasks of this chapter to show that approaching ecology from a spiritual and an esoteric perspective will indeed make a positive difference.

On the way to forming one's own individual ecological perspective, it will be worthwhile to explore the similarities and differences between Teilhard and Berry, two great Earth-loving thinkers. I want to hold and recommend a continuity from Teilhard's (and Steiner's) pre-ecological spiritual cosmology to Berry's passionate humanistic ecological vision. A well known Buddhist teaching says there is no time to discuss fire when one's house is burning. But because there are other houses and potentially other fires to burn them, it is essential to know why houses burn and how they can be prevented from burning. Berry excelled at analyzing why Earth is burning, and what to do about it. In service of this double commitment he increasingly ignored Teilhard as a solution because he considered Teilhard to be too optimistic, too much in favor of technology, and too affirmative of some Roman Catholic teachings.

The chapter concludes with a summation of Steiner's esoteric ecology, including his account of spirit and matter, the reality of the etheric, biodynamic farming, and his conviction that the etheric body of Christ has encircled the Earth.

CHAPTER TWELVE: SPIRITUAL PRACTICE

This book assumes the truth of Sri Aurobindo's maxim, "All life is a secret yoga," which I take to mean that all life is spiritual practice. All religious traditions teach core practices such as the golden rule, and all spiritual disciplines affirm these same practices as preconditions for spiritual progress. While some individuals on a spiritual path dismiss religion as a lower level of aspiration, this chapter emphasizes the continuous recursive relationship between religious traditions and mysticism. The four approaches presented here represent the synthesis of spiritual teachers with specific religious traditions: Sri Aurobindo with Hinduism, His Holiness the Dalai Lama with Tibetan Buddhism, the Roman Catholic tradition represented by Teilhard de Chardin, and Rudolf Steiner's Anthroposophy mixed with significant Christian components. In the Christian section I recommend the Mass or Eucharist, which has been powerfully affirmed by Teilhard, Jung, and Steiner.

In the section on anthroposophic practice, the tradition that I know best and practice, I include a discussion of practices that seem to me especially efficacious: the integration of thinking, feeling, and willing (a modern Western version of the yogas of the Bhagavad Gita); the practice of forgiveness; the use of verses and meditations; the discipline of attending to the mysterious reality of karma and rebirth; the disciplined expression of the etheric, astral, and "I" by manifold arts; the spiritual discipline of loving relationships; the conscious attention to a wide variety of religious and spiritual traditions; and all of these in the context of the divinely guided evolution of consciousness.

This entire chapter is an attempt to transmit advice to be found in the writings of these teachers, Steiner foremost but not exclusively. I trust their advice because I have learned to trust their respective syntheses of new ideas with their lifelong manifest virtue. I believe that any one of them can lead any one of us to an increase in wisdom and compassion, and that when we learn to work with all of them for different purposes, they can lead us even more effectively. It is also important, I believe, to develop and serve a spiritual home, and to use the terms of the Buddhist three jewels, to have a primary teacher, to have a primary *dharma* (teaching and practice), and to serve a primary *sangha* (spiritual or religious community).

Rudolf Steiner
Helena Petrovna Blavatsky

2

STEINER ALONE
APPROACHING RUDOLF STEINER

Rudolf Steiner's life can be read in exoteric (immediately observable) terms: birth, family, education, profession, marriages, friends, and influence. But it is important to try to understand the esoteric (hidden or secret) meaning of his life as well. The esoteric events in Steiner's life include the apparition of an aunt who had committed suicide, his experience of geometry, experience of the healing power of herbs, his meetings with Felix Kogutsky[1] and the one he refers to as M [Master],[2] his experience of Christ, and twenty-five years of esoteric research, writing, and teaching. In Steiner's life esoteric and exoteric experiences are entwined; both are necessary, true, and significant. The external events and activities of Steiner's life are mixed, often mysteriously, with his mission, contact with spirit guides, and ability to see spirit life in both the most mundane and the grandest phenomena.

Rudolf Steiner contributed an enormous body of thought, one that covers at least a dozen disciplines, including spiritual practices and a combination of deep insight with practical impact. To follow Steiner's life, thought, and works is to be led from one field to another, from immediately accessible and useful knowledge to the extremely profound and mysterious. It would take a lifetime to understand all that Steiner contributed during his twenty five years as a spiritual-esoteric teacher. By his clairvoyant ability he was able to investigate realities inaccessible to all but a few

---

1. For a revealing portrayal of Felix, see Emil Bock, *The Life and Times of Rudolf Steiner. Vol. 1: People and Places*, ch. 1.

2. Sri Ramakrishna also referred to his spiritual guide as M. See *The Gospel of Sri Ramakrishna*.

individuals. He made disclosures which, if true, reveal a world that is deeper, wiser, more mysterious, and yet more fathomable than the world as understood by the dominant paradigm. As Hamlet said:, "There are more things in heaven and earth, Horatio, Than are dreamt of in your philosophy" (*Hamlet,* 1.5.167–8).

In relation to all such situations that he researched and described, Steiner tried to lead his audiences and readers from the biography (as in karma) and the event (the subtle relationships between spiritual and physical) to the source, divine beings unseen except to someone like Steiner. The idea that there is a divine, and that it intervenes in human and cosmic events is considered unintelligible, unlikely, or impossible by the dominant modern Western way of thinking. According to Steiner, the intervention of the divine in cosmic, earthly, and human realities is difficult to know, but not impossible. Such interventions and subtle relationships deserve to be affirmed and described with reverence and humility. This was Steiner's life work: to put the spiritual dimension of the human individual in thinking and loving contact with the spiritual in the universe.

Clearly, some of Steiner's claims are surprising and resistant to evidence. Without an ability similar to Steiner's it is difficult to assess some, but not all, of his claims. Because he exhibited capacities far outside the usually acceptable range of knowledge and insight, there has been a tendency to question, and more typically to avoid, even his contributions that are as evident as great works of art. As we can see Michelangelo's *Pieta* and Raphael's Madonnas, and as we can read Dante and Shakespeare, we can observe the Waldorf approach to education and biodynamic farming: We observe the children attending Waldorf schools and follow them in later life, and we can view and taste fruits and vegetables from a biodynamic farm. Similarly, we can observe Steiner's architecture, read his mystery dramas, experience the language of the sacraments that he gave to the Lutheran priests; observe a performance of eurythmy; consider his lectures on economics, on heat and light, or philosophy. Evidence of many of his amazing capacities abounds in full view for anyone who would consider it dispassionately.

Perhaps the best way to approach the commonality between Steiner and the "kindred spirits" in this book would be to say that they all (or almost all) celebrate the numinous, the irreducibly mysterious, awesome, and inspiring. Or, we might say that they are all pointers: in a wide variety of ways they all say, "Look, keep looking, empty the ego and the habit of ordinary thinking, and you will see deeper and higher, perhaps all the way to spiritual insights and spiritual beings." Wherever Steiner went, whether in lecture halls, meeting rooms, drafty trains through the night, whether talking with the first Waldorf students, teaching eurythmy, or sculpting, he pointed to depth and height, to etheric, soul, and spirit. He did not begin at a remove from the ordinary: He pointed to the spiritual in the ordinary as well as in the purely spiritual realm, and then he brought them together. He is a guide as well as a teacher. He found hundreds of ways to say "Look, listen, imagine: Spirit is real, it is here, and it is specific; here is an angel, an ancestor, an ideal shaping a civilization."

As one reads and ponders, the most helpful thought might be, "How far out (or how high, or how deep) am I willing to go?" The line one draws might move, or it might not. Either way, reading and pondering with humility and reverence is a worthwhile spiritual practice in its own right, independent of whether it brings one into closer contact with Steiner's insights. Steiner's most important contributions, irrespective of whether he might be an example of a clairvoyant, are probably his spiritual qualities and the methods he provides for his readers to improve their own spiritual lives. It might be very sensible to ignore his esoteric ideas at first and go directly to his spiritual practices.

Since so much of Steiner's work was made possible by his clairvoyance, the remainder of this chapter offers an explanation of this esoteric capacity and its results. "Esoteric" typically refers to knowledge that is accessible only by an individual with a rare capacity to know the invisible and the profound. Steiner was clearly an extremely original and prolific esoteric researcher and teacher. He wrote approximately twenty books (or perhaps thirty or forty depending on how and what one counts), beginning in 1891 with *Truth and Knowledge,* his doctoral dissertation in philosophy, and ending with his unfinished autobiography, written in 1924, the year before his death. He delivered more than six thousand lectures, most of which were posthumously published in German, and about two hundred of which have been translated into English.[3] Some of his books of lectures, e.g. on the Gospel of St. John or on the Gospel of St. Luke, are extremely esoteric, while others are either entirely exoteric—i.e., generated by intelligence as distinct from clairvoyance—or a mix of esoteric and exoteric without indications of how to distinguish these two levels of thinking and insight.

Contrary to anthroposophists who claim that every word that Steiner spoke and wrote is true simply because he was clairvoyant, this book holds the view that much of what Steiner wrote and spoke included exoteric (ordinary intellectual) content, and further, that even his clairvoyant disclosures were limited by the process of translation from vision to words. The same is true of mystics who experience unity but then need to find a way to describe their experience. If artists claimed truth for their creations the same argument would have to be made against such claims. What Steiner was able to disclose as a result of his spiritual-esoteric capacity was truly astonishing and calls for gratitude from non-clairvoyant humanity, but it does no service to him or to other clairvoyants to insist that all of their translations from vision to verbal expression are necessarily true.

It seems to me evident that there are many doors into Steiner, and many doors out into the world of work as a result of his anthroposophic teachings and our anthroposophic practice. Choosing a way in and a way out of Steiner's teaching and anthroposophic practice is like focusing on one of the traditional yogas—knowledge, action, love, or contemplation. Ideally, whichever yoga we might practice will lead to the others. Similarly, a person can begin with a tour of a Waldorf school, or a biodynamic farm, or the Goetheanum, and work toward the center or foundation of

---

3. Gene Gollogly and Christopher Bamford, publisher and editor respectively of SteinerBooks, are committed to publishing Steiner's *Collected Works* in more than 300 volumes. For a list, see SteinerBooks.org or the last pages of each volume of the *Collected Works*.

Steiner's thought: philosophy of freedom, evolution of consciousness, or Steiner's conception of Christ. It is probably a good idea
to begin with his biography, some of which is exoteric, and some
very esoteric.

FAMILY AND EARLY YEARS

Rudolf Steiner was born on February 25, 1861,[4] in Kraljevec, Cro-
atia, within the Austro-Hungarian Empire. His parents, Johann
Steiner (1829–1910) and Franziska Blie Steiner (1834–1918), were
both born in southern Hungary. Young Rudolf's life seemed similar to that of any child of a working-class family in rural Austria,
but in terms of his karma and clairvoyant capacities, it clearly
was not ordinary. At age seven he was visited by a ghostly female
figure who requested his help and then suddenly disappeared.
Two days later, the boy's father received a telegram stating that
his cousin had committed suicide the day she had visited young
Rudolf in search of assistance as she made her way in the afterlife.
By remaining silent about this and similar experiences, he continued through his boyhood as though his life were indistinguish-
able from that of other boys his age. In fact, however, it was quite
unusual and lonely.

When he was eight years old, Steiner's teacher lent him a
book on geometry, wherein he found for the first time ideas
that expressed his own intuitive knowledge of a world of formal realities and sensory-free ideas. Steiner was grateful for
his experience of geometry not only because it validated spiritual forms behind or within physical realities, but also because
it enabled him to link the two worlds in which he lived: the
spiritual, with which he was immediately comfortable, and the
physical, of which he gained knowledge only by concentrated
effort. In his youth Steiner's thinking was more akin to the intuitive seeing that he considered characteristic of the early Greek

---

4. The date of Steiner's birth is ordinarily given as February 27, but this
    was actually the date of his baptism. Steiner was quite ill immediately
    after his birth. Fearing that he might not live until the scheduled bap-
    tism date two weeks later, his parents rushed him to baptism two days
    after his birth.

philosophers—clairvoyance accompanied by reflective analysis and explanation.

According to Steiner's description of evolution of consciousness that he developed in the last two decades of his life, the way of receiving intuitive ideas and images such as in the Book of Exodus or the *Iliad*, directly without doubt or analysis, was exactly right for human consciousness prior to the beginning of the Axial Age (approximately the sixth century B.C.E.).[5] Steiner was born into modern European consciousness characterized by rational-scientific inquiry, a consciousness that requires explanation and evidence. Steiner's experience of geometry signaled the beginning of his lifelong attempt to translate spiritual experience into intelligible vocabulary and argument.

While serving as an altar boy for the celebration of the mass in the local Roman Catholic Church, Steiner was saddened to see the disbelief that lived in the soul of the priest. He attended a scientific high school and graduated from a polytechnic college in Vienna. When he was fourteen, he endured a boring history teacher by reading Kant's *Critique of Pure Reason* in class. He continued to read the German philosophers, from Kant to Hegel and Schelling, throughout his teen and early adult years. During those years, he sought to reconcile his spiritual perception with his hard-earned knowledge by sensory perception. As a college student, Steiner tutored to a family with several boys, the youngest of whom, Otto Specht, had virtually been abandoned by his parents because of his hydrocephalic condition. After two years of patient work, Steiner not only brought the boy into normal family life, but also educated him on a par with those of his age and equipped him for productive life. Otto eventually became a physician. This successful pedagogical experience prepared Steiner to give instruction toward the end of his life to teachers of children in need of special care, a work that was subsequently advanced by Karl Konig, an Austrian physician who founded the Camphill Movement for "people in need of special care."

---

5. Karl Jaspers introduced the concept of Axial Age which is now in common use. See Karl Jaspers, *The Origin and Goal of History*, 1–21.

From Steiner's first years, as described in his autobiography written during the last year of his life, he was able to see into the world of spirits. Like Krishna, who was able to see, or know, his own previous lives and the previous lives of Arjuna (Bhagavad Gita, IV: 4–7), Steiner was able to see human souls, such as his aunt who appeared to him seeking his help, as well as the spiritual forces within the plant world. On his walks to and from school through the hills of Kraljevec on the Austrian-Hungarian border, Steiner saw the life force of plants, which he later referred to as etheric.

ROOTS IN GERMAN PHILOSOPHY

German Idealism: Self and History

In 1893, at age 33, seven years before he emerged as an esoteric teacher lecturing regularly to groups of theosophists, Steiner completed a doctorate in philosophy. His dissertation, entitled *Truth and Knowledge*, focused primarily on Johann Gottlieb Fichte, and it also included his original philosophical ideas concerning freedom in thinking. One year later he wrote a full-length philosophical treatise, *Philosophy of Freedom*. This work was the result of his own research on the history of Western philosophy, especially the explosion of philosophical genius called German Idealism that includes, in addition to Fichte, Immanuel Kant, Friedrich Wilhelm Joseph Schelling, and Georg Wilhelm Friedrich Hegel. In the "Barr Document" (1907), written for Édouard Schuré, Steiner refers to his reading in his early years:

> My attention was drawn to Kant at an early age. At fifteen and sixteen I studied Kant intensively, and before going to college in Vienna I had an intense interest in Kant's early nineteenth century orthodox followers.... In addition, I immersed myself in Fichte and Schelling....Then came acquaintance with the emissary of M (the Master). Then intensive study of Hegel. Then the study of modern philosophy as it developed from the 1850s onward in Germany, particularly the so-called theory of knowledge with all its various branches.[6]

---

6. Rudolf Steiner, "The Barr Document," in Robert McDermott, *The New Essential Steiner*, 80–90.

The philosophies of Kant, Fichte, Schelling, and Hegel continued to influence Steiner's worldview and his commitment to the creation of a new epistemology.

Steiner's first systematic philosophical books—his doctoral dissertation *Truth and Knowledge* (1891) and *Intuitive Thinking as a Spiritual Path* (1893)—are not themselves explicitly esoteric but serve as a foundation for his subsequent esoteric books. These early philosophical works, which are essentially epistemological, support his claims for knowledge of the spiritual world, but they do not refer to his conception or experience of higher beings such as Christ, the spiritual nature of the human being, or karma and the afterlife. He developed these ideas in lectures that he began to deliver in 1900, after accepting an invitation to lecture to members of the Theosophical Society first in Germany and then throughout Europe. His lectures on esoteric topics all presuppose philosophical writings influenced by Goethe and the German idealists—Fichte, Schelling, and Hegel.

In 1901 Steiner published *World and Life Conceptions of the Nineteenth Century*. In 1914, when it was time for a new edition of this work, Steiner used the 200-page book as the second half of a new book, *Riddles of Philosophy*, and wrote another 200 pages on the history of philosophy from the ancient Greeks until the end of the eighteenth century. Steiner's original philosophizing presupposed the standard history of modern philosophy: Descartes tried to replace philosophical confusion and religious superstition with mathematical certainty and philosophically distinct ideas. David Hume, arguing that Descartes's certainty was impossible, introduced an atomistic ontology and epistemology. In Hume's view, despite the appearance to the contrary, causality is not a law; it is rather the habit of seeing certain processes in such close proximity that one appears to be causing the other. He replaced causality with conjunction. Hume was a brilliant writer and a deep skeptic.

As a result of recognizing the force of Hume's critique of certitude in science and ethics, Kant set out to save some degree of certainty, especially concerning "the starry heavens and the moral law." Immediately following Kant, the German idealists—Fichte,

Schelling, and Hegel—tried to create philosophies built on a conception of the self in relation to natural, cultural, and historical
processes. In Steiner's study of German idealism there are perhaps two ideas, or perspectives, that proved to be defining for his
later thought:

1. The conviction, developed by Fichte, Schelling, and Hegel,
   and against Kant, that it is possible to break through the
   limits of knowledge that Kant set in his *Critique of Pure
   Reason* (1791)
2. The affirmation of a transcendent self as the source and
   guarantee of the effort to attain higher knowledge.

Although these convictions and his experience of Christ exercised significant influence on Steiner's philosophical writing, he
found that philosophical idealism needed to be supplemented by
a more direct and detailed account of the natural world. This
affirmation of nature is the other foot on which Steiner's philosophy stands, or other eye that provided him the possibility of an
in-depth and precise vision of both self and nature. Throughout
his life Steiner continued to build on Goethe, first on the details
and method of Goethe's philosophy of nature, and subsequently
on his aesthetics.

Goethe: Natural Science and Aesthetics

Prior to Steiner, spiritual or meditative thinking applied
to nature finds its fullest expression in the writings of Goethe,
who pioneered the work of observing the metamorphosis of
plant forms. Goethe's highly conscious receptivity enabled him
to observe plant structure and growth thoroughly, deeply, and
sympathetically. He was able to "see/think" what he termed the
Urpflanze, or fundamental generating principle of the plant. This
is an example of what Steiner means by a path of knowing "to
guide the spiritual in the individual to the spiritual in the universe." As Steiner's thought can be described as Goethean, it can
also be called Emersonian: Both Emerson and Steiner were deep
students of Goethe. Emerson read the entire fifty-five volumes of
Goethe's collected works in German. Emerson and Steiner were

also influenced by Schelling, particularly his attempt to develop both a philosophy of the "I" and a philosophy of nature—the very philosophical task shared by Emerson and Steiner.

Although their works are separated by a century—Goethe (1749–1832) and Steiner (1861–1925)—these two artist–philosophers of nature are united in their affirmation of the positive roles that disciplined subjectivity, true individuality, and enlightened volition play in the process of gaining scientific knowledge. Precisely because Goethe had the power to see the ideal form in the physical world, Steiner regarded him as the most modern thinker of his age. It is also true, and a sign of the enormity and complexity of Goethe's influence, that he was at the same time a major force for reclaiming the riches of classical Greece. In Goethe, Steiner found spiritual knowing in and through rather than separate from the external world. Steiner agreed with Goethe's insistence that the individual "is the most powerful and exact physical apparatus there can be" for observing the natural world. Goethe and Steiner also agree that natural phenomena reveal themselves fully to a person who approaches them with both an unbiased spirit of observation and a developed inner life in which the ideas of things manifest themselves.[7]

The natural philosophies of Goethe and Steiner should be seen as a neglected alternative to the conventional view that excludes the knowing subject from attempts to gain scientific knowledge. Steiner's approach to nature is thoroughly Goethean, but because it utilizes philosophically precise terminology and argument, it is closer to William James and Alfred North Whitehead. Steiner sought to provide an epistemology for Goethe's methodology, the result of which is a rich appreciation and understanding of the cosmos—every particular and every particle of it. Steiner's epistemology proceeds through three levels. Goethe excelled at the first level, imagination, through his disciplined experience of the natural world, including plants and animals. Steiner developed

---

7. See Arthur Zajonc, "Spirituality in Higher Education: Overcoming the Divide" (July 25, 2002).

the next two levels, inspiration and intuition, beyond the levels developed by Goethe.

Contemporary scientists influenced by Steiner's approach regard Goethe's natural science as a needed corrective to the paradigm that stands for separation and dualistic independence of self and world, or of mind and matter. Owen Barfield, one of the most distinguished anthroposophists, offers a clear account of the transformation of the concept of knowledge as a result of the Scientific Revolution:

> The vaunted progress of "knowledge," which has been going on since the seventeenth century, has been progress in alienation. The alienation of nature from humanity, which the exclusive pursuit of objectivity in science has entailed, was the first stage; and was followed, with the acceptance of man himself as part of nature so alienated, by the alienation of man from himself. This final and fatal step in reductionism occurred in two stages: first his body and then his mind. Newton's approach to nature was already, by contrast with older scientific traditions, a form of behaviorism; and what has since followed has been its extension from astronomy and physics into physiology and ultimately psychology.[8]

Goethe's natural science is primarily concerned with establishing a method of empirical science rooted in the knowing subject. It is worth pondering Ronald Brady's summary of Goethe's living, immediate empiricism regarding color in contrast to Newton's more reductionist conception of color:

> Even a cursory reader of Newton's *Optics* and Goethe's *Farbenlehre* (color theory) will quickly discover the difference between the two works. By his premises, Newton had to reduce color to the relations of primary qualities in order to explain it. His text is not about the experience of color but of the other angles of refraction of paths of light. In Goethe's pages, however, we find considerations of color as given: felt polarities of tone, of brightness and darkness, and

---

8. Owen Barfield, "The Coming Trauma of Materialism," in *The Recovery of Meaning, and Other Essays*, 188.

of saturation. While Newton attempts to understand color as a reductionist, Goethe performs an examination of immediate appearances, which Husserl would term a "descriptive morphology." Some hundred years before Husserl formulated the epistemological principles of such a science, Goethe had already begun to practice it.[9]

Along with other aspects of Goethean natural science, Goethe's *Farbenlehre* is also championed among scientists and artists influenced by Steiner. More important than the conclusions that Goethe and Steiner share, however, is their commitment to an approach or method, one that assumes and strives to advance the unity of science and art in "life and immediacy." For Goethe and Steiner, scientific knowing, indeed all knowing, begins with imagination, or more precisely, suprasensory or etheric thinking. In his essay on Goethean science, Hans Gebert recounts the following story, perhaps apocryphal, that exemplifies Goethean imagination:

> During his stay in Strasbourg, Goethe had been fascinated by its cathedral. He had examined it under all possible lighting conditions. Reflecting on the way in which its architecture combined the majestic with the agreeable, he developed a view new to him about Gothic architecture in general and, in particular, about its importance for Germany. He not only observed and sketched the cathedral, but also went so far as to use the tower to cure his predisposition to vertigo. He repeatedly climbed to a small, unprotected platform just below the top of the tower, fighting the giddiness until it no longer occurred. He tried to experience the building in as many ways as he could. When he was about to leave Strasbourg, he remarked to his friends that the tower was incomplete. He also sketched what it would have looked like had it been finished. Drawing on the original plans, one of Goethe's friends confirmed that he was right in his projections. When asked who told him about the original design Goethe replied, "The tower itself. I observed it so long

9. Ibid., pp. 149–150.

and so attentively and I bestowed on it so much affection that it decided in the end to reveal to me its manifest secret." Through observation, exercise, and mental effort he had penetrated to an imperceptible reality, to the idea of the architect.[10]

Goethe's experience of the ideal, physically incomplete steeple might be classified as fantasy or mysticism, but Steiner maintains that such an experience is exactly the kind of knowing that Goethe exemplified. It is precisely this capability that Steiner took as foundational for Anthroposophy, and particularly for his philosophies of nature and art.

Carl Jacobi, a friend of Goethe, espoused that "Nature conceals God"; Goethe responded that it is precisely through one's relation to nature that it is possible to know God in the form of eternal or divine ideas. These ideas are concealed to ordinary observation but can be revealed by practice of *gentle empiricism,* the term for Goethean sympathetic, imaginative observation of nature. Thinkers of the last two centuries have agreed with Jacobi against Goethe. An approach to science that requires even a trace of suprasensory perception is not likely to gain acceptance in the foreseeable future. It is understandable that Steiner, a clairvoyant from childhood, should be one of the few scientific thinkers of the past century to take up Goethe's determined attempt to derive ideas from the direct experience of natural phenomena. Eschewing the spectator role characteristic of modern science, the Goethean approach to science—like the Goethean approach to art—emphasizes the indispensable role of imagination in scientific thinking.

It is the recombination or reunification of the material and spiritual that gives significance to the Goethe–Steiner approach to science and art. Goethe, however, did not study his own powers of intuition, and did not develop a systematic methodology by which others could attain his ability. Standard biographies of Goethe note that after a severe illness at age eighteen he turned to introspection, mysticism, and alchemy. To this description

10. Hans Gebert, "About Goetheanistic Science," *Journal for Anthroposophy* (spring 1979), 45–46.

Steiner adds an esoteric explanation: During this illness Goethe's etheric body was loosened from his physical body, and thereafter, in a physical and etheric realignment appropriate for his destiny, Goethe was better able to permeate the etheric level of the physical world. Ever the scientist of spirit, Steiner sought to use Goethe as an example of the method and results of the *etheric thinking* necessary for progress in science and art. Through Anthroposophy, or spiritual science, Steiner advanced on Goethe's elementary efforts at suprasensory perception. In effect, Steiner begins where Goethe leaves off. Steiner also makes this power systematic and shareable.

Whereas Goethe was a poet and naturalist, Steiner was a philosopher of the self and nature and the ideal relationship between the two. While Steiner shared Goethe's interest in plants, and in fact shared virtually all of Goethe's interests, it was not in relation to plants that he sought to give imaginative thinking its most important role. Rather, Steiner claimed to show that this kind of inner penetration of the natural world would reveal to the observer a capacity for thinking that is self-confirming. Steiner contends that individuals conducting such exercises as Goethe conducted on plants—though it would be equally effective on any object as well as on the process of thinking itself—would eventually begin to notice their own new, more highly developed capacity for the intuitive-seeing-knowing of interiors.

Steiner's serious involvement with art and aesthetics dates to 1888 when at age twenty-seven he lectured before the Goethe Society of Vienna and published his lecture under the title, "Goethe as the Founder of a New Science of Aesthetics." The full extent to which Steiner's aesthetics issued from Goethe's is evident in this lecture and in several subsequent full-length studies, including *Goethe's Worldview* (particularly the sections on "Goethe and Schiller"), "The Phenomena of the World of Color," and "Goethe's Standard of the Soul as Illustrated in *Faust* and in the *Fairy Story of The Green Snake and the Beautiful Lily*."[11] For

---

11. For Steiner on Goethe's *Green Snake and the Beautiful Lily*, see Frederick Amrine, "Goethe's Spirituality as Revealed in 'The Fairy Tale of the Green Snake and the Beautiful Lily,'" *Being Human* (August–winter,

a deeper understanding of the significance of Goethe for Steiner's aesthetics, it is best to study Steiner's artistic works based on Goethean principles, especially the first Goetheanum. This building, of which only drawings and models survive, is the most impressive endeavor by which Steiner sought to join the physical and the suprasensory.

Nietzsche: Integrity in an Age of Alienation

In 1895, Steiner visited Friedrich Nietzsche who had been comatose for six years due to a breakdown he suffered in 1889. Steiner reported that he experienced Nietzsche's soul and spirit (the two higher "bodies," or principles) floating above Nietzsche's physical and etheric bodies in a way resembling accounts in the literature of near-death experiences. Thereafter, Steiner sought to solve the problem with which Nietzsche had wrestled throughout his brilliant and tortured life: the complacency and self-deception of conventional, contemporary Western morality. Steiner wrote a full-length study, *Friedrich Nietzsche: Fighter for Freedom*, depicting him as the archetypal cultural figure at the close of the nineteenth century. He affirmed the significance of Nietzsche's announcement of the "death of God" at that time. Steiner considered it to be part of his own mission to examine more systematically Nietzsche's announcement.

While Nietzsche's influence on Steiner was significant at the time, the influence of the natural philosophy of Goethe and the philosophies of the German Idealists was more comprehensive and enduring. The impact of Nietzsche on Steiner was due mostly to Steiner's direct experience of Nietzsche while he was in a coma, as a great suffering soul. Steiner's philosophical convictions and precision worked against Nietzsche's extreme subjectivity. It is important to note that Steiner's position is committed to the ideal of objectivity, though it remains thoroughly pluralistic, and even relativistic and individualistic. The double discipline of reverence and humility allows one to attain a personal and individual objective knowledge with respect to spiritual reality. As Steiner developed in his *Philosophy of Freedom*, objectivity is guaranteed by

2013), 30–38.

spirit itself and the subjective is provided by the individual karma of each inquirer.

From Theosophy to Anthroposophy

Isis was the goddess of the Mediterranean world for three millennia, from the first Egyptian kingdom to early Christian centuries. Her image was veiled because she held many secrets that were forbidden to be revealed. In 1879 Madame Helena Petrovna Blavatsky, or H.P.B. as she was called, wrote an enormous two-volume treatise, *Isis Unveiled*, that claimed to reveal the very same secrets that Isis had held for almost three thousand years. In mid-nineteenth century, Madame Blavatsky (HPB) traveled alone to the Middle East, Tibet, and across the United States. In 1875 Blavatsky cofounded the Theosophical Society with Col. Olcott in New York City. During the next half century, the Theosophical Society became a significant esoteric influence in the United States, Britain, Europe, and India (where in 1882 it established its international headquarters). The secrets that HPB unveiled concern the evolution of the earth, including humanity; esoteric teachings of early civilizations, especially Egyptian, Hebrew, and Greek; and the exalted teachers of each of these civilizations. HPB also provided a positive account of the teachings of Krishna, Buddha, and Christ. Blavatsky, and theosophists generally, regard all religious traditions as true expressions of the eternal revelation of the divine.

Blavatsky's life, which reveals her genuine esoteric, clairvoyant capacity, was controversial, influential, and tragic. Steiner is one of many clairvoyant/esoteric teachers to have been profoundly influenced by her research and writing, but almost certainly many more would have benefitted from her esoteric teachings had there not been a false accusation against her. The event in question decisively limited her legacy. The American Society for Psychical Research, a prestigious organization founded primarily by William James, sent Richard Hodgson to Adyar, India, to investigate the claims for and against HPB's esoteric abilities. Hodgson did not meet HPB because she had moved to London. Instead, he interviewed a husband and wife, former employees whom

HPB had fired because they had stolen from the Society house they were tending. They contrived a way to convince Hodgson to believe that HPB was a fraud. Hodgson subsequently wrote his so-called findings in the prestigious journal of the Society of Psychical Research, destroying HPB's reputation. Her closest colleagues abandoned her; she died in disfavor in London, 1891, at age 59. One century after the charge of fraud was published in its journal, the Society for Psychical Research admitted that the accusations against HPB were unfounded,[12] but current encyclopedias continue to cite the charges against her without mentioning the retraction. This event might be an example of Steiner's concept of "occult imprisonment," a takeover by a spirit hostile to the spiritual evolution of humanity.

From 1902 to 1909 Steiner served as general secretary of the German branch of the Theosophical Society on condition that he could speak from his own experience even if his ideas would contradict the official teaching of the Theosophical Society. It is worth noting that Steiner did not officially join the Theosophical Society—a fact that Steiner's followers tend to emphasize, just as they tend not to acknowledge Steiner's use of terminology and insights found in Madame Blavatsky's two double volumes, *Isis Unveiled* (1878) and *The Secret Doctrine* (1888). Steiner clearly saw his own esoteric teaching as contiguous with that of HPB, whom he regarded throughout his life with gratitude and respect. When Blavatsky died in 1891 Steiner was finishing his doctorate in philosophy, a full decade before he began his own esoteric teaching. In 1886, while editing Goethe's scientific writing and preparing his book, *Goethe's Theory of Knowledge,* he read A. P. Sinnett's *Esoteric Buddhism* (1883) a classic theosophical text written under the direct guidance of one of the discarnate masters of Theosophy.

In his fortieth year, immediately following his experience of Christ in cosmic manifestation, Rudolf Steiner began to use his natural clairvoyance to conduct esoteric research into a wide range of historical events and intellectual topics. Steiner's

---

12. See Vernon Harrison, *H. P. Blavatsky and the SPR: An Examination of the Hodgson Report of 1885.*

writings prior to his experience of the Mystery of Golgotha in 1899 were concerned principally with philosophy of nature, particularly Goethean natural science. Thereafter he began his career as an esoteric teacher. In his first esoteric lecture Steiner revealed the obscure symbolism in Goethe's fairy tale, "The Green Snake and the Beautiful Lily."[13] In 1901 he offered a series of lectures in the Berlin Theosophical Library that were published as *Mystics after Modernism.*[14] He then published *Christianity as Mystical Fact* in 1902 in which he sought to recount the origin of Christianity in relation to the esoteric teachings of Egyptian and Greek mystery centers that were transmitted secretly by initiates to their students. It would seem to be of some significance that the publication of this volume was the same year as the publication of William James's *The Varieties of Religious Experience,* the unsurpassed study of individual religious experience. Throughout the first decade of the twentieth century, Steiner was a prominent leader of the Theosophical Society, which was emerging in Europe as a significant organization for the development and dissemination of esoteric teachings. He clearly had developed important ideas, and especially the esoteric vocabulary of HPB.

From 1904 to 1909, Steiner published the other three of his four foundational works: *How to Know Higher Worlds* (1904), *Theosophy: An Introduction to the Spiritual Processes in Human Life and in the Cosmos* (1904), and the most systematic and detailed of his books, *An Outline of Esoteric Science* (1909). These carefully prepared works serve as the foundation for Steiner's practical insights in the sciences, arts, religion, social sciences, and education given to those who asked for Steiner's advice. They also offer many spiritual disciplines and practices through which individuals can strive to develop

---

13. For the complete text with illustrations, see Rudolf Steiner, *The Green Snake and the Beautiful Lily: A Fairy Tale,* tr. Julius E. Heuscher; illus. Hermann Linde. On its esoteric relationship to Anthroposophy, see Paul Marshall Allen & Joan deRis Allen, *The Time Is at Hand!*

14. Also published as *Eleven European Mystics, Mysticism at the Dawn of the Modern Age,* and *Mystics of the Renaissance and their Relations to Modern Thought.*

"clear seeing," or capacities for higher knowledge. During those same years, Steiner began to lecture on a wide variety of themes within the history of Western esotericism, including events depicted in the Gospels, the spiritual guidance of the individual and humanity, the influence on human beings of the cosmos and spiritual beings such as Krishna and Buddha, and the mission of four archangels (Gabriel, Michael, Raphael, Uriel). Steiner's foundational books and the thousands of lectures that followed all serve the essential task of Anthroposophy, namely, the attempt to gain loving and creative knowledge of the spiritual in the individual and the spiritual in the universe, and their interrelationship.

Col. Olcott served as president of the Theosophical Society from 1891 until his death in 1907. Olcott recognized Steiner's esoteric capacity, and Steiner recognized Olcott's organizational contributions, publicly praising them at the 1907 Theosophical Society meeting in Munich. When Steiner lectured on esoteric topics, members of the Theosophical Society were his sole audience. Until 1907 he spoke from within Theosophy in concert with its discarnate teachers, particularly the Indian master Morya and the Tibetan master Koot Hoomi, both of whom were called Masters or Mahatmas ("great souls") and both of whom had been the source of the teachings and activities of Blavatsky, and subsequently of Olcott.[15] Just before his death in 1907, Olcott disclosed that he had received a message from these masters that Annie Besant should succeed him as president of the Theosophical Society. During the 1907 meeting, Besant, having just assumed the presidency of the Theosophical Society, made it clear that Rudolf Steiner's teachings concerning the importance of Christ and his emphasis on the Western esoteric tradition were not consonant with her focus on Hindu and Buddhist spiritual sources.

Owing to Besant's negative attitude toward Christianity, a schism between Besant and Steiner, as well as theosophical and anthroposophic esotericism, was virtually inevitable. As Rudolf Steiner explained in 1907, there would be two esoteric

---

15. Rudolf Steiner, *From the History and Contents of the First Section of the Esoteric School 1904–1914: Letters, Documents, and Lectures*, 41.

schools, one headed by Annie Besant, whose focus would be on Hindu and Buddhist spirituality and be guided by Indian and Tibetan masters, and the other headed by Steiner and guided by "Master Jesus and Master Christian Rosenkreutz." Rudolf Steiner made it clear that members would have to choose between these two schools. In addition to her opposition to the esoteric Christian path that Rudolf Steiner was developing, and her commitment to a Hindu and Buddhist path that she was developing, Annie Besant resisted Steiner's emphasis on artistic practice and productions to which he was committed and that he introduced at the 1907 Munich International Conference of the Theosophical Society.[16]

Steiner wrote four mystery dramas, the first of which was performed in Munich in 1910. Throughout the years that he directed the German branch of the Theosophical Society, Steiner collaborated with Marie von Sievers, a Russian actress and linguist, who in 1900, on the recommendation of Édouard Schuré, had heard Rudolf Steiner lecture in Berlin. It was von Sievers who asked Steiner at that time why there was no Western esoteric school. Because esoteric teachers should await such a question before they offer an answer or initiative, a rule that Steiner followed faithfully throughout his life, this question by von Sievers proved to have profound implications for the destiny of Rudolf Steiner and the Theosophical Society. Four years later Steiner created the Western esoteric school, and twelve years later his followers founded the Anthroposophical Society. The question also had profound implications for Marie von Sievers, whom Rudolf Steiner married in 1914, and with whom he subsequently collaborated on many anthroposophic works, especially in the arts.

In 1912, Annie Besant, at the prompting of her colleague, C. W. Leadbeater, pronounced the sixteen-year-old Jiddu Krishnamurti (1895–1986) as a reincarnation of Jesus, the vessel for "Christ Maitreya," who would become the World Teacher.[17] They

---

16. See Rudolf Steiner, *Rosicrucianism Renewed: The Unity of Art, Science, and Religion; The Theosophical Congress of Whitsun 1907.*

17. Rudolf Steiner, *From the History and Contents of the First Section of*

announced the creation of a new esoteric society, the Star of the East, with J. Krishnamurti as its head. When Steiner, who was lecturing in Copenhagen, was informed of this development, he replied by giving three lectures in which he offered his own account of the spiritual destiny of the West, clearly in contradiction to the view of Besant and Leadbeater. He then carefully revised and published these important lectures under the title *The Spiritual Guidance of the Individual and Humanity*.[18]

Steiner did not discourage his followers, most of whom were former members of the Theosophical Society, from founding the Anthroposophical Society in December 1912. The process of separation, which has been under way for at least five years, resulted in the forming of two separate esoteric societies: Theosophy which has focused primarily on ancient Hindu and Buddhist sources, and Anthroposophy which has focused mainly on the Western esoteric tradition, including Egyptian, Hebraic, Greek, Christian, and modern Western esoteric sources, all understood within the guidance of higher beings allied with Christ. From the early twentieth century until the present the worldwide Theosophical Society and movement have continued to focus more on Krishna and Buddha and of course on the writings of HPB, Annie Besant, and other theosophical authors. The Anthroposophical Society and movement have continued to focus primarily on Christ, very secondarily on Krishna and Buddha, and of course on the writings of Steiner and authors influenced by him. Anthroposophy is intensely devoted to the evolution of human consciousness toward freedom and love.

The separation of the Anthroposophical Society from the Theosophical Society was not accomplished without loss. To this day, Steiner's name is almost entirely absent in books by theosophists.[19] Anthroposophists tend to ignore the obvious continuity

---

the *Esoteric School 1904–1914*, 264.

18. Rudolf Steiner, *The Spiritual Guidance of the Individual and Humanity: Some Results of Spiritual-Scientific Research into Human History and Development*.

19. Even Sylvia Cranston's *H.P.B.*, an exhaustive and judicious biography, gives only a cursory account of Steiner's relationship to the Theosophical Society.

between theosophical and anthroposophic teachings, especially concerning the evolution of consciousness and life after death, and tend to understate the years that Steiner spent as a teacher within the Theosophical Society which served as a preparation for his life as the primary teacher of Anthroposophy. Fortunately, the publication of *Spiritualism, Madame Blavatsky, and Theosophy*, twenty-one lectures by Steiner on Blavatsky and his view of the relationship between Anthroposophy and Theosophy aims to correct this ignorance on the part of both theosophists and anthroposophists.[20] This volume includes lectures primarily from 1904 to 1916 and as late as 1923, showing the abiding respect Steiner held for HPB, and leaves the reader with the impression that, if he had been able to collaborate with her instead of with her successors, Steiner might have been able to remain a teacher, perhaps *the* teacher, of the Theosophical Society. This would have been possible, of course, only if HPB had been able to accept Steiner's conviction that Christ has been the central spiritual reality for the West, albeit in close collaboration with Krishna and Buddha and other important spiritual beings.

STEINER'S CLAIRVOYANCE AND MISSION

The remaining three sections in this chapter on "Steiner Alone" focus on his singular capacities and commitments. In 1879, at age eighteen, Steiner met an herb gatherer, Felix Kogutski, with whom he was at last able to discuss his confident knowledge of spiritual realities (more accurately, the etheric world of plants, or world of subtle bodies). Prior to this meeting, he had no language by which to discuss the inner life of plants. Felix provided Steiner his first opportunity to share with another human being the reality of the etheric world as it manifests in nature, particularly in herbs. It was a great joy for Steiner to communicate a part of his experience that had been so important to him from his earliest years. More importantly, Felix Kogutski sent Steiner to one whom Steiner referred to as "M," his Master in relation to his

---

20. Christopher Bamford, ed., intro., *Spiritualism, Madame Blavatsky and Theosophy: An Eyewitness View of Occult History.*

esoteric tasks, or life mission. In a brief autobiographical sketch called "The Barr Document," which he wrote in 1906 at the request of Édouard Schuré, a prominent French esotericist whom Steiner was visiting in Alsace, Steiner acknowledged but did not identify this individual from whom he had received knowledge of his life work:

> I did not at once meet the M. [Master], but first someone sent by him [i.e., Felix Kogutsky, the herbalist] who was completely initiated into the mysteries of the effects of all plants and their connection with the universe and with human nature. For him, converse with the spirits of nature was a matter of course, which he described without enthusiasm, thereby awakening enthusiasm all the more.[21]

Steiner's spiritual master, or initiator, presumably discarnate, whom some students of Rudolf Steiner speculate might have been Christian Rosenkreutz,[22] gave him several tasks. We know from his autobiography that his mission, that for which he was initiated, can be summarized as follows:

1. To articulate his instinctual clairvoyance so that it might be used by others deliberately and systematically
2. To work for the loosening of the materialist grip on modern Western thought and culture
3. To reintroduce the teaching of karma and rebirth to the West and to Christianity.

The first and second tasks, both of which occupied him throughout his life, summoned him decisively at age twenty-one when he was invited to edit the natural scientific writings of Goethe. The third task, having to do with karma and rebirth, was certainly central to all of his work, but he was unable to give it full treatment until the year before his death, during which he gave ninety

---

21. Robert McDermott, ed., intro., *The New Essential Steiner*, 6.
22. For Steiner's account of the significance of Christian Rosenkreutz, see Christopher Bamford, ed., *The Secret Stream: Christian Rosenkreutz and Rosicrucianism*.

lectures on the successive earthly lives of historically important personalities.[23]

Not at all unrelated to his effort to fulfill his mission, Steiner was trying to earn a living and find the colleagues with whom he could work and enjoy a normal social life. In 1899, Steiner married Anna Eunike, the widowed mother of the five children for whom he had been a resident tutor. Steiner maintained his own section of the Eunike home for his work and for meetings with colleagues. Anna Eunike died in 1911. In 1914, at the outbreak of World War I, Steiner married Marie von Sievers immediately after she crossed the border from Germany into Switzerland. For the next ten years, Marie Steiner shared every detail of Steiner's work on behalf of Anthroposophy, especially with respect to the arts. She was also a problematic figure in the fractious history of the Anthroposophical Society from Steiner's death in 1925 until her death in 1948.

Steiner poured forth his research, both theoretical and practical, in more than 6,000 lectures on natural sciences, the arts, education, social theory, psychology, cosmology, and, most important, his account of the central role of Christ in the evolution of consciousness. From 1909 to 1913, he delivered more than a hundred lectures on events depicted in the Christian Gospels. In 1913, Steiner laid the foundation stone for the Goetheanum, an enormous wood auditorium he designed to be built on an imposing hill in Dornach, near Basel, Switzerland. He put into the building every conceivable artistic form that might enable the ordinary observer to glimpse the spiritual reality he saw in full force, particularly the ways in which the spiritual nature of the human being can be made manifest through the arts. In all of this research and teaching, Rudolf Steiner advanced a Goethean aesthetic. He chose the name *Goetheanum* to honor Goethe's understanding of metamorphosis, the natural and artistic processes of change.

The Goetheanum was perhaps the most impressive physical example of Steiner's creative genius. The architecturally unprecedented and influential interlocking double-cupola domes,

---

23. Rudolf Steiner, *Karmic Relationships*, 8 vols.

Above: *The first Goetheanum, a double-domed wooden structure, was opened in 1920 and destroyed by fire on New Year's Eve, 1922.*
Below: *The second Goetheanum, a formed-concrete structure, was built between 1925 and 1928.*

made of woods from all over Europe and North America, included architectural forms that subtly revealed the spiritual dimension of wood and glass. This building had been under construction for ten years by workers from seventeen countries, including Austria, Germany, France, and England, whose soldiers were battling in World War I in the hills around Switzerland. Steiner hoped that the first Goetheanum would give future generations of spiritually searching visitors some clues about the healing capacity of spiritually based arts.

The Goetheanum had just been completed when it was burned to the ground on New Year's Eve, 1922. Steiner's attempt to manifest spirit in architectural and sculptural forms was destroyed in one night. Steiner is said to have known the person who had caused the fire, but he did not disclose the person's name. He is reported to have seen the etheric body of the Goetheanum ascend in the smoke of the conflagration. As his own etheric body was so deeply attached to this building, it seems evident that something of Steiner drifted away as well. This depletion of his etheric forces resulting from the grief he suffered might well have hastened his death two years later. Insurance on the building made possible the construction of the second Goetheanum, built on the same hill, which serves as the headquarters of the Anthroposophical Society. Though imposing and artistic, the second Goetheanum, which is concrete, lacks the spiritual transformative intent, as well as the esoteric insight, sacrifice, and effect of the original Goetheanum.

Both in the Goetheanum and wherever Anthroposophy is fostered throughout the world, the arts are an important component. Steiner taught that the etheric, or life body, can be nourished and made healthy through sculpture and eurythmy, that the soul, or astral body, is strengthened by painting, and that the "I," or individual spirit, can be nourished especially by poetry. In response to the mother of a young dancer who asked for a new art form of movement, Steiner developed eurythmy. Superficially resembling modern dance, eurythmy is usually described as speech and music made visible. Like all true art forms, eurythmy is spiritually restorative. It is a way of forming and strengthening the performer's subtle body, the etheric life forces that surround and pervade the living physical body. Steiner developed eurythmy as a performance art, for therapeutic work, and for pedagogical use in schools, particularly Waldorf schools.

Steiner developed many of his contributions due to requests for help. In addition to eurythmy, Steiner also proposed new methods and creative innovations in a variety of traditional arts, including sculpture, architecture, painting, and music. Bruno Walter, the famed conductor of the Berlin Philharmonic Orchestra, and Wassily Kandinsky, a pioneer of abstract expressionism, among many other artists, were influenced by Steiner's worldview and his esoteric approach to the arts. From 1910 to 1913, Steiner wrote four mystery dramas so that modern Western audiences could experience dramatically the karma of paradigmatic individual lives through several incarnations. First performed in Munich, the dramas continue to be performed by anthroposophic communities and in the Goetheanum, whose enormous auditorium and stage Steiner designed specifically for performances of eurythmy and mystery dramas.

In answer to a plea from farmers, Steiner lectured extensively on a method of agriculture based on his suprasensory knowledge of the etheric forces operating in the Cosmos, Earth, plant, and animal worlds. This "biodynamic" method of farming has become an increasingly important agricultural alternative to chemically dominated farming in Europe, North and South America, India, New Zealand, and Australia.

The economic and social ills of the decade surrounding World War I led Steiner to develop an elaborate social, political, and economic philosophy that he called the "threefold social order." He based this ideal commonwealth on the three components of society: economic, legal/political, and spiritual/cultural. Among the many significant implications of this division is the protection of the cultural sphere (including religion, education, and the arts, and all other expressions of individual freedom and creativity) from the control of both the political and economic spheres.

In 1919, Emil Molt, owner of the Waldorf-Astoria Cigarette Factory in Stuttgart, Germany, asked for Steiner's help in educating the children of his employees. In response, Steiner developed an approach to education based on anthroposophic wisdom concerning the inner life and development of children. The Waldorf schools are especially significant for reconciling the sciences with the arts on the basis of a triple source and methodology—heartfelt thinking, conscious feeling, and responsible willing. The Stuttgart school became the model for the Waldorf school movement, which today includes several thousand schools throughout the world (including 300 Waldorf schools in the People's Republic of China), and constitutes, after Montessori, the second largest nonsectarian private school movement in the world. Waldorf schools are characterized by the attempt to integrate the work of head, heart, and hand (the disciplined cultivation of thinking, feeling, and willing), with the aim of educating the whole child in freedom and responsibility for nature, for the individual, and for the global human community.

Steiner responded to the requests of ministers and theology students who asked him for help in their effort to renew Christian life and liturgy. He inspired and helped fashion an institutional and ecclesiastical structure called The Christian Community (also called the Movement for Religious Renewal). He disclosed seven sacraments, including a liturgy called the Act of Consecration of Man, a ritual similar to the Roman Catholic mass. In contrast to Anthroposophy, whereby human beings strive essentially on their own to experience spiritual ascent, the intent of the Act of Consecration of Man[24] is to enable participants to experience a descent of the divine into the assembled community.

In response to requests from doctors for a course of lectures on homeopathic and anthroposophic healing, Steiner classified numerous herbs and other natural substances with various healing powers. There are now several hundred physicians who enjoy the advantage of a double training and methodology—standard medical training for allopathic prescriptive treatments, as well as the development of a capacity for insight and an image of the human being based on the teachings and discipline of

---

24. Evelyn Francis Capel and Tom Ravetz, *Seven Sacraments of the Christian Community*, 47–60.

Anthroposophy. Both Weleda and Wala, two worldwide phar-
maceutical companies, have developed and continue to distribute
products based on Steiner's esoteric research.

It is important to notice that Steiner lectured on a wide variety of topics not merely to general audiences, but to experts in the
disciplines on which he was asked to lecture.

Written in 1924, the last year of his life, Steiner's autobiography covered the years until 1907, when he was forty-six. Both
Steiner and Jung dictated their autobiographies during the last
year of their lives, Steiner at age sixty-four and Jung when he
was eighty. Both of these autobiographies focus primarily on their
interior lives. Sri Aurobindo, too, expressed none of the biographical details that others wanted him to reveal. The Dalai Lama has
written about his life in relation to Tibet, and Thich Nhat Han
has written about his life as a Vietnamese monk, but neither has
written or spoken about any intimate relationships they may have
had, nor did they reveal what it meant to have had or not to have
had such experiences.

Steiner did not have children, but it was widely reported
that he was tremendously fond of children, both the children of
his friends and those in the Stuttgart Waldorf School, which he
founded and guided in his last years. We know that Steiner was
attentive and generous concerning the welfare of his unmar-
ried younger sister Leopoldine, particularly in later life when
she was losing her sight. He had a compassionate relationship
with his younger brother Gustav, who was deaf and unable
to speak. It seems that Steiner's deepest personal relationship,
one that he described as having extended through previous lifetimes, was with Ita Wegman, a Dutch physician with whom he
collaborated on medical research for more than two decades.
This collaboration led to the publication of their book *Extending Practical Medicine: Fundamental Principles Based on the
Science of the Spirit.*

Steiner's research concerning medicine, like his research concerning agriculture, child development, economics, and history,
all typify his lifelong devotion to the practical results of esoteric/
clairvoyant research. His mission was simultaneously spiritual,

scientific, and practical. His teaching and spiritual discipline is different from but not opposed to either mysticism (understood as the experience of the unity of self, or unity of self and world, or self and divine) or to traditional religious belief. His esoteric path aims primarily at the kind of knowledge that can lead to the transformation of the human being and the revitalization of human culture.

Anthroposophical Society

Steiner neither founded nor joined the Anthroposophical Society that his followers formed in 1912, but he did work intimately on a daily basis with its leaders and members. Ten years later, during Christmas week of 1923, he reestablished the General Anthroposophical Society and assumed the position of its leader. Anthroposophy, a term that was introduced in the mid-nineteenth century by Robert Zimmerman,[25] was adopted by Steiner and his followers as early as 1906. It seems odd that one of the most stubborn obstacles to widespread knowledge of Steiner is the name Anthroposophy. While the English-speaking world is comfortable with the term *anthropology,* the term *Anthroposophy* is frequently found to be unpronounceable. *Anthropos* (Greek) means ideal human; *logos,* as in the suffix *–logy,* means knowledge; hence, *anthropo(s)-logy,* as in anthropology, which means knowledge of the human. Sophia, and the suffix *–sophy,* means wisdom, particularly divine feminine wisdom, as in *philosophy*—love of wisdom. *Anthropos-sophia,* or Anthroposophy, means human wisdom, as well as wisdom of the ideal human: knowing in a way that is itself the essence of the human.

Rudolf Steiner offers a spiritual path, a method of practice for the difficult process of attaining significant insights. His spiritual and esoteric teachings claim to be both life-affirming and life-knowing. Several months before his death, in a series of letters written to members of the Anthroposophical Society, Steiner wrote the following characterization of Anthroposophy:

---

25. Rudolf Steiner, *Autobiography,* 25–27, and 259 note 74.

Anthroposophy is a path of knowledge to guide the spiritual in the human being to the spiritual in the universe. It arises in the human being as a need of the heart, of the life of feeling; it can be justified only inasmuch as it can satisfy this inner need. Only those can acknowledge Anthroposophy who find in it what they themselves in their inner lives feel impelled to seek. Only they can be anthroposophists who feel certain questions on the nature of the human being and the universe as an elemental need of life, just as one feels hunger and thirst.

Anthroposophy communicates knowledge that is gained in a spiritual way. Yet it does so only because everyday life, and the science founded on sensation and intellectual activity, lead to a barrier along life's way—a limit where the life of the soul in the human being would die if it could go no further. Everyday life and science do not lead to this limit in such a way as to compel the human being to stop short at it. For at the very frontier where the knowledge derived from sense perception ceases, there is opened through the human soul itself the further outlook into the spiritual world.[26]

Steiner preferred this term *Anthroposophy* to *Theosophy* (divine wisdom) as a way of emphasizing that at this time in the evolution of consciousness human beings must gain a knowledge of the divine by their own effort rather than by divine revelation. While it is literally correct to understand the term *Anthroposophy* as the knowledge of the human, or human knowledge, we must understand that Steiner is here referring to the knowledge of the ideal or spiritually alive human. Such knowledge is produced by the higher, spiritually active self. Steiner aims to enable each human being to develop his or her spiritual faculties and thereby to develop knowledge of the spiritual in the cosmos.

Like Buddhist spiritual practice, it fosters wakefulness; like shamanism and earth-based religion, it fosters a direct relationship with nature spirits; it also fosters characteristics of consciousness such as nurture and embodiment. In his lectures published as *Awakening to Community,* Steiner suggested that he intended Anthroposophy to refer to the truest and most profound

26. Rudolf Steiner, *Anthroposophical Leading Thoughts: Anthroposophy as a Path of Knowledge: The Michael Mystery,* 13.

consciousness of one's humanness. Steiner developed Anthro-posophy for anyone who saw the need for a third way between religious faith and scientific knowledge. Steiner was born with the ability to excel at this third way, he then developed it further, and he learned ways to teach it to others. While he himself did not need techniques and practices, he did practice: He prayed, meditated, studied, practiced arts, and attended to his own con-sciousness with complete dedication. Steiner taught that the achievement of thinking one's own thoughts requires a strenuous exercise of will and a feeling akin to love.

Although mixing love with serious thinking might seem oxy-moronic, and certainly not ordinarily considered an ideal com-bination for the advancement of philosophy or science, Steiner insisted that this mix is needed precisely to overcome the limi-tation of modern Western thinking in general, and the peculiar limitations of philosophy and science in particular. His entire life's work was an attempt to show that the separation of think-ing from feeling and willing has proven disastrous for modern Western culture, and that their reintegration is needed for the survival of humanity and the Earth. The deepest and most imme-diate problem of contemporary thinking is simply that the exact nature and causes of this separation of thought from will and affect go largely undetected, and therefore uncorrected.

To enable the rest of humanity to develop the clairvoyance that came naturally to him, Steiner struggled to develop prac-tices he could share. Steiner's task resembles the mission and consciousness of Socrates in that he sought to begin a new tradi-tion. As Socrates led Western consciousness from myth to reason, Steiner sought to lead human consciousness from reason to intu-ition. He insists that no thinker of the ancient world—not even Socrates, Plato, or Aristotle—could have achieved, or would have needed to achieve, the kind of intuitive thinking that he, as a twentieth century esoteric teacher, sought to exemplify and justify. Steiner's spiritual-scientific way of thinking resembles the divine clairvoyance of Krishna as well as the highly reflec-tive analytic mind of Socrates. In its ability to render clairvoy-ance deliberate and verifiable it is obviously the creation of a twentieth-century thinker and teacher, at once scientific and in living relation with spiritual realities.

If one takes karma and rebirth seriously, one would admit that Steiner did not just happen to be born clairvoyant: he entered the world with this high power precisely because he had attained it—or some earlier version of it—in a previous life. Of course, not everyone is comfortable with the idea of a soul reborn. Steiner asks that we work with this idea, and specifically the idea that a soul carries abilities from one life to the next. According to Steiner, those who enter this life with a low capacity for spiritual discernment will be unable to know whether spiritual and esoteric teachings are valid, and whether practices based on such teachings are efficacious. More pointedly, such individuals will have little inclination to want to know! Those who exhibit little or no clairvoyance in daily life will avoid an attempt at esoteric discernment in favor of either religious belief, or skepticism, or perhaps a mix of both.

Steiner argues for and strives to demonstrate a mode of thinking that is at the core of great advances in science, art, religion, self-knowledge, and personal relations. One of the difficulties facing a person first approaching Anthroposophy in search of spiritual sustenance is simply that it appears to be a call primarily, or even exclusively, to thinking, an activity and practice that some spiritual seekers might consider too intellectual and academic, and thus antithetical to spirituality. But Steiner's concept of thinking is essentially spiritual, affective, and artistic.

Rudolf Steiner's entire life work was in response to the requests of others for help, and in all of his initiatives he waited for an actual question or request. This is an important mark of his esoteric legitimacy. There appear to be two exceptions to Steiner's observation of this rule but a closer examination shows them to be completely in conformity with it. The first apparent exception is his dozens of lectures on karma and rebirth which he delivered not in response to a human request but rather in response to the charge given him by his Master as part of his initiation. The second seemingly unsolicited contribution was his reestablishment of the Anthroposophical Society, a deed he explained was in direct response to a charge by the spiritual world, presumably by the Archangel Michael. In 1923 he founded the General Anthroposophical Society and the anthroposophic movement as ways of providing increased opportunities for collaboration and mutual support for individuals who feel called to practice suprasensory, heart-filled thinking. The General Anthroposophical Society—whether local branches, national societies, or its world center in Dornach, Switzerland—does not teach a set of beliefs, ideas, or positions. Anthroposophic teaching involves a free attempt to know and serve the spiritual world but the results of such inquiry should not then become dogmas or objects of unquestioning belief. Steiner stated anthroposophists should not say "we as anthroposophists hold" any particular idea.

Steiner did not deny his importance to his followers, but he tried to prevent the results of his research from being a bar to each person's own research and discernment. This works better in theory than in practice, for the simple reason that most individuals cannot actually attain significant esoteric insight, and so fall back on Steiner's. In this respect, it would perhaps be more accurate if students of Anthroposophy would refer to themselves not as anthroposophists, with its connotation of an ideological set of beliefs, but as "anthroposophers," a group of individuals who share compatible spiritual approaches and aspirations, as well as an accompanying worldview, and typically perform a certain set of spiritual practices such as meditation or the imaginative exercise of art or science, all irrespective of religious, political, and cultural commitments.

By 1923 Steiner's followers had spent ten years trying to implement his insights and, to a lesser extent, their own, but the results had proven uneven. After the destruction of the Goetheanum at the end of 1922, Steiner saw that his followers were not advancing Anthroposophy to the extent that he had hoped and expected. In some respects, Steiner's life work was nearly in ruins. The loss of the Goetheanum and the limitations of the anthroposophists themselves, who had a habit of dissension as well as dependence on him as a kind of guru, indicated that the task of bringing Anthroposophy into the world was more difficult than its founder had anticipated. In light of this limited success, Steiner reestablished the General Anthroposophical Society at a meeting in December 1923, in a carpentry shop next to the burnt concrete slab that had been the foundation of the Goetheanum.

The General Anthroposophical Society is an esoteric community continuous with the Christian esoteric tradition, modernized by its emphasis on individuality and freedom. Steiner understood the General Anthroposophical Society as an esoteric as well as an exoteric body, a mystery school to express the will of the spiritual world. He created this school in the conviction that it would further the mission of the Archangel Michael, whom Steiner regarded as Christ's emissary and as the regent and guide of the present time.

As reestablished by Steiner at Christmas 1923, the General Anthroposophical Society is open to anyone who wishes to join. A prospective member needs only to express support for the research conducted at or by the Goetheanum. Individuals are welcome to join irrespective of spiritual training, intellectual capacities, social standing, or religious commitment. Jews and Muslims, Hindus and Buddhists, as well as agnostics are no less welcome than Christians—though it must be admitted that much of the content of Anthroposophy, both its somewhat assumed worldview and specific practices, are more rooted in a Christian legacy, and more compatible with Christian than with non-Christian traditions. Perhaps Anthroposophy is not entirely compatible with other traditions because it has not yet fully evolved. Nonetheless, compatibility between Anthroposophy and each of the world religions remains important in principle though not yet entirely successful in practice. And because Anthroposophy has experienced numerous conflicts with various Christian denominations, particularly with the Roman Catholic Church, compatibility between even Anthroposophy and Christianity also awaits a fuller realization of the spiritual mission of both.

In a daring, selfless decision Rudolf Steiner united his own karma to the karma of the General Anthroposophical Society. Although he knew that it might be at great expense to his own spiritual destiny and to his esoteric-spiritual mission, not only for the remainder of his life but also for his life after death and presumably for future incarnations, he nevertheless created and assumed leadership of the General Anthroposophical Society as a mystery school open to all, including those who may be unprepared and unfaithful. Steiner's second gift to the members of the Anthroposophical Society was to present a four-part verse, subsequently called *The Foundation Stone Meditation* (see chapter 12, "Spiritual Practice").[27]

Steiner's Esoteric Research

It is unclear in advance for whom Steiner's *dharma* (his research and practice) might prove extremely important. For a start, a consideration of Steiner's ideas in comparison to the ideas of other twentieth- and twenty-first-century religious and spiritual thinkers might establish that there is at least one individual (and surely many others) who has attained important knowledge considered impossible by the dominant paradigm. You might decide that Steiner was a genuine clairvoyant, a clear seer concerning research on topics (e.g., karma, afterlife, and rebirth) widely regarded as unknowable. He was able to see spiritual realities, including something about exalted spiritual beings such as Krishna, Buddha, Christ, and Sophia. He reported on individuals who had died as well as the causes and meanings of important events.

Clearly, each person is unique in some respects, but individuals such as Steiner can be considered unique in the additional, more significant sense of exhibiting qualities and capacities that are rare, incomparable, even astonishing. Steiner and a very few other spiritual teachers, such as Sri Aurobindo and the Dalai Lama, exhibit capacities extremely dissimilar to us and even to most other spiritual teachers. Similarly, Steiner's ability to give four lectures a day, 6,000 lectures in twenty-five years, without notes yet ready for publication, on myriad subjects, is surely rare. More remarkably, Steiner's lectures and more than twenty (or thirty) books cover widely, even wildly, diverse subjects, including

---

27. For the full text, including three English translations and the original German version, see Rudolf Steiner, *The Foundation Stone Meditation*.

philosophy, science, the evolution of consciousness, spiritual practice, higher beings such as Christ, Sophia and archangels, karma and rebirth, the arts (especially painting, architecture, and mystery dramas), society (including economics), education (specifically the Waldorf approach), psychology, health and healing, the Earth, and the future.

Because Steiner offered a profound and systematic defense of his insights, he became a magnet for skeptical opposition. His writings are mostly ignored not only by academics but equally by religious thinkers, including *all* of the thinkers discussed in this book. Consequently, the skeptical opposition can argue not only against Steiner's claims; he or she can also argue that even religious and spiritual thinkers pay very little attention to many of Steiner's claims. Steiner's ideas are not only by far the most numerous, they are also the most "far out."

While the range and depth of Steiner's thinking seem to me far more vast than any of the teachers with whom he might be compared, such emphasis on the uniqueness of his capacities has proven unhelpful. Such counterproductive insistence lacks *upaya*, skillful means. Steiner wrote on philosophy, history, education, sciences, and the arts, and therefore he faced most, if not all, of the same challenges that any teacher does when attempting to offer advice on spiritual practice, on ways of attaining higher knowledge, on education and community, on ways to respiritualize the arts, and on ways to rejoin spirit and matter. Steiner is indeed distinctive in having bequeathed to humanity so many deep and truthful teachings on many important and challenging issues, all taught with compelling reverence and humility. Steiner's abilities and significance certainly do appear to be more comprehensive and detailed than those of comparable spiritual thinkers. It is important, however, that he not be isolated and made to appear strange.

Most of Steiner's perspectives and insights, while perhaps surprising and unusual, are worth considering, but some contained in this book may seem to you, the reader, implausible. On behalf of such claims I am essentially saying, "Yes, these are surprising ideas but you needn't focus on them, at least not at the outset. You can go a long way into Steiner's disclosures, methods, and advice without accepting, or even seriously considering, the ideas that you consider implausible. But if you stay with Steiner patiently and gently, even initially implausible ideas might gain in plausibility, perhaps by their association with ideas that are evidential and by association with Steiner, an honest, self-sacrificing servant of humanity and the spiritual world.

Steiner wanted all of his ideas to be affirmed, rejected, or revised by comparable esoteric investigation. As so few of us, and in fact scarcely any of us have the kind of clairvoyance that Steiner possessed from birth, however, we cannot adequately investigate these ideas. In deference to a truly great spiritual-esoteric researcher we might at least try to hold them respectfully. Anyone who cannot take these ideas seriously can nevertheless see the effectiveness of Waldorf education, the transformative power of biodynamic agriculture, the healing effect of eurythmy, and the sanity of Steiner's approach to society and money. As these innovations are increasingly accepted by the mainstream, perhaps the initially "impossible" ideas from the same source will merit a second look, or at least a gentle laying aside instead of a confident dismissal.

It is precisely Steiner's esoteric research and worldview, exercises, books, and thousands of lectures, that stand behind the Waldorf approach to education, biodynamic agriculture, eurythmy, innovations in architecture, and his analyses of past and current cultures. As a result, anyone interested in the Waldorf approach to education is likely to be led to Steiner's writings about karma and rebirth, angels and gnomes, the soul development of the child, and the tempters Lucifer and Ahriman. A person interested in biodynamic farming will soon be led to a consideration of etheric forces in composts and the esoteric meaning of Gaia. An interest in comparative study of religion will lead to Steiner's unusual claims concerning the relationships between Krishna of the Bhagavad Gita, the Buddha and bodhisattvas before and after the birth of Gautama, and an entirely unprecedented account of the entering into the body of Jesus of Nazareth of the souls of Adam, Zarathustra, Moses, Krishna, and Buddha.

Few of the thinkers discussed in this book affirm Steiner's dramatic claims. For Steiner's followers, this contrast typically leads to the conviction and claim that Steiner's disclosures are singular, that no other philosopher, religious, or spiritual teacher knows at the height, depth, or extent of Steiner. For anyone influenced by thinkers such as William James, Teilhard de Chardin, Sri Aurobindo, Gandhi, Rabindranath Tagore, or C. G. Jung, on the other hand, the singular claims of Rudolf Steiner are reason to avoid him. This can be, and usually is, a great either/or divide, but it needn't be.

A person can remain cautious, even somewhat skeptical, and still benefit from Steiner's esoteric thinking and spiritual practices. Steiner's "far out" claims might come closer when one is scarcely paying attention. But even if they do not—even if they stay out of reach after reading many books by Steiner or some of his followers such as Owen Barfield, Sergei Prokofiev, Peter Selg, Christopher Bamford, Arthur Zajonc, and Robert Powell— there are many hundreds of insights in Steiner's lectures that are entirely in reach even of someone whose thinking is formed by mainstream assumptions. The remainder of this book treats topics on which Steiner's views are comparable to the views of thinkers closer to mainstream, and in some cases to thinkers, with little or no spiritual insight but whose views are nevertheless compatible with some of Steiner's.

Some of Steiner's ideas are not shared by any of the great religious and spiritual thinkers discussed in the following ten chapters. Steiner's body of work is also rare in the volume of ideas, insights, creations, and recommendations. He contributed to the spiritual renewal of the individual and of Western culture in ways comparable to other important thinkers, but because he thinks more deeply and more widely than any of them, he can also be shown to provide support for the contributions of other esoteric claims and spiritual ideals as well as his own. One difficulty surrounding claims for his insightful contributions is simply that their number and range render them rather overwhelming. Steiner described the mysteries of life in sleep and between death and rebirth, he offered remedies for illnesses, recommendations concerning economics, directions for agricultural soil preparation, and the ideal fairy tales for five-year-olds. Who would want to believe that one person could know so much and make so many effective recommendations in so many different fields and endeavors? As Owen Barfield, philologist and cultural critic, asked,

> Why should we accept that one man was capable of all these revelations, however meaningful they may be? But there is also the other side of the coin. If those revelations *are* accepted, they entail a burden of responsibility on humanity which is itself almost beyond description.[28]

Steiner's claims to the truth of his method and teaching are backed and tested by his willing sacrifice on their behalf. He did not simply make claims; he reached important truths through strenuous and selfless effort, and then offered them freely to anyone who asked for them. All of his claims arose from experience won by diligent effort, and held up against frequent intellectual opposition. Toward the end of his life opposition became increasingly personal and violent. When a teacher or leader offers insights selflessly and peacefully that prove effective, and are backed by a demonstrated willingness to suffer on their behalf, such a person would seem to warrant a respectful hearing, certainly more than Steiner has received to date.

Academics are sometimes humorously ridiculed for allegedly asking, "Yes, it works in practice, but will it work in theory?" Steiner's contributions in education, farming, architecture, and medicine, as well as his volumes of philosophy and spiritual insight, are efficacious in both theory and practice. Steiner's followers, and others partially influenced by him, believe that he was sent by the spiritual world to do something significant. An increasing, though still relatively small number of individuals are convinced that he was sent on a mission to show the reality of spirit to a culture committed almost exclusively to materialism. As a twentieth-century central European thinker with a

---

28. Owen Barfield, "Introducing Rudolf Steiner," in Robert McDermott, ed., *The New Essential Steiner,* 94.

doctorate in philosophy and a deep knowledge of several sciences, Steiner sought to bring the ideals and methods of modern scientific objectivity to the experience and study of spirit in its myriad manifestations. A small number of contemporary Western scientists elicited his attention and respect. He taught them methods by which to break through perceived boundaries and gain direct knowledge of spirit. He also offered numerous solutions to stubborn practical problems.

The teachers in Waldorf schools continue to draw guidance from the hundreds of lectures that Steiner delivered on child development, curriculum, and pedagogy, all made possible by his ability to see and to communicate the realities of the inner lives of children. Secondarily, he is known for biodynamic agriculture. In time, he will be known for his economic theory and medical recommendations. On his deathbed during the first months of 1925, he asked every day for the latest books in the sciences, social sciences, and the arts.

This book assumes that anyone interested in the thought of Rudolf Steiner should also be interested in other twentieth- and twenty-first-century world-class spiritual thinkers. The book also contends that anyone interested in one or more of these thinkers should be interested in Rudolf Steiner's contributions to philosophy, education, arts, sciences, interpretations of exalted beings, and recasting of society (legal, financial, and cultural). These are all doors into Steiner's thought as well as doors out from Steiner's thought to its practical implications. Steiner offers claims and descriptions concerning everything from evolution of Earth to the activities of angels and archangels; the influence of planets on the soil of Earth, to the physical and spiritual development of the child. Following Steiner's request to his readers, audiences, and followers, this book does not ask for belief. It presents these and dozens of other unusual ideas in the hope that the reader will consider them in reverence and humility, the first steps of the spiritual discipline that Steiner recommends in his foundational book *How to Know Higher Worlds* (1904).

Despite his inspiring example of engagement with social issues and academic research, his followers—perhaps because they have been so in awe of his capacities and achievements—too often treat him as their absolutely single source of spiritual and esoteric insight. Contrary to his own attitude and example, Steiner's followers often expound his ideas in separation from, and often in contrast to other great thinkers and movements. This book attempts to forge new relationships between Steiner and comparable thinkers, to place him in explicit relation, and to remove the perception of Steiner's isolated singularity.

It is worth recalling that at the end of his life, Steiner reported that almost all of the major tasks that he had taken up as his own, beginning with editing five volumes of Goethe's natural scientific writing, were actually tasks that others, both consciously and unconsciously, had avoided. Steiner generated his leading ideas in response to appeals for help from followers, colleagues, and the public that came to him daily. He generated his entire teaching and practical innovations in response to the needs of the human community, including needs that were and are desperate, yet dimly perceived by most of humanity. He bequeathed both commonplace and highly esoteric teachings, all intended to increase human self-understanding. It would be difficult to find an author, teacher, or activist responsible for a body of work more generative of positive results in so many fields. By almost any criteria of intellectual and practical significance, Steiner should be taken very seriously, particularly in this extremely precarious time.

Ralph Waldo Emerson
William James
Josiah Royce

PHILOSOPHY

RALPH WALDO EMERSON: THE ACTIVE SOUL

Students of Rudolf Steiner are fond of quoting Steiner's comment that the whole of Anthroposophy can be found in seed form in the writings of Ralph Waldo Emerson (1803–1882). But it is not well known that Steiner's philosophy also bears significant resemblance to the philosophies of William James and Josiah Royce. Like Steiner, Emerson was steeped in the thought of Goethe, and sought to overcome the limitations to "Pure" (theoretical) knowledge set by Kant's *Critique of Pure Reason*. As a prophet and exemplar of original thinking and the active soul, in the mid-nineteenth century Emerson gave to America, and thereby to the world, a vision of culture based on ideals thoughtfully reviewed and freely affirmed. In Emerson we observe a figure schooled in history, literature, and thought. By the time he was ordained a Unitarian minister in 1829 at age twenty-six, the Calvinist theology of Jonathan Edwards had begun to lose favor, but an emphasis on individual religious experience championed by Edwards remained central to the evolving conception in New England of religion and human nature.

Emerson wrote two major declarations of American cultural and epistemological independence: "Nature" (1836) and "The American Scholar" (1837). His defining task was to convince his American listeners to overcome dependence on dogmas, religious institutions, and the great European intellectual tradition. Emerson taught that it is better to think one's own thoughts poorly than borrow from the wisdom of sages—though Emerson himself, along with most authors writing in nineteenth-century New England borrowed extensively from Goethe and other European thinkers. Prophet and critic of the new culture, Emerson expressed most of the ideals developed by the thinkers grouped as the New England Renaissance.

Although Emerson is identified with transcendentalism, perhaps the surest entry to Emerson's thought is the relationship that he establishes between thinking and democracy. Emerson teaches that all individuals in the still new democratic American culture can think their own thoughts, and can thereby participate in the ideal and practice of democracy. Emerson created a democratic epistemology according to which a free-thinking person can create a new world, one which will prove worthy of coming generations. In a way that anticipates William James and John Dewey, both of whom consciously built on him, Emerson understood democracy and original thinking to be coextensive. He contended that the ideal of original thinking was not only a possibility but, in a culture committed to the democratic ideal, a necessity. He wrote:

> Original thinking is and should be ordinary: "the genius is our most indebted man"; a genius should accept no awards; the idea is to get in, render the situation more workable, and then get out before you get in the way.
>
> Why should not we have a poetry and philosophy of insight and not of tradition, and a religion by revelation to us, and not the history of theirs? ... There are new lands, new men, new thoughts. Let us demand our own works and laws and worship.[1]

Emerson has ever since been prized for this declaration of American intellectual and religious freedom of thought, freedom of expression, and freedom to trust one's own experience. Many of the quotations influential on American thought and culture are to be found in Emerson's essays. Perhaps the most famous of

---

1. Ralph Waldo Emerson, "Nature" in Stephen E. Whicher, ed., *Selections from Ralph Waldo Emerson*, 16.

these quotations is the following: "Why should not we also enjoy an original relation to the universe?"

Emerson's individualism focused on the relationship between personality and the transcendent Self which is universal and infinite. Gertrude Reif Hughes offers this summary of Emerson's advice:

> Noting that many people feel defeated by circumstances, he recommended that they counter their melancholy by remembering their own infinitude. "As fast as you can," he urged, "break off your association with your personality and identify yourself with the Universe." Why does such self-transcendence make one both freer and more oneself, rather than less so? Because— and this is the paradox of "the infinitude of the private man"— "I could not be, but that absolute life circulated in me, and I could not think this without being that absolute life."[2]

Such is the message of Transcendentalism: The self that I am is comprised of my double membership in the world of personality and in the world of the absolute infinite. This double citizenship is very close to *Critique of Practical Reason*, Kant's second great philosophical treatise in which he established an alternative to his first *Critique*: whereas the first *Critique* set the limits to pure knowledge, the second *Critique* established the possibility of reaching the noumenal (transcendent) realm by a free moral choice, one with a maxim worthy to be universalized. The Romantic tradition, of which Emerson is the primary American representative, follows from Kant's second *Critique*. What is not possible by pure reason is possible by moral and aesthetic experience. Steiner's philosophy is solidly in this same tradition—but in his *Philosophy of Freedom* he is also arguing, against Kant's *Critique of Pure Reason*, for certitude concerning one's experience of the spirit, freedom, and immortality. According to Emerson, we are the creator of our truth and meaning, and at the same time we are that because we are, in a prior and fundamental way, the

---

2. Gertrude Reif Hughes, "Emerson's Epistemology with a Glance at Rudolf Steiner," in Kate Farrell, ed., *Anthroposophy and Imagination, Classics from the Journal for Anthroposophy*, 35.

absolute infinity that circulates in each of us, without which we could not think or be a person at all.

Admittedly, during the century and a half since Emerson developed this defense of individualism, American culture has not shown itself to be a faithful example of or environment for the Emersonian ideal. Yet, to the surprise of its observers, American thought and culture returns repeatedly to a transcendentalist ideal remarkably like Emerson's. In the present generation, in response to the poverty of behaviorist images of the human being, transpersonalism, a late twentieth-century Romanticism, has risen as a modern transcendentalism. Emerson is thoroughly transpersonalist in that he talks about a kind of altered state, not one made possible by hallucinogens, but one which is significantly different from our received thinking. To the extent I think a true thought, or commit a free moral deed, I am able to do so because of my relationship to the universal and absolute life. It is a tiny step from Emerson's transcendentalist epistemology to William James's transpersonalist concept of a "'Something More' through which saving experiences come," and another small step to contemporary transpersonalism.

WILLIAM JAMES: MULTI-PERSPECTIVE AMERICAN

Throughout its history, America has been characterized by its radical pluralism and evolving character. It is appropriate, and perhaps necessary, that these qualities should also characterize the philosophies of William James (1842–1910) and John Dewey (1859–1952),[3] the two most representative of American philosophy in the twentieth century. Extending the Romantic vision and epistemology of Emerson, at the turn of the twentieth century William James celebrated every form of pluralism—varieties of religious experience, philosophical perspectives, and psychological types. Like America, James was open to possibilities and alternatives, determinedly resisting any one metanarrative that would exclude others. It is James who gave us the definition of philosophy as "the habit of always seeing an alternative," a definition

---

3. For the philosophy of John Dewey see chapter Nine.

with a distinctly American ring. In his Phi Beta Kappa Oration at Harvard, June 1911, Josiah Royce explained that only two great American thinkers had made novel and notable contributions to general philosophy, Jonathan Edwards and Ralph Waldo Emerson. He then offered that his friend and senior colleague, William James, should be considered the third "representative American philosopher... the interpreter of the ethical spirit of his time and of his people." Royce then offered a wish that has largely come true: "Let him, too, be viewed as a prophet of the nation that is to be."[4]

William James, the philosopher most associated in the popular mind with American philosophy, was born in New York City where he was visited soon after his birth by Emerson, a friend of his father, Henry James, Sr. William was the oldest son in a famous family with friends throughout the intellectual world. His brother was Henry James the novelist. For James, the essence of religious experience is conversion and mysticism. James studied painting and biology (during which time he went on an influential and complicated year-long trip to the Amazon with Louis Agassiz), and then he became, successively, a physician, a psychologist, a philosopher, and a psychical researcher. He traveled throughout New England in search of "one white crow" who could transmit messages from "the other side."[5] James wrote on psychical research every year until his death in 1910; it was one of his most consuming intellectual passions. Even during the current revival of interest in his thought, however, James's contribution to psychical research remains largely ignored by philosophers and psychologists. Had James not been influenced by the report on HPB for the (American) Society of Psychical Research (see chapter 2), and thereby discouraged from taking seriously her clairvoyant writings, he might have taken a step closer to an appreciation of Steiner. Or, if Jung had been more respectful of Steiner's esoteric research, he might have passed such an opinion

---

4. Josiah Royce, "William James and The Philosophy of Life," in *William James and Other Essays on the Philosophy of Life*, 44–45.

5. See Robert McDermott, "Introduction," William James, *Essays in Psychical Research. The Writings of William James*, xxii.

on to James when they met in 1909, a meeting which, by the way, was reportedly excised from the published version of Jung's *Memories, Dreams, Reflections.*

James had an overabundance of intellectual interests and talents: He was equally psychologist by virtue of his classic study *Principles of Psychology* (1890), religious thinker by virtue of his classic study *The Varieties of Religious Experience* (1902), and philosopher by virtue of his major works, *Pragmatism* (1907), *Pluralistic Universe* (1909) and *Essays in Radical Empiricism* (1912). In all these works, James shows himself the carrier of the American impetus toward overcoming dualism: especially mind/matter, organism/environment, individual/society, and human/divine—precisely the task of Steiner's epistemology. In its focus on individual experience, James's philosophy lends support to Steiner's *Philosophy of Freedom*, but it is difficult to find in James's writings an affirmation of an enduring self. In this respect James contrasts with Steiner whose primary philosophical aim was to establish an immortal self in the context of a spiritual universe.

In the tradition of David Hume, the eighteenth-century skeptical Scottish empiricist, James conceived of the self as a recurring phenomenon, or nexus of relations, the forerunner of the self in Whitehead's *Process and Reality.* In his study of religious experience, for example, he focused entirely on the varied experiences of individuals as the instrument of certain consequential attainments, but he did not affirm a continuing self. He explained the so-called sick-soul temperament, religious conversion, saintliness, and mysticism as examples of dramatic experiences, of particularly meaningful relations, in the sphere of religion. Temperamentally and philosophically a pluralist, James regarded the religious experience of each individual to be evidence that human experience is resistant to a single summary.

All of James's philosophical writing is vivid, but perhaps none so vivid as the first chapter of *A Pluralistic Universe*, "The Types of Philosophic Thinking." It is important and enjoyable to experience James's thinking and mode of expression:

> Let me repeat once more that a man's vision is the great fact about him....A philosophy is the expression of a man's intimate

character, and all definitions of the universe are but the deliberately adopted reactions of human characters upon it.[6]

In the same lecture James declares himself on the side of the empiricists:

> Empiricism means the habit of explaining wholes by parts, and rationalism means the habit of explaining parts by wholes. Rationalism thus preserves affinities with monism, since wholeness goes with union, while empiricism inclines to pluralistic views.[7]

It should be easy for the reader to see that the best way to explain James is to quote him. Not only is he unfailingly felicitous, he is always convincing, even if one holds a position opposite to his. It could not have been easy for Royce, his younger colleague, to deal with James's overwhelming philosophical charm. Further, James's argumentation is not merely clever, but also genuine. James reduced the fundamental philosophical divide between rationalism (which he ascribed to Hegel and Royce, the attribution to Royce being increasingly inaccurate) and his own empiricism:

> But all differences are minor matters which ought to be subordinated in view of the fact that, whether we be empiricists or rationalists, we are, ourselves, part of the universe and share the same one deep concern in its destinies.[8]

Like Emerson, who considered himself to be "an artist in the medium of theory," James, an accomplished painter in his early years, vividly depicts relationships and processes. James is devoted to the universe in its many parts, and not at all in terms of a Hegelian absolute:

> We humans are incurably rooted in the temporal point of view. The eternal's ways are utterly unlike our ways. "Let us

---

6. William James, *A Pluralistic Universe*, 20.

7. Ibid., 7–8.

8. Ibid., 12.

imitate the All," said the original prospectus of that admirable Chicago quarterly called the *Monist*. As if we could, either in thought or conduct! We are invincibly parts, let us talk as we will, and must always apprehend the absolute as if it were a foreign being.[9]

For Hegel and Royce, of course, as well as for Steiner, the absolute, the eternal, infinitude, is neither separate nor foreign. It is to be distinguished but not separated from the relative, temporal, and finite. The absolute and infinite was experienced by Hegel and Royce (until his last decade), but not by James.

If James rested in a position, the following would probably be its most accurate summation:

> Every bit of us at every moment is part and parcel of a wider self.... There are religious experiences of a specific nature...that point with reasonable probability to the continuity of our consciousness with a wider spiritual environment from which the ordinary prudential man...is shut off.[10]

Steiner deeply appreciated the thought of Emerson but unfortunately knew the writings of William James only by a poor translation of his *Pragmatism*. Had James read Steiner's writings on Goethe, or on German idealism, or his *Philosophy of Freedom*, one hopes that he would have been more amenable to Steiner's philosophic probity and thereafter his esoteric research. After all, Steiner really was the "one white crow" that James sought so conscientiously. In my essay on "James and Steiner" in *American Philosophy and Rudolf Steiner*,[11] I offered three points of comparison, though on rereading them now I notice that they are primarily points of contrast: their conceptions of experience, particularly at the outer and most significant reaches of consciousness, where contact (James) and extraordinary knowledge (Steiner) can be attained; their views of process (James) and evolution of consciousness (Steiner); on James's inattention to the kind of spiritual

---

9. Ibid., 40.

10. Ibid., in William James, *A Pluralistic Universe* (Harvard U. P.1977), 135.

11. Robert McDermott, in *American Philosophy and Rudolf Steiner*, 60.

discipline that Steiner practiced and taught. The remainder of this essay ignores these points of contrast between James and Steiner and focuses on the ways in which James's philosophy indirectly makes the case for Steiner's essential philosophical and esoteric claim, that the entire goal of human life, particularly for Western humanity, is to strengthen the spiritual in the individual in relation to the spiritual in the universe.

In his *Varieties of Religious Experience,* James offers an unsurpassed account of individual religious experience. It could serve as a prolegomena, or preparation for, Steiner's *Philosophy of Freedom* or his *Knowledge of Higher Worlds.* The difference, of course, is that James relied on documents and Steiner relied on his intuition. These are different and complementary, not incompatible. The deeper affinity between James and Steiner, however, would seem to be between their philosophies, specifically: empirical (evidential), phenomenological (based on individual human experience, not abstract systemization), pluralistic (radically multiple perspectives), though also monistic (anti-dualistic, unity and complexity of consciousness), and open ended (philosophy more as process than a systematic set of conclusions).

Turning to Steiner, he seldom if ever mentions an absolute reality; he speaks of spirit and divinity, but always in varieties of images, grades, functions, and deeds. James and Steiner both wrote in and to a culture divided between religious theism and scientifically inflected atheism (or atheistically inflected science), and both sought a middle position—middle or alternative choice, what James Joyce referred to as "one aneither."[12] To the extent that James maintained a position—always a question with him—he favored pluralism, but of a spiritual and idealist variety against a materialism that excludes spirit. Against an idealism that affirmed too much unity, too absolute, he advocated for a radical pluralism. He sided with consciousness over matter and within the consciousness perspective he sided with facts, particulars, and data over abstraction and too tight of a unity. Pluralism, after all can account for imperfection and the reality of myriad particulars, incomplete and imperfect:

12. Thanks to my brother Ray (R. P.) McDermott, a deep reader of Joyce.

My conclusion, so far, then, is this, that although the hypothesis of the absolute, in yielding a certain kind of religious peace, performs a most important rationalizing function, it nevertheless, from the intellectual point of view, remains decidedly irrational.[13]

For James the concept of the absolute is irrational because it is thought to be perfect whereas its parts are manifestly imperfect. This leads James (and Whitehead after him) to conclude that the only God worthy of the name must be finite.

JOSIAH ROYCE:
LOYALTY AND THE BELOVED COMMUNITY

In 1855, during the Gold Rush in the Sierras, Josiah Royce was born in Grass Valley, in a community, as he said, only a few years older than himself. His family moved to San Francisco where Royce, a precocious teenager, attended Lowell High School, and in 1875 received his BA from the University of California, Berkeley where he soon after taught literature and writing. A group of businessmen sent Royce to Germany to study philosophy. He then earned a doctorate in philosophy from Johns Hopkins University, the first doctoral program in the United States. While teaching at Berkeley, Royce wrote to William James at Harvard explaining that he wanted to be a philosopher but as he was in California he had no one to talk to. James invited Royce to replace James while he would be on sabbatical. Royce was given a permanent position in the Harvard philosophy department in 1884, and continued there as the younger colleague and philosophical sparring partner of William James, with whom he is invariably associated. The friendship of James and Royce—who lived next to each other on Auburn Street, Cambridge, for twenty-five years—is endlessly fascinating. They both taught at Harvard during the last decade of the nineteenth and first decade of the twentieth century, and both were original philosophers with deep and wide knowledge in other fields, including the sciences and religion.

---

13. Ibid. 123.

In his inspiring and scholarly book, *Reverence for the Relations of Life: Re-imagining Pragmatism via Josiah Royce's Interactions with Peirce, James, and Dewey*, Frank Oppenheim, S. J., shows that Royce's devotion to community, in this case a community of brilliant philosophers, advanced the dialogue that established the years 1885 to 1910 as one of the great periods in the history of philosophy. Royce valued and sought community but was ill suited to social life or fame, two of the many ways in which James excelled. For Royce, religious experience issues from and returns to the community. The essence of religion is triadic, two poles brought into relation by a third. His core text was the words of Jesus: "Where two or three are gathered in my name, there I am in the midst of them" (Matt. 18:19–20). James could appear cheerful and intensely social as a way of masking a profound depression; he celebrated recovery from melancholia and a divided soul. Despite health and family challenges, Royce based his entire life on hope and the atoning power of community.

Royce understood that the desires of the individual and the ideal of community can be complementary, even ideally so, but they can also conflict, and often do. While a morally sensitive person might find it sufficient to rely solely on his or her own conscience, almost everyone needs guidance. The purpose of this guidance is to make a person loyal. Without using the term, Royce is offering *virtue ethics*—i.e., a theory of ethics that focuses not on the rule (as, for example, Kant's categorical imperative) or consequences (as, for example, the utilitarianism of John Stuart Mill or the pragmatism of William James), but rather one that focuses on the development of character, specifically the loyal person who faithfully and habitually serves worthy causes.

Among the causes most worth serving are those that have proven to be, or are likely to be, "lost," causes that do, or will live in memory:

> Loyalty to lost causes is, then, not only a possible thing, but one of the most potent influences of human history. In such cases the cause comes to be idealized through its very failure to win temporary and visible success. The result for loyalty may be vast. I need not remind you that the early Christian church

itself was at first founded directly upon a loyalty to its own lost cause—a cause which it viewed as heavenly just because here on earth the enemies seemed to have triumphed, and because the Master had departed from human vision.[14]

Loyalty to a lost cause, furthermore, can lead the loyal servant of the lost cause to a deeper reality: "Sorrow, defeat, disappointment, failure, whenever these result from our efforts to serve a cause, may all be used to teach the same lesson," namely, that we can learn whether we are truly devoted to this cause. If so, our cause will be transformed and idealized, as the lost throne of David was idealized by Israel, and as the departed Master's cause was idealized by the early church. Royce's philosophy of loyalty encourages us to regard defeat and sorrow as a deep opportunity.[15]

With respect to lost causes, sorrow, defeat, and bereavement, Royce knew whereof he spoke. In the midst of a life well acquainted with tragedy, death, and disappointment that filled Royce's life, two deserve special mention. First, surely, is the incredible family trauma Royce enduring when he was forced to commit his oldest son Christopher at age 21 to an insane asylum. Secondly, he saw his philosophy losing attention and influence because of the spread of anti-idealist and anti-Christian thinking, including in his beloved Harvard department of philosophy. Royce remained loyal, and in fact increased his explicit loyalty, to both loyalty as a bridge to religious experience, and to the specific religious life based on the reality of Christ the Logos–Spirit as described in the letters of Paul and the Gospel of John. Surely some of the disinterest in Royce from his time until recently has been due to his explicit affirmation of the Logos–Spirit found in the Epistles of Paul and the Gospel of John. Royce's mature thought, the metaphysics, ethics, and philosophy of religion (logic was also a preoccupation) that he developed during the last five years of his life, must be seen as empiricist and pragmatic as well as affirmative of the reality of the eternal, and particularly

---

14. Ibid., 130–31.
15. Ibid., 130–33.

the eternality of the Beloved Community. Royce's later works, especially his *Problem of Christianity*, is too complex and subtle to permit any of the usual labels.

Ever the professor of philosophy (as well as a loyal servant of worthy causes), Royce leads the reader to a level, at which we are invited to integrate our moral life with metaphysics and religion:

> Human life taken merely as it flows, viewed merely as it passes by in time and is gone, is indeed a lost river of experience that plunges down the mountains of youth and sinks in the deserts of age. Its significance comes solely through its relations to the air and the ocean and the great deeps of universal experience. For by such poor figures I may, in passing, symbolize that really rational relation of our personal experience to universal conscious experience.[16]

Royce criticizes a pragmatic approach to truth that omits this eternal dimension, one that is close to the noumenal realm manifest by a loyal implementer of Kant's categorical imperative and perhaps even closer to Steiner's *Philosophy of Freedom* (with which Royce was apparently unfamiliar). Here is Royce's conclusion to the chapter in *Philosophy of Loyalty* entitled "Loyalty, Truth, and Realty":

> Truth, meanwhile, means, as pragmatism asserts, the fulfillment of a need. But we all need the superhuman, the city out of sight, the union with all life—the essentially eternal....My cause partakes of the nature of the only truth and reality that there is. My life is an effort to manifest such eternal truth, as well as I can, in a series of temporal deeds. I may serve my cause ill. I may conceive it erroneously. I may lose it in the thicket of this world of transient experience. My every human deed may involve a blunder. My moral life may seem one long series of failures. But I know that my cause liveth. My true life is hid with the cause and belongs to the eternal.[17]

---

16. Ibid., 179–80.
17. Ibid., 161–62.

RUDOLF STEINER, *PHILOSOPHY OF FREEDOM*

It is important to emphasize that just as the classical period of American philosophy, essentially Emerson to Dewey and Whitehead, exhibits a wide range of assumptions, perspectives, themes, and methods, there is no one anthroposophic method or perspective in philosophy. Anthroposophy is a method with many practices; each of these practices can be applied to many different philosophies in many different ways. There is, however, one honored primary source, Steiner's *Philosophy of Freedom* (1893), the text by which Steiner sought to bridge and articulate the reality of spirit (by whatever designation) in relation to the cosmos, Earth, humanity, and individual lives. Steiner's philosophy is a preparation for, and a subset of, the method and goal of Anthroposophy, namely, awakening the relationship between the spiritual in the individual and the spiritual in the Universe. Steiner offered a variety of methods and perspectives such that in this one respect Steiner's philosophy is entirely postmodern. He refused to see one approach as definitive; he invariably sought to see every problem, question, and phenomenon from several perspectives. This habit of seeing alternatives is characteristic of Anthroposophy as Steiner understood it. Steiner practiced, as well as recommended, multiperspectivism.

Epistemology: Free Thinking

In the 1890s, when Rudolf Steiner was in his thirties, before he began his career as an esoteric researcher and author, he wrote scholarly, carefully argued books on metaphysics, epistemology, and ethics. These books have been almost completely ignored by philosophers from his day until the present. It is worth wondering whether if he had not changed focus from epistemology to esotericism he would have been so ignored. Would his doctoral dissertation, *Truth and Knowledge* (1891) and his full-length philosophy book, *Philosophy of Freedom* (1893), have received the attention of philosophers had he not followed their publication by *Theosophy* (1904), *How to Know Higher Worlds* (1904), and *An Outline of Esoteric Science* (1909)? It seems likely that Steiner's later works as an esoteric teacher lead philosophers to respond that if Steiner had actually thought that he knew about the ancient world, or angels, and the experiences of the dead, then surely his philosophy books are simply not to be taken seriously.

Or, if some philosophers and professors of philosophy read his philosophical writing, might it be that they put these writings aside because these books revealed that Steiner had already been thinking and writing somewhat esoterically, and already demanding of his readers a patient, meditative reading that might lead from philosophy to esotericism? While his predecessors, the representatives of German Idealism—Kant, Fichte, Schelling, and Hegel—are also generally ignored by analytic philosophers, they are not kept entirely off the canon of philosophers, as Steiner clearly is.

In his philosophical writings, Rudolf Steiner tried to show how spiritual thinking leads to an experience of freedom. His major work, *Die Philosophie der Freiheit*, has been translated accurately with three synonymous titles: *Philosophy of Freedom, Philosophy of Spiritual Activity,* and *Intuitive Thinking as a Spiritual Path.* For Steiner, to be free is to be capable of thinking one's own thoughts—not the thoughts merely of the body or of society, but thoughts generated by one's deepest, most original, most essential, spiritual self. Free thinking is a spiritual and intuitive activity, as distinct from activities that are social, physical, and intellectual.

The Philosophy of Freedom is Steiner's first systematic attempt to establish a philosophical path by which an individual might access spiritual realms by thinking. The active, intuitive thinking he recommends necessarily and significantly includes will and affect. While this free intuitive thinking concerns the results of sense-free experience, its primary goal is to enable the meditative reader to develop the ability to think, and indeed the habit of thinking, in a way that accesses the realm of ideas independent of the sense world. One part of Steiner's argument is aimed at naïve realism, the view that says the world is "out there," and that there is really nothing more to it than the way it appears sensually.[18]

---

18. Steiner is here objecting to the commonsense view that thinking, and the acquisition of knowledge, is not very complicated. A version of this perspective can be found in the English philosopher, G. E. Moore, a contemporary of Steiner who was as unaware of Steiner as Steiner was of him.

His position is equally opposed to materialist thinking, the view that regards matter as the sole reality, such that mind is identified with the brain.[19]

Because Steiner's *Philosophy of Freedom* is written in a style that stimulates active thinking and places certain demands upon the reader to grasp it, upon first reading the book may seem not particularly rewarding to the standard intellectual method of reading a philosophy text. For the reader willing to engage actively in study, the book becomes tremendously rewarding. Steiner was trying to show the causes of alienated thinking and the possibility of thinking in a new, more creative, and integral way. Intuitive thinking is generative; our everyday thinking tends to be derivative, sifting through mental pictures of previous experiences and correlating them to new events. This experience is perhaps most vividly presented by Owen Barfield at the conclusion of his remarkable book, *Unancestral Voice*. Barfield distinguishes "creative thoughts" as being one's substance and one's life, "so that to perceive them is verily to perceive the spirit within you in the act of creating."[20]

Philosophy of Freedom is intended to be its own verification. If one follows the guidance offered in this book, it is possible to experience oneself initiating a genuinely new thought, or the beginning of a new chain of thoughts, one not controlled by external circumstances. Such thoughts are free from the assumptions of one's culture, historical legacy, or biography. Without such an effort, *Philosophy of Freedom*, like a religious text or a work of art, can seem unintelligible, or devoid of significance. By lack of effort in reading Steiner's philosophical writing, just as in a dull response to any new and profound idea, anyone can reduce the intuitive to the ordinary—i.e., the spiritual to the self-interested. The intended result of working conscientiously through Steiner's *Philosophy of Freedom* is none other than what the book's title suggests: to think freely and to intuit

---

19. Although Freud wrote brilliantly on the reality, and influence, of the unconscious, he nevertheless held a completely materialist view of the mind, that is, that mind and brain are identical terms.

20. Owen Barfield, *Unancestral Voice*, 162.

ideas and ideals that live in the spiritual world—the world of thinking of which the free thinker is a creative member. As this work teaches the practice and the results of intuitive thinking, it serves as a sure foundation for Steiner's lifework and for its continuance by the efforts of others.

To think one's own thoughts, it turns out, requires a tremendous amount of will—and, perhaps more surprising, the kind of relationship that is best described as love. In his addendum to the 1918 edition of *Philosophy of Freedom*, Steiner wrote:

The difficulty of grasping thinking in its essence by observing it consists in this: when the soul wants to bring it into focus of attention, this essence has all too easily already slipped away from the observing soul. All that is left for the soul then is the dead abstraction, the corpse of living thinking. If we look only at this abstraction, we can easily feel drawn to the mysticism of feeling or the metaphysics of will, which seem so "full of life." We find it strange if anyone seeks to grasp the essence of reality in "mere thoughts." But whoever truly manages to experience *life within thinking* sees that dwelling in mere feelings or contemplating the element of will cannot even be compared with (let alone ranked above) the inner richness of the experience, the inner calmness and mobility, in the life of thinking. Feeling and willing warm the human soul even when we look back and recollect their original state, while thinking all too easily leaves us cold. It seems to dry out the life of the soul. Yet this is only the sharply contoured shadow of the reality of thinking—a reality interwoven with light, dipping down warmly into the phenomena of the world. This dipping down occurs with a power of love in spiritual form. One should not object that to speak of love in active thinking is to displace a feeling, love, into thinking. This objection is actually a confirmation of what is being said here. For whoever turns toward essential thinking finds within it both feeling and will, and both of these in the depths of their reality. Whoever turns aside from thinking toward "pure" feeling and willing loses the true reality of feeling and willing. If we experience thinking intuitively, we also do justice to the experience of feeling and will. But the mysticism of feeling and the metaphysics of will cannot do justice to the penetration of existence by intuitive thinking. Those views all too easily conclude that it is *they* who stand within reality, while intuitive thinkers, devoid of feeling and estranged from reality, form only a shadowy, cold picture of the world in "abstract thoughts."[21]

In Steiner's view, ordinary thinking is characterized by so fundamental a flaw that it disastrously limits our feeling and willing. He is trying to show that free, spiritual, philosophical thinking engages both feeling and willing, and can lead to knowledge of the ordinary as well as to inner and transcendent realities.

Beginning with his *Philosophy of Freedom* and continuing for the remainder of his life, Steiner argued on behalf of more than one level of thinking. In this regard, his epistemology is continuous with the line of Western philosophic thought traceable to the Greeks (specifically Platonism and Neoplatonism), as well as with the Christian epistemology (particularly Augustine and Aquinas). At the dawn of philosophy there was a need to explain both levels of knowledge—what Plato referred to as sensory knowledge useful for physical objects and pure thinking (or intuition) needed to apprehend Ideas and Ideals—but there was little doubt that the higher form of knowledge was possible. This conviction prevailed in the West until John Locke and David Hume in the eighteenth century, both of whom argued that all knowledge comes only through the senses, and not through intuition. This view, generally known as empiricism, has prevailed against the claim for intuition or higher knowledge, the kind of knowledge espoused by religious believers, mystics, and esotericists of all centuries, as well as Romanticism of the nineteenth century, and a few twentieth-century philosophers, certainly Henri Bergson and Karl Jaspers, and to some extent, James, Royce, and Whitehead.

Steiner was addressing twentieth-century European consciousness and culture that had collectively denied the kind of thinking and knowledge of which he was certain. In his early years Steiner was capable of an automatic intuitive knowing, the kind that was standard in earlier centuries. In later life, as a mature thinker and philosophically trained, he assumed the task

---

21. Rudolf Steiner, *Intuitive Thinking as a Spiritual Path*, 132–134.

of breaking through the generally accepted limits to knowledge shared by philosophers at the end of the nineteenth century, and continuing into the twentieth. Then, for the remainder of his life, he applied his counter-cultural knowledge to natural and social sciences, education, and various arts.

Steiner suggests that one can only answer a question such as, "Is the human being free?" by first establishing an epistemology affirming the possibility of certain knowledge gained by intuition and by thinking from many points of view. In the first half of *The Philosophy of Freedom* Steiner argues that certainty is possible, and the second half of the book he sets out the conditions by which human freedom can be achieved. Steiner points out that the purpose of *thinking* is to form, or discover, the correct inherent *concept* that lies hidden within the *percept* (the content of what is perceived). Every object presents certain qualities to be observed or perceived, but the *concept* of an object can be discovered only by *thinking* about its observed qualities. Intuitive thinking awakens the observer to the reality and meaning of an object.

In modern Western consciousness, individuals typically experience themselves as separate from nature, Earth, and other human beings. In contrast to Kant who first emphasized this separation and then denied a possible reunification by knowledge (except by moral experience, also called practical reason), Steiner sought to demonstrate that the essential unity between the inner self and nature can be known by higher thinking. He urged that every thinking individual can confront and then find a way beyond the confines set by Kant and European positivism, and other paradigmatic framers of modern consciousness. He recommended that each modern Western individual should experience his or her own soul life in action so as to know first-hand the nature and activity of spiritual realities, beings, and ideals—the existence and accessibility of which are denied by the dominant thinkers of the present age.

Knowledge arises by the intuitive affirmation of the lawful relationships between percepts and corresponding concepts. The correctness of the exact fit between *percept* and *concept* is often accompanied by our excitement and feelings of certainty. The *cognitive concept* belongs lawfully to the *objective percept* from the outset, prior to human cognition, but the concept is not "given" as immediately as the observed percept, but requires thinking to discover it. For Steiner, our human organization requires that we experience percepts and concepts in two distinct stages. Within the interval between our perceiving the percept and thinking the concept, we can become aware of our self's own activity. We recognize that *we* are observing and thinking—that the human individual emerges as the one participating in cognitive activity. We cognize and identify our self or individuality with the name "I."

Steiner argues that we can actively, or truthfully, think about concepts such as virtues. We can intuit, as Aristotle did, that courage lies midway between the extremes of rashness and cowardice. We can intuit ideas and concepts that are free of the influence of the senses. By living thinking, or moral imagination, we can break patterns of passive behavior. We can form a motive to act out of the universal realm of ideas. Freedom of action is possible by a free moral intuition followed by moral technique. At the highest level of life, a free and true action is characterized by love for the action, or deeds of love, worthy to be considered free artistic creativity in life and society.

Ethics: Free Deeds

Some of the best practitioners of what Rudolf Steiner meant by freedom are discussed in this book, perhaps especially Emerson, James, and Royce, C. G. Jung, Marjorie Spock, Rachel Carson, Gandhi, the Dalai Lama, and Archbishop Tutu. Steiner intends freedom to be practiced and realized by starting a new chain of cause and effect, one that is not reactive to social or physical causes but is expressive of one's karmic situation and destiny. In ethics as in epistemology, Steiner developed a view that is opposed to Kant's. Whereas Kant's categorical imperative defined a moral deed as one governed by a maxim worthy to serve as a universal law that would govern any moral agent in the same situation, Steiner emphasized the uniqueness of each moral agent. For Steiner, the morally right action is the one that issues from an individual's karmic relationship to the spiritual world. This position is probably closer to Kant's formulation than Steiner admits.

Kant did affirm that a moral choice is by definition an act made possible by a moral agent's ability to express the noumenal realm, the realm of moral law awaiting manifestation by the agent, the moral lawgiver, the one who formulates and implements a maxim worthy to serve as a universal law. Kant's conception of practical reason is also closer to Steiner's ethics than Steiner admits. But the difference is also important: whereas Kant emphasizes the articulation of a moral law, with the universalization of one's maxim, leading to self-imposed law and duty, Steiner emphasizes the originality of each moral action by each unique moral agent.

In the chapter on "Moral Imagination," Steiner contrasts free and unfree moral deeds:

> Before coming to a decision, unfree spirits remember what someone did, or recommended, or what God commanded in such a case, and so forth. Then they act accordingly. Free spirits have other sources of action than these preconditions. They make absolutely *original* decisions.[22]

And further,

> To be free means: to be able—on my own, through moral imagination—to determine the mental pictures (motives) underlying an action.... I am free only when *I* produce these mental pictures myself, not merely when I *can* carry out motives that another has placed within me. Free beings are those who can *will* what they themselves hold to be right.[23]

As with Steiner's Goethean philosophy of nature, the individual perspective is essential for knowing. In the moral sphere this means knowing right action, but in the knowledge of nature, right knowing is completely dependent on the accomplished discipline and clarity of the perceiver. It takes a highly practiced moral agent to detect obstacles to free choice and more importantly, to

---

22. Ibid., 180.
23. Ibid., 191.

one's inner life, one's karma and one's true relationship to the world of moral ideals right for oneself. When Gandhi, for example, was thrown off the train in Durban, South Africa, in 1908, he was sufficiently intuitive concerning his own life and the world of ideals, and right relationship between them in that situation, that he was able to intuit a new course of moral action, a strategy of nonviolence that he named *satyagraha*, moral truth force. Subsequently *satyagraha* served as the defining ideal of Gandhi's life and message. Similarly, in response to the Montgomery segregated buses and the arrest of Rosa Parks, Martin Luther King, Jr., intuited the core identity of Gandhi's *satyagraha* and the gospel of love taught by Jesus.

Friedrich Wilhelm Hegel
Sri Aurobindo
Pierre Teilhard de Chardin
Owen Barfield

4

Evolution of Consciousness

Hegelian Background

Like Emerson, James, and Royce, Rudolf Steiner was pro-foundly influenced by the philosophy of Friedrich Hegel (1770–1831). Even Dewey started his philosophical career as a Hegelian; he remarked that Hegel had "left a permanent deposit in his thought." Hegel left more than a deposit in Steiner's thought: He influenced both the method and content of Steiner's philosophizing. In "The Barr Document," the autobiographical sketch that Steiner wrote for Édouard Schuré in 1907, he wrote that in his early twenties he studied Hegel intensively.[1] Hegel also influenced Steiner's conception of history as the development from lesser to greater freedom. Although Hegel's thought is notoriously difficult, his philosophy of history can be grasped, or pictured, perhaps because it has been widely influential. Almost any large (i.e., metaphysical or theological) philosophy of history that includes an affirmation of a spiritual source and purposive unfolding is almost inevitably Hegelian.

For Hegel, history is the history of consciousness; it is human-ity becoming aware of its past and present—and thereby increas-ing its ability to participate in shaping its future. In Hegel's view, creating the future requires will as well as intellect, exactly as Steiner contends, although Steiner adds that increasingly love is also required. In Hegel's *Introduction to Philosophy of History*,

---

1. Rudolf Steiner, "The Barr Document," in Robert McDermott, ed., *The New Essential Steiner*, 80.

he explains that there are three methods of understanding history.[2] The first method, called Original History, is limited by the time of the historian. The Original Historian "is not concerned with reflection about events. He lives the spirit of the events; he does not transcend them." The second method, Reflective History, includes surveys, analyses of the present, and critiques. The third method, Philosophical, which is the primary method of Hegel and Steiner, aims at a deeper level than the first two, and consequently "seems to require some commentary or justification." Hegel continues: "The most universal definition would be that philosophy of history is nothing but the thoughtful contemplation of history." If we substitute Logos (Christ) for Reason in the following passage, it is clear that Steiner's philosophy of history is thoroughly Hegelian. Further, as we know from his *Philosophy of Religion*, Hegel himself reads the Rational Idea, including Rational History, as the philosophical term for Christ, so that his philosophy of history is also a Christian theology of history. Hegel wrote:

> Only the study of world history itself can show that it has proceeded rationally, that it represents the rationally necessary course of the World Spirit, but one whose nature unfolds in the course of the world....To him who looks at the world rationally the world looks rationally back.[3]

Steiner might say, "To one who looks at the world with the idea of the Incarnation of Christ, the Incarnation looks back," and not only looks back, but takes up residence in the inquiring soul. Writing one century after Hegel, Steiner offers a more expansive and participatory view of history, certainly one less State-dominated and more positive than Hegel's concerning historical evolution toward freedom. Equally importantly, at the present time, a century after Steiner, an even more expansive and participatory view of history and freedom is coming to the fore, one that includes the rights for women, LGBT, racial and

2. G. W. F. Hegel, *Reason in History: A General Introduction to the Philosophy of History*, tr., int., Robert S. Hartman, 8–11.
3. Ibid., 12–13.

ethnic groups, and nature, significantly and exactly to the extent that thinkers and leaders consider such an expansion of rights to be possible. This is the point that James and Royce joined in emphasizing: the belief in a particular future is essential for its realization.

Perhaps the most dramatic insight bequeathed by Hegel is his conviction that because human history endures it affects divinity itself. It is Hegel who introduced a philosophical position subsequently known as panentheism, a term introduced by Charles Hartshorne in *Philosophers Speak of God*, which is a comprehensive treatment of this philosophical and theological position. The accounts of the relationship between divinity and the history of creation offered by Sri Aurobindo, Teilhard de Chardin, and Rudolf Steiner are all versions of panentheism and are all influenced by Hegel. Panentheism is a position midway between theism and pantheism. In contrast to theism, Hegel and subsequent panentheists hold that the transcendent divinity is affected by creation, including particularly by human consciousness. In this view, the divine permeates the Earth and humanity, evolves in that relationship, and sustains that relationship into eternity.

Unlike pantheism, according to which the divine is coextensive, or identical, with creation, panentheism holds that the divine permeates the Earth and humanity yet these do not exhaust divinity. There is no Earth, no cosmos, no humanity, no time and no space that is not filled with the divine, but the divine has always been and always will be, whereas creation had a beginning and will come to an end. For Hegel and all panentheists, particulars are irreducibly real, and so will not cease absolutely; they will be included in the divine in some way forever, and the divine will be changed by this endurance of creation, by what has accumulated as a result of the divine having once involuted (involved) itself in creation.[4]

While Hegel's influence is evident in Steiner's view of both history and its deeper version, evolution of consciousness,

---

4. This position has been advanced most effectively by the concept of the consequent nature of God as proposed by A. N. Whitehead in his *Process and Reality*.

Steiner's clairvoyant research led him to describe actual spiritual beings such as the Archangel Michael (whom Steiner considered to be the regent of Christ and guiding spirit of the modern West), and the tempters, Lucifer and Ahriman (since the beginning of human history opponents of Christ and of human freedom and love). Hegel's conception of Christ is philosophical and for most believing Christians too abstract (intelligible but not particularly worshipful). In contrast, the conception of Christ that Steiner articulated in more than a hundred lectures vividly details Christ's influential actions in history, and in individual human lives as numinous, inspiring, and worshipful. There are no reports of Hegel, as there are of Steiner, reciting the Our Father aloud every day. It was one of Steiner's central commitments to show the evidence of Christ in all aspects of earthly and human history. That said, Hegel definitely gave to Steiner and to some other nineteenth- and twentieth-century philosophers an approach to history that is so deep and broad that it transcends the usual bounds of both philosophy and theology, and leads philosophers and theologians to encounter evolution of consciousness—i.e., a view of history that requires some amount of intuition and esoteric thinking.

SRI AUROBINDO

Aurobindo Ghose was born in Calcutta in 1872. His mother was mentally ill; his father was a physician and an anglophile who arranged for his three sons to be educated in England. After being in England for 14 years, Aurobindo, on his return to India at age 21, embraced Indian languages, culture, politics (under British rule), and what he considered to be India's destiny. From 1893 until his departure for French India in 1910 Aurobindo was the most impressive and dangerous leader of the movement for Indian independence from British rule. During these same years, Gandhi was emerging as a leader of nonviolent protest against social injustice in South Africa. The British Government of India arrested Aurobindo for insurrection in 1909; he spent a full year in the Alipore Jail. Immediately on being freed in 1910, in order to be free from British rule, he sailed for the southeast section of India then controlled by the French. This location proved karmically significant because it was Paul Richard, a French diplomat, who found Aurobindo in 1914 and immediately wrote to his colleagues in France that he had found "the spiritual teacher whom we have sought." Several days later, when Richard's wife Mira met Aurobindo she recognized him as the Krishna who had appeared to her in her dreams. Mira was destined to be the Mother of the Sri Aurobindo Ashram. Departing for France, Richard paid for the publication of the Indian journal *Arya* in which Aurobindo wrote monthly installments.

From 1914 to 1921 Aurobindo's monthly installments coalesced into his major works: *The Life Divine* (his philosophy), *Essays on the Gita*, *Synthesis of Yoga* (on the yogas of knowledge, love, action, and the yoga of the evolution of consciousness), and *Savitri: A Legend and a Symbol* (a poetic account of the Mother's attempt to transform matter and to conquer death).[5] *The Life Divine*, Aurobindo's yoga experience expressed in language of Hegelian philosophy and the Upanishads, is a brilliant 800-page metaphysical treatise. As his writings include no references to sources, it is difficult to discern just what he absorbed during his years of study at Cambridge and what he read in subsequent years. Aurobindo continued to expand and revise *Savitri* for the remainder of his life until in its final form it became one of the longest poems in the English language.

Once Aurobindo established himself in Puducherry (formerly Pondicherry) and began to write based on his yoga experience, he did not leave the city for forty years and did not leave his apartment for his last twenty-four years—despite the pleas from Gandhi (who had returned to India from South Africa in 1914) and Jawaharlal Nehru that he should join their movement against British rule. In response to them and to others, Aurobindo explained that he was working intensely on behalf of Indian independence, and on behalf of many other causes, but at the psychic level. In 1926 after his definitive experience that he attributed

---

5. See Robert McDermott, editor, *Six Pillars: Introductions to the Major Works of Sri Aurobindo.*

to the presence and revelation of the god Krishna, he came to be called Sri Aurobindo. Mira Richard, after spending the years of World War I in Japan, joined Aurobindo as director of the ashram. In the same year he gave her the name Mother of the Sri Aurobindo Ashram. Aurobindo combined Bengali and British masculine consciousness, to which Mira Richard brought Egyptian–Turkish–French feminine consciousness. They joined their karmic destinies in the service of the evolution of consciousness.

Aurobindo continued his yoga practice and writing from 1914 until 1950 when he died (or, as his followers say, "until he left his body"). His writings, in more than thirty-five enormous volumes, are characterized by a florid, Victorian style with very lengthy sentences and extremely complex thought development. Uncharacteristically, his three-page essay "The Teachings of Sri Aurobindo," written the year before his death, though still florid, offers a concise summation in the third person of Aurobindo's ideas, including a succinct account of the evolution of consciousness:

> The teaching of Sri Aurobindo starts from that of the ancient sages of India: that behind the appearance of the universe there is the reality of a being and consciousness, a self of all things, one and eternal. All beings are united in that one self and spirit but divided by a certain separativity of consciousness, an ignorance of their true self and reality in the mind, life and body. It is possible by a certain psychological discipline to remove this veil of separative consciousness and become aware of the true Self, the divinity within us and all.
>
> Sri Aurobindo's teaching states that this one being and consciousness is involved here in matter. Evolution is the process by which it liberates itself; consciousness appears in what seems to be inconscient, and once having appeared is self-impelled to grow higher and higher and at the same time to enlarge and develop toward a greater and greater perfection. Life is the first step of this release of consciousness; mind is the second. But the evolution does not finish with mind: it awaits a release into something greater, a consciousness which is spiritual and supramental. The next step of the evolution must be toward the development of Supermind and spirit as the dominant power in

the conscious being. For only then will the involved divinity in things release itself entirely and it become possible for life to manifest perfection.

But while the former steps in evolution were taken by nature without a conscious will in the plant and animal life, in man nature becomes able to evolve by a conscious will in the instrument. It is not, however, by the mental will in man that this can be wholly done, for the mind goes only to a certain point and after that can only move in a circle. A conversion has to be made, a turning of the consciousness by which mind has to change into the higher principle. This method has to be found through the ancient psychological discipline and practice of yoga.[6]

In telling his own spiritual biographical details Sri Aurobindo gives significant prominence to the god Krishna revealed in the Bhagavad Gita. He also focuses on the descent of a Supramental consciousness revealed, or perhaps incarnated, through the collaboration of the Mother and himself beginning in 1956, even though—or perhaps made possible by the fact that—Sri Aurobindo died in 1950. By contrast, the accounts of the evolution of consciousness by Steiner and Teilhard assign profound significance to the incarnation of Christ. Had Rudolf Steiner known the work of Sri Aurobindo and the Mother it seems likely that he would have researched their karmic destinies, as he often did with persons whose lives and works indicated a significant spiritual capacity and mission. I like to think that Steiner would have seen them as co-avatars, and specifically as a twentieth-century expression of Krishna.

Many modern Western thinkers, including Hegel, Schelling, Henri Bergson, Teilhard de Chardin, and Jean Gebser have written an account of the evolution of human consciousness comparable to Steiner's. Sri Aurobindo seems to be the only non-Western thinker associated with this perspective, perhaps due to his having absorbed Hegelian philosophy while a student at King's College, Cambridge. During the remainder of his life in India, he created a vast and original spiritual philosophy which is a

---

6.   Robert McDermott, editor, *The Essential Aurobindo*, 39–40.

rich synthesis of Hegelian and Nietzschean philosophy with the Indian spiritual tradition, particularly the Upanishads, mystical texts that were literally sung into existence in the eighth to sixth centuries BCE. Both Hegel and Sri Aurobindo emphasize absolute unity, but in a way that is expressive of nineteenth-century European Romanticism—i.e., thoroughly historical and evolutionary. The Upanishads resemble the monist or pantheist philosophy of Spinoza in the seventeenth century. With the influence of Hegel and Nietzsche who breathed history and personal will into Spinoza, Sri Aurobindo breathed history into the Upanishads.

Aurobindo's evolutionary philosophy establishes three processes: First, Involution, wherein the divine empties itself into time and space, including all of the permutations that follow as a result. The divine, called Brahman or *Sat-Chit-Ananda* (Being Consciousness Bliss), not only involves itself in the first moment of creation, it continues to be involved as creation proceeds from inconscient matter to a vast variety of living forms, and on to the incremental emergence of mind. The second process is evolution, the process by which the divine brings about its fuller and more sublime self-expression. The third process is Transformation, whereby each of the three stages of the evolution above matter—life, mind, and Supermind—reaches down to the preceding level to lift it to a higher synthesis. In Sri Aurobindo's view, these three processes are continuous.

In addition to these three processes of evolution Sri Aurobindo's account of the evolution of consciousness focuses on four major phases: matter, life, mind, and Supermind. Further, between mind and Supermind he posits several minor phases: illumined mind, intuition, Overmind and Supermind. Overmind is the phase that helps to cause the transformation, or enlightenment, of great spiritual individuals. Like Steiner, Sri Aurobindo saw spiritually evolved persons receiving the inspiration of higher beings in a lineage. He was convinced that the descent of the Krishna and the Overmind made possible his own transformation from Aurobindo Ghose to Sri Aurobindo, as well as the transformation of Mira Richard into the Mother, and the lifting of their work through the agency of the Sri Aurobindo Ashram on behalf of the whole of humanity.

The Involution of Supermind, or what Sri Aurobindo and the Mother refer to as Supramental Manifestation of consciousness, descended into human consciousness at a particular time (according to the Mother, in 1956). However, it was always "there," a latent reality, not directly available to humanity until Sri Aurobindo (reportedly from the spiritual world) and the Mother (reportedly working with Sri Aurobindo "on this side") were able to serve as instruments of this transformation comparable in significance to the transition from matter to life or life to mind. The Mother reportedly continued to work with the Supramental Manifestation through her physical and psychic experience until her death in 1973.

Anyone who lectures on Sri Aurobindo's concept of Supermind (as I have done steadily since 1970) is invariably asked, "Who else knows about this?" Or, "Is there any evidence that such a world-changing transformation has actually occurred?" To answer these and other reasonable questions about the Supermind I tend to compare this presumably transformative descent of the divine into Earth and humanity to the incarnation of Christ. Perhaps not even the faithful at the crucifixion (probably three Marys and John the Beloved Disciple) really understood the transformation that was subsequently defined by Paul in his influential letters to communities of Christians throughout the Mediterranean world. One argument says there is no reason to believe in what Steiner refers to as the Mystery of Golgotha, the profound spiritual transformation wrought by the crucifixion and resurrection of Christ). This same view will argue that the Supramental descent predicted by Sri Aurobindo and announced in 1956 by the Mother was also no great positive change. A counter argument says that the world (i.e., human ignorance and cruelty) would be even worse if not for the Incarnation—or descent of Supermind. In the face of such huge claims by impressive individuals such as Steiner and Aurobindo, would seem that caution as well as reverence and humility are both necessary and, it seems, not sufficiently in evidence.

PIERRE TEILHARD DE CHARDIN, S.J.

Pierre Teilhard de Chardin (1881–1955), a French Jesuit priest and world-class paleontologist, is perhaps best known for his views on the spiritual source, process, and goal of evolution. His vision is distinguished by an intensely personal account of his experience of the presence of Christ permeating the cosmos and Earth. Teilhard is perhaps the single major alternative to Steiner with respect to a foundational and comprehensive reunification of science and spirit. His unifying vision, expressed in beautiful evocative language, is the most original and extensive attempt to reunite matter and spirit, science and religion, and specifically science and Christ. In the process, by means of his devotion to describing the evolution of both Gaia and culture, Teilhard also offers profound revisions of Christian theology, particularly an original understanding of Christ as both cosmic and personal.

Pierre Teilhard de Chardin, S.J., to use his full name, is almost always referred to as Teilhard. "S.J." (Society of Jesus, or Jesuit) signifies an order of highly educated, influential Roman Catholic priests to which Teilhard belonged from age eighteen until his death at age seventy-four. Teilhard's unwavering loyalty to the Jesuits is itself significant evidence of his spiritual discipline. He faithfully practiced his vows of poverty, celibacy, and obedience even to the prohibition by his Jesuit superiors against publication of his philosophical and spiritual writings. Fortunately, upon his death (on Easter Sunday, 1955, in New York City) Teilhard's friends began to publish his writings. His influence began to spread immediately. His writings exercised a significant influence on the Second Vatican Council (1962–1965), the worldwide assembly that succeeded partially in opening the Roman Catholic Church to the modern world. In a survey of New Age communities Teilhard was voted the most significant thinker of the twentieth century.

In *The Heart of Matter* Teilhard recounts the interplay of spirit and matter in his life beginning with his earliest memories. He hoped that his account of his intellectual career and spiritual striving might either "make it possible for other similar cases to be recognized or even to be brought into being." He set out to show how:

Starting from the point at which a spark was first struck, a
point that was built into me congenitally, the World gradually
caught fire for me, burst into flame; how this happened all during my life and as a result of my whole life, until it formed a
great luminous mass, lit from within, that surrounded me.[7]

He wrote that at six years of age he was drawn to something
that shone at the heart of matter, to "the Incorruptible, Irreversible, Necessary, as opposed to the contingent." After discover-
ing that iron, which he thought was eternal, could rust, nothing
could satisfy him "that was not on the scale of the Universal."[8]
He had "an insatiable desire to maintain contact (a contact of
communion) with a sort of universal root or matrix of beings."
He continues:

The truth is that even at the peak of my spiritual trajectory I
was never to feel at home unless immersed in an Ocean of Matter.... Thus, between the ages of ten and thirty, at the heart of
my absorbing interests and of my secret delights lay a continued
and increased contact with the Cosmic "in the solid state."[9]

Teilhard begins his major work, *The Human Phenomenon*
(1955/1999), by explaining that it "represents an effort *to see*
and *to show* what the human being becomes, what the human
being requires, if placed wholly and completely in the context of
appearance."[10] He sets out to recount "the world's becoming in
time; the entire story from start to future." Further, he intends
his focus to be "on humanism that arose within Christianity,
then separated, and now needs to be reunited with it." Exactly
like Steiner, Teilhard's purpose is to enable others "to see the
Within of Things," and thereby to see "the mutual interdependence of matter and spirit in the overall movement of evolution."
In Teilhard's vision, matter is the matrix of consciousness; consciousness is born from the womb of matter. Teilhard wrote his

---

7. Pierre Teilhard de Chardin, *The Heart of Matter*, 15.
8. Ibid., 19.
9. Ibid., 20–22.
10. Pierre Teilhard de Chardin, *The Human Phenomenon*, 3.

Human Phenomenon in order to convince the non-Christian of the deep and purposive meaning of evolution. His only reference to Christ is in a six page "Christian Epilogue." This strategy follows from his desire to help the reader to "see." Thomas Berry used the same strategy in many of his essays on ecology that contain scarcely any mention of Christ or Christianity.

Teilhard felt "at home in precisely this world of electrons, nuclei, and waves"; it gave him "a sense of plenitude and comfort."[11] When Teilhard was age twenty-eight Henri Bergson's *Creative Evolution* (1909) provided him "fuel at just the right moment, and very briefly, for a fire that was already consuming" his heart and mind. Whereas Teilhard's Catholic education to that point had instilled in him a dualism of matter/spirit, as well as body/soul, as two substances, Bergson enabled him to dissolve this dualism and to replace it by "the primacy of Spirit or, which comes to the same thing, the primacy of the future."[12]

As a result of working with Bergson's concept of *e'lan vital*, or vital force, Teilhard developed a philosophy of "directed Evolution," with matter transformed into thought. At this time he no longer doubted that the supreme happiness he had formerly looked for in iron "was to be found only in Spirit."[13] This statement, and others like it, does not at all negate Teilhard's devotion to matter. For Teilhard, matter is suffused with spirit and constitutes the other half of consciousness. The Creator needs the cosmos to manifest Itself. Earth and humanity are two glorious manifestations of God, and most particularly of the incarnate Christ.

Teilhard's account of the evolution of consciousness is presented in four major phases. The three phases from the genesis of the cosmos to the present are the same as described by Sri Aurobindo—matter, life, and mind. As Sri Aurobindo affirms an emerging and future phase, Supermind, Teilhard similarly affirms a future phase, called the Omega Point, which he describes as the fullest possible expression of spirit in matter, and the goal of the evolution of consciousness. Despite the word *point*, which would

---

11. Teilhard de Chardin, *The Heart of Matter*, 23.
12. Ibid., 27.
13. Ibid., 28.

seem to indicate a particular moment in time, the Omega Point might be better understood as a phase, a long period of development toward the blissful fulfillment of the mission of Christ in service of humanity and Earth. Like Rudolf Steiner, Teilhard saw the incarnation of Christ as the defining event in the whole of creation. For Teilhard, the material world, including the rocks and metals that he learned to love as a boy, proclaims God's love for the world particularly in Christ.

Teilhard didn't simply announce an evolutionary view; he carefully researched fossils, digging by hand in many parts of the world to support his case for the evolution of matter, plants, animals, and humanity. He knew his theory would be and has been opposed on one side by atheistic materialists for whom evolution is without an intelligent cause or meaningful purpose, and on the other side by biblical creationists who hold to literal interpretations of the Genesis story of creation. Teilhard's deep theological and philosophical reflections on the evolutionary process, particularly on the ancient past, enabled him to argue that creation, or cosmogenesis, continued to evolve because of its *telos*, its inherent purposeful drive. The cosmos is striving to evolve, and humanity is the latest and most advanced stage of this evolution. For Teilhard, humanity is the universe become conscious of itself.

In his detailed account of the evolution of consciousness, Teilhard identifies two faces of cosmogenesis: The first is described variously as complexification, or disorganized (and disorganizing) tendencies of matter; he refers to this process as tangential. The second process, which he calls radial, refers to expanding consciousness, the energy of evolutionary ascent. On the basis of his scientific research and sympathetic imagination, Teilhard was convinced that the evolutionary process has a stable, irreversible goal and ultimate meaning. His profoundly spiritual relationship to all aspects of the material world enabled him to offer a view of evolution that affirms a divine source and purpose as well as an open *telos* (end or goal). Because he had studied the past, and the mysterious energy that drives each level or phase to greater realizations, it seemed obvious to Teilhard that the whole of creation is groaning to attain ever more perfect expressions of the divinity in and by which creation evolves.

For Teilhard, although a person's action, or the action of a group, even a nation, might seem completely free of divine or spiritual influence, there has always been, and there will always be, an underlying general sense, perhaps unconscious, that all action is spiritually guided and can lead to a creative advance. In order to act there must be meaning built into the evolutionary process itself. To strive, or aspire, is to be on the side of the universe.[14] Teilhard was convinced that if the Universe has undertaken this work, has evolved from prelife to life, and then to thought, it must be aiming at Omega: "It can bring it to completion, using the same methods it began with and with the same infallibility."[15] Again: "Regardless of what they say, there is no 'energy of despair.' ... All conscious energy, like love [and because it is love] is founded on hope."[16]

When, in *The Human Phenomenon*, Teilhard turns to themes such as faith, hope, and love, it is clear that despite his claim to be writing "purely and simply ... a scientific treatise,"[17] he is arguing for a religious perspective on scientific insights. Ultimately, Teilhard's vision centers on love:

> Love alone is capable of completing our beings in themselves as it unites them, for the good reason that love alone takes them and joins them by their very depths—this is a fact of daily experience. For actually is not the moment when two lovers say they are lost in each other the moment when they come into the most complete possession of themselves? Truly, in the couple and the team, and all around us at every moment, does love not accomplish that magic act, reputed to be contradictory, or "personalizing" as it totalizes. And if it does this on a daily basis on a reduced scale, why could it not someday repeat it in the dimensions of the Earth?[18]

---

14. Ibid., 230–31.
15. Teilhard de Chardin, *The Human Phenomenon*, 163.
16. Ibid., 162.
17. Ibid., 1.
18. Ibid., 189.

Teilhard believes in a positive outcome to history, or more generally to the evolutionary process, but despite his hope and optimism, he does not claim to see the future with any degree of confidence: He admits that the end of the world defies imagination. In this respect his vision is quite different from Steiner's confident, clairvoyant description of consciousness, and even specific events, hundreds of years into the future.

Without offering a time frame, Teilhard affirms the virtual certainty of the eschatological kingdom of God. For Teilhard, as for Royce, Steiner, Aurobindo, and Whitehead, the universe has a spiritual center. It is a universe governed by a kind of freedom that God respects. But while for Bergson and Whitehead the universe is evolving towards an ill-defined unification, for Teilhard it is eschatological. The final unity of the universe is the precondition for the return of Christ. Teilhard's evolutionary vision celebrates the human in the context of the physical. The Noosphere is "the Earth's thinking envelope." While Goethe asserted that "matter is never without spirit; spirit is never without matter." For Teilhard, all matter is permeated by spirit. Before matter there was spirit—and after matter there will be spirit. In this respect, Teilhard's position, along with Steiner's and Aurobindo's, is neither theist nor pantheist, but panentheist, as discussed at the beginning of this chapter.

RUDOLF STEINER ON EVOLUTION OF CONSCIOUSNESS

Reading the Akashic Record[19]

Steiner was one of the rare individuals such as Emmanuel Swedenborg and Madame Blavatsky (HPB) who was able to "read" (which can also be understood as seeing suprasensorily) the essential events recorded in, or by, what is known in esotericism as the *akashic record* or cosmic memory stored in an astral light. It seems that the essence of one's life is preserved and can be accessed by extraordinary mental capacities, the kind possessed both by esoteric teachers and by ordinary individuals in the moments near

---

19. This section and the next section are indebted to Brian Gray.

death. Writings by Steiner on the akashic record are quite different from books chronicling near death experience but both require a serious effort by the reader beginning with a suspension of standard contemporary Western skepticism. These ideas require at least the beginning of a "what if" or "well, perhaps" attitude.

As we know from Steiner's autobiography, from an early age he possessed a rare capability to perceive spiritual realities, including beings, events, and ideas both current and in the ancient past. Through conscientious and diligent esoteric-scientific training he improved his organs of perception and strengthened his ability to think clearly and logically about what he perceived. Steiner referred to his research as Spiritual Science. He researched several important insights about the past and present, and to some extent, the future. He assigned himself the task of recovering the capacity of ancient atavistic perception and developing it into exact clairvoyance, clairaudience, and clairsentience. He described the path that any modern human being can follow to initiation into suprasensible consciousness. Because these capacities are almost completely absent in the modern West Steiner gave exercises to help develop these capacities and use them to research higher worlds.

This book accepts as true that Steiner was able to experience a world teeming with spiritual beings. It is difficult for those of us lacking perception to know and express exactly what it means to say that he experienced spiritual beings. Yet Steiner perceived and described in vivid detail the workings of lofty divine beings who coordinate the creative efforts of nine levels of other spiritual beings who have gradually formed individual humans, animals, plants, and minerals on planet Earth. He further described the workings of elemental beings who constitute an entire hierarchy "below" the human being. In more than 300 volumes of lectures Steiner spoke of these beings as knowable both in their actions and in their nature—who or what they are in themselves, as beings—but as so few other humans have a capacity for such detailed perceptions and descriptions, some skepticism or doubt is likely to characterize one's initial response.

Because he lived in communion with spiritual realities Steiner strove throughout his life to assist those of us who cannot perceive the spiritual world. He dealt with skeptics his entire life, carefully addressing each objection. In *An Outline of Esoteric Science* Steiner explains his research method and results:

> Although suprasensory facts can only be *discovered* by means of suprasensory perception, once they have been discovered and communicated by the science of the suprasensory, they can be *understood* by ordinary thinking, at least if it attempts to be truly unbiased.[20]

Steiner used the names and descriptions of various beings affirmed by Christianity and Theosophy only after checking and testing these descriptions through his own direct spiritual perception. He accepted leadership of the German-speaking branch of the Theosophical Society with the condition that he would speak only out of his own spiritual experiences. In HPB's massive books, *Isis Unveiled* and *The Secret Doctrine*, she described her experiences of numerous spiritual beings, including Isis whose "veil" she uncovered. The statue of Isis in Turkey was covered because she and the esoteric secrets she held were to be protected from the uninitiated. Stimulated by HPB's lead in attempting to describe ancient mystery wisdom, Steiner continued to "lift the veil" by continuing his research and further developing it with logical and scientific methods. Perhaps more importantly, he gave exercises on ways one can develop the ability to see or know spiritual beings and past events with scientific certainty.

Steiner insisted that progress on these topics is possible neither by the old atavistic clairvoyance, which he considered too dreamy to generate precise knowledge, nor by standard scientism, which lacks the ability to see spiritually, and consequently limits considerations to the physical world perceived by the senses. Accordingly, the true, full, account of the evolution of consciousness requires a new synthesis of rational and intuitive ways of thinking, and requires spiritual perception and communion with spiritual realities. Steiner argued that the dominant theories of cosmic and human evolution fail to answer the most fundamental questions, because at the present time the scientific method

---

20. Rudolf Steiner, *An Outline of Esoteric Science*, 122.

is applied only to measurable sense data, and thereby completely misses the spiritual origins and principles of development at play in the cosmos and humanity.

Like Aurobindo and Teilhard, Steiner attempts to assist his hearers and readers to supplant materialistic theories of evolution with descriptions based on the reality of spiritual influences. He perceived the cosmos that is not only unimaginably vast but also, and more importantly, populated by a multitude of spiritual beings who are wise, significant, active, and at times embattled. He insisted that the cosmos is enchanted and that true knowledge of cosmology could become a source of healing, especially for modern Western humanity.

Steiner perceives and describes many phases of cosmic evolution, including the cooperative deeds of spiritual beings that are reflected in the origin of the zodiac and starry heavens, our solar system and planets, many phases of Earth evolution, and of human consciousness. Even a brief outline of Steiner's chronicle of evolution would have to include the following:

- the causative spiritual beings who created primal warmth and light
- the archetypal spiritual and psychic dimensions of cosmic bodies, including sun, moon, planets, stars, and their influences on humanity
- the course of cosmic evolution from ages preceding the formation of the Earth and its present constituents—fire, air, water, and solid matter
- etheric or formative forces working in the plant and animal worlds, as well as, "'subearthly" forces such as gravity, magnetism, and electricity
- the complex and exquisite evolution of the human body
- the development and eclipse of civilizations
- great events in human history, from his surprising account of Atlantis to his insightful account of the emergence of modern nations and World War I
- some premonitions of the overall direction of cosmic and human evolution from the early twentieth century into the distant future

Steiner's analysis of the modern West describes a gradual decline in human atavistic clairvoyance, particularly during the past three millennia of Western civilization alongside simultaneous increase in the capacity for and reliance on sense perception of the material world interpreted by rational intellect.

The gradual loss of spiritual perception allowed a strong sense of individual selfhood to emerge, along with the possibilities to act out of freedom rather than under the compulsive influences of certain spiritual beings. Steiner further states that all human beings have the potential to become Spirits of Freedom and Love, if we strive to transform ourselves. Our present state of spiritual ignorance could gradually be supplanted by our emerging individuality and creativity as we learn to cooperate with other spiritual beings in shaping future worlds. Steiner stated repeatedly that it is possible and essential for humanity to know the entire arc of evolution, from divine beings who form the solar system, to Earth and *anthropos*, and to the ever evolving, ever complex relationship between humanity and Earth.

Steiner never wanted anyone to accept his ideas on the basis of his authority, but rather hoped that by reading and studying these accounts—which requires open-mindedness others would gradually win their way into perceiving and testing the ideas themselves. It might seem that Steiner's ideas are not easily corroborated, because contemporary cosmology tries to explain evolution merely as a colliding sequence of chance physical events. As the phenomenal world consists of both realms simultaneously, however, Steiner was convinced that in the future matter-based natural science would gradually merge into Spiritual Science.

Fortunately, the case for Steiner's approach to Waldorf education, biodynamic agriculture, or anthroposophically extended medicine can be made without assenting to his account of the evolution of cosmos, Earth, and humanity, and the evolutionary struggle for control of human consciousness by adversarial beings. Many followers of Steiner are researching the relationship between the results of his clairvoyant research and scientific cosmology. His pictures of the universe are worth looking at and reflecting on carefully. They might help us accelerate past our usual view of the world in a similar way that the Hubble telescope also accelerated scientific cosmological knowledge when the telescope began to be used. We might want to think of Steiner as the Hubble telescope of the interplay between the spiritual and physical in cosmic evolution.

Steiner maintains that deliberate and affectionate living thinking needs to perceive the whole of creation. He characterizes Anthroposophy—the spiritual in the individual in relation to the spiritual in the universe—to include the living and non-living, individuals and the whole of humanity, Gaia in its many expressions, and the many levels of divinity. He hopes that the next phases of the evolution of consciousness will include growing understanding of spiritual as well as physical realities, but he also affirms the reality of tempters against humanity. The Luciferic temptation leads to a presumptuous spirituality in which everything is already divinized, thus steering human beings away from participating in further evolution on Earth, while the Ahrimanic temptation hardens the intellect into a defeatist "nothing but" materialism.

To all of this a perfectly reasonable reaction might be, "How could he, or any one, possibly know this?" I have found that it makes all the difference whether Steiner's disclosures can be compared with accessible intellectual knowledge that I possess. As I have some quite specific knowledge of the period he calls the fourth cultural age, eighth century BCE to fifteenth century CE, I feel that I can check his insights. I am even more confident verifying the fifth cultural age, which he maintains began in the fifteenth century in the West. These historical periods, along with his explanations of the Bhagavad Gita and events in the New Testament, are topics I have pondered independently of Steiner. Based on standard knowledge we can assess the extent to which his claims illumine or seem irrelevant to contemporary understanding. Because I find his insights on Western thought and culture both plausible and insightful, I am willing to take seriously his account of the contribution of spiritual beings and forces behind planetary evolution prior to Earth.

There are certain foundational ideas that are assumed, whether explicitly or implicitly, by all of Steiner's lectures and written books. One of these is the continuing influence of the past, including the ancient past. In Steiner's view, the past does not completely determine the present, and the present does not completely determine the future. In this sense, the potential for human freedom is wide and deep. Nevertheless, perhaps because he reports so extensively on what he perceives as having happened in the past, and specifically on causes and processes that he identifies as the deeds of specific spiritual beings, his analysis of the present and his vision of the future are closely tied to the past and to the continuity of past-present-future.

EVOLUTION OF EARTH AND HUMANITY

Almost immediately after his experience of the Cosmic Christ in 1899 when he was thirty-nine years of age, Steiner began to lecture and write on the evolution of the cosmos, Earth, and humanity. By the end of his life a quarter of a century later, Steiner had bequeathed an esoteric account of the evolution of consciousness unsurpassed in extent and detail, not least because it includes an account of the sacrificial deeds by many exalted beings. Steiner's research on the evolution of planetary stages that preceded the evolution of Earth might seem odd and irrelevant, except that in many subsequent lectures Steiner emphasizes that these early phases, including Ancient Saturn along with the successive stages of Old Sun, Old Moon, and Earth, all continue to exercise significant influence on the present constitution of the human being and kingdoms of nature, as well as on human evolution and human behavior.

According to Steiner the cosmos reveals itself to humanity and humanity is urged to cooperate with the cosmos in the great struggle for meaning over alienation, or for relation over disenchantment. It is this struggle that ought to make a crucial difference for individuals and cultures at the present time. To be alive in the twenty-first century is to know something of Pascal's experience. Although Pascal lived in the seventeenth century, he wrote:

When I consider the short duration of my life, swallowed up in the eternity that lies before and after it, when I consider the little space I fill and I seem engulfed in the infinite immensity of spaces of which I am ignorant, and which know me not, I rest frightened, and astonished, for there is no reason why I should be here rather than there. (*Pensees*, 206)

In response to the disorienting experience of the unfathomable extent of the cosmos, Steiner describes stages of planetary evolution that are profoundly meaningful and inspiring, but they are also quite startling in nature and extent. Students of contemporary cosmology are familiar with the idea of millions and billions of years and stars, but not with the pre-evolution of humanity or the role of spiritual beings in relation to planets.

For most evolutionary thinkers, it is perfectly obvious that humanity evolved from earlier forms, from inorganic entities to kyriotes to multicelled animals to humans. According to most accounts of evolution, humanity evolved from physical (mineral, chemical) to life (plants and animals) to thinking (humanity). A few evolutionary cosmologists and metaphysicians, however, including Steiner, Aurobindo, and Teilhard, hold that the formal or primordial spiritual idea of humanity preceded and made possible the physical evolution toward historical humanity. This evolution was possible because the idea of humanity was (and is) there as a source, guide, and goal. Steiner refers to this formal or ideal being as *anthropos*, the archetype of the ideal human. This archetype lived in the spiritual beings who helped birth humanity, which was a creative force seeking its own incarnation, and was realized on three planetary conditions that preceded Earth: Old (or pre-earthly) Saturn, Old Sun, and Old Moon.

According to Steiner, Old Saturn, Old Sun, and Old Moon, are three planetary stages that preceded and evolved into Earth, and into our entire solar system. They were also necessary to form what Steiner describes as the four basic parts of the human being—the physical body, which first evolved on Old Saturn; the etheric (or life body), which began to evolve on Old Sun; the astral body, which began to evolve on Old Moon; and the human "I," which was kindled for the first time during Earth evolution.

Steiner claimed that Christ performed three pre-earthly deeds, each ensouled in an Archangel, two during the Lemurian and one during the Atlantean phase.[21] Each of these sacrifices were necessary for the development of human beings and each is recapitulated in the first three years of a child's life: standing upright, walking, speaking. Steiner also taught that by the fourth sacrifice, the one on Earth in the human life of Jesus of Nazareth, Christ enlivened the "I" (or spirit) within all human beings. If accurate, this account obviously reveals an enchanted and enchanting Cosmos. (For Steiner's description of the relationship between Jesus and Christ, see the next chapter.)

According to Steiner's cosmology, the cosmos, Earth, and humanity cooperate from the beginning to the present, and presumably until the end of time, to purposefully evolve toward the ultimate triumph of love. In addition to the Trinity, Steiner perceives the outpouring of love and wisdom by the Nine Hierarchies (as named by the Christian tradition since Dionysius in the sixth century): Seraphim, Cherubim, Thrones, Dominions, Virtues, Powers, Principalities (Archai), Archangels, Angels. By pouring their wise and loving forces into the cosmos, the Trinity and the Nine Hierarchies have enabled humanity to evolve from unity with the divine to the temporary separation in order to attain reunification with the divine. Owen Barfield refers to this dialectic as original participation, loss of participation, and final participation. All nine hierarchies are alive, wise, and creative, and serve as the meaningful, influential source of human intelligence and striving, and capacity for love. But for human love to achieve freedom requires humanity to first undergo the experience of being distanced from the divine. In this way, human love can arise not out of compulsion from divine influence, but rather generated out of the human heart and given freely to others.

Steiner's account of the evolutionary process by which cosmic intelligences poured their wisdom into Earth—into light, warmth, form, movement, growth, thought, and personality—is one of the most distinctive and important revelations that Steiner

---

21. Rudolf Steiner's "The Four Sacrifices of Christ," 1981.

bequeathed. For most readers new to Steiner, it is a dividing line. While no one need slam closed Steiner's writings on philosophy, whether his own *Philosophy of Freedom*, or his writings on Goethe or Nietzsche, his account of esoteric cosmology is likely to strain most readers. Yet if we could imagine Steiner's descriptions of the formation of pre-earthly Saturn, Sun, and Moon, we would be treated to a kind of cosmic face on the billions of galaxies discovered in the last hundred years. Contemplation of these early phases and their contributions to the evolution of Earth and humanity might help everyone suffering the enormity of the cosmos to picture it as various phases and planetary influences. Steiner's vast cosmology is more than most people can imagine, but perhaps it opens significant possibilities through which one might relate to the cosmos in more spiritual terms.

Whereas the usual cosmological argument either affirms or denies the existence and role of a creator—an either/or choice with no middle position—the Nine Hierarchies account for the gradual evolution of the cosmos, Earth, and humanity. In addition, highly individualized beings such as Krishna, Buddha, Zarathustra, Christ, and Sophia have similarly given of themselves in order to enable Earth and humanity to realize their shared destiny. In Barfield's account of original participation, love refers primarily to the divine love for humanity. In the beginning (another term for original participation) humanity in its infancy was not yet capable of love, because its consciousness was not at all separated from the divine. At present this separation would seem to be complete or nearly so; the journey to love, to chosen reunification with the divine, as Steiner knew so well and depicted so convincingly, certainly appears to be a long way from realization.

Yet for Steiner and Barfield (as well as for Teilhard), love is essence of divinity as well as the ideal and hope of humanity. Love will not be the essential characteristic of humanity until humanity can act in harmony with love's many manifestations—especially the Trinity (including Christ and the Holy Spirit), Sophia, and the Nine Hierarchies. Steiner often invoked the Christian conception of the Divine Trinity in the following terms:

The Father God be in us;
The Son God create in us;
The Spirit God enlighten us.

Steiner understands the fourth planetary phase, the evolution of Earth and humanity, as the time for consolidation of the conditions of Old Saturn, Old Sun, and Old Moon. During the various phases of Earth evolution, the Cosmic Christ will unite with humanity and increasingly make it possible for human beings to develop the "I" within the physical, etheric, and astral bodies. Like all preceding evolutionary stages, Earth has seven major phases:

1. Polaria: Recapitulation of conditions of Old Saturn; further development of the physical body in preparation to receive a refined etheric body.
2. Hyperborea: Recapitulation of Old Sun; further development of the etheric body in preparation to receive a refined astral body.
3. Lemuria: Recapitulation of Old Moon; further development of the astral body in preparation to receive the "I."
4. Atlantis: The first real Earth stage, not a recapitulation; middle of the seven Earth phases.
5. Post-Atlantis: The current phase of evolution consists of seven cultural ages, each approximately 2160 years in duration. Leading evolutionary stages are identified by Steiner with cultures that most clearly initiate new stages of consciousness, beginning with Ancient India and continuing into Ancient Persia, Ancient Egyptian–Babylonian–Chaldea, and Greco–Roman Medieval civilizations.
6, 7. Steiner foresees future stages of Earth evolution, which will consist of human beings who have developed their capacities for compassion and love trying to heal and assist those human beings who have not achieved such transformations.

The cosmos was and is characterized by the outpouring of tremendous gifts by spiritual beings who bring to the human being the possibility to gain wisdom and overcome conflict through a persistent striving toward love and freedom. Much of this drama in Steiner's account focuses on the Earth, in which Christ and the tempters, Lucifer and Ahriman, have been spiritually combatting, affecting the evolution of humanity. Far from being disenchanted, this cosmos is a realm in which a constant war of worlds can set up alternative futures for humanity. It is important to note: even the tempters, Lucifer (who leads humanity to blinding pride and egotism) and Ahriman (who leads humanity to a lust for power) are indirectly working on behalf of human evolution. By negative influence, these fabulously wise and powerful beings, with legions of allies, take turns and sometimes join forces in setting challenges such that by overcoming them, human beings emerge who can attain greater awareness, independence, and an opportunity to generate greater love. (For a discussion of evil, see chapter 7, "God, Evil, and Suffering.")

EVOLUTION OF CULTURES

Steiner's attempt to track and characterize the evolution of consciousness provides more detail and more powerful examples than can be found in any comparable account, including those generated by Sri Aurobindo, Pierre Teilhard de Chardin, Jean Gebser, or Ken Wilber. Steiner (following Johann Herder) acknowledges that each culture has its own particular task, destiny, or karma, each of which is necessary for the evolution of consciousness. Consequently, he considers it better for a culture to perform its own duty poorly than to perform well the duty of another culture. (This position is also found in the Bhagavad Gita, but without the context of evolution of consciousness.) Steiner was convinced that the spiritual and evolutionary task of contemporary Western civilization should not be to attempt to create (or to try to recreate) a culture based on dreams or primal/shamanic practices, but rather to create a culture based on a will-filled and heart-filled living connection between self and universe.

Steiner's account of the evolution of human consciousness affirms a double process: Consciousness both evolved toward greater intelligence, and simultaneously devolved with respect to its noetic relationship to all interiors and to the divine in itself and in creation. Steiner attempts to show that over the course of human history, consciousness expanded and deepened with respect to knowledge, individuality, complexity, inventiveness, and power over nature, while it proportionately and painfully lost its capacity for shamanic and mystical immediacy. Steiner holds that ancient ways of experiencing a transcendent world were true in their time and context even though they might not appear so from a contemporary perspective. In Steiner's view, ancient consciousness was characterized by direct experience of the divine made possible by dreams, mythic images, and other forms of revelation. The commandments of Moses and the epic adventures sung by Homer reveal their respective experiences of divine realms. Because that capacity has been greatly diminished, it is now necessary to develop a way of relating to the world of gods and goddesses, angels and ancestors, avatars and Buddhas, through loving and free intuitive thinking, a kind of knowing that is awake and will-filled. For a person born into modern Western consciousness, the spiritual thinking espoused by Steiner is difficult to attain.

In his description of a double evolutionary process, Steiner characterizes earlier consciousness (shamanic, for example) as being closer to spiritual realities and later consciousness (particularly the modern Western) as more alienated, individualistic, and materialistic. He considered the first quarter of the twentieth century (the exact years in which he researched and lectured) to be a time of exceptional spiritual darkness and thereby an extraordinary opportunity for the development of human wisdom (*anthropos-sophia*) made possible by human will and love. As humanity gradually lost its innate spiritual home and capacities, what Owen Barfield refers to as loss of participation, humanity simultaneously gained new intellectual capacities. Over the course of several millennia, human beings developed greater independence from divine beings and their influence. This independence enabled an increase in conscious awareness and individual will. Such awareness, though it has caused the prevailing darkness and alienation, provides humanity the opportunity to share freely in the deliberate, though difficult, creation of spiritual knowledge that is distinctly human and necessary for future evolution of consciousness.

In a mix of broad strokes and very specific detail, Steiner recounts the evolution of humanity up to the extraordinary cultural and material changes of the nineteenth and twentieth centuries. He repeatedly adds to his understanding of the Greeks, of the history of Christianity, or modern Western thought and culture, but except for his treatment of Krishna and Buddha, he unfortunately omits from his account a sustained treatment of the great civilizations of India, China, and the Islamic empire. From the Greek originators of philosophic thought from the sixth to fourth centuries BCE. there evolved a tradition of rational thinking, and a corresponding loss of spiritual awareness culminating in the philosophical and cultural "death of God" announced by Friedrich Nietzsche at the end of the nineteenth century. Steiner saw this loss of spiritual awareness in the modern world as a necessary price for the evolution of consciousness toward "I"-based, free thinking. He frequently affirms the methods and achievements of modern science while he seeks to overcome its limited materialistic presuppositions. His claims for the evolution of consciousness provide an excellent example of how a new post-scientific, or spiritual-scientific, mode of consciousness can reveal important truths.

Steiner offers descriptions of the salient characteristics of Western civilization, including historically significant and paradigmatic individuals. He describes the role of great spiritual beings such as Krishna and Buddha, the tempters Lucifer and Ahriman, the Archangel Michael, and Sophia (the complement to Christ) in providing wisdom and compassion to struggling souls. Steiner also traces the contributions of the pharaohs of ancient Egypt, the Hebrew patriarchs, Moses and the prophets of Israel, Zoroaster, Socrates, Plato, and Aristotle. He particularly emphasizes the descent into history of the Sun being, Logos or Christ, in union with the human life of Jesus of Nazareth. He uses the phrase "the Mystery of Golgotha" to refer to the redemptive world-transformative presence of Christ in the death and resurrection of the etheric body of Jesus. He refers frequently to several influential Christian personalities, including the mother of Jesus, John the Baptist, John the Evangelist, Mary Magdalene, the Apostle Paul, Augustine, Thomas Aquinas, and St. Francis. Unfortunately, he does not refer to Mohammed, Rumi, Avicenna, Averroes, or the Muslim tradition generally.

Readers who are new to Steiner's vast and sometimes astonishing writings might find it difficult to know how to evaluate, or even understand, the accuracy or the implications of his account of events he reportedly derived from the Akashic Record. The key point is his overall intent to explain how modern Western consciousness lost the clairvoyance it possessed in ancient civilizations and how this loss can be made a gain by developing a clairvoyance that is simultaneously scientific (deliberate, objective, systematic, evidential) and spiritual (free from sense-based thinking, intuitive).

Unlike many New Age enthusiasts and others who long for a return to ancient clairvoyance (referred to variously as primal, primordial, mythic, or archaic consciousness), Steiner traces the loss of ancient clairvoyance without regret. He sees that it is precisely this loss that has made possible the development of the rational intellect and scientific objectivity, and also the free and creative individualism characteristic of modern Western humanity. The cause for regret, according to Steiner, lies not in the admittedly profound loss of a cosmic intelligence—wisdom transmitted by higher beings to shamans, teachers, prophets, and sages—but in the failure of modern Western consciousness to develop imagination, inspiration, and intuition by which to overcome the distance between the individual person and his or her environment. In Steiner's view, the great religious traditions are not universally or permanently true; their truth value changes over time. The truth, meaning, and effectiveness of ideas, as well as the consciousness of all thinking beings—including exalted beings—are all decisively affected by their evolving contexts and destinies.

Ken Wilber's pre-/trans- fallacy begs comparison with Steiner's account of the evolution of consciousness. Wilber states that it is a mistake to attempt to overcome contemporary human alienation and loss of meaning by reverting to pre-personal, pre-modern, or indigenous modes of consciousness. More than a half century before Ken Wilber contributed this useful "pre-/trans-fallacy,"[22] Steiner recognized the need for individuals and cultures to meet the distinctive challenges of their context-specific mode of consciousness. In Wilber's terms, contemporary thinking should proceed from personal thinking to transpersonal, from ordinary rational thinking to intuitive thinking that transcends the personal. Steiner's vast body of writings and recommendations for the renewal of contemporary culture are congruent with the principle nicely summarized by Wilber. Steiner exemplified as well as articulated various methods of Spiritual Science, which in many ways synthesize ancient shamanic intimacy and modern Western rationality. From this synthesis Steiner developed not only his method of esoteric science but the full range of anthroposophic practices and endeavors. The shamanic is essentially a spiritual and cognitive method based on the reality of the etheric realm. Steiner, of course, researched and advocated for the integrated human experience of the "I," the soul (astral), and the physical body, and between the soul and the physical, the important etheric body, which is tragically neglected by modern Western consciousness.

Human-divine relationships such as between Moses and Yahweh, or Arjuna and Krishna, were not as separate as our current way of experiencing and conceptualizing relationships between humans and divinity. In our modern experience of the everyday world, meaning and intelligibility are contingent upon shaping by the human mind. During each particular phase of collective human development, the sun, moon, and stars, physical earth, and nature in all of its variety of spatially and temporally determined forms, all have had meanings given them by the mode of consciousness prevalent in each historical period. In the ancient past, consciousness was not individualized as it is currently. Steiner sought to show the complex interplay between knower and known as well as to show ways to overcome the duality of subject/object, or matter-bound/transcendent thinking, which is characteristic of contemporary alienated, fragmented consciousness.

---

22. See Ken Wilber, *Sex, Ecology, and Spirituality*, 205ff.

The separation between "out there" and "in here" has become more pronounced throughout history. The relationship between "in the mind" and "out there" has evolved so dramatically that perceiving and thinking are fundamentally different activities for a modern Western person as for a person living at the time of the Hebrew scriptures or classical Greece. Modern Western thinking has largely lost contact with and faith in the inner reality and meaning of what it perceives. Advocates of nominalist epistemology argue that all meanings are merely terms that the culture agrees to use. Whereas contemporary Western theories of evolution presuppose that the universe and all of its constituent parts—including planets, the ecosystem, Shakespeare, Mozart, trains, planes, the atom bomb, and computers—evolved from matter, Steiner argues that every atom, every moment, and all creation is made possible by mind or spirit, which precedes them and is the necessary source of physical evolution. Language and music, to take only two of countless examples, came into existence because sound already existed as an eternal potentiality in the original spiritual source of all that is. According to Steiner, evolution of consciousness is only possible because of its source and agency, whether referred to as spirit, mind, Nous or Word (Logos), and its double goal (lure, or *telos*) of freedom and love. The realization of freedom and love is not guaranteed; it requires cultivation through the spiritual thinking, feeling, and willing espoused by Steiner and other great teachers of humanity, at least two of whom, Sri Aurobindo and Teilhard de Chardin, are discussed in this chapter.

The most important contribution of Steiner's account of evolution of consciousness may be simply that it can help twenty-first-century people to understand why they have come to think, feel, and will as they do. From Steiner's perspective, most of the distinctive features of modern Western consciousness are traceable to the early centuries of the West, when it experienced the transition from late Hebraic and Greco–Roman to Christian thought and culture. Steiner named this period the Intellectual Soul Age, as well as the fourth cultural age, the eighth century BCE to the fifteenth century CE. Karl Jaspers introduced the term

Axial Age[23] for the first half of this period, approximately the eighth to third centuries BCE. In his account of the Axial Age Jaspers does not grant a significant transformative role to the arrival of Christianity, but he does recognize that in the fifth century CE Augustine of Hippo (North Africa) created a powerful synthesis of Christian and Neoplatonic thought.

During this period, the Hebraic tradition witnessed the prophecies of Jeremiah and Isaiah and the mystery of Job. Greek thought in the early Axial Age represents a remarkable transition from Homer's *Odyssey* to Sophocles' *Oedipus* and *Antigone*, and the execution of Socrates by a corrupt Athenian court, each of which stand as iconic moments in the evolution of human self-consciousness. Steiner's account of the evolution of consciousness during the Graco–Roman–Christian epoch provides important insights concerning the evolution from Socratic myth and inquiry to Platonic dialectic to Aristotelian logic. (Unfortunately, he does not recognize the importance of the Stoics.) Steiner claims that Socrates was influenced by the teachings of the mystery centers wherein the clairvoyance of previous centuries was preserved in secrecy.

Although Socrates historically represents the beginning of rational, philosophical thought, it is also important to note that he was called to philosophy by the prophecy of an oracle (a divinely inspired prophet of an ancient Greek cult through which the gods spoke directly to human petitioners). When on trial for his life, charged with heresy and corrupting the youth of the Athenian state, Socrates argued that he had acted on the authority of his *daimon*. An interpreter limited to a scientific or modern frame of reference would understand Socrates's *daimon* as individual conscience, the distinctly modern subjective moral sense that has no independent authority or existence outside of a person's own socially generated values. For Steiner, the *daimon* of Socrates had an independent existence and was not his own creation. Steiner reports that Socrates, and to some extent Plato and Aristotle, still had access to spiritual realities, and therefore in varying degrees their consciousness combined both the fading

---

23. Karl Jaspers, *Origin and Meaning of History*, 1–21.

clairvoyance of the previous age and the beginning of non-clairvoyant rational thinking.

Steiner maintains that Plato saw the Forms or universal Ideas as real and existing independent of (but also fashioned by) the knowing mind, while Plato simultaneously argued for the possibility of building up to that vision by rational dialectic. In his *Philosophy of Freedom* Steiner himself performed a service similar to the contribution of Plato: He articulated a method of thinking for ordinary, scientifically-minded people. Steiner's clairvoyance is continuous with the clairvoyance of Socrates, Plato, and Aristotle, for whom the Forms or Ideas were in the cosmic order and in *Nous* (the intellect), but Steiner's clairvoyance is necessarily more deliberate.

Steiner's thought is reflective of both Plato's intuitive capacity to see Ideas, or essences, and Aristotle's empirical method and scientific sensibility. Raphael's famous painting of the School of Athens accurately depicts Plato and Aristotle in polar positions—Plato gesturing to the heavens and Aristotle gesturing toward Earth. From the perspective of the evolution of human consciousness, and more specifically, of human thinking, Aristotle's contribution was as important as Plato's. The two-thousand-year period that began with classical Greek genius and the Hebrew prophets and then evolved through the early and middle Christian centuries refers to a way of thinking that is midway between the imaginal immediacy of the third cultural age that ends with Homer and the Book of Genesis, and the fifth cultural age that began with the scientific revolution in the West.

It is characteristic of Christian and particularly Euro–American thinking to ignore Asia when describing the broad sweep of human history. Steiner's account of this fourth cultural period ignores the two dominant paradigms of classical China: Confucianism which tries to harmonize the Tao with the rhythms of nature and the rhythms of moral and social processes; and Taoism which tries to reconcile the Tao with the inner experience of humanity. *Religion in Human Evolution*, the *magnum opus* of the late Robert Bellah, includes India and China as well as Hebrew and Greek civilizations. Both the general and the particulars of Steiner's interpretation of the evolution of cultures must be rethought in light of inclusive scholarship such as Robert Bellah's.

Continuing with his characterization of the fourth cultural age, Steiner refers to the Incarnation of Christ in the first century as "the turning point of time." But what evidence is there that the time turned, and what would count as evidence? The life and teachings of Christ did not gain visible significance in the larger ancient world for several centuries, most evidentially in 325 when the emperor Constantine declared Christianity to be the official religion of the Roman Empire.[24] Exactly opposite to Steiner's interpretation of the Incarnation of Christ, the Jewish philosopher Martin Buber wrote that the Christian holds a presumptuous position which affirms redemption in a manifestly unredeemed world. Buber and others could retort to Steiner that the time does not appear to be turned. But consistent with two thousand years of Christian thought, Steiner claims to see a decisive, if subtle turning, from a state of consciousness on rapid descent to one that is in tension between descent and ascent. Hence, Steiner's similarity to Hegel's maxim: "To him who looks at the world rationally the world looks rationally back." Steiner looked at the world incarnationally, and the world look incarnationally back.

Steiner reads the last three thousand years of history as a steady decline in the intimacy between human and divine in favor of a steady increase in independent, humanistic thinking. How, then, can the Incarnation of Christ in the first century signify "the turning point of time"? Steiner's answer is that new capacities and possibilities have been introduced, whether or not they have been realized. According to Steiner, Christ brought a new "I," a new spiritual relationship, but, as Buber noted, to an unredeemed world. Jesus of Nazareth was prepared to receive the divine Christ, the Logos and Sun Being, but except for a few spiritually advanced souls such as the mother of Jesus, John the

---

24. For the import of Constantine, and particularly for the beginning of establishment of Christian anti-Semitism, see James Carroll, *Constantine's Sword*.

Baptist, John the Evangelist (the Beloved Disciple), Mary Magdalen, and later Paul the Apostle, very few were prepared to recognize or collaborate with the teachings, death, and resurrection of Christ.

The capacities of great souls can not be diminished by the neglect of others. But the impact of such souls requires that they be recognized and served. The history of Christianity, including the epistles of Paul, the gospels of Matthew, Mark, Luke, and John, as well as the writings of the Latin and Greek Church Fathers, showed the effects of the Incarnation to the extent possible at that time. As we know from both Greek literature and history, and from the Hebrew scriptures, the permanent characteristic of nations and empires during the Axial Age was war and slavery, with only an occasional ineffectual voice against the status quo. The *Meditations* of emperor Marcus Aurelius, written in the midst of war, was not against war (which he presumed to be inevitable), but in favor of *amor fati*, the peaceful "love of fate."

Jesus taught and exhibited love and peace but even he accepted slavery as a fact of the time. Slavery is still widespread, especially involving girls in Southeast Asia and the Middle East— but approval of slavery is mostly past. Gross economic inequity is also widespread, but this, too, is generally recognized to be a failure of widely accepted democratic values. It seems that the world is both still unredeemed and in the process of redemption. God is dead and yet Christ lives in the souls of millions. When asked his opinion of Christianity, Gandhi famously replied that it ought to be tried. And so it has: I believe that it has been the best possible result, however inadequate and even tragic, of the teachings and presence of Christ and inspiration of the Holy Spirit when combined with frail humanity in an advanced stage of loss of participation.

Steiner states that modern Western humanity, and increasingly the rest of humanity—is in what he calls the fifth cultural age, the Consciousness Soul Age, characterized by increasingly intense competition between individual freedom and materialistic collectivity. By his account, the primary task of the present age is to replace the cold rational and scientific thinking that has been ascending since the fifteenth century by thinking that will be increasingly individual, free, will-filled, and full of affection. Through Steiner's several hundred volumes of lectures delivered to specialists in the natural sciences, social sciences, and the arts, he sought to show that modern science as well as currents in modern arts and humanities share a single paradigmatic that has been emerging in European cultures of the last six centuries. This perspective began with the explosion of individualized genius referred to as the Renaissance and continuing to the eighteenth-century Enlightenment: These two periods include the contributions of Nicholas of Cusa, Pico della Mirandola, Ficino, Leonardo da Vinci, Michaelangelo, Raphael, Copernicus, Luther, Bacon, Galileo, Shakespeare, Descartes, Newton, Kepler, and Locke. In the United States, the six Founding Fathers—Franklin, Washington, Adams, Hamilton, Jefferson, and Madison—represent a similar burst of genius. (Note: All of this genius totally failed to see and support the inestimable potential and talent of women and people of color. Worse, Steiner made many comments on race that are not true and quite offensive by twentieth- and twenty-first-century standards.)

One of the obvious obstacles in attempting to revive an enchanted cosmos within modern culture continues to be dazzled by the success of science. Even thinkers who lament and oppose the scientific worldview and its negative fallout must admit that humanity cannot return to a pre-scientific way of thinking. Still, many individuals living in the midst of scientific and technological security and conveniences seem to long for the values and abilities of pre-scientific forms of life: intimacy with nature, dream life, spirits, shamanic practices, and other powers studied by C. G. Jung, Claude Levi-Strauss, Mircea Eliade, Joseph Campbell, and a host of mythologists, anthropologists, and historians of religion.

The modern scientific paradigm is generally regarded throughout most of the world as the one that will continue to serve as a basis for an endless series of elaborations and extensions, none of which will alter its shared scientific methods and assumptions. This confidence in science in the face of ecological devastation will produce fascinating as well as urgent consequences. Though Steiner contributed to and appreciated much of Western scientific thought, he regarded the presuppositions and achievements of the modern scientific West as temporary and limited. He saw the entire scientific revolution—from Francis Bacon's *New Organon* in 1620, to Descartes' mathematical philosophy in 1637, to Darwinian evolution in 1858, to Freudian psychoanalysis in 1900—as a dramatic manifestation of a new and powerful mode of consciousness that followed from centuries of careful growth. He was confident that it would lead to an entirely different mode of consciousness in the future.

One of the tasks of the modern age, therefore, is to bring to fruition a new kind of spiritual thinking, as well as cultures characterized by peace and justice. Spiritual perception can be developed through the cultivation of the cognitive powers appropriate for the present stage of cultural and psychic evolution—imagination, inspiration, and intuition. Compared to these more spiritual and intentional modes of thinking, the thoughts of the modern person tend to be determined by impersonal forces such as culturally engendered habits or biophysical impulses. Steiner refers to our ordinary thinking as dead thinking, or, as in Plato's allegory, as cave-like. The modern person is generally incapable of the kind of clairvoyance that was standard for individuals in past epochs and typical of a few highly evolved individuals today, such as Rudolf Steiner, but with the assistance of such individuals one can still develop capacities that guide humanity safely past immanent challenges.

In addition to analyzing the ills of contemporary civilization, Steiner adds a deeper interpretation, one not found in other academic or religious thinkers, nor even in contemporary spiritual teachers such as His Holiness the Dalai Lama. Steiner's completely unusual analysis of the present situation concerns the two spiritual tempters, Lucifer (who, with legions, tempts humanity to ignore natural and social requirements) and Ahriman (who, also with legions, tempts humanity to think that matter is all there is, with no depth and no interior). These tempters typically lead humanity to misinterpret or fail to serve the species's distinctive task. For example, it seems likely that the French Revolution as a task, passionately embraced, was premature: late eighteenth-century France was not ready for Liberty, Equality, and Fraternity. Similarly, the seventy-year communist experiment by the Soviet Union would seem wrongly timed: Steiner states that the sixth cultural age, beginning in the thirty-fifth century, will be ideal for the implementation of communal values. Of course, in the midst of a possibly fatal ecological demise, talk of the thirty-fifth century might also well be wildly presumptuous.

Each advance in consciousness (e.g., from tribal to national to global) brings new challenges. It was the great task of the third cultural age (third millennium to eighth century BCE) to transition from tribal identity (and constant warfare between tribes) to larger identities, primarily national. The challenge of the fourth cultural age (eighth century BCE to fifteenth century CE) was to transition from constant warfare among nations to a more international consciousness. The challenge of the fifth cultural age (beginning in the fifteenth century West) is the transition from autocratic to democratic governments and to establish a lasting peace among people and nations. In general, humanity has proven incapable of peace for a variety of reasons, the most important of which, according to Steiner, is related to concurrent increases since the nineteenth century in individual freedom.

In Steiner's view, the West is caught in a great struggle with Ahriman, the tempter on behalf of materialism, not merely concerning actions but more importantly concerning thinking. Under Ahriman's influence, Western consciousness focuses primarily, and almost exclusively, on externals. This blindness has overtaken parts of cultural life such as religion, arts, and education that are inextricably related to the inner life and spiritual realities. Religions succumb to the materialist temptation by reducing spiritual realities to mechanistic functions, to magical fix-alls and tribal commitments in service of ignorant, and selfish ends. The arts, too, can fail to connect the spiritual and the material, and education can serve the political and economic aims of society at the expense of freedom and creativity.

The fear of Ahrimanic deception can send seekers, artists, and educators into an opposite, Luciferic deception which involves the neglect, and even denial, of the material, e.g., spiritual practice oblivious of social justice, or of physical well being, or of human relationships. Religions have generally failed to serve the cause of justice in advance of the rest of the culture. In the 1950s and 1960s the Black churches worked to end segregation, but white churches were generally working against equality. Evidencing a mix of Luciferic presumption and Ahriman materialism, religions have a history of siding with as well as opposing the proponents of violence, intolerance, and injustice. In response to both the Ahrimanic and Luciferic temptations Steiner recommends the balancing function of Christ, a purely spiritual being who entered fully into the material world—and in the person of Jesus with whom Christ was perfectly joined, suffered the fullest possible effect of human cruelty.[25]

---

25. The influence of Lucifer and Ahriman is discussed in chapter 7, "God, Suffering, and Evil," and in chapter 10, "Art and Aesthetics."

Tenzin Gyatso, the 14th Dalai Lama

5

KRISHNA, BUDDHA, AND CHRIST

INTRODUCTION: CONFLICT OF RELIGIONS

To the extent that religious believers have been forced to consider religions other than their own, they have tended to treat other religions as entirely foreign, as competitors, and even as abominations. Education at every level, however, along with personal contact, has helped to diminish the mutually negative perceptions among religions. In the Christian-oriented West, college courses on religion typically treat the world's major religions respectfully. Understandably, they consider Hinduism and Buddhism to be entirely separate from each other and from Christianity. Christian theologians and church leaders tend to consider it obvious that since Christ is divine claims for other would-be divine beings such as Krishna and Buddha must be mistaken. If Christ is divine, then the Jews need wait no longer for a messiah, and both Judaism and Islam should abandon their conviction that no person is both human and divine.

Throughout the nineteenth century, despite the challenge posed by Darwinian theory of evolution, European and North American Christians were able to sustain without challenge their conviction that the Bible was the sole valid revelation by the divine. It was not until 1893 at the first Parliament of Religions in Chicago that Protestant leaders and theologians had to face for the first time the possibility of multiple valid revelations. This case was made brilliantly by the reformer of Hinduism, Swami Vivekananda (1863–1902). Not yet thirty years old, Vivekananda amazed (and probably alarmed) the hundreds of scholars and religious leaders with his rich language, deep experience, and oratorical skills in defense of Hinduism and the unity of diverse religious traditions.

Vivekananda's speeches brought both good news (a powerful case for harmony of religious essentials and tolerance of differences), but also showed the need for Christians to confront the possibility that a non-Christian religion might also be true, and that Krishna or Buddha might be divine, if not instead of, in addition to, Christ. The Roman Catholic Church, by far the largest Christian denomination whose members number twenty-percent of the world's population, was not forced to acknowledge the validity of non-Christian religious traditions until the Vatican council, 1962 to 1965 when the Roman Catholic Church conceded that non-Christian religions can offer a positive way to salvation.

Hindus and Buddhists, fortunately, never taught that theirs was the only way to enlightenment or liberation, nor did they attribute divine status to only one being. The Hindu tradition affirms many gods and avatars (sometimes including Buddha and Jesus), and Buddhism, which has many branches, has no single teaching on Buddha or on divine beings. Further, throughout their histories, Hinduism and Buddhism, like Confucianism and Taoism, have been entwined with other major religions. Each of these religions has a history—though certainly not a perfect history—of tolerance toward other religions. Perhaps partly because it has not until recently had military power, Judaism also has a peaceful history toward other religions. It is only Christianity and Islam that have insisted on an exact definition of divinity and the status of various religious figures. Islam claims that Mohammed is Allah's last prophet, but is not divine. Only Christianity has claimed throughout its history, and by all of its branches, that only one being, Jesus Christ, is "the only Son of God," fully human and fully divine, as expressed in the dogma of the hypostatic union.

It follows from the Christian claim to be "the sole way to salvation" that Krishna and Buddha are not, and could not be, divine beings in any significant respect. Non-Christians, including Hindus and Buddhists, consider the exclusivist claim for

Christ's divinity to be presumptuous. In varying degrees, many great religious thinkers have expressed inclusiveness toward Krishna, Buddha, and Christ. Sri Ramakrishna, Swami Vivekananda, Mahatma Gandhi (not accidentally all Indian), and also Thich Nhat Hanh and His Holiness the Dalai Lama (both Buddhists) are comfortable with the attribution of a similar status, whether divine, enlightened, or simply special and inspiring, to Krishna, Buddha, and Christ.

Toward the end of his short life, Thomas Merton, the well-known Roman Catholic monk who befriended both Thich Nhat Hanh and His Holiness the Dalai Lama, developed a special relationship with the teachings of Krishna and Buddha. Thanks to the research of Ursula King, we now know that Teilhard, during his twenty years in China, developed a relationship with both Confucianism and Taoism. Sri Aurobindo held that Krishna is divine but not the only divinity in the Hindu pantheon. Unfortunately, some of his references to Jesus and Buddha, which admittedly are more anecdotal than systematic, are dismissive. The Dalai Lama holds that all three, Krishna, Buddha, and Christ, are enlightened beings, the approximate equivalent of divine, but he does not seem particularly interested in classification and even less interested in competition among religions or claims on behalf of their founders.

Rudolf Steiner considers Christ to be fully divine, one with the Father and the Holy Spirit in the Christian conception of the Trinity. He regards Krishna and Buddha as sublime spiritual beings who have brought essential teachings to humanity appropriate to their time and culture. In his view, these three beings have collaborated from before their appearance on Earth, and continue to be essential for the evolution of humanity. It appears that Steiner developed a clairvoyant relationship with Krishna and Buddha but not particularly with Hinduism or Buddhism, nor with the cultures within which they flourish. I tend to think that Rudolf Steiner was able to contact Krishna and Buddha simply because their souls are so numinous. While he was able to see Krishna, his knowledge of the Bhagavad Gita appears to be almost entirely exoteric—i.e., standard knowledge such as found in books. He does not mention Sankara or Ramanuja, roughly equivalent to Augustine and Aquinas in the history of Christianity. Similarly, Steiner connected with Buddha, but does not mention Zen or Pure Land, nor great Buddhist thinkers such as Nagarjuna, Shantidev, Dogen, or the Tibetan tradition of the Dalai Lama.

It is not unusual for a contemporary person, especially one who holds a skeptical postmodern worldview, to think that it does not matter if beings such as Krishna, Buddha, or Christ actually lived. This view claims that we need only know that their influence is felt. This book holds the view that in the long run (throughout an entire life and not just in an emergency) it is not likely to be efficacious to pray to or supplicate an unknown, and perhaps unknowable, image that is real in one's subjective belief but not in objective reality. (A pragmatic approach might show the need to believe in a particular being on the way to knowledge of a spiritual being but such belief produces neither knowledge nor the being, but only the belief.)

How might we gain real relationships to objective-transcendent beings? Throughout this book I suggest that the best way is through active, patient, and disciplined imagination—i.e., by seeing-knowing-feeling one's way into real images. This seeing-knowing is definitely akin to love. Note the title of the book by Arthur Zajonc: *Meditation as Contemplative Inquiry: When Knowing Becomes Love.* Such knowing turned to love is difficult for a contemporary person because most of us think materialistically and reductionistly such that we habitally consider images to be less real than physical objects. C. G. Jung, among others, is especially helpful in enabling us to experience the reality of images and symbols. In the dominant worldview, imagination and images are all equally unreal, whereas the thinkers I am recommending, especially in this regard Steiner and Jung, are arguing that some symbols participate in real invisible beings. Whereas Ulysses, Hamlet, and Moby Dick are the creations respectively of Homer, Shakespeare, and Melville, and depend on us for their continued existence as important fictional creations, spiritual beings such as Krishna, Buddha, and Christ have their own existence in addition to their existence in the lives of those who believe in them. This chapter discusses these three figures both as they have revealed themselves, as they continue to affect the lives of their followers, and especially in light of Rudolf Steiner's esoteric-intuitive research.

SRI AUROBINDO ON KRISHNA AND THE BHAGAVAD GITA

When one first reads the Bhagavad Gita ("Song of the Lord," the Lord being Krishna), initially it appears to be a story. In the middle of a civil war in ancient India, the warrior Arjuna turns to his charioteer Krishna and says in effect, "This is crazy; almost all of the warriors on both sides will soon be dead, leaving families without care and communities without leadership."As we know from the great Indian epic the *Mahabharata* ("the great tale about ancient India"), Krishna was not an ordinary charioteer. It is only in the Gita, however, which evolved out of the *Mahabharata*, that He reveals Himself to be a god, or more technically, an avatar, a divine being who helps humanity when it loses its way. As Krishna says in a famous passage,

> Whenever *dharma* [right order] declines and the purpose
>   of life is forgotten, I manifest on earth.
> I am born in every age to protect the good,
>   to destroy evil, and to reestablish *dharma* (4.7–8).[1]

Herein lies the first question, and perhaps mystery, of the Gita, and perhaps of all religion and spirituality. What is happening in this text? Did such an event actually occur? Was there ever a god named Krishna who revealed Himself, and His offer of help, to a warrior in a civil war in ancient India? Is the Gita a fictional story of an imagined being similar to Achilles, Hamlet, and Ahab, or an accurate account of a revelation that took place in time, and perhaps in space. Was the Gita a revelation from the spiritual world, perhaps through a dream or an inspiration of an author?

---

1.   The Bhagavad Gita, translated by Eknath Easwaran, reprinted in Robert McDermott, ed., intro., notes by Robert McDermott, *The Bhagavad Gita and the West*, CW 142/146.

Was it similar to the annunciation to the Virgin by the Archangel Gabriel, or by Christ to Saul (on the road to Damascus)? If so, might it have happened in space as well as in time, by one flesh and blood being to another, for example as Buddha to His disciple Govinda or by Jesus to his disciples at the last supper?

Although Gandhi said that he based his entire life's work on the teaching of the Gita, he did not affirm the avatar passage above or the war. In his commentary Gandhi considers the war to be a metaphor for the struggling self, a conflict between the higher and ordinary self, and between good and evil. He refers to the avatar passage as the voice of reason leading the embattled Arjuna from his lower to his higher self. By strong contrast, Sri Aurobindo regards Krishna as a real being, in fact a uniquely exalted being, perhaps the highest of all spiritual beings, an avatar or god who made a real revelation of Himself and His yogas (the disciplines of knowledge, action, love, and contemplation) to a historically real warrior in the midst of a historically real war. Aurobindo also thinks that Krishna said, and meant, that Arjuna should turn around and prepare to throw, and if necessary receive, a spear in the gut.

Gandhi's and Aurobindo's respective interpretations of the Gita are consistent with their basic disagreement about violence: Gandhi spent his entire life practicing and advocating nonviolence whereas in response to World War II Aurobindo advocated for India to join the Allies militarily against the Axis powers. In the course of his counsel Krishna tells Arjuna to recommit to his duty as a warrior. Several times He says to Arjuna, "therefore go and fight." Gandhi argues that an Indian scripture could not advocate war as Krishna might seem to be doing. Consequently, the war must be internal. Sri Aurobindo, however, with no aversion to war, believes that Krishna's advice should be considered both a historical event and truthful contemporary advice. This disagreement between Gandhi and Aurobindo extends to their understanding of Krishna and their differing view of the yogas that Krishna teaches in the Gita: For Gandhi, Krishna teaches karma yoga, or selfless action, the teachings in the first three of eighteen chapters. Aurobindo regards Krishna's teaching of karma yoga to be subordinate to Krishna's revelation of His divine status in chapters nine to eleven, after which all four yogas come to the fore culminating in the profound mystical statement at the end of chapter eighteen:

> Make every act an offering to me; regard me as your only pro-
> tector. Relying on interior discipline, meditate on me always.
> Remembering me, you shall overcome all difficulties through
> my grace. But if you will not heed me in your self-will,
> nothing will avail you.
> If you egotistically say, "I will not fight this battle," your resolve
> will be useless; your own nature will drive you into it. Your
> own karma, born of your own nature, will drive you to
> do even that which you do not wish to do, because of your
> delusion.
> The Lord dwells in the hearts of all creatures and whirls them
> round upon the wheel of maya.
> Run to him for refuge with all your strength, and peace pro-
> found will be yours through his grace.
> I give you these precious words of wisdom; reflect on them and
> then do as you choose.
> These are the last words I shall speak to you, dear one, for your
> spiritual fulfillment. You are very dear to me.
> Be aware of me always, adore me, make every act an offering
> to me, and you shall come to me; this I promise; for you are
> dear to me.
> Abandon all supports and look to me for protection. I shall
> purify you from the sins of the past; do not grieve. (18:57–65)

In 1908 to 1909, while in the Alipore Jail on charges of trying to bomb the offices of the British Government of India, Aurobindo Ghose (his given name) memorized and recited the Gita. He had a vision of Krishna holding in His embrace the jailers and the jailed. Such a vision of reconciliation, however, did not lead Aurobindo to avoid taking sides either against the British Government of India or on the side of Britain against Nazi aggression through-out Europe. Rather, he maintained a view of Krishna as being above warring factions, while at the same time believing that in any conflict a follower of Krishna should take the side that seems right. It was clear to Aurobindo that Arjuna was on the side of justice and so Krishna encouraged him to fight, while Krishna Himself by definition remains above opposing sides.

In Aurobindo's view, Arjuna's initial argument against fighting because the other side included cousins and uncles, and families would be left bereft, is superseded by the revelation of Krishna as avatar, the display of Krishna's divine extent, and the concluding verses in which Arjuna's ordinary consciousness has been transformed by the love between him and Krishna. While the civil war in the Gita is real, a much larger set of historical, spiritual, and cosmic forces are at work. Arjuna should do his part, and most importantly, he should do so in conformity with the yogas: He should know his karma; he should act without attachment to any benefit to himself or to his side; he should act out of love for Krishna; and he should act in a meditative or contemplative state—while throwing, ducking, and if necessary being hit fatally by enemy spears.

In his *Essays on the Gita,* Aurobindo explains his approach to scripture:

> Only those scriptures, religions, philosophies which can be thus constantly renewed, relived, their stuff of permanent truth constantly reshaped and developed in the inner thought and spiritual experience of developing humanity, continue to be of living importance to mankind. The rest remain as monuments of the past, but have no actual force or vital impulse for the future.[2]

When Gandhi returned to India after twenty years in South Africa he joined the movement for Indian independence from Britain. Soon after, he sent his son to ask Sri Aurobindo to come out of his ashram and join the movement that was then forming around Gandhi's leadership. Aurobindo explained to his young visitor that he was very busy fighting for India against the British on the level of consciousness. This conflict of approach powerfully sketches the difference between Gandhi's practice and advocacy of karma yoga and Sri Aurobindo's synthesis of all four yogas within the context of the evolution of consciousness (of

---

2. Sri Aurobindo, *Essays on the Gita,* 2

which Gandhi seems to have had no awareness). For Aurobindo personally, Krishna was and is the teacher of the yogas and the avatar of the successive phases of human evolution, including the one that Aurobindo and the Mother considered themselves to be assisting. But in his public writing and his teaching to disciples Aurobindo does not enjoin any necessary acknowledgement to Krishna or any other God, leaving individuals free for their revelation of God.

Like Steiner's lectures on the transformative revelations by higher beings, Sri Aurobindo's account of divinity sees the divine—specifically, *Sat-Chit-Ananda* (Being Consciousness Bliss)—continuing to inspire matter, life, and mind to ever higher modes of consciousness. He particularly sees Krishna as the great transformer—initially of Indian consciousness and culture, but ultimately of humanity. He does not attribute to Buddha or to Christ a role in the evolution of consciousness comparable to the significance he ascribes to Krishna.[3] Yet he also does not consider the Bhagavad Gita to be an adequate guide for the spiritual needs of modern humanity. The Gita does not include anything like Aurobindo's conviction concerning the evolution of humanity through stages of consciousness aiming at the universal realization of Supermind, the most thorough and conscious permeation of the divine into humanity and material creation. Sri Aurobindo wrote *Essays on the Gita,* as well as a masterpiece of spiritual direction, *Synthesis of Yoga,* in the first half of which he explains the disciplines of the Gita, and in the second half addresses those three disciplines in relation to the evolution of consciousness (see chapter 12, "Spiritual Practice").

Aurobindo suggests that subsequent to Krishna's revelation in the Bhagavad Gita, He has continued to inspire the evolution of humanity, including the transformation of all mind, life, and matter. Rather than recommending a focus primarily on the Gita, Aurobindo recommends an intimate transformative experience of Krishna like his own in the Alipore Jail. He referred to his second experience of Krishna, on November 24, 1926, as the Descent of the Overmind into his own consciousness.

---

3.   See Sri Aurobindo, *Problem of Rebirth,* 41–45.

Disciples of Sri Aurobindo understand the descent of Krishna into Aurobindo to be a twentieth-century reenactment of the Bhagavad Gita, an event whereby Aurobindo, the recipient of Krishna's grace, came to know Krishna by the triple yogas of knowledge, action, and love, and by the modern revelation of the evolution of consciousness.

When Aurobindo Ghose (not yet "Sri") went for instruction to Lele, a Maharastrian who was thought to be one of the most advanced yoga masters in India at that time, Lele told Aurobindo that he was already too accomplished for further instruction. Can we avoid asking just who Aurobindo might have been in his previous life? Isn't it obvious that he brought spiritually advanced capacities with him? It certainly seems (at least to me) that Teilhard and Steiner similarly came with advanced capacities: They knew the spirit world from childhood. Aurobindo does not say very much about his childhood or early years when he was in England separated from Indian soil, language, and spirituality, but he does speak about the early life of Mira whom he referred to as "divine even in childhood." While it is not exactly clear what "divine" means in this claim, it would seem to give the suggestion of avatar status, perhaps similar to initiate, the label usually ascribed to Rudolf Steiner.

Sri Aurobindo and the Mother collaboratively directed the work of the ashram, including the hundreds of disciples who lived and worked there, presumably all under the inspiration of Krishna. We can think of the Dalai Lama's work on behalf of wisdom and compassion as being under the guidance of Avalokiteshvara, an emanation of Buddha. Like Steiner, who has described the work of Christ through the Archangel Michael at this time, and the Dalai Lama, who has described the work of Buddha through Avalokiteshwara, Sri Aurobindo and the Mother were directed by Krishna to prepare the way for the descent of the Supermind, a universal transformative power and the next major phase of the evolution of consciousness. It is generally misleading to separate a discussion of the Mother of the Sri Aurobindo from a discussion of Sri Aurobindo himself, but the Mother, in addition to her exalted life in intimate spiritual relationship with Sri Aurobindo, is also a distinct manifestation of *shakti,* the divine feminine, and as such is discussed in the next chapter on Sophia.

His Holiness The Dalai Lama on Buddha and Christ

The life of the Dalai Lama is probably as well known as that of any twenty-first-century spiritual leader. The details of his amazing life began when he was found in eastern Tibet, across the whole of Tibet from Lhasa where the search for the next incarnation had begun. At two years of age, in a very simple house—not a stable exactly, but the parallel comes to mind— Tenzin Gyatso was able to identify several objects, including the cane and beads of his old teacher, from several other look-alikes intended to trick him. He also identified several objects that had belonged to the Thirteenth Dalai Lama, that is to say, that had been possessions of Tenzin Gyatso in his previous life as the Thirteenth Dalai Lama. There is no similar story for the birth of any other modern person, not Gandhi, or Teilhard, or Aurobindo, or Steiner—although there are such stories of other Tibetan tulku, reincarnate lamas. How much different must the world be from either the mainstream secular worldview or even from the Judeo-Christian worldview, if it is true that the Great Thirteenth Dalai Lama, who lived from 1876 to 1933, was reborn with sufficient memories of his life as the Thirteenth that he could be identified as the Thirteenth reborn. What's more, the Great Thirteenth had been a returnee from his life as the Twelfth, etc. back to the rather unclear origin of this lineage in the fourteenth century.[4]

What is thought to be clear—and altogether mysterious—is that after the first, the next thirteen Dalai Lamas, each found by a similar process, has been a spiritual teacher (*lama*) perceived to be as vast as an ocean (*dalai*). The entire line—may it endure!— is a physical, historical, and above all spiritual manifestation of Avalokiteshvara, the goddess of wisdom and compassion in the Buddhist tradition, possibly the same being as Quan Yin (Chinese),

---

4.   For an account of all fourteen Dalai Lamas, see Glen Mullin, *The Fourteen Dalai Lamas: A Sacred Legacy of Reincarnation.*

Tara (Tibetan), and Kannon (Japanese). That said, the Dalai Lamas
have not been equally impressive: Only a few come close to the
"The Great Thirteenth." It seems well assured that Tenzin Gyatso
will be universally referred to as "The Great Fourteenth." Anyone
who does not know his story should log on to the home page of
the Dalai Lama.[5] Birth stories in mythic time can be more amazing
but considering that we are talking about a flesh and blood human
being in the present time, one whom hundreds of thousands have
heard speak, and even met, this is a birth story capable of seriously
altering one's worldview. (How confusing is it that the atheist government of the People's Republic of China insists that the Dalai
Lama reincarnate as the Fifteenth Dalai Lama, and in Tibet, the
better to gain control of his life from infancy.)

To be in the presence of His Holiness, and especially to
meet him face to face, is to experience *darshan* of an ocean of
spirituality. The presence of the Dalai Lama is referred to as *jin
lap,* "blessings," or "gift waves." Despite worldwide adulation
(by virtually everyone except the government of the People's
Republic of China), the Dalai Lama deals humbly with claims
made on his behalf:

> His Holiness is considered to be the reincarnation of each of
> the previous thirteen Dalai Lamas of Tibet (the first having
> been born in AD 1391), who are in turn considered to be mani-
> festations of Avalokiteshvara, or Chenrezig, the Bodhisattva of
> Compassion, holder of the White Lotus. Thus His Holiness is
> also believed to be a manifestation of Chenrezig, in fact the sev-
> enty-fourth in a lineage that can be traced back to a Brahmin
> boy who lived in the time of Buddha Shakyamuni. I am often
> asked whether I truly believe this. The answer is not simple to
> give. But as a fifty-six-year-old, when I consider my experience
> during this present life, and given my Buddhist beliefs, I have
> no difficulty accepting that I am spiritually connected both to
> the thirteen previous Dalai Lamas, to Chenrezig and to the
> Buddha himself.[6]

5. See www.dalailama.com/biography/a-brief-biography.
6. His Holiness the Dalai Lama, *Homepage.*

That the Dalai Lama has had thirteen previous successive life-times to practice Tibetan Buddhist spirituality surely gave him an excellent start on his spiritual path, but he nevertheless has had to practice further—and he does. As he has explained countless times, he spends at least five hours a day in meditation and study. He has also repeated many times his conviction that "religious practice is a twenty-four-hour occupation."

As the historical Buddha has not been on Earth for 2500 years, it is sensible to inquire: just how can the Dalai Lama be said to know him? Or, what is it about Buddha that he knows? When a Hindu such as Sri Aurobindo refers to Krishna he is likely to recall and perhaps quote one or more *shlokas* (three- or four-line verses) from the dialogue between Krishna and Arjuna in the Bhagavad Gita. Teilhard de Chardin and Thomas Merton are likely to refer to the life and teachings of Jesus in the New Testament or a conception of Christ developed by a major Christian theologian such as Augustine, Aquinas, or Karl Rahner. In a similar situation, the Dalai Lama refers to one of the major Buddhist texts such as Shantideva's *Bodhicaryāvatāra* (entry into the way of the bodhisattva),"[7] but he does not often focus on the life of Gautama who became Buddha, the enlightened one.

Both of the major traditions of Buddhism, Theravada and Mahayana, embrace the Three Jewels: Buddha, *Dharma* (teaching and practice), and *Sangha* (community of practitioners). The conception of Buddha according to Theravada Buddhism, The Way of the Elders, can be compared to the Jewish conception of Jesus, or to the view of Jesus of the early non-Pauline Christians. In this view, Buddha is understood in terms of the life and teachings of Gautama, a view similar to those who focus on Jesus without affirming the divinity of Christ. The Theravada school is predominant in southeast Asia; the Mahayana tradition is predominant in China, Tibet, Mongolia, Korea, and Japan. Until the arrival of His Holiness the Dalai Lama in the 1980s, Buddhism in Europe and North America was predominantly Zen Buddhism from Japan and also Theravada, particularly the Thai practice

---

7. The Dalai wrote commentaries on the full text, *The Flash of Lightening in the Dark of Night*, and on the last chapter, *Practicing Wisdom*.

of Vipassana, or "insight meditation." Japanese Zen as taught by D. T. Suzuki who first came to Europe and North America in the 1930s, is part of the Mahayana tradition. In Herman Hesse's short novel *Siddhartha*, Gautama Buddha teaches the Theravada conception of Buddha: He is not divine, he will die, and that each person should do as he did—meditate and overcome attachment to the ego—but should not call on him for help. The main character in the book, Siddhartha, follows Buddha's advice, goes off on his own, but then loses his way. He has a son, becomes a self-indulgent merchant, takes up gambling, and loses track of his spiritual commitment until he meets a ferryman who reminds him of the Buddha's teaching. In the end, Siddhartha attains enlightenment, just like Gautama who became a Buddha.

In contrast, according to the Mahayana (the Greater Way) tradition, Buddha is understood to have three bodies:

Dharmakaya: truth body; infinite and eternal body of Buddha;
Sambhogakaya: transformation body; spiritual body of a
    bodhisattva;
Nirmanakaya: emanation body; biography of Gautama [8]

In the Mahayana version, "Buddha" is more than a name, as "Christ" is more than a name: both "Buddha" and "Christ" describe the divine natures, respectively, of Gautama and Jesus. Gautama and Jesus answer to "who"; "Buddha" and "Christ" answer to "what." In the Theravada tradition, "Buddha" is a title rather than a proper name. According to Tibetan Buddhism, after Buddha's death he was still present in the form of his *nirmanakaya*, which His Holiness refers to as "a form of perfect resourcefulness." As the Dalai Lama explained at the John Main seminar: Buddha "continues to emanate and manifest in various forms that are most suited and beneficial to other sentient beings. From that point of view, although Buddha Sakyamuni as a historical figure has ceased to exist, Buddha's presence is still there." [9]

---

8.   Rudolf Steiner, *According to Luke: The Gospel of Compassion and Love Revealed*, 231.

9.   His Holiness the Dali Lama, *The Good Heart*, 119.

It is revealing that Thich Nhat Hanh, a Zen master who teaches from a perspective that often seems closer to Theravada than to Mahayana, has written a book entitled *Living Buddha, Living Christ* which is actually about Gautama and Jesus, and not at all about Buddha and Christ. Similarly, Thich Nhat Hanh's *Old Path White Clouds*, which tells stories about the life of Gautama, gives no indication of the Buddha of the Mahayana tradition—i.e., there is no reference to Buddha living and aiding humanity after his death. The Mahayana tradition holds that the early texts contain Buddha's exoteric teachings but that he also taught esoteric truths to his closest disciples, just as Jesus presumably taught esoterically to his Mother, Mary Magdalen, and John: "But privately to his disciples he explained everything" (Mark 4:34).

The core of the Buddha's teaching in both Theravada and Mahayana is the Buddha's first sermon consisting of the Four Noble Truths:

> There is suffering. Existence is painful, transient, limited, and unsatisfactory.
> The arising of suffering is due to causes and conditions.
> There is cessation of suffering.
> There is a path that brings about the cessation of suffering [the Eightfold Path].

The Eightfold Path can be considered the whole of Buddhist practice, the other half of Buddhist *dharma*. Essential to Buddhist *dharma*, both teaching and practice, is the need to overcome attachment to self. At an ordinary level, this overcoming refers to habitual desires, the ones that take the form of "I want," and "I need," as well as "I don't want," and "I hate." The opposite to such desiring, of course, is selflessness, compassion, and love. Daily selfishness is difficult to transform, especially if, as the Buddhist tradition holds, each of us is born with a karmic debt and negative tendencies in the form of fear, hatred, and delusion. The attachment most difficult to cure, of course, is to a belief in one's independent and lasting existence. Release from attachment, which the Buddha preached, is the most fundamental teaching of all Buddhist traditions. In the most radical formulation of this thought, Buddha is thought to have preached that there is no enduring self, no *atman* (*an-atman*), or *anatta* in Pali, the language of the earliest Buddhist texts. The Dalai Lama has explained that in teaching the *anatta* doctrine, Buddha taught according to the spiritual need of individuals, all of whom are to some degree attached to their illusory individual selves.

Because it is difficult for Western audiences to accept the concept of non-self, Thich Nhat Hanh and the Dalai Lama, the two major Buddhist teachers in the West, both believe that it is not important to know exactly what Buddha taught about the self (or non-self). Instead, they teach that it is absolutely essential to reduce, and if possible eliminate, the attachment to one's belief in one's enduring self—irrespective of whether in fact the self is real and enduring or illusory. What follows the elimination of one's attachment is bliss (*ananda*). This is the point: Overcome the self and attain liberation from attachment, the cause of *dukkha*. This is exactly what the Buddha did and taught, after which, according to Theravada, he died; according to Mahayana, the Buddha essentially is his *dharmakaya* state such that at the end of his life his *nirmanakaya* simply dissolved, leaving him, as always, in *dharmakaya*.

One's understanding of the first jewel—the teacher Gautama who awoke, taught, was called Buddha, and died, forever to be imitated but not to be contacted, *or* an infinite and eternal Buddha—affects the other two jewels, the *dharma* (teaching and practice), and *sangha* (the community). As a teacher of Mahayana Buddhism, the Dalai Lama focuses on the spiritual reality of Buddha as manifest in his two higher bodies: his *sambogakaya*, or subtle body, and his *dharmakaya*, or infinite and eternal body. It is also true that the Dalai Lama, with typical humility, says that he focuses on the Buddha in his historical nature, as *nirmanakaya*: "I prefer to relate to Buddha as a historical figure and personality—someone who has perfected human nature and evolved into a fully enlightened being." Following the Mahayana tradition, the Dalai Lama affirms the *trikaya*, the Buddha's three bodies, and with the Theravada tradition, he focuses on Buddha as a model to be imitated. In speaking to Vajrayana (Tibetan) Buddhist communities, His Holiness includes descriptions of the Buddha's cosmic dimensions. When speaking to Western audiences he emphasizes *dharma*, teaching and practice.

The third jewel, or *sangha* refers to the spiritual community, or monastery, to which a practitioner goes for refuge. In the Theravada tradition, *sangha* consists primarily of monks, with some lay practitioners. For the Mahayana tradition *sangha* is primarily lay people. In the West *sangha* increasingly refers to spiritual community irrespective of the spiritual attainment of its members. In this expanded meaning, *sangha* might not count as the third jewel of the Buddhist tradition. When the Dalai Lama lived in Tibet (before he escaped the invading Han Chinese at age seventeen) his *sangha* consisted of Tibetan Buddhists. As an adult in exile, based in Dharamsala, northern India, he is claimed as a teacher by many *sanghas* and many Westerners who do not identify as Buddhist. According to the Bodhisattva vow that His Holiness shares frequently, he has devoted his life, and if necessary an infinite number of rebirths, to the eradication of suffering of all sentient beings. Here is the vow, as stated by Shantideva in *The Bodhisattva Way of Life*:

> And now, as long as space endures,
> As long as there are beings to be found,
> May I continue to remain
> To soothe the sufferings of those who live. (*Shantideva* 10:55)

His Holiness the Dalai Lama, foremost spiritual teacher of humanity at the present time, is devoted to generating the mind of enlightenment in all communities and in all countries—especially in the People's Republic of China where the government continues to prevent its people from experiencing the healing presence of His Holiness. One of the communities of practice that His Holiness especially appreciated was the John Main Seminar in Ireland hosted by Father Lawrence Freeman. The Seminar, a community of Roman Catholic contemplatives, asked His Holiness to comment on eight passages in the New Testament. The Dalai Lama spoke from a Buddhist mountain top to men and women on a mountain top of Christian spirituality. He said that at this seminar he learned more about Christian spirituality than at any time since his conversation with the Catholic monk Thomas Merton thirty years earlier.

In the course of his comments on the eight passages, His Holiness admitted that on several important points the two traditions appear to be in conflict. He stated, for example, that "one must admit that, at the theoretical level, the conceptions of God and Creation are a point of departure between Buddhists and Christians."[10] In fact, however, the differences go deeper: Christian theology conceives of God not only as Creator, but more distinctly as Trinity (three Persons equally divine and in absolute oneness), a conception central to Christianity that is clearly incompatible with the Buddhist conception of dependent co-arising that does not affirm the agency of a creator, and most certainly does not affirm divine trinity.

His Holiness acknowledges more similarities than differences between Jesus and the Buddha, the most important of which focus on their teachings. He emphasizes that the life of Jesus exemplified his teaching of love in the way that the life of the Buddha exemplified compassion. Both the Buddha and Jesus taught the necessity of hardship, dedication, and commitment to attain enlightenment or salvation. More specifically, the Dalai Lama emphasizes that just as to see Christ is the way to the Father, so to see the Buddha as *dharmakaya* is to see Buddhahood.[11] He writes: "For me, as a Buddhist, my attitude toward Jesus Christ is that he was either a fully enlightened being or a bodhisattva of a very high spiritual realization."[12]

STEINER ON KRISHNA, BUDDHA, AND CHRIST

Steiner's pantheon includes the Trinity, Nine Hierarchies, Sophia, the tempters Lucifer and Ahriman and their legions, many exalted beings such as Moses, Melchisadeck, Zarathustra, and Christian

---

10. Ibid, 81.
11. Ibid., 112.
12. Ibid., 83.

Rosenkreutz. This arrangement of divinities is traditional in its inclusion of Hebraic and Christian beings in hierarchical order. It is also radical because it includes Krishna and Buddha and some figures that are known only in esoteric literature. Steiner's vision of these and other exalted beings appears not to be systematic. His account emerged in one series of lectures at a time, heavily from 1909 to 1913, and amplified until his death in 1925. Steiner portrays the highest beings, particularly the Trinity, as inclusive of other beings. He portrays smaller beings as included in the higher ranks of the Hierarchies. Despite the intervention of exalted, spiritual, sacrificial beings, human beings are quite separate, and increasingly so, from these divine beings. This separation of human beings from divine beings and from the cosmos and Earth is necessary, according to Steiner, in order for humanity to attain freedom and love.

It is by Steiner's own experience aided by the language of St. Paul—"Not I but Christ lives in me"—that Steiner is able to affirm repeatedly that Christ is active in the spiritual world, on Earth, and in relation to the "I" of all human beings able and willing to receive His influence directly. Human beings also receive the guidance of beings closely allied with Christ such as Sophia and the Archangel Michael. Sophia is closely allied to the Holy Spirit as well as to Christ. There is more sharing, cooperating, and opposing among higher beings than traditional theology suggests. There is also greater mystery. We are not dealing with human creations, but rather with vast, non-physical, eternal yet evolving beings. As in all anthroposophic research and practice, a true understanding of these divine beings requires reverence and humility.

Steiner delivered more than one hundred lectures on the *events* in the New Testament—which is not the same as lectures on the New Testament. We might say that Steiner's lectures are like gospels—or not, depending on whether, or the extent to which, one is willing to ascribe to Steiner the same authority that tradition ascribes to Paul, Matthew, Mark, Luke, and John. Steiner regards the Gospel of Luke as a greater revelation of love than any other Christian text. He states that the Gospel of Luke reveals "love transformed into deed." He prizes the Gospel of Matthew for its direct line to Matthew's spiritual teacher, Jesu ben Pandira, who, Steiner says, will return to earth as the Maitreya Buddha some 2500 years from now. He considers John, the author of Fourth Gospel to be one of the most advanced spiritual beings around Christ and John's Gospel to be profoundly intuitive and mystical. Perhaps because Steiner is focused on Christ (as distinct from Jesus) and particularly the trans-Hebraic significance of Christ, Steiner is also very close to Paul's letters, especially those that announce the continuing work of Christ and the Holy Spirit in relation to human beings and Earth.

The Incarnation of Christ foremost into Jesus of Nazareth as well as into each human person who receives Christ into his or her life (by affirmation, prayers, sacraments, and deeds) involves transformation at all four levels of the human being—physical, etheric, astral, and "I." One surmises that this transformation of the entire person is possible because, according to Steiner (and probably no one else), at the baptism of Jesus of Nazareth, who was fully human, the divine being Christ joined with Jesus and transformed his physical, etheric, astral, and "I." Although difficult to understand and to visualize, it is important to consider Steiner's further explanation that at the baptism by his cousin John in the river Jordan Christ replaced the Zarathustra "I" which until that moment had served as the "I" of Jesus as described in the Matthew Gospel.

Paul's transformation included his physical body (which was blinded), his etheric (which heard the voice of Christ say to him "Saul, Saul"), his astral/soul that experienced remorse for attacking Jews who had become followers of Christ, and his "I" that changed course, reversing his destiny from an anti-Christian Jewish teacher to a vocation for the remainder of his life as the Christian "Apostle to the Gentiles." Similarly, because Mary Magdalen had transformed her etheric body, she was able to see the etheric resurrected Christ whom she took for a gardener, and was able to hear his etheric voice say "Mary." Of course, the mother of Jesus possessed throughout her life an etheric body that was able to recognize in her son Jesus the future Jesus Christ. By receiving into her womb the body of Jesus, her astral body was transformed by the Holy Spirit. Steiner reports that Jesus was conceived by a sexual act between the couple traditionally known as Joseph and Mary, and that the mother was overshadowed by the Holy Spirit. (As explained below, Steiner claims that there were two mothers, one described in Matthew and one in Luke, clearly very different from each other but fused in the evolution of Christian piety.)

Preachers and New Testament scholars are generally at a loss as to how to interpret the raising of Lazarus from the dead. Without the concept of the etheric, there can only be a choice between Christ calling forth someone who had been dead for several days and its opposite, that Lazarus was not really dead and consequently not raised. John's Gospel is perfectly clear that Lazarus's body had been wrapped and in a tomb for several days. (In Israel–Palestine, a tomb was not a grave but rather a large room cut into the side of hill or small mountain at the entrance to which was placed an enormous round stone that could be rolled away.) Mary is quoted as saying, "Master, if you had been here my brother would not have died." When Christ asks to have the stone rolled back in order to call forth her brother Lazarus, Mary rightly protests, "The body will stink" To preach that Christ brought back to life a friend who had been literally dead for several days clearly strains credulity; to regard it as fictional is also problematic for the veracity of the scripture, akin to denying the crucifixion or the resurrection. But consider that the raising of Lazarus, or Mary's conception of Jesus ("overshadowed by the Holy Spirit"), the resurrection of Christ, Mary Magdalen's sight of the resurrected, the conversion of Paul are all etheric events, neither fictional nor physical, but absolutely real at the level of the subtle body between the physical and soul. According to Steiner, the etheric body of Lazarus was in an initiation coma from which Jesus called him forth. Mary Magdalen saw the etheric body of Jesus, the same body that appeared to the disciples on the way to Emmaus.

It is in the etheric that illness and recovery take hold in the human body. Steiner's characterization of Anthroposophy as a path of knowledge to lead the spiritual in the individual to the spiritual in the Universe significantly affirms the etheric as one of the levels on which this relation is generally broken and in need of restoration. He recommends several arts as being effective remedies for a depleted etheric body, along with spiritual thinking, feeling, and willing, and meditation, prayer, and contemplation of the natural world. As explained below, Steiner reveals an astonishing account of the development of Jesus from birth until His baptism based on the incompatible nativity accounts in Matthew and Luke. Steiner developed his conception of Christ on the language and images offered by the concept of the divine Logos (Word) in John, and the account of the resurrected Christ in Paul. The Prologue to the Gospel of John introduces the Logos, Christ:

> In the beginning was the Word, and the Word was with God, and the Word was God. This one was in the beginning with God. All things came into being through him, and apart from him not one thing came into being that has come into being. (John 1:1–4)

Paul offers a conception of Christ similar to John's. In his letters that show the results of the overwhelming conversion that he experienced on the road to Damascus, Paul offers a passionate account of the reality of Christ in his experience and in the minds and hearts of Christians with whom he came in contact during his extensive travels throughout the Mediterranean world.

With John and Paul as his primary foundational sources, Steiner then develops a conception of Christ intended to foster love and freedom, karma, and reincarnation within the context of the evolution of consciousness. Steiner's self-assigned task is similar to those of Sri Aurobindo who spoke of Krishna in the context of the transformation of the material world, and also similar to that of His Holiness the Dalai Lama who speaks of Buddha in the context of world religions. Both Steiner and Aurobindo teach that each individual soul will return in order to draw from and contribute to the evolution of consciousness. For Steiner, Christ, evolution of consciousness, karma, and rebirth, and the struggle against the tempters, are all very thickly entwined.

As we know from Steiner's biography, his Master gave Steiner the tasks of opposing modern Western materialism and restoring karma and rebirth to the West. Both of these tasks are to be understood in the context of the fifth cultural age, the one that began in fifteenth-century Europe. Steiner was critical of mainstream Christianity because he considered it to be caught in the age in which it originated, or centuries prior to the dawn of the modern West. It is easy to agree with him that the Roman Catholic Church, despite its impressive learning and sacramental life, clings to moral ideals that are stuck in the Middle Ages. When Pope John Paul stated that the ordination of women could never be discussed even in the future, such thinking is obviously contrary to the current cultural age: It denies history. Other Roman Catholic teachings, especially on sexual morality, also clearly show thinking characteristic of an earlier period.

By contrast, Steiner sees Christ, the Archangel Michael, and Sophia on the side of history, and especially on the side of freedom of conscience. In this respect, Steiner is closer to Protestant Christianity than to Roman Catholicism. Yet, with respect to the affirmation of exalted beings, particularly the mother of Jesus (whom the Protestant Reformation essentially expelled from dogma and practice), Steiner is closer to Roman Catholicism. In respect to karma and rebirth, of course, he is on his own. He is convinced that one of the essential practices of a Christian should be to try to experience not only the presence of Christ but also the reality of one's karmic past and present, and even an intuitive sense of one's future task. In his view, it is not necessary to belong to a church but it is necessary to try to make a relationship with exalted beings, whether Krishna, Buddha, Christ, or Sophia, and by so doing to be aware that to revere one of these beings is to draw near to the others. (In my view, belonging to a church, and especially participating in its sacramental life, is an important aid in this effort. While Steiner presumably did not need a church, I do.)

Steiner himself apparently did not pray to Krishna or Buddha but he was convinced that when he focused on Jesus Christ he was also focusing on the ways that Krishna and Buddha had collaborated with Christ. I believe that Christ and the Archangel Michael have inspired spiritual teachers such as Sri Aurobindo, the Mother, Teilhard, Jung, His Holiness the Dalai Lama, and advocates of Sophia and feminist spirituality. Steiner was convinced that Christianity is still at the beginning of its mission: It needs to evolve from past ways of thinking to a universal spirituality affirmative of informed, free thinking as well as by a free expression of love.

Based on his own experience of the revelation of the continuing activity of Krishna, Buddha, and Christ in individual human lives and in human history, Rudolf Steiner affirms the reality of all three of these exalted beings. Steiner also discloses the results of his research concerning these three divine figures working collaboratively on behalf of the evolution of Earth and humanity. He claims that far from serving as an excuse for the religious intolerance that leads to violence, these three deities have revealed their teachings to particular civilizations in ways that are intended to benefit, and ideally serve, the whole of humanity. In Steiner's account of the evolution of consciousness, Krishna, Buddha, and Christ each entered human history at a particular time, in a logical sequence, and in cultures that were able to receive them effectively—though, obviously and alas, very imperfectly. One of the tasks of the present age is to understand the contribution of each of these divine beings on behalf of the entire human community.

Steiner stated many times that the Jesus described in the Gospel of Luke contained the soul of Krishna. As we know from the Bhagavad Gita, on which Steiner delivered fourteen quite learned and insightful lectures in 1912 and 1913, Krishna taught four yogas: knowledge, action, love, and contemplation. It is more often stated that he taught the first three of these with the fourth as an accompaniment. Steiner taught the same yogas, usually stated as: thinking, feeling, willing, and contemplation in relation to these three. Further, Steiner states that it was these three yogas taught by Krishna that Christ communicated to Saul, soon to be Paul, on his way to Damascus. Paul, Apostle to the Gentiles, then taught these three yogas himself. The basic spirituality of the Gita flowed through the most influential teacher sent to fledgling Christian communities. As the foremost exponent of the revelation of Christ, Paul preached first to the Hebrews of Israel and then to the entire non-Jewish Mediterranean world. One answer to the question, "What is Steiner's spiritual practice?" is transformed thinking, feeling, and willing. These are precisely the yogas of the Gita as taught by Krishna, except of course, in relation to Christ. In Steiner's teaching these three yogas need to be understood and practiced within the evolution of consciousness: In Steiner's reconceptualization, thinking requires free individual thinking, feeling requires transformation into love, and will requires free service aimed at a loving relationship to Earth and betterment of the human community.

Steiner's relation to Buddha is as unusual as his relation to Krishna. Additionally, it has an intensely personal quality, filled with awe and numinosity. In Krishna Steiner found the announcement of the "I" essential for human evolution toward love; in Buddha he found compassion, at the very edge of the divine love brought by Christ. He recounts at least five or six instances of collaboration between Buddha and Christ, all of them suffused with compassion and love. Perhaps most remarkable of these is his account of the appearance of the subtle body of Buddha present at the nativity of Jesus! In one of his more astonishing claims, Steiner reported that at the nativity of Jesus as told in the Gospel of Luke the heavenly host that sang "Peace on Earth to people of good will" was the subtle *nirmanakaya*, or truth body, of Buddha. The disciple Luke, a physician and close colleague of the apostle Paul, clairvoyantly saw or clairaudiently heard the sublime celebration by a heavenly choir of the birth of Jesus. To Luke's thinking, such a celebration could only be the work of angels as experienced in the Hebraic tradition. Had Luke been able to attribute this celebration to Buddha, his fellow Jews with no knowledge of Buddha would have found such an attribution unintelligible. Unknown to Luke and his fellow Jewish Christians, Buddha (according to Steiner) was one of the highest collaborators of Christ, such that this connection at the Nativity of Jesus was part of a continuing relationship.

Some of the connections between Jesus (not Christ until his baptism) and Buddha are minor but worth recounting and considering. Steiner repeats the story of the presentation of Prince Gautama to Asita, a Hindu *sadhu* (holy man).[13] On several occasions Steiner told the story of Asita's prophecy, the unsuccessful attempt of Gautama's father to prepare his son for a life as a great prince, and Gautama's experience of the four sights, all exactly as it has been told for 2,500 years in every Buddhist community. But Steiner then adds to this story that Asita was reborn as Simeon in Bethlehem, where he was presented the infant Jesus. Simeon had the pain and privilege of foretelling the mother of Jesus that because of the destiny of her son "a sword would pierce her heart."

As often happens to fathers who try to manage their children's lives, Gautama's father's plans did not work out as he intended, due to the power of karma. While karma presumably does not prevail in every life, karma with respect to such an elevated prelife as Gautama would almost certainly insinuate itself, and so it did. At age twenty-nine, while married (to Yasodhara) with a son (Rahula), Gautama went outside the princely grounds accompanied by his teacher, whereupon he experienced four karmically powerful sights including the famous three sorrows: He saw a person who was seriously ill, a person who was very old, and a person who had died and was being carried by his or her sons to the burning *ghat* for cremation. Gautama was overwhelmed with sorrow. He then saw a line of monks in walking meditation. This experience spoke to him with great force at the deepest possible level of his self-conception. On his return home he announced to his father and his wife that he must retreat to the forest to solve the problem of suffering.

As Steiner retold on many occasions, Gautama went to the forest to meditate and practice austerities. There are many sculptures of Gautama, not yet Buddha, looking emaciated from fasting. He had jumped from luxury to deprivation. After seven years of asceticism, at age thirty-five, Gautama discovered the truth of

---

13. Though often thought of as Hindu, Gautama's family would more accurately be referred to as Vedic or Brahmanic, followers of the Vedas and Upanishads.

the middle way: One attains liberation, as he did, not by indulgence and not be starvation, but by sensible self-discipline. Under the Bo tree, the tree of Enlightenment, Gautama had a great struggle with Mara, the tempter, who offered Gautama nirvana, eternal selfless bliss disconnected from earthly existence. As has often been pointed out, probably first by Huston Smith, Gautama was tempted to leave the world whereas Jesus was tempted to gain control of the world. Unfortunately, these somewhat opposite stories tend to strengthen the simplistic idea that Buddha and Buddhism are world-negating whereas Christ and Christianity are world affirming. This too-easy contrast fails to note that Buddha, with infinite compassion, continued to teach for his next forty-five years, clearly not an abandonment of the world. Similarly, Christ refused Satan's (i.e., Ahriman's) offer of an earthly kingdom. He spent his next three years preaching that his kingdom was not of this world. In short, the missions of Buddha and Christ are very close: They both teach a positive combination of spiritual enlightenment and service, or wisdom and compassion.

Amazingly, or absurdly, Steiner reports that his esoteric research revealed there were two children named Jesus with two sets of parents named Joseph and Mary. Steiner refers to the mothers as the mother in the Luke Gospel and the mother in the Matthew Gospel. A quick check of the first three chapters of Luke and Matthew will confirm that the two nativity stories are entirely different. The Christian tradition has been able to fuse them into one story, the one that is told every Christmas season. According to Steiner (and probably no other interpreter), the family described by Matthew was middle or upper class, was visited not by shepherds but by three magi (astrologers) from afar, probably Persia, and he was child hunted by Herod.

Six months after the Matthew child, the Luke child was born in a stable in Bethlehem and visited by local shepherds. During the slaughter of male children under the age of two, the Matthew child was with his parents hiding in Egypt. Again, according to one of Steiner's most dramatically singular accounts of spiritual events, the child described in the Luke Gospel carried the souls of Krishna and Buddha, and was the very essence of purity, innocence, and compassion: "The 'Gloria' heard by the shepherds in the fields proclaimed from the spiritual world that the forces of Buddha were streaming into the astral body of the Jesus child described in St. Luke's gospel."[14] Steiner says that etheric and astral bodies of high beings are available for other individuals whose karma leads them to great tasks in future lives. For example, the etheric body of Zarathustra (one of the high beings who had guided the building of civilizations) had been given to Moses and his astral body had been given to Hermes. Similarly, at age 12, the pure Luke child was suddenly able to teach the rabbis in the temple because, according to Steiner the wise Zarathustra ego had joined with the soul of the Luke child, thereby creating an exquisite individual characterized by wisdom as well as compassion. The Matthew child, abandoned by the Zarathustra "I," dies, leaving one cosmically crafted twelve-year-old boy known thereafter as Jesus of Nazareth. The Luke mother also dies. Steiner adds that the *nirmanakaya*, infinite body of Buddha joined to the astral body of the Luke child at his death.

The story continues. At the baptism of Jesus by John, again according to Steiner, Christ (part of the Trinity, as the Logos and Sun Being) entered the Jesus that included the astral bodies of Krishna and Buddha. The Zarathustra "I" vacated this being and is replaced by Christ, who for the next three years would be the "I" of Jesus of Nazareth. Christ also permeated the astral, etheric, and physical bodies of Jesus. The Matthew mother, spiritually a Sophia being from before her life as the mother of Jesus, will live with Jesus for the rest of His life. Along with Mary Magdalen and his apostles, especially John the Beloved disciple, the mother Mary will be his disciple during the three years of His teaching and miraculous healings. In his lectures entitled *From Jesus to Christ* and *The Fifth Gospel*, Steiner recounts deep conversations between Jesus and the Matthew mother. This mother stood at the foot of the cross and was entrusted by the crucified Christ to John the Beloved disciple, and he to her. Mary is the Notre Dame (Our Lady) to whom countless cathedrals in European cities and towns were dedicated in the

---

14. Rudolf Steiner, *According to Luke: The Gospel of Love and Compassion Revealed*, 115–117.

late Middle Ages. She is the Madonna envisioned by the Renaissance painters and Michelangelo's *Pieta*. Whether she is related to Quan Yin/Avalokiteshwara as Christ is related to Buddha is one of the great mysteries discussed in the next chapter.

In addition to many references to Buddha in the life of Christ, particularly during the years prior to the founding of the Anthroposophical Society in 1912, Steiner delivered five lectures exclusively on Buddha, 1909 to 1912. As these lectures indicate, Steiner confirms the Mahayana interpretation of Buddha—i.e., as a spiritual being who continues to guide humanity toward compassion. Almost all of these lectures were delivered during the same years when he delivered fourteen lectures on the Bhagavad Gita. He did not speak about the continuing spiritual influence of Krishna after the Bhagavad Gita—e.g., he was unaware of the relationship between Krishna and Sri Aurobindo—but he regularly mentioned the continuing influence of Buddha.

One wonders who the four evangelists were such that they could vividly record events that they had not observed at the time they occurred. Steiner spoke at length about John the Beloved Disciple. He explained that "beloved" is a title for one who was initiated. Steiner described at length, and several times, that the author of the Fourth Gospel, clearly the most mystical and advanced of the four, or of any gospels discovered in the last half century, John the Evangelist was Lazarus who was not raised but was initiated by Christ. Christ called him forth, as He said, "for the glory of God" (John 11). As a high initiate, clearly close to Christ throughout His three years of teaching and miracles, and as the one to whom the crucified Christ karmically entrusts His Mother, John was able to write an authoritative gospel, at the end of which he wrote: "This is the disciple who is bearing witness to these things, and who has written these things; we know that his testimony is true" (John 21:24).

Similarly, Steiner tells us that in preparation for his role as an evangelist Matthew was the spiritual-esoteric student of Jesu ben Pandira who, if the future would unfold as Steiner envisions it, will be reborn as the Maitreya Buddha in the middle of the fifth millennium CE, fulfilling the expectation among esoteric

Buddhists that the Maitreya will incarnate 5,000 years after the life of Gautama Buddha. (Admittedly, Steiner dates future events with a confidence that is entirely contrary to contemporary thinking. As I have no way to verify or falsify such statements, I simply allow them to be. I also hold to the possibility that Steiner's prevision might come to pass and that the Maitreya Buddha will incarnate as Steiner and many Buddhists predict.)

Steiner's account of the next interaction between the Buddhist and Christian traditions after the life of Christ is on the Black Sea in the sixth century. For admirers of Francis of Assisi (one of the few saints whom Christians can confidently brag about and recommend to non-Christians—even though his horror of sex is rather fanatical) Steiner's description of the life of Francis before his conversion should be a source of delight. If true, it would also help to explain how Francis was able to embrace a life completely opposite to his early years and to the values of everyone around him. Here is Steiner's lengthy and fascinating account concerning the continuing spiritual influence of Buddha and the reincarnation of St. Francis:

> When this individuality who has passed through many lifetimes as a *Bodhisattva* [one who attains enlightenment but continues to reincarnate in order to help others] advanced to the rank of Buddha, that incarnation [as Gautama] became his last incarnation on earth in a physical body....
>
> Some centuries into the Christian era, a kind of occult school was founded on the shores of the Black Sea [in which] pupils were instructed in doctrines and principles which had originated in Buddhism, but which were permeated by the impulses that came into the world through Christianity....
>
> One such pupil of the occult school on the Black Sea was born in his next incarnation as Francis of Assisi. It is not surprising, then, that there lived in him the wisdom he had received [from Buddha] about brotherhood and human equality, about the need to love all human beings equally, and that his soul was permeated and strengthened by the Christ Impulse.[15]

---

15. Rudolf Steiner, *The Spiritual Foundation of Morality*, 33–35.

In a previous lecture, Steiner stated:

> The characteristic quality of Francis of Assisi and of the life
> of his monks, which is so similar to that of the disciples of
> Buddha, is due to the fact that Francis himself was a pupil of
> Buddha.[16]

To understand this picture one needs to know something
about Christian Rosenkreutz, the initiator of the Rosicrucian
spiritual-esoteric tradition since the fifteenth century in the West.
The Rosicrucian esoteric teaching and influence is continuous
with esoteric Christianity but with a distinctively modern Western character. Steiner frequently refers to Christian Rosenkreutz
as the devoted servant of Jesus Christ and as the teacher of Buddha. Steiner related the following:

> Left to itself without intervention, human history would inevi-
> tably have taken this course. But in the wise councils of the
> spiritual worlds, steps were taken to avert the worst form of
> this evil on earth.
>
> A conference of the most advanced inidividualities was
> called together by Christian Rosenkreutz. His most intimate
> pupil and friend, the eminent teacher Buddha, participated
> in these councils and in the decisions that were reached. At
> that spiritual conference it was resolved that henceforth Bud-
> dha would dwell on Mars and there unfold his influence and
> activity....
>
> Christian Rosenkreutz realized that to bring about a cer-
> tain purification needed on Mars, the teachings of Buddha were
> eminently suitable. The Christ being, the essence of divine love,
> had once descended to Earth to a people who were in many
> respects alien; in the seventeenth century, Buddha, the prince of
> peace, went to the planet of war and conflict, Mars, to execute
> his mission there where souls were warlike and torn by strife....
>
> Through the deed of redemption performed by Gautama
> Buddha on Mars, it is possible for us, when passing through the
> Mars sphere between death and new birth, to become follow-
> ers of Francis of Assisi without causing subsequent deprivation

---

16. Rudolf Steiner, "The Mission of Gautama Buddha on Mars," in *Esoteric Christianity and The Mission of Christian Rosenkreutz*, 176.

to Earth. Though it may seem fantastic it is nevertheless true that since the seventeenth century every human being is, in the Mars sphere, for a time a Buddhist, and Franciscan, and an immediate follower of Francis of Assisi....

Because Christian Rosencreutz was able to transfer the work of Buddha from Earth to Mars, it is possible for the influences of Buddha to pour down to human beings from outside Earth.[17]

At the conclusion of this remarkable lecture Steiner recommends:

Those who are able to draw near to Christian Rosenkreutz see with wondering veneration by what consistent paths he has carried through the mission entrusted to him. In our time this is the Rosicrucian–Christian path of development.[18]

All of the parts of this astonishing event are difficult to understand and difficult to accept. Perhaps the most astonishing is the role of Christian Rosencreutz, so high in this circle of spiritual leaders that, according to Steiner, that he instructed Buddha, yet so little known outside of Rosicrucian esotericism. The other challenging part of this text is the idea of souls on Mars. In Steiner's cosmology, human souls have experienced other planetary dimensions, in this case the warring influence of Mars. Given the sacrifice of Buddha on the spiritual or etheric planet Mars and the sacrifice of Christ on Earth, one wonders, if there is any truth to this account, how much more violent human nature would have been, or would be still, if those sacrifices had not taken place.

While leaving no doubt about the exalted status and contribution of Buddha, Steiner nevertheless attributes to Christ, building on Buddha, an even greater transformation than the wisdom and compassion brought by Buddha:

There is a difference, however, between wisdom, knowledge, or thoughts and an active, living force. There is a difference between knowing what an "I" should be like and imbuing

---

17. Ibid.
18. Ibid., 184.

ourselves with a living force that can then flow from the "I" into the entire world, as the force emanating from the Christ influenced the astral, etheric and physical bodies of those around Him. Humankind learned the content of the doctrine of compassion and love through the contribution of the great Buddha. In contrast, the Christ's contribution is not a doctrine but a living force. He sacrificed himself and descended to earth to pervade not only the astral body but also the "I," teaching it to exude the substance of love. The Christ brought to Earth love's substantial, living content, not merely its wise content. This is the essence of His mission.[19]

For three years, from His baptism to His crucifixion, Christ the Sun Being lived in union with Jesus of Nazareth, teaching, healing, manifesting divine love, showing the way to the Father, and forming the community of disciples who would serve as the vessel of the transformation that Christ incarnated to effect. Steiner asserts that Christ has a transformative effect on every human being, on humanity in its totality, and on Earth. Beginning in the twentieth century, the etheric body of Christ has been surrounding Earth, which is an important fact in relation to the current ecological crisis. In concert with Christ, and the evolution of Earth and humanity, Krishna and Buddha continue to evolve.

It is apt that Steiner refers to Christ as the Light Being: like light, Christ appears in relation. As it is difficult to imagine light apart from that on which it shines, it is difficult to contemplate Christ alone, apart from the Father (Ground of Being), apart from the Holy Spirit, apart from Sophia, apart from His regent, the Archangel Michael, apart from his Mother, the Virgin Mary. Christ is love, a relational being. Relationality in the form of love begins with the Trinity and continues, because it was generated by the Trinity, throughout all creation. For both Teilhard and Steiner, Christ permeates the Cosmos as well as every human soul: they also believe that it is the opportunity of each soul to experience the presence of Christ.

---

19. Rudolf Steiner, *According to Luke: The Gospel of Love and Compassion Revealed*, 187–188.

Mary, Mother of Jesus
Kwan Yin (Bodhisattva Avalokitesvara)
Anne Baring
Thomas Merton

6

THE GODDESS SOPHIA

THE RESURGENCE OF SOPHIA

Happy are those who find Wisdom...
She is more precious than jewels,
And nothing you desire can compare with her...
Get wisdom, get insight: do not forget.
—BOOK OF PROVERBS

Sophia is the ideal of perfect humanity,
eternally contained in the integral divine being.
—Vladimir Solovyev

The Mother was divine even in childhood.
—SRI AUROBINDO

[On Kuan Yin's birthday] ...the splendidly robed and bejeweled figure could almost have been mistaken for that of Mary arrayed as Queen of Heaven...
—JOHN BLOFELD

Whenever I see an image of Mary, I feel that she represents love and compassion; ...the goddess Tara occupies a similar position.
—THE DALAI LAMA

Isis–Sophia,
Wisdom of God
Lucifer has slain her,
And on wings of cosmic forces
Carried her away into the depths of space.
Christ-Will
Working in us
Shall tear her from Lucifer
And on grounds of spiritual knowledge
Call to new life in human souls
Isis–Sophia
Wisdom of God.
—RUDOLF STEINER

Over the past centuries the being of Sophia,
or feminine Divine Wisdom,
Has been emerging from the mists of ancient history,
like Venus from the waters,
to become a sign and mystery of our times.
Though it is difficult to say who she is, wherever we turn,
we see traces of her coming
—as if tracking the fringes of her mantle as it brushed aside
    the tangled,
sclerotic cobwebs of centuries of cerebration.
As she draws near, much that was forgotten is reentering
    consciousness,
not only as memory but also from the future, as possibility.
A new mood is abroad, a kind of heart's yearning for what
    Sophia
has traditionally always provided
—seamless vessel of harmony and meaning, uniting Heaven
    and Earth,
within which we may live, move, and have our being.
Sophia gives us this ethical directive, calling upon us to
    sacralize
—consecrate, make spiritual
—the whole world and all our lives, not just Sunday.
"Everything that lives is holy," said Blake.
She is, we may say, the very soul of God,
of the world, and of humanity.

Sophia lies at the esoteric heart of Steiner's mission.
Beginning with the earth phase of evolution,
the wisdom of the outer cosmos
becomes inner wisdom in the human being.
"You must be Mary and give birth to God in you
If God is to give you eternal bliss too."
Angelus Silesius
By the radiant light of the being that ensouled her,
Mary recognized intuitively in her completely changed Son
the power of the Sun being, Christ.
This it is that brought about the miracle of Cana.
I am humanity. I am the past, present, and future.
Every mortal should lift my veil.
— CHRISTOPHER BAMFORD[1]

These quoted passages, deliberately varied, serve as an introduction to this chapter on the divine feminine, the goddess, here referred to as Sophia, who is equally one and many. Sophia mysteriously embodies many fundamental polarities, finite and infinite, temporal and eternal, named and unnamable, visible and invisible. As *Laotse* teaches: "The Tao that can be named is not the eternal Tao." Of course, Tao is named infinitely by *te,* the creative process (as in Tao te Ching, the classic of Tao and changes). Complementing the Confucian tradition of naming, and particularly its doctrine of the rectification of names, the Taoist tradition both names and resists naming. It prefers metaphor and image, and invites imagination. As this book espouses many ways of pointing to the divine, Sophia, the goddess, is represented as a single being who manifests in all cultures and all times, but in every culture she is seen by only a small minority. She is Isis–Mary–Sophia of the West and Tara–Quan Yin–Kanon of Asia; she is Lady Philosophy of the Christian Middle Ages; and perhaps the Mother of the Sri Aurobindo Ashram, and just as likely Amma (Mata Amritanandamayi), the living goddess who on any

---

1.   From Christopher Bamford's introduction in Rudolf Steiner, *Isis Mary Sophia,* 7–44.

given weekend heals by hugging thousands of seekers, one at a time.

The Myth of the Goddess: Evolution of an Image (1991) introduced me to the feminine archetype in the history of religious traditions of the West. In the early 1990s, while I was president of California Institute of Integral Studies, I was a colleague of Charlene Spretnak, author of *Lost Goddesses of Early Greece: A Collection of pre-Hellenic Myths* (1981) and Elinor Gadon, author of *The Once and Future Goddess: A Symbol for Our Time* (1989). In the mid-1990s all of these scholars of the divine feminine, including Anne Baring, participated in a memorable public conference titled "The Return of the Divine Feminine," cosponsored by The California Institute of Integral Studies and Grace Cathedral.

If this chapter needed justification, the indices of *The Myth of the Goddess* would be more than sufficient. *The Myth of the Goddess* depends very prominently on the account of the evolution of consciousness by Owen Barfield which, as Barfield indicates in every one of his books, is based on the writings and published lectures of Rudolf Steiner, yet in its more than 700 pages, *The Myth of the Goddess* includes no references to Steiner. Thomas Schipflinger, a Roman Catholic priest who served in Austria and Germany where knowledge of Steiner's writings and influence is very widespread and easily available, similarly makes no reference to Steiner in the text or bibliography in his book *Sophia–Maria*. At my invitation Andrew Harvey, who was at that time a colleague and friend, was writing *The Return of the Mother* (1995), based on his exciting lectures to standing room audiences. Harvey's book traces the virtual disappearance and the gradual contemporary reappearance of the Goddess tradition in world religions. That book similarly includes no reference to Steiner. Steiner's name and publications are also absent in Caitlin Matthews, *Sophia, Goddess of Wisdom, Bride of God* (2001) and Rosemary Radford Ruether, *Goddesses and the Divine Feminine* (2005). If these authors—Gadon, Baring and Cashford, Harvey, Matthews, Schipflinger, Ruether—did not mention Steiner, if only to disagree with his esoteric research, I wonder why they did not do so. The omission of Steiner's name on books about Sophia is similar to the omission of his name in books on philosophy and psychology, on education, or on various arts. Books that show Steiner's influence without acknowledging him seem to me lacking integrity as well as pedagogy.

DIVINE MOTHER, EAST AND WEST

Myth of the Goddess: Evolution of an Image

In the process of recounting the actual history of the goddess in Western thought and culture, *Myth of the Goddess* draws from and strengthens two crucial interpretative paradigms: First, it draws from the Jungian conception of archetypes as a source of diverse symbols and images manifest in successive cultures of the West. The authors, both Jungians, refer to Jungian research as psychological and spiritual archeology, the digging up of myths that are still alive even though buried beneath conscious memory. As Jung remarked many times, "Nothing in the psyche is ever lost." Unconscious archetypes, myths, symbols, and images can be retrieved in religion and art where they continue to function effectively even if, and to some extent because, they are unconscious. *Myth of the Goddess* belongs in this chapter both because it presents the history of Sophia in ways comparable to Steiner, and also because Jung's thought is comparable to Steiner's.

The second crucial interpretive paradigm that Baring and Cashford utilizes is the account of the evolution of consciousness in Owen Barfield's *Saving the Appearances* (1957). As explained in chapter 4, "Evolution of Consciousness," Barfield interprets the evolution of consciousness in three phases: original participation, loss of participation, and final participation. "Final" in this context is the Aristotelian concept: an end point, *telos*, or goal rather than temporal end. By this account, the experience of the divine feminine during the Paleolithic and Neolithic periods was direct and effortless. The break in this original participation first came slowly, and then intensely in one dramatic period: In approximately the twelfth century BCE the male sky gods essentially replaced the mother Goddess in the minds and hearts of Mediterranean cultures. This distancing between the Goddess and human consciousness is what Barfield refers to as loss of participation. During original participation this Goddess was experienced as a wife and mother, sacred, generative, and the original source of nature. The generative power associated with the Goddess by the image of mother and son as well her depiction as cave, moon, life, death and rebirth, are essential images in the very early stage of the evolution of consciousness. Baring and Cashford found that over several thousand years the goddess gradually transferred (or was forced to transfer) her primary activity, and perhaps her identity, from a goddess of nature to a goddess of wisdom.

The Goddess Isis, who represents suffering and vulnerability as well as a synthesis of transcendence and immanence, was worshipped throughout the Roman Empire: Isis was the greatest goddess in Egypt and was worshipped for over 3,000 years, from pre-dynastic times (before 3000 BCE) until the second century CE, when her cult and many of her images passed directly on to the figure of Mary.[2] The end of the Bronze Age brought with it the end of the *hieros gamos*, the sacred marriage of the mother to her husband Osiris and son Horus. The Iron Age was a major moment in the loss of divine feminine participation in the evolution of consciousness. Thereafter the male gods dominated: The divine mother was no longer a sacred marriage partner and no longer a creator. In *Enuma Elish*, written in Bagdad, in approximately the twelfth century BCE, the goddess Tiamat does not sacrifice, but is sacrificed by her conqueror, Marduk, who hangs Tiamat on a hook for three days. The ascendency of Marduk signals predominance of warfare as "given," and an inevitable component of human experience.

In six empires of the Iron Age—Egyptian, Assyrian, Persian, Greek, Roman, and Hebraic, father gods established dichotomy, warfare, darkness, and death over the life-giving mother, who was depicted as helpless. The West has ever since accepted the culture of warfare established by Yahweh in the Hebrew scriptures

---

2. Anne Baring and Jules Cashford, *The Myth of the Goddess: Evolution of an Image*, 225.

and Zeus in Homer. The sky gods are amoral, pro-war, and lack-ing compassion. Yahweh is a "jealous and vengeful god." At the dawn of the Abrahamic religions (Judaism, Christianity, and Islam), Yahweh was tribal, entirely male, and granted to human-ity dominion over Earth and all other species.

The presentation of creation in Genesis is especially problem-atic as a conception of the divine feminine. The only divinity is male, a god who creates entirely by Himself. He creates Adam first; Eve is created as a subordinate companion, rather as an afterthought, and primarily to fill Adam's desire for a mate. Gen-esis replaced life-affirming images—garden, river, serpent—with fear and guilt. Eve came to represent the devil's work, especially with regard to the sexual temptation of males. She also came to represent the body, while males represented the mind. Eve was transformed from source of life to cause of death, and instead of naming living beings was named by Adam. The feminine was irrationally rejected as a source of birth and identified with (origi-nal) sin and death. According to the Epistles of Paul, male mir-rors God, while the woman is the glory of man. Eve is intuitive and sinful in contrast to Adam who is rational and more the victim than the agent of the Fall.

Unfortunately, despite their use of Jung and Barfield, Baring and Cashford do not try to explain why or how it came about that the feminine divine gave way to patriarchy. Did the masculine gods overwhelm the goddesses? Was the switch from feminine to masculine intended by a higher and wiser power for a posi-tive, and perhaps temporary end? Is it a sensible question to ask whether the evolution of consciousness is itself conscious of itself such that it might know what it does? Was the creative energy of the Hebraic and Greek cultures, followed by the powerful build-ing of Christendom made possible by this change in hierarchy? In a similar way, is the apparent resurgence of the divine feminine at present the result of the effort by the divine feminine or by another higher power?

Any account of evolution of consciousness should at least raise and try to answer this double question: Is there guidance and a goal in this process? Neither Baring and Cashford nor

Schipflinger discuss this topic. To say that patriarchy was an appropriate change is a huge claim, a commitment to guidance at the highest level; without such affirmation, however, we are left with the fact of change without any particular reason. In the extensive literature on the evolution of Sophia, it appears that Steiner is the only researcher to offer insights on this topic. Steiner, and Barfield following Steiner, think that a process such as the loss of Isis and the ascendency of the masculine was somehow appropriate, a high-level change of consciousness in order to bring about a new possibility, rather like a change of *dharma* at the divine level. The loss of divine participation involved terrible suffering for all human beings, and particularly for women. At the same time, it led to a slow, very slow, gain in human intelligence, independence, and freedom. According to Steiner, humanity can find Sophia again, this time in increased freedom and love.

Boethius and the Consolation of Philo-Sophia[3]

In the history of Western consciousness the compassion of Sophia appears in many forms and diverse circumstances. She might arrange a pregnancy—or an escape from torture or starvation. In the example of the inspiring figure of Boethius, an early sixth-century student devoted to Plato, Aristotle, and the Stoics, Sophia might bring serenity to a philosopher about to be executed on false charges of treason in Rome. By his lone work, *The Consolation of Philosophy*, which he wrote in prison while awaiting execution, Boethius bequeathed to his contemporaries, and all interested in wisdom and justice thereafter, a dramatic affirmation of the Christian love of wisdom. With echoes of Job's experience of the Voice from the Whirlwind that affirmed the wisdom of God's ways, or the calm, resolute fortitude of falsely accused Socrates when forced to drink hemlock, or the suicide of Seneca under pressure from the emperor Nero, Lady Philosophy (Sophia) convinced the ill-fated—and increasingly

---

3. A similar account of Boethius's *Consolation of Philosophy* appears in my essay, "Wisdom in Western Philosophy," in Roger Walsh, ed. *The World's Great Wisdom*.

equanimous—Boethius that even his execution could be understood in the light of divine wisdom. Lady Philosophy reveals herself to be an inspiring image and presence in the mind and heart of the doomed Boethius. She provided wise consolation that Boethius would presumably not have been able to generate without her influence. Boethius in conversation with Lady Philosophy would seem to provide a convincing example of the compassion brought by Lady Philo-Sophia Herself.

John Blofeld, Bodhisattva of Compassion:
The Mystical Tradition of Kuan Yin

John Blofeld, Sinologist and scholar of Taoism, "set out to discern whether it was wholly symbolic or whether Kuan Yin could, in some sense, be said to *be*." His delightful book, *Bodhisattva of Compassion: The Mystical Tradition of Kuan Yin,* offers an honest and revealing, but not simple, reply. Here are three typical statements, the first slightly reverential but confused, the second expressing simultaneous devotion and Western academic skepticism, and the third a twist typical of Quan Yin and John Blofeld's complex relation to her.

> ...the goddess, so I could have sworn, deigned to address me! Imagination?
> Thenceforth I was her devoted follower, which does not mean, however, that I quite believe in her . . .Years later, with an insight stemming from the teaching of my Chinese and Tibetan masters, I came to understand what I still think is her true significance—or part of it. She is real! (11–12)[4]

After decades of searching and wondering, Blofeld asserts that Kuan Yin is both mysteriously Avalokiteswara (the bodhisattva of wisdom and compassion) and Tara, two deities warmly cherished by the Tibetans. She is also the Chinese Princess Miao Shan, and remarkably also what Laotse calls the Nameless and the Mahayana Buddhists call Mind. In thinking of Quan Yin it is essential to soften boundaries, to think porously. She is male and female,

---

4. Page references to this work are in parentheses.

human and divine, temporary and eternal. To know Kuan Yin is to know compassion. "The goddess would not deny so harmless a request without good reason." To say that she is Avalokiteshwara is to say that she is Wisdom and Compassion. Because Sophia or Quan Yin by whatever name cannot be isolated and objectified, any experience that claims to identify her manifestation might be faulty imagination. There might be reason not to inquire too closely or intellectually. Blofeld writes:

> Seeing her as a benevolent goddess into whose nature it would be discourteous to inquire, [her devotees] rejoice because she is lovely in herself and generous in heeding supplications (25).

Reverent belief is the essential precondition for an experience of Quan Yin. Blofeld explains: "No special degree of piety or strict conduct was required of the petitioners beyond firm belief in Kuan Yin's power to aid" (20).

Sophia is interpreted as Isis first through the iconographic and linguistic lens of Egypt, and then for the entire Mediterranean civilization for three thousand years, and then as Mary, mother of Jesus, in the Christian civilization, Kuan Yin is interpreted in the Mahayana tradition of China as Void, Pure Land, and Mind. These concepts enabled John Blofeld to establish a resting place in relation to the Quan Yin for whom he searched and, in a mixture of reluctance and surprise, he found. Here is his summation:

> Having disposed of caviling logic, my mind soared, leading me to a state bordering on ecstasy. I had a foretaste of the wisdom born of full realization that only mind is real; the demons of duality were temporarily vanquished so that it became possible to entertain simultaneously two opposing facets of truth....for the plain truth is that the statue answered me at once, saying: "Look not for my reality in the realm of appearance or in the Void. Seek it in your own mind. There only it resides." I felt sure that I had received an intimation that Kuan Yin exists—to the extent that "exists" is a fitting description of her subtle nature. Using the word thus is perhaps to overstate the case, just as to say that she does not exist would be to understate it (28–29).

Following John Blofeld's inquiry concerning Kuan Yin, we observe the fusion of several gods such that they are both distinct and united as one. At the conclusion of Blofeld's inquiry he comments:

> I have had much to say of Kuan Yin's three progenitors—Avalokiteswara and Tara, two deities warmly cherished by the Tibetans, and the Chinese Princess Miao Shan, for Kuan Yin is mysteriously all of these together!" (12).

Blofeld writes: "Until recently, shrines to Kuan Yin stood in all kinds of places throughout the length and breadth of China and in several neighboring countries as well" (18). Although she assimilated Tara (and Miao Shan), Quan Yin retains in the minds of her Chinese devotees full identity with Avalokateshwara, so what is said in the sutras about him is, as it were, said of her. This relationship of identity is similar to the statement of Sri Aurobindo that his consciousness and the Mother's are one and the same. Kuan Yin and Avalokiteshwara are "the secondary emanation of the energy of compassion." Either or both can be invoked with equal efficacy.

The intellectual problem concerning the reality of Quan Yin might be the key to understanding her status: She is herself, but she is also Avalokiteshwara (a male bodhisattva). She is also a fragment or component of Buddha, perhaps the *sambogakaya* (subtle body) of Buddha. From an anthroposophic perspective we might understand Kuan Yin as an etheric form or power, and as such she is likely to be seen by seekers but not by skeptics. Similarly, skeptics do not see the apparitions of the Virgin Mary but the faithful presumably do. Like Isis, Kuan Yin, Mary, and Sophia are available to every person who seeks her. She is compassionate to all who acknowledge her. To all others, because she appears inconsequential as well as invisible, she does not exist. She is between the physical and spiritual: "Avalokita, bearing a lotus flower, was born from a ray of light that springs from Amitabha Buddha's right eye" (102).

When Mahayana Buddhism was introduced to Tibet by Padma Sambhava in the first century, the bodhisattva Avalokita was adopted as Tibet's tutelary deity, and chief guardian of the *dharma*. Note that "adopted" does not mean created; it means recognized, as Isis was recognized in a new form as Mary. Some people kill devotees who either cling to the old recognition or introduce a new one, but there is no reason for alarm: Isis is alive in Mary, and both are alive as Sophia. Like other goddess figures, Kuan Yin is to be approached, not argued about. Once one experiences her compassion, the name matters little; what matters is the reality of the archetypal goddess behind the specific manifestation—the source of the real, efficacious existence of Isis, Mary, Kuan Yin, Anthroposophia. At the conclusion of his inquiry, Blofeld is left with a certain ambiguity, an irreducible tension between Quan Yin being symbolic and really existing: "There is a whole range of experience that would be difficult to classify as purely objective or subjective" (134).

Does it not seem that Kuan Yin is real and efficacious in the etheric realm, available to all who have ears to hear and eyes to see etherically (as Mary Magdalen had etheric eyes to see and to hear the risen etheric Christ)? In the sense of a true image, an *imago*, really existing, Blofeld imagines Kuan Yin's final reply:

> In universes countless in number as Ganges sands there are gods and goddesses who have heard the voices of their devotees more often. Thus was it in your world with Isis, Artemis and Aphrodite; so is it now with that Mary who is worshipped in many climes as Queen of Heaven, so, too, with Kali who rejoices still in the blood of sacrificial victims, and many, many others (135).

Mira Richard, The Mother of the Sri Aurobindo Ashram

It is tempting to think that the goddess Sophia came to humanity only in the olden times, as some believe that prophets, saints, and sages belong only in the Hebrew Scriptures or in ancient India or China. But of course all exalted beings continue to incarnate; the Dalai Lama has reincarnated fourteen times. Buddha is expected to come again as Maitreya. Presumably, individuals who lived in the twentieth century such as Rudolf Steiner, Sri Aurobindo, C. G. Jung, and Pierre Teilhard de Chardin will be, or have been, reborn, quite possibly all as women. We can expect that Hildegard of Bingen, Catherine of Sienna, and Margaret Fuller will be or have been reborn, perhaps as males. When we observe a child who exhibits extraordinary capacities it seems sensible to wonder who such a person might have been.

Anthroposophists who know about those individuals such as Ita Wegman who were close to Rudolf Steiner, cannot help but wonder who they were previously and who they might be now (assuming that she has reincarnated.)[5] Steiner delivered more than a hundred lectures indicating the previous lives of various individuals. Sri Aurobindo did not identify previous incarnations of Mira Richard, but he did assert that "she was divine even in childhood." Her prayers, meditations, and dreams certainly give one reason to think of her in extraordinary terms, perhaps even as a manifestation of Sophia, or of *shakti*, the Sanskrit term that Sri Aurobindo used to designate her divinity.

In *The Mother*, Sri Aurobindo's book that he wrote in 1926, the same year that he had an extraordinary experience of Krishna and the year in which Mira Richard took responsibility for the Sri Aurobindo Ashram (essentially as the Shakti to Sri Aurobindo), he attributed to the Mother four powers and four states of transformation, summarized as follows:

1. As *Maha-Sarasvati* the Mother is the agent of transformation of the material realm. She is responsible for the creation and evolution of the human body, especially its beauty and harmony.
2. As *Maha-Lakshmi* the Mother is responsible for transformative power and strength expressed by the vital, or life force.[6]
3. As *Maha-Kali* the Mother is responsible for the transformation of mind.
4. As *Maha-Ishwari* the Mother transforms the psychic being by the power made possible by Supermind.[7]

---

5. The mystery of Ita Wegman in particular was revealed by Steiner himself in a series of letters, for which see the beautiful book by Thomas Meyer, *Rudolf Steiner's Core Mission*.
6. The vital (life) force would seem to be synonymous with Steiner's concept of etheric.
7. Sri Aurobindo, *The Mother*, 25–35.

According to Sri Aurobindo, the Mother is able to realize each of these stages of transformation because from all eternity she has been *shakti*, not as Mira Richard but as the Mother/*shakti*, in 1876 manifested as Mira Richard.

The powers that Sri Aurobindo attributes to the Mother are so unqualified that it is rather difficult to know exactly what he intends. By identifying her as *shakti*, he is ascribing to her a divine spirit coursing through consciousness, affecting history and matter. He also states that the Mother has three ways of manifesting: as transcendent, universal, and individual. Sri Aurobindo and the Mother would seem to offer the furthest claims, the ones most in need of the question I have asked repeatedly in this book: "How far do you want to go?" If you want to go as far as possible, the claims by and on behalf of Sri Aurobindo might be the answer to your search! Sri Aurobindo and the Mother clearly resemble Krishna both as co-avatars and by the divine qualities they themselves claim and that continue to be attributed to them by disciples.

It is not clear what a person who has not experienced the Sri Aurobindo Ashram and Auroville is likely to make of the claims by and for Sri Aurobindo and the Mother. Conversations between Aurobindo disciples and non-disciples usually do not advance very far. In my experience, these conversations are far more difficult than conversations between followers and non-followers of Steiner. The reasons are not hard to see: if an inquirer comes across Steiner's extraordinary (and on first hearing wildly implausible) claim that there were two Jesus children, or that Buddha made a sacrificial deed on Mars, either of which could stop a conversation cold, it is usually easy to bring the conversation back to some of Steiner's more accessible contributions such as his sophisticated epistemology, biodynamic agriculture, Waldorf approach to education, impressive architecture, and sensible insights concerning money and social organization. In the case of Sri Aurobindo and the Mother, to appreciate them one has to have an unusual affinity for the karma of spiritually highborn souls. If one has even a little such affinity then association with Sri Aurobindo can be very inspiring, because it suggests the continuity of the divine working in the world through the kind of souls described in the sacred texts of the world's religions.

ROMAN CATHOLIC SOPHIOLOGY

Thomas Schipflinger: Sophia–Maria

The single most helpful book on the history of Sophia in relation to Christianity is Thomas Schipflinger's *Sophia–Maria*, an ideal complement to Baring and Cashford, *The Myth of the Goddess*. Schipflinger's book is a treasure of texts and explanation; it also includes more than thirty color plates. Schipflinger presents the many manifestations of Sophia historically but not with reference to the evolution of consciousness. No book has to meet every test, but as it is such a valuable book it is a pity that Schipflinger does not take an interest in these questions. It would be so helpful if we could learn (from someone other than Steiner) whether the evolution, devolution, and reemergence of Sophia is spiritually appropriate, correct, or part of a larger development. That said, this book, so obviously done with great care and scholarship, is the ideal source for an introduction to many Sophia texts, including Boehme (who is difficult to understand); Anne Catherine Emmerich (1774–1824), the stigmatist and clairvoyant; the Russians—Vladimir Solovoyev (1853–1900), Mikhail Bulkakov (1891–1940), and Pavel Florensky (1882–1937)—and well chosen texts from the Hindu, Buddhist, and Taoist traditions. Curiously, Schipflinger does not refer to Jung's case for the importance of the dogma of the Assumption of Mary. As *Sophia–Maria* was published in 1998, before Christopher Pramuk's *Sophia: The Hidden Christ of Thomas Merton*, it is not surprising that Merton is not included.

Thomas Merton: Sophia, the Hidden Christ

Sophiology is the domain of Russian Orthodoxy, especially the late nineteenth- and early twentieth-century mystics, Vladimir Soloviev (1853–1900), Mikhail Bulkakov (1891–1940), and Pavel Florensky (1882–1937). Rudolf Steiner's understanding of

Sophia was deeply influenced by Soloviev; several modern sophiologists—Valentin Tomberg, Sergei Prokofieff, Christopher Bamford, and Robert Powell—have been influenced by both Steiner and Soloviev. In his thoroughly researched study, *Sophia: The Hidden Christ of Thomas Merton*, Christopher Pamuk describes Merton's devotion to Sophia, and especially to his conception of Sophia as *Hagia Sophia*. To the fabulous range of Merton's spiritual reading, we can now add his deep knowledge of the Russian Sophiologists, especially Soloviev, Nicolas Berdyaev (1874–1948), and Paul Evdokimov (1901–1970).

Steiner often mentioned the need to pay attention to a moment of grace, or revelation. This is exactly what Merton did, as Pamuk recounts. While visiting the home of his friends Victor and Carolyn Hammer, "Merton noticed a triptych that Hammer had painted, its central panel depicting the boy Christ being crowned by a dark-haired woman." In response to Merton's inquiry, Hammer explained that he did not know the identity of the woman behind Christ. Merton then replied: "She is *Hagia Sophia*, Holy Wisdom who crowns Christ. And this she was—and is." Subsequently, in a letter to Hammer, Merton explained:

> The first thing to be said, of course, is that Hagia Sophia is God Himself. God is not only a Father but a Mother. He is both at the same time.... [To] ignore this distinction is to lose touch with the fullness of God. This is a very ancient intuition of reality which goes back to the oldest Oriental thought.... For the 'masculine–feminine' relationship is basic in all reality—simply because all reality mirrors the reality of God.[8]

In this same letter to Victor Hammer, Merton expressed his deep conviction concerning Sophia, especially Her role as God's love and mercy. He describes Sophia as the expression of each of the three Persons of the divine Trinity. His letter continues,

> In the sense that God is Love, is Mercy, is Humility, is Hiddenness, He shows Himself to us within ourselves as our own

---

8. Quoted in Christopher Pamuk, *Sophia: The Hidden Christ of Thomas Merton*, 194, from William H. Shannon, *Witness to Freedom: The Letters of Thomas Merton in Times of Crisis*, 4

poverty, our own nothingness (which Christ took upon Himself, ordained for this by the Incarnation in the womb of the
Virgin) (the crowning in your picture), and if we receive the
humility of God in our hearts, we become able to accept and
embrace and love this very poverty, which is Himself and His
Sophia.[9]

In his deeply mystical prose-poem, "Hagia Sophia," Merton
identifies Mary the Mother of Jesus as she reveals Sophia:

> Now the Blessed Virgin Mary is the one created being who
> enacts and shows forth
> in her life all that is hidden in Sophia. Because of this she can
> be said to be a
> personal manifestation of Sophia....

As Sophia, Mary with the full awareness of what she is doing,
sets up the Second Person, the Logos, with a crown which is His
human nature. Thus her consent opens the door of created nature,
of time, of history, to the Word of God.[10]

Teilhard de Chardin: "The Feminine or the Unitive"

Teilhard was devoted to the divine feminine in the image
of the Virgin Mary, a prominent part of French Catholic piety.
Young Pierre was nurtured by his mother to honor a simple, pious
version of the Mother of Jesus; that nurturing remained with him.
In his mature years as a mystic and scientist he was able to add
to it an original expression of the mystery and numinosity of
"The Feminine or the Unitive." Teilhard sees a close relationship
between the divine feminine and matter, a relationship that is
expressed in his intensely personal and poetic writings on the
divine feminine. In reading these pages it occurs to me that his
description would have been clearer if he had known Steiner's
concept of the etheric. What is clear, however, is Teilhard's deep
reverence for the divine feminine, mostly in relation to the mother
of Jesus whom he, following standard Roman Catholic terminology, referred to as the Virgin Mary. Whether or not related to

---

9. Ibid.
10. "Hagia Sophia," in Pamuk, 305.

this reverence, Teilhard also exhibited obvious affection for the human feminine, including deep friendships with several women, in light of which his lifelong observance of the vow of chastity is more remarkable.

In March 1918, while on leave from fighting at the front in World War I, Teilhard wrote a ten-page essay entitled "The Eternal Feminine." Remarkably, written after three years in the midst of constant battles, suffering, and death, this essay is essentially about love, both human love and love that serves as a force of unification throughout the universe. Here is a typical sentence from this poetic essay:

> For every monad, be it ever so humble, provided it is in very truth a center of activity, obeys in its movement an embryo of love for me: The universal Feminine.[11]

To be understood this essay would need to be read repeatedly, and even then its meanings will be too subtle to summarize. Consider: "I am the unfading beauty of the times to come—the ideal Feminine." And: "I am Mary the Virgin, mother of all human kind." And:

> When you think I am no longer with you—when you forget me, the air you breathe, the light with which you see—then I shall still be at hand, lost in the sun I have drawn to myself.[12]

C. G. Jung: Assumption of Mary

I have included Jung in this chapter because of his remarkable claim at the end of his book *Answer to Job* (1955), on behalf of the Roman Catholic doctrine of the Assumption of Mary proclaimed by Pope Pius XII in 1950 to be an article of Catholic faith. Jung's enthusiastic response to this papal declaration follows from his having affirmed the divine mother as an archetype. While the archetype itself is unknowable, its manifestations are evident at many levels and in diverse modes of expression. An archetypal image such as Mary, the mother of

---

11. Pierre Teilhard de Chardin, *Writings in Time of War*, 193.
12. Ibid., 199–201.

Jesus, has revealed itself all the way up to the edge of the divine mother archetype itself, as well as all the way down to popular myths, symbols, and images, from the sublime Madonna of the Renaissance painters to the litany of Mary, the rosary, and simple prayers such as the "Hail Mary." Jung chided Protestant theologians and church leaders, including the Lutheran Church with which his forebears were associated for five generations, for having driven Mary out of Christian theology and practice. Jung seems to be one of the rare Protestants (to the extent that he is Protestant, or even Christian), who has emphasized the importance of the divine feminine, specifically by the archetype and many images of the Mother. In *Answer to Job*, a work that Jung wrote in a frenzied ten-day outpouring of insight and opinion, argument and advocacy, he refers to the papal declaration of the Assumption of Mary into heaven (following the Ascension of Christ) as the single most important religious event since the Protestant Reformation—i.e., in 500 years![13] Jung's reason for this claim is simply that as defined by the papacy Mary's physical body was granted unique status close to Christ's.

In Jung's opinion, this declaration in effect restored the *hieros gamos*, the sacred marriage, or divine *conjunctio*, between a divine mother equal to her divine son.

Jung saw the papal declaration as a response to the widespread devotion among Roman Catholics to the Virgin. In this respect, this upsurge of devotion resembles the popular demand for cathedrals dedicated to Notre Dame, in every town and city in Europe from the tenth to the twelfth centuries. These are psychic events arising from the unconscious. It seems unclear how Jung himself understood the doctrine of the Assumption; what could it possibly mean to declare that the physical body of the mother of Jesus was preserved in heaven, as though heaven were a physical place capable of supporting human bodies? In such discussions Steiner's concept of the etheric is crucially important. Without this concept, Jung dismisses the need to understand the status of the body of the Virgin assumed into heaven:

---

13. C. G. Jung, *Answer to Job*, para. 752.

It does not matter at all that a physically impossible fact is asserted, because all religious assertions are physical impossibilities....But religious statements without exception have to do with the reality of the *psyche* and not with the reality of *physis*.... The feminine, like the masculine, demands an equally personal representation.[14]

From Jung's archetypal perspective the papal declaration restores Mary as "functionally on a par with Christ." It is less clear whether Jung's psychological account of the feminine puts the feminine on a par with the masculine, and women on a par with men. For a fair and insightful account of this issue Debaris Wehr, *Jung and Feminism* is especially important.[15]

ANTHROPOSOPHICAL SOPHIOLOGY

Valentin Tomberg and Sergei O. Prokofieff[16]

In his teen years, Valentin Tomberg (1900–1973) was involved with Theosophy in Russia and first wrote to Rudolf Steiner at age twenty. He was an anthroposophist during the 1920s and 1930s and withdrew from the General Anthroposophical Society in 1938 and soon after joined the Roman Catholic Church. In the 1930s he wrote essays that have been beautifully published under the title *Christ and Sophia: Anthroposophic Meditations on the Old Testament, New Testament and Apocalypse* (2011). Unlike his magnificent volume on Tarot (written during the 1960s), this volume, written under the influence of Steiner's esoteric research on the events depicted in the Bible, includes many references to

---

14. Ibid.
15. See also Ann Ulanov, *The Feminine in Jungian Psychology and in Christian Theology*, and Susan Rowland, "Anima, Gender, Feminism," in Kelly Bulkeley and Clodagh Weldon, eds., *Teaching Jung*, 169–182.
16. In this brief discussion of Russian Sophiology I cannot resist mentioning that to enter the Russian Orthodox Holy Virgin Cathedral in San Francisco is to be enveloped in a womb of Sophianic images. Curiously, one of the most complete collections of Sophia icons in the United States is in The Museum of Russian Icons in Clinton, MA, forty miles west of Boston.

Steiner. Christopher Bamford suggests that it might have been difficult for Tomberg, a thorough Christian Platonist, to fit in with the thoroughly Aristotelian perspective of the leadership of the Anthroposophical Society.[17] This is probably so but it is also easy to imagine that it would be even more difficult for such an advanced and sensitive esotericist to collaborate with the leaders of the Anthroposophical Society after Steiner's death while those leaders, particularly Steiner's widow, were caught in conflicting currents for and against National Socialism.

Meditations on the Tarot, by the anonymous author, offers a compendium of esoteric–mystical insights that combine Roman Catholic and Sophianic perspectives. In this same book, Robert Powell's afterword presents two Trinitarian triangles: Father, Son, Holy Spirit, and Mother, Daughter, and Holy Soul.

Sergei O. Prokofieff (1954–2014) was the author of several deep esoteric books beginning with a book on Steiner and continuing through an insightful book on forgiveness. Unfortunately, he is also the author of a regrettable book, *The Case Against Valentin Tomberg: Anthroposophy or Jesuitism* (1997). Particularly relevant for this chapter is his profound book, *The Heavenly Sophia and the Being Anthroposophia* (1996). In the foreword to this volume Prokofieff makes the following disclosure concerning the meaning of Anthroposophia for his life:

> Many years of living with this question in connection with an intensive study of Anthroposophy and a constant practice of meditation on the basis of Rudolf Steiner's writings and lectures led gradually to a wholly new experience of Anthroposophy. It revealed itself as not only a contemporary spiritual-scientific teaching issuing from the sources of esoteric Christianity but also as a living being of the spiritual world, as Anthroposophia, who bring to human beings of the twentieth century the new revelation of the heavenly Sophia, the divine wisdom.[18]

---

17. Christopher Bamford, "Introduction," Valentin Tomberg, *Christ and Sophia*.
18. Sergei O. Prokofieff, *The Heavenly Sophia and the Being Anthroposophia* (1996), 1.

Prokoffieff's book does not at all lend itself to summary, let it simply be said that it provides the most advanced exploration of Steiner's experience of and revelation concerning Anthroposophia.

Christopher Bamford: Isis Mary Sophia

Christopher Bamford is an author of and the editor of several important books on Christ, Sophia, the Archangel Michael, Celtic and Russian spirituality, the history of the Anthroposophical Society, anthroposophic practice, and a book with the revealing title Isis Mary Sophia—with no punctuation between these names. In his beautiful introduction, many lines of which are quoted at the beginning of this chapter, Bamford repeats Steiner's statement that behind Steiner's thirty-three–foot wooden sculpture of Christ (The Representative of Humanity) "there was a fourth, invisible, figure, a being, Isis."[19] Steiner reportedly indicated:

> Mostly she was invisible, but sometimes especially intuitive visitors glimpsed her. They saw that, in fact, she was asleep and that beneath her was the inscription "I am humanity. I am the past, present, and future. Every mortal should lift my veil."[20]

Isis Mary Sophia, following Bamford's inspiring introduction, contains Rudolf Steiner's references to Sophia as the new Isis, the divine feminine wisdom reemerging in contemporary consciousness. Bamford summarizes his and Steiner's understanding of Isis–Mary–Sophia:

> The feminine divine is clearly present everywhere in the founding civilizations of our present moment. She is called by many names—Inanna in Sumeria; Astarte among the Hittites; Ishtar in Babylon; in Egypt (among many others), Isis, Maat, Hathor, Nut, and Neith; in Greece, Demeter, Persophone, Artemis, Athena, Hecate. The list is endless—Sophia and Mary are only two more. The more one seeks, the more Goddesses one

---

19. Christopher Bamford, Isis Mary Sophia, 22.
20. Ibid., 22.

finds. This apparently riotous confusion should *not* be taken as evidence of polytheism—far from it. These figurations—all of whom may be said to be aspects of Sophia—represent different states of one and the same primal principle, acting according to successive phases of becoming.[21]

It would be difficult to summarize this complex set of fifteen texts by Steiner featuring his many descriptions of Isis, Mary, and Sophia, the relationships among them as well as their unity, and their relationships with Christ, the Holy Spirit, Mary Magdalene, Archangel Michael, and Anthroposophia. Some texts, such as "The Nature of the Virgin Sophia and of the Holy Spirit," from Steiner's lectures on the Gospel of St. John, are quite challenging on first reading. The entire book is at another level of mystery and profundity from most of the literature on Sophia—though not at another level from *Mary and Sophia*, a recent book by Michael Debus, which organizes Steiner's references to Sophia that Bamford has presented.

Michael Debus, *Mary and Sophia*

Mary and Sophia: The Feminine Element in the Spiritual Evolution of Humanity, by Michael Debus, a Christian Community priest, clearly explains Steiner's esoteric research on Sophia, particularly in relation to Christ and to the Mother of Jesus, as well as in other important relationships. Early in the book Debus explains the deliberations and decision of the Council of Nicaea in 325 CE and the Council of Constantinople in 381 CE concerning the theology of Christ: at His birth was Christ of the same substance as the Father, or as the Son of God was He created by the Father? Did Mary give birth to a god (such that she was a *theotokos*, a god bearer), or was she an *anthropotokos*, mother of a human being?[22] Debus explains the import of the Council of Ephesus in 425 for the devotion to Mary throughout the history of Christendom:

---

21. Ibid., 23–24.
22. Michael Debus, *Mary and Sophia: The Feminine Element in the Spiritual Evolution of Humanity*, 58.

In the dogma of Ephesus, Mary is responsible for Christ's human aspect. As the Mother of God, *theotokos*, she bestows humanity upon Christ. Just as Adam received his body made from Earth, Christ as the 'second Adam' (1 Cor.), now received his body from Mary, the 'good soil.' Through the decisive rejection of ascending Christology in Ephesus the human Jesus disappeared from religious view, but this human element then returned in the person of the virginal Mother of God. The nearness to humanity that Christ had lost was given back to the religious longing of Christians by Mary's presence that was felt in devotion to her.[23]

One of the great advantages of this book is simply that Debus knows the esoteric research of Rudolf Steiner on the individuals and events depicted in the New Testament (Steiner delivered dozens of very esoteric lectures to the priests of the Christian Community), and he also knows the history of Christian theology, especially concerning the theology and spirituality of Mary–Sophia. The influence of Steiner on Debus is especially prominent in the idea of ascending Christology, and with it ascending Mariology: Debus laments the proclamation of the Assumption of Mary by the Roman Catholic Church in 1950 (the same declaration that Jung celebrates in his *Answer to Job*) because it denies to Mary the possibility of further development. Steiner, and Debus following him, emphasizes the development of Jesus after his transformative experience in the temple at age twelve and after his baptism in the river Jordan at age thirty. Echoing Steiner, Debus writes: "The essence of Christianity, however, lies not in preserving but in transforming guilt."[24]

Debus describes Steiner's account of the raising of Lazarus, specifically Steiner's account of the dramatic, transformative revitalization of the etheric body of Lazarus so that thereafter Christ called him John, the Beloved Disciple—i.e., he who was initiated. In esoteric Christianity, "beloved' refers to someone who was initiated, as Lazarus–John had been in the event depicted as a raising from the dead. According to Steiner, it was the initiated,

---

23. Ibid., 61
24. Ibid., 77.

beloved disciple Lazarus–John who was able to write the Gospel of John and the Apocalypse (Book of Revelation). It was also this Lazarus–John, with his transformed etheric body, who was able to join with the mother of Jesus, also with a pure etheric body, in a community in Ephesus for several decades after the crucifixion and resurrection of Christ. Mary–Sophia lived in this community of the Beloved Disciple that became the primary source of mystical and esoteric Christianity, ever in tension with the exoteric strand of Christianity headed by Peter, the first bishop, in Rome. Steiner tells us that Mary–Sophia possessed not only a pure etheric body, but a unique physical body, soul, and "I." Every chapter of Debus's very precise, profound book reveals aspects of the Marian–Sophianic mystery worthy of meditative reading.

THE DIVINE FEMININE AND FEMINISM

It appears that the various images and attributes of the divine feminine, whether or not under the heading of Sophia, do not *directly* support feminist critiques and goals—i.e., women's rights and gender justice. If only they did. It seems to me that Isis–Mary–Sophia, or Kuan Yin, or *Philo-Sophia,* who brought equanimity to Boethius, or the Mother of the Sri Aurobindo Ashram, do not address or directly affect the social structures that sustain male privilege. Effective opposition to large-scale male domination and gender injustice almost certainly requires a knowledge of the analyses and critiques of gender imbalance and social dynamics that have been and continue to be generated by social scientists, particularly feminists. A hierarchy of males that forbids women full participation in its leadership and sacraments is not in a strong position to tell the faithful to imitate Mary's "I will" in response to the angel. A feminist might reasonably object that *Philo-sophia* could have put less effort into calming Boethius and more effort into freeing him. There are also many good reasons to be impressed by the Mother of the Sri Aurobindo Ashram but feminism and feminist spirituality are not among them.

Contrary to what one hears from divine feminine devotees, male and female, I am emphasizing the limitations of loyalty to the divine feminine: Devotion to Sophia or another image of the divine feminine on its own appears to be powerless against the subtle, ubiquitous power of patriarchy and male privilege. Worse, focus on the divine feminine can privilege the feminine at the spiritual level while masking abuse of the feminine in social life. Masculine power and privilege do not tire and seldom yield voluntarily. Devotion to the feminine divine needs to be complemented by feminist critiques and by listening to individuals and groups adversely affected by gender imbalance. Even those so affected must learn effective language to express their experience. It helps to have access to concepts such as patriarchy, male privilege, or Buber's "I–It." It does not require a lot of learning, however, for a woman to observe that she is blocked from decisions affecting her body, or her pay scale, or extent of influence in social and political issues. But it does require knowledge to understand the entwined causes of these injustices and the powers that sustain them. This knowledge is not available from images or descriptions of the divine feminine, and might even be masked by them.

Male opposition to both the feminine divine and to justice toward women might be analogous to the relationship between feminism and ecology. Violation of nature and violation of women have many characteristics in common, most obviously that they have the same cause: both are inflicted by male passion for control and power. The similarity between male abuse of Earth and of women was first established powerfully by two books of enduring value: Susan Griffin, *Woman and Nature: the Roaring Inside Her* (1978) and Caroline Merchant, *Death of Nature* (1980), but it must be added that a person can be sensitive to Earth and not to women, and vice versa. Similarly, one can worship Sophia and be insensitive to women and to justice generally. The Roman Catholic hierarchy, for example, has sustained a strong affirmation of the exalted status of Mary but continues systemically to treat women unjustly. It is unconvincing to regard the Mother of Jesus or the Mother of the Sri Aurobindo Ashram as models of gender equality or exponents of economic, sociological, or sexual feminist values.

Worshiping Mary is a matter of spirit and archetype, not necessarily a matter of justice for females, which requires a reform of social context. Jung's affirmation of the divine mother or feminine archetype, for example, is a contribution to the psychology of the feminine, but this conception was not particularly advantageous to the women in his own life—he appears to have taken full advantage of his privilege as a powerful male. Irrespective of how one answers the difficult question concerning essentialism (gender differences are built in, encoded in the gender) or contextualism (gender differences are socially and culturally taught and learned) every culture and every person has the responsibility of social justice for all persons, certainly including all females. Despite the apparent failure of the divine feminine to serve feminism directly, it does important work indirectly, at the level of the unconscious, concerning what Jung refers to as the God image.

I believe the great problem in this discussion, far from resolution, involves the disconnect between the essentialist theory of the feminine as espoused by Jung and the contextual theory preferred by most feminists. With Jung, advocates of the divine feminine tend to favor essentialism, with little or no concern for its contextualist critique, but if the general attitude toward the divine feminine were to be uplifted (the point of this chapter) this improvement might indirectly, and perhaps profoundly, affect the perception and treatment of women, and thereby both men and women. Inclusion of the feminine divine is not the only way to diminish gender injustice but it is a way consistent with the aims of this book and probable values of its readers. The divine feminine might make a strong case against divine patriarchy, or at least provide an attractive (as well as true) alternative to it, and thereby *indirectly* stand against patriarchy at the social level. Mary Daly's remark that the Christian Trinity consists of "two men and a bird," and Elizabeth Johnson's re-conceptualization of God as "She" do not directly address gender injustice, but they do unsettle concepts deeply lodged in the unconscious use of language that has distorted Christian theology and behavior for many centuries.

If Sophia or the divine feminine can be shown to be efficacious on behalf of women, then patriarchy would seem diminished to that same extent. Unfortunately, this is not necessarily so. There are negative as well as positive examples of the impact of devotion to the divine feminine. In the case of India, where there is a strong tradition of female gods, where every god has a female consort of comparable power (Kali and Durga, for example, are consorts of Siva), there is widespread generally condoned violence against women. The Roman Catholic hierarchy is similarly devoted to the divine feminine and opposed to women's rights. Nevertheless, overall and however indirectly, it would seem a good development for the cause of feminism if the divine would be conceived equally in feminine and masculine terms and function as a support for the indispensable social scientific critique of gender injustice. To the extent that Sophia in Her many manifestations breaks the presumed but mistaken and deleterious characterization of the divine in exclusively masculine terms (and masculine preference for power and violence), Her images and any homage to her might contribute to the rebalancing of masculine and feminine. It is also true and important that males and females need to be inspired by at least some (and perhaps all) of the qualities thought to be characteristically feminine as embodied in images of the divine feminine. An increased awareness of Sophia, the divine feminine, could seem to be an antidote at the subtle and unconscious level where the distortion between genders resides all too comfortably—*could be* but the connection needs to be made between the unconscious archetype and gender justice in social structures and processes.

Exactly which qualities can safely be called feminine is a fraught topic but on the basis of the history provided by Baring and Cashford and ascribed to Kuan Yin, Philo-Sophia or the Mother of the Sri Aurobindo Ashram, these qualities probably include nurturing and natural generativity, creative relationality, subtlety and nuance over single pointed power, inspiration over domination, compassion over atomism, etc. Note that I did not mention the sun as masculine and the moon as feminine; this attribution, frequently cited by Jungians, seems to me unhelpful to the cause of feminism because the sun is the source of heat and light whereas the moon is merely its reflection. Even if the application of generally acceptable qualities to archetypal masculine and feminine are indirectly influential, they are positive in many important ways in their own right. Because the divine feminine has been missing, and because it seems to be an antidote to excessive masculinity in many cultures at both archetypal and social levels, the divine feminine would seem to be an image that is healing and needed.

Elizabeth A. Johnson appears to me a theologian who ideally combines a deep theological account of the relationships among Christ, Sophia and Mary with an equally informed analysis of the role of gender. A Roman Catholic professor of theology at Fordham University, Elizabeth Johnson is the author of several books on the Trinity, Sophia, and Mary from a feminist perspective. Although not at all strident or exaggerated, Johnson offers a powerful expose of the misogyny endemic in the Roman Catholic hierarchy and theologians from Tertullian and Augustine through Thomas Aquinas to the present. In addition to this necessary and obvious critique, Johnson also offers a positive feminine spirituality that utilizes new terminology, as by the title of her major work, *She Who Is.* In Johnson's writings the Archetypal Sophia–Maria is presented in precise theological terms in relation to each Person of the Trinity, and in relation to an ideal spiritual conception and experience of these divine beings in the twenty-first century.

I will end this chapter with my own tribute to the resurgence and the influence of the divine feminine.[25]

ꩰ

---

25. I first read this invocation in 2007 at a Sophia conference at the Sophia Center, Charleston, South Carolina, cosponsored by the Fetzer Institute and the Sophia Foundation of North America. The version on my website, ciis.pcc faculty publications, includes 60 footnotes.

INVOCATION TO SOPHIA

I. Sophia, We Call to You

We invoke you, divine mother,
humanity's first image
and first word.

You were Demeter and Persephone,
the goddess Zoe,
and the mother of the lunar cycle.

As Ishtar and Inanna you waged war
—and you'd better again
to save the Earth.

As Inanna you were Queen of Heaven,
a title and identity
you lost in Christendom.

Before the garden of Eden
and Plato's cave
you held spirit and matter as one.

You hear with the aged sagacity of the Psalms,
of *Hokhmah*, essential Hebraic wisdom,
who was there when God created heaven and Earth.

As Isis you were sacred cow, pig, and bird;
guardian of the underworld,
Sirius and loving mother of your son Horus.

We recall the litany of your images as Mary—
holy mother of God, mother ever faithful,
queen of angels and saints, portal of heaven.

As Isis you weep,
as Mary you suffer and comfort,
as Sophia you inspired Plato's Diotima.

These many names and more point to you.
Tao, *sunyatta*, Kuan Yin, *shakti* also name you,
but not one is your eternal name.

Water, womb, silence, and mother,
the inner and subtle, soul and spirit,
mystery and secret, all try to name you.

You reigned as Isis for three millennia,
as Mary you inspired the Christendom
of Dante's Beatrice and the Grail.

II. *That We Lost You*

We are too accustomed to the guy project,
a brilliant Faustian bargain ending too slowly.

Steiner taught "we have not lost Christ, we have lost Sophia."
Cosmic alienation has seized the modern mind.

We didn't lose you in a day or a year.
A profound cosmic transformation takes a century or two.

A Cartesian–Newtonian billiard ball cosmos,
not to mention the quest for gold,
fueled passion for control and power.

The modern project can't handle interiors and subtleties:
bring on the visible and solid, surfaces only;
nothing too soft, fluid, or flexible.

They say the takeover started with *Enu Elish*,
in Baghdad—still in the news—
as Inanna you hung on a hook for three days.

Crucifixion has been a male specialty;
no more the generative goddesses,
give us the thunderbolt gods.

As goddess, you're assigned to girls and crones,
but empires need Marduk;
a god's gotta do what a god's gotta do.

On he came morphing and starring—
as Zeus, ruling the sky and mountain tops,
as YHWH, vengeful god of the garden.

Your daughter Eve made a bad marriage.
In the Garden Adam was a loser;
Eve, a scapegoat.

All sin then traceable to a woman,
childbirth a curse, males in charge,
sin and salvation over service and generation.

Your archetypal image surfaced
in Medieval European towns,
hundreds of cathedrals to Notre Dame.

Too good to go unopposed,
from Notre Dame of Paris
to the Temple of Reason.

Bacon is our Man:
nature on the rack,
control at all cost.

By the shadow of the Enlightenment,
knowledge and power over wisdom,
analysis and argument over insight.

We will have knowledge,
get the secret, blow the atom,
take charge, go the limit, no price too high.

And we did, and it feels good.
We have dominion, even over death—sort of.
Why are we so depressed, fearful, and violent?

What shall we make of the hard images
Are you really Kali with a company of destroyers?
Are they you, embracing all opposites?

Should we accept your embrace of suffering and evil—
war, hunger, rape, HIV/AIDS, cancer, Parkinson's,
ALS, Alzheimer's, addiction, despair, suicide?

Does your hard mother-love find these useful?
Are you the source of pain, illness, and loss?
—alienation, dead ends, Beckett's *Endgame*?
We really need to know this!

Were you behind Gettysburg, Pear Harbor, Hiroshima?
Could you have stopped them?
What are you doing about sex slaves?

We believe you bind each nation's wounds,
comforting soldiers slain,
and their widows and orphans.

But why are these? Why?
Is this your way to make us conscious?
For us to try harder? What a strange way!

And what of spiritual suffering?
Have you led the West
to suffer the loss of your comfort?

III. *By Sight and Sound We Call to You*

As your Christopher has written,
you are again arising like Venus.
Some are seeing the hem of your mantle.

Searching for inner realities,
seeing behind, and within,
are we seeing signs of your presence?

We practice philo-sophy,
looking to interiors and a single vision,
participating subject and object.

We know such sightings are rare
in a culture of denial,
a passion for "nothing but."

What about the books on your behalf?
Are they seeing you,
or fantasizing your mantle, your image, and sound?

Leonardo, Michael Angel, and Rapha-el
renaissanced your sacred image,
Mama and Bambino, for all times and all hearts.

We see you through the holy Fra,
Duccio and the Sienese School,
and the American Henry Ossawa Tanner.

You've sent healing cosmic sounds
to Bach, Mozart, and Beethoven.
Deo gratias for Schubert's "Ave."

Shakespeare has revealed you:
"There are more things under heaven and earth...."
They are the hidden, subtle, and mysterious.

Dante, Shakespeare, and Goethe,
the greatest three, all know you
in ambiguity, artistry, inner *anthropos*.

Goethe's poetry and *urpflanze*, gentle science,
alchemy, mysteries, polarities—
and Faust, the rascal—all approach you.

Your Gretchen, Faust's victim and savior,
in the end reveals your grace:
"The Eternal Feminine draws us onward."

You've sent us the mantras of wise women,
mothers, teachers, poets, and children.

Abigail wrote to John, "Remember the Ladies."
Henry Adams, son and grandson of presidents,
looked past the dynamo to the Virgin
and saw the secrets of Chartres.

We still learn from Laotse,
a correction for Confucian rigidity,
bringing grace to order, surprise to tradition.
Not mere chaos, Tao weaves subtly.

After enlightenment the river remains.
Jack teaches laundry after ecstasy.

You've shown the interiors of exteriors.
You are *shakti*, a hot knife through butter;
you slice as needed, and at the joint.

No Rama without Sita,
no Krishna without Radha,
no Buddha without Quan Yin.

No Jesus without you,
no Aurobindo without the Mother;
His Holiness, verily Avalokiteshvara.

We know you break through concrete,
like the lily in the wall,
and grass on Madison Avenue.

As *prajnaparamita* you teach us "gate', gate',"
"Go beyond, beyond,
Wisdom beyond knowledge, Emptiness beyond form."

With Blofeld we see you as Quan Yin, in the crevice,
arranging pregnancies, auspicious births,
tending to the bereft.

Long before Lovelock, you knew you were Gaia.
long before permaculture
the farmers of Assam rotated crops.

You taught Derzu Uzala to know the river and the wind,
Francis to celebrate the sun
and befriend the wolf of Gubbio.

You led Teilhard and Thomas to reverence Gaia,
Mary Evelyn and John to teach religion and ecology,
Joanna to teach the truth of Chernobyl and deep time.

Surely you led Al to teach,
and the Norwegians to applaud,
the inconvenient truth.

Will fundamentalist Christians,
held by Calvin's misanthropy and the Rapture,
replace "dominion" by "protection"?

When New York State sprayed DDT,
Marjorie sued, Rachel took notes
and wrote *Silent Spring*.

Despite these whistle blowers,
as Gaia you burn.
Are you *Pieta* forever?

His Holiness knows you as Tara,
faithful to the *bodhisattva* vow,
he holds Tibet as you held your Son.

We know you as Notre Dame in blue veil,
as the Virgin of Chartres, as Guadalupe in gold,
revealed by the peasant, the pure, the peaceful.

We still need our guide books,
and fabulous Icons—Greek, Russian, Bulgarian;
we study the Grail, Dante, Hildegard, Julian.

We call to you by your many names,
knowing you as Isis–Mary–Sophia,
three names for your singularity.

IV. *Gaiasophia's Response*

Save my body; it burns from greed.
turn the Ganges from brown to green,
plant trees in Africa.

Spread *Blessed Unrest*,
save the rainforest,
speak truth to power.

My mantle will do for some of you,
others of you need a good smack
and a "Thou Shalt Not."

Thou shalt not poison my blood,
Thou shalt not hammer my bones,
Thou shalt not commit deicide.

I am the sucking infant and the Alzheimer patient,
I am the Mississippi and the Hudson,
I am Mt. Tam and Mt. Kailash.

Recall the forgotten ancient wisdom:
HPB announced my unveiling;
her Indian and Tibetan masters knew me.

Heed Steiner's divine *coniunctio*
—Anthropos and Sophia—
and Sophianic thinking.

And my Sophiologists,
Soloviev, Bulgakov, Florensky,
and the wise Tarot meditator, Valentin Tomberg.

Read the profound Prokofieff.
Robert Powell knows me as
Trinosophia—Mother, Daughter, Holy Soul.

I am the Primordial Flaring Forth,
Steiner's etheric, Jung's *anima mundi*
and Thomas's Great Work.

Know me,
come to me and love me,
as I have loved you.
Your Mother,
GaiaSophia.

Martin Buber
Carl Gustav Jung
Richard Tarnas

GOD, EVIL, AND SUFFERING

INTRODUCTION: MARTIN BUBER, C. G. JUNG, AND RUDOLF STEINER

This chapter compares some of the leading ideas of three great religious thinkers on the topic of theodicy—the philosophical attempt to explain the existence of suffering and evil in relation to belief in a just and loving God. I feature three deep thinkers who devoted their lives to curing the spiritual ills of modern Western humanity: Martin Buber, who was deeply related to Judaism, had an affinity with several existentialist themes, and offered the practice of "I and Thou" and dialogue as cures for modern Western malaise; C. G. Jung, who sought to heal the psychological ills of individuals and modern Western culture; and Rudolf Steiner who brought spiritual and esoteric insights for the enlivening of thinking, feeling, and willing.

These three great twentieth-century European religious thinkers wrote in the German language, though none was of German nationality: Martin Buber was Polish–Jewish, C. G. Jung was Swiss, and Rudolf Steiner was Austrian. Because of their religious and spiritual orientations, they each struggled with challenges posed by the Enlightenment, the philosophy of Immanuel Kant, twentieth-century positivism and skepticism, and more generally the secular worldview of twentieth-century European thought and culture. In a remarkable coincidence Buber, Jung, and Steiner each at the age of fourteen began to read, and confront in a life-defining way, Kant's *Critique of Pure Reason* (1781). This work defined the philosophical task for the nineteenth and twentieth centuries, and more specifically set the limits to theoretical knowledge concerning God, human freedom, and human immortality.

In the opinion of these three thinkers, modern Western humanity suffers from a variety of illnesses including disenchantment, alienation, fragmentation, anxiety, and meaninglessness, all due to a broken connection with the divine (variously understood). To address these and other profound illnesses, Buber brought biblical faith and an "I–Thou" way of life. In his classic text *I and Thou*, Buber inspires the reader to respond to another so as to experience in that person the presence of the Eternal Thou, understood in the Jewish tradition as the God of Abraham, Isaac, and Jacob. Because his commitment was to religious and moral experience, and not to pure theoretical knowledge, Buber did not object to Kant's denial of theoretical knowledge of God, human freedom, and human immortality.

Jung developed methods by which to contact the wisdom of the unconscious psyche. Despite his amazing plunge into psychic depths for several years, Jung wrote as though he were observing Kant's restrictive epistemology. Philosophically minded readers of Jung recognize that his analysis of archetypes, images, myths, and especially synchronicities reveals that Kant's epistemological strictures did not limit Jung's spiritual and esoteric insights. In response to modern Western spiritual poverty, Rudolf Steiner contributed many complementary ways to lead the spiritual in the individual to the spiritual in the universe. In his doctoral dissertation *Truth and Knowledge* (1891) and *Philosophy of Freedom* (1893), his original epistemology and ethics based on his clairvoyant experience, Steiner set out to refute Kant's restrictive epistemology. For the last twenty-five years of his life he developed religious, moral, and artistic practices by which his followers might experience divinity, human freedom, and an experience of oneself enduring over lifetimes.

It is also true that Kant helped to liberate all three of these great thinkers: He established that despite common-sense appearances to the contrary, the world is as much in the mind as "out there." According to Kant, the human mind does not create the world, but it does organize it according to fixed categories, beginning with time and space. This claim, for which Kant argued brilliantly, set the terms for the explosion of philosophic genius called German idealism and subsequently for the English and American Romantic traditions in philosophy, science, and art. It was the *Critique of Practical Reason* (1788), and Kant's successors, especially Fichte, Schelling, and Hegel, that led to the pragmatism of James, Peirce, and Royce and to the Romantic conception of a higher, wider realm. It is this realm that Emerson refers to as the Absolute and the Oversoul, James refers to as "Something More," and Royce refers to as "The Beloved Community." In his *Philosophy of Freedom*, especially in Part One, Steiner showed the way to break through Kant's epistemological ceiling. In the second half of *Philosophy of Freedom* he argues that by intuitive thinking about moral experience an individual can gain access to truths beyond the reach of ordinary thought— i.e., it can break through phenomenal, determined experience to free, noumenal experience.

Buber, Jung, and Steiner reveal a mix of similarities and interesting differences. Buber was educated in Jewish and German culture, Jung was the descendent of five generations of Lutheran pastors, and Steiner's parents were Roman Catholic. All three were students of Goethe and Schiller. All three devoted their lives to healing the ills that arise from faulty Western thinking. Yet there is an important difference between Buber and Jung: As is evident in his disagreement with Jung, Buber is committed to the real (not what he considered merely symbolic) presence of God, including the Judaic conceptions of divine creation, revelation, and redemption. Unlike Jung's conception of God as changing, and in fact evolving in concert with the evolution of human consciousness, Buber's conception of God is more in conformity with the Abrahamic conception of God as unchanging. That said, Buber's philosophy of I–Thou applied to God established the possibility and ideal of a more personal relationship between an individual person and God as person. For Jung, God is a psychologically real entity but he insisted that human beings should not speak of God as independent of psyche. Jung spoke of the "objective psyche"—collective, archetypal, trans-human, and a repository of the numinous and of the evolution of God in dialogical interdependent relationship with human consciousness. For both Buber and Jung God is an authentic "Other" to human consciousness. For Buber, God is personal and in charge of history while for Jung God is contacted in the numinous depths of the archetypal psyche, the experiential source of "everything one could wish for in the psychic Thou." Steiner's conception of God falls roughly between these two.

Jung's concept of the divine–human relationship is more dialogical and intimate, in the sense of mutual influence, than Buber's religious philosophy can uphold given its wholly "Other," transcendent, self-contained, monotheistic God. Speaking of the "God image" allowed Jung to have an understanding into why the God of the Hebrew Bible could at times be so loving and caring, at other times so angrily punitive, and yet at other times tell the Hebrews to kill and maim enemies, and so forth. The God image evolved. Jung was trying to observe the strictures set in Kant's *Critique of Pure Reason* while also remaining true to his empirical approach to his own religious experience, the noetic experiences of his clients, and the evidence of religious knowledge worldwide. Steiner partly agrees with Buber and partly with Jung: With Buber, Steiner conceives of God as an infinite and eternal being and the creator of psyche, not, as Jung argues, the reverse. But Steiner is close to Jung in his conviction that the images of God, and of other exalted beings evolve, and further in his affirmation of many exalted beings, whether the Christian Trinity, or the Christian hierarchy, or Sophia, Krishna, Buddha, or the two tempters, Lucifer and Ahriman.

Each of these three profound religious thinkers offers a worldview that is important in its own right and also important as a type or category, respectively: Buber's traditional Abrahamic faith, Jung's post-traditional psychological spirituality, and Steiner's esoteric approach that draws on both traditional Christianity and panpsychic numinous beings. All three thinkers offer their respective worldview as a solution for the ills of modern humanity.

Buber's worldview is a synthesis of the Hebraic biblical faith, Hasidism, and German-language philosophy and culture; Jung's worldview is essentially psychological extended to Christianity, Romanticism, alchemy, Gnosticism, the *I Ching*, and esotericism; Steiner's worldview is esoteric, influenced by Theosophy, German philosophy (especially Goethe and German Idealism) and with a definite overlap with Christianity. All three thinkers attempted to articulate a new consciousness that is both affirmative of a transcendent divine realm higher and wiser than humanity yet consonant with human individuality and freedom. All three missed each other: Buber and Jung participated in an exchange of letters that reveals neither of them was able to grasp the deepest intellectual commitment of the other. Steiner's volume of lectures on Jung are definitely not among his best, and Jung completely dismissed Steiner's esoteric research with a shrug similar to Freud's dismissal of Jung's descent into "the black tide of mud...of occultism."[1] Yet, all three of these learned, original thinkers have contributed insights that are positive for our understanding of suffering and evil, and are remedies for contemporary alienation and loss of direction.

It is worth noting that all three lived "between": Buber between Judaism and German culture, Jung between simultaneous commitments to empirical science, religious experience, and psychological healing, and Steiner between spirit (which came to him naturally) and matter (which he had to befriend). Teilhard is not in this chapter but it is worth mentioning that he lived between Christian mysticism and paleontology. Sri Aurobindo lived between Indian spirituality and Western philosophy, and His Holiness the Dalai Lama lives between Tibetan Buddhism and Western science, philosophy, and religion. Tagore lived between matter and spirit, and Gandhi, Dewey, and Buber all lived the tension between individual and community. "Between" might be a fertile location from which to generate a creative worldview.

---

1. Carl Jung, *Memories, Dreams, Reflections*, 150.

MARTIN BUBER: "I–THOU" WAY OF LIFE

The life and thought of Martin Buber (1878–1965) are characterized by a play of polarities. He is deeply devoted to biblical faith, yet generally critical of all religion, including Judaism. His *I and Thou*, one of the great works of twentieth-century philosophical and religious literature, reveals traces of both existentialism (a philosophy of radical individualism) and Marxism (a philosophy of radical collectivity). His careful social and moral philosophy is balanced by his translations and retelling of simple, pious Hasidic tales. From these Hasidic masters of eighteenth- and nineteenth-century Eastern Europe, Buber learned to appreciate the life-affirming power of small, tight communities.

Martin Buber was born in Vienna, then the capital of the Austrian Empire and rivaled only by Paris as the intellectual and cultural capital of Europe, but Buber regarded neither Vienna as his native city nor Austria as his native country. He referred to himself as a "Polish Jew." In addition to German and Polish, Hebrew and Yiddish, Buber also learned Greek, Latin and French while a youth, and in later years lectured and wrote in English. In one of his last essays, "The Word that Is Spoken" (1961), Buber attempts to show that the word that is spoken establishes "the between" by which persons establish themselves as persons.[2] This concept of between, like relation and dialogue, are at the core of Buber's worldview.

Although Buber was blessed in his paternal grandparents who raised him from age three to fourteen, his parents' divorce provided him with a painful experience of the failure of relations. Writing of this experience some eighty years later (just prior to his death in 1965), Buber does not gloss over its impact on his early life or on his philosophy of dialogue. He recalled at approximately age four he stood next to an older girl, perhaps seven, on the veranda of his grandparents' home:

> I cannot remember that I spoke of my mother to my older comrade. But I hear still how the big girl said to me: "No, she will never come back." I know that I remained silent, but also

2. Martin Buber, *The Knowledge of Man*, 112.

that I cherished no doubt of the truth of the spoken words. It remained fixed in me; from year to year it cleaved ever more to my heart, but after more than ten years I had begun to perceive it as something that concerned not only me, but all men [and women]. Later I once made up the word *vergegnung*, mismeeting, or miscounter to designate the failure of a real meeting between individuals. When after another twenty years I again saw my mother, who had come from a distance to visit me, my wife, and my children, I could not gaze into her still astonishingly beautiful eyes without hearing from somewhere the word *Vergegnung* as a word spoken to me. I suspect that all that I have learned about genuine meeting in the course of my life had its first origin in that hour on the balcony.[3]

In addition to the negative experience of "non-meeting" his mother, Buber was formed by his negative experiences as a Jew in overwhelmingly Catholic Galicia. As a Jewish student in the public yet essentially Catholic elementary school he attended, young Buber keenly felt the power of a community bond and the impact of being left outside that community. To an extent that could not have been foreseen at the time of his childhood, this experience of alienation as a Jew in a Christian culture prefigured the violence of Christians against Jews in twentieth-century Europe. Because of this experience of Christian anti-Semitism, Buber remained steadfastly opposed to all missionary activity and open to dialogue among adherents of various faiths. He was also introduced to conflicts between various factions within the Jewish tradition.

As is often the case with a liberal position, Buber's attempt to steer a middle course between orthodoxy and assimilation failed to satisfy either faction. (Jung experienced a similar tension between theologians and psychoanalysts.) Buber was so often in this position that he characterized his entire life and teaching as a "narrow ridge," the path that carries one forward while trying to avoid the extremes on the left or the right.[4] Buber's warning concerning the state of Israel put him on an especially narrow

---

3. "Autobiographical Fragments," in Paul Arthur Schilpp and Maurice Friedman, eds., *The Philosophy of Martin Buber*, 3–4.
4. Martin Buber, *Between Man and Man*, 184.

ridge in relation to the Israeli political right wing. He "warned of excessive nationalism in Zionist thought and counseled against the creation of a 'tiny state of Jews, completely militarized and unsustainable.'"[5]

Like his grandfather, Buber was an intellectual descendent of Moses Mendelssohn (1729–1786) who symbolized the Jewish enlightenment (called *Haskalah*) and who had translated the Pentateuch, the first five books of the Bible, from Hebrew to German. For Buber's bar mitzvah speech, he chose not the customary biblical reading but a text from the German poet, Friedrich Schiller. From age fourteen to eighteen, while he lived with his father, Buber grew increasingly estranged from Jewish practice. He explains that until his twentieth year his spiritual life was in constant turmoil, "in versatile fullness of spirit, but without Judaism, without humanity, and without the presence of the divine."[6]

Buber struggled with Kant throughout his teen years, and then at age seventeen he encountered the writings of Friedrich Nietzsche who affirmed the primacy of passion, or in Nietzsche's terms, the Dionysian over the Apollonian. Whereas Buber had found in Kant a conception of human nature as essentially a lawgiver, or a being capable of universalizing the maxims of one's action, Nietzsche's *Zarathustra* introduced Buber to the ideal of a heroic individual, one capable of enacting a will to power. Nietzsche's original ideas—the death of the God of the Abrahamic religions, passion over reason, and the individual heroic will—all continued to exercise significant influence on Buber's thought for the remainder of his life.

Martin Buber's classic text *I and Thou* (1923) teaches that human responses fall into two types, or two attitudes: The first, "I–Thou," is spontaneous, personal, genuine, and receptive; the second, "I–It," is routine, impersonal, closed, fixed, and other qualities ranging from neutral to negative. We have all found ourselves in relationships in which we feel that we do not count for

5. David Remnick, "The One-State Reality," *The New Yorker*, November 17, 2014, 51.
6. Martin Buber, *Hasidism and Modern Man*, 57.

very much, in which we feel replaceable by someone else, or in which we feel either invisible or used. The civil rights movement and the women's rights movement have powerfully articulated the feelings of people of color and women who feel themselves to be treated as an "It." The most obvious examples of a predominantly I–It existence are the slave, prisoner, and abused child, but even individuals of power, prestige, and security are occasionally treated as things. A more thorough understanding of Buber's I–It relationship should begin with Hegel's influential master–slave dialectic according to which master and slave depend on each other for their identity. Whereas Marx sought to liberate the worker enslaved by the capitalist master, Nietzsche lamented that slave morality had replaced the master ideal of classical Greece.

Steiner and Buber both try to philosophize between Marx and Nietzsche.

Most individuals also occasionally have experiences which deserve to be called I–Thou. This wonderfully positive relationship occurs whenever a person responds to someone or something so as to affirm the other being's unique meaning and integrity. The essential core of Buber's I–Thou philosophy is contained, in crystalline form, in the first page of *I and Thou*. The following passage, translated by Walter Kaufman, uses "I–You," but I am convinced that "I–Thou" is so well established in English that it better serves Buber's meaning:

> One basic word is the word pair *I–Thou*. The other basic word
> is the word pair *I–It;* for this basic word is not changed when
> *He* or *She* takes the place of *It*. Thus the I of man [a person]
> is also twofold. For the I of the basic word *I–Thou* is different
> from that in the basic word *I–It*.[7]

Neither people, things, nor events are in themselves either "I–Thou" or "I–It." Rather, persons, things, and events are rendered one way or the other by individual human choices. What Buber calls "words"—"the two basic words a person can speak"—are not necessarily spoken words at all, but are modes of response, kinds of relationships. It is not only the person, thing, or event to

7.   Martin Buber, *I and Thou*, 53.

which I respond that becomes a "Thou" or an "It." I myself as the respondent am essentially different according to my response. Apart from these two definitions or characterizations of self, I am or have no other self. I am what I choose myself to be: Either an I–Thou person or an I–It would-be person. Or, more likely, some combination of these two. By responding to another person in an I–Thou way, I am made whole, personal, human. In the moment of my I–Thou response or relationship, I take myself and that to which I respond into the world of genuine relation, of meeting and dialogue. When I respond from within an I–It attitude, however, neither I nor that to which I respond is affirmed in wholeness, in authentically relational terms.

I–Thou and I–It relations define all reality, even our relationships with God, the Eternal Thou. The Eternal Thou of one moment can be turned into an "It" by anyone who reduces a concept of the divine to a functionary or a warlord, or any other role that suits limited purposes. A husband and wife, parent and child, or any intimate combination, may appear to others, and even to themselves, to be responding to each other in an I–Thou way when in fact one or both of them may be using the other as an "It." Lovers may be rapt in tender embrace, but neither might be I–Thou to each other: one may be doing power and the other self-denial.

The task of creating oneself as a person (and not as a thing that looks like a person) is never fully successful, nor fully and finally a failure. With the existentialist, Buber denies essential human nature: my life, my existence, is given (by my parents and all subsequent influences) but my essence as a person can only be achieved by authentic responses that render both agent and recipient as a Thou. Whereas the world of "It" is ineradicable— we are almost always in "I–It" relations—an I–Thou relationship is like a mystical experience: it does not last but it leaves a profound impact. In a world of objects and restrictions, it is profoundly transformative to break through "It-ness" to mystery, to the unlimited. In person-to-person relations, an I–Thou can reach the level of love, and in fact might be what love essentially is: unqualified, boundless, mysterious affirmation.

In his lecture "The Man of Today and the Jewish Bible" (1926), Buber laments what he considers to be the inability of religion to bring about a new union between spirit and the world, and contrasts this inability with the power of the Hebrew Bible itself to communicate an I–Thou experience. According to Buber, "religion" itself is often part of the detached spirit: "It is one of the subdivisions.... It has lost its unity and so it cannot lead man to inner unity."[8] For Buber, Hebraic faith is essentially an I–Thou relationship. By faith, Buber means "not the so-called faith which is a strange mingling of assumptions and cognitions, but that faith which means trust and loyalty."[9] This is a faith that requires encounter, decision, and deep personal commitment even at the cost of intense suffering. Perhaps the most powerful, and representative figure of this faith in biblical literature is the suffering servant depicted in the book of Job.

In most treatments of the problem of suffering or evil, the victim, whether an individual or a community, can typically be understood as in need of purification, education, or punishment for transgressions. The book of Job excludes such obvious answers, and forces a far more difficult question: Why, as in the case of Job, do the virtuous suffer? In that he is rebuffed not merely by the world around him, but specifically by his friends, his wife, and by the supposedly just God who sends him suffering without explanation of any kind, Job stands as one of the first representatives of existential dread. It seems likely as well that the anonymous author of this book intended Job to represent both the individual and Israel. As this book was almost certainly written during the early years of the Babylonian captivity (587–538 BCE), Job's fate suggests a victim larger than himself:

> Job's question comes into being as the question of a whole generation about the sense of its historic fate. Behind this "I" made so personal here, there stands the "I" of Israel.[10]

---

8. Martin Buber, *Israel and the World,* 90–91.
9. Ibid., 13.
10. Martin Buber, *The Prophetic Faith,* 189.

What answer does God finally supply to Job's impassioned plea to know the cause and meaning of his suffering? According to Buber's interpretation, this great poetic dramata proceeds through a dialectic of four views of God's relationship to human sufferings.

In the first view, presented in two chapters, the author establishes Job's righteousness not only in Job's eyes, but also in the eyes of God. Job is made the test case in a rather unedifying battle of egos between God, who claims Job as a faithful servant, and Satan, who contends that Job will abandon God if given sufficient enticement to do so. The second position is developed by three friends of Job who, in three sets of speeches (chapters 4–14, 15–21, and 22–27), develop the same positions which most of us, if we were Job's friends, would probably bring to him. In the third view, Job exposes the irreconcilability of human justice and God's actions. In the face of this irreconcilability, however, Job resists the temptation to give up on either side. Although Job "is no longer able to have a single faith in God and in justice," he nevertheless clings to both God and justice. This irreconcilability of two values essential for Job's sane survival forces him, and the dialogue, to yet a higher level. In the fourth view Job sends an anguished plea to God, to which God responds by listing His infinite powers as Creator. Thereupon Job confesses: "I despise myself, and repent in dust and ashes" (42:2–6).

Mystery remains, but Job does get an answer to his cry. He doesn't get what he asks for, but he does get what he needs. Buber offers the following interpretive summary of the entire book:

> It is not the revelation in general which is here decisive, but the particular revelation to the individual: the revelation as an *answer* to the individual sufferer concerning the question of his sufferings, the self-limitation of God to a person, answering a person.[11]

In the end, the book of Job holds out the possibility of genuine contact with God, but only at the price of sacrificing the support of both logic and religion. By Job's suffering, and by his steadfast

---

11. Ibid., 195–96.

commitment to the God of faith (as distinct from the God of religious dogmas and belief), he attains a vision of God, and is clearly justified in God's sight. God doesn't answer why there is suffering, or why it frequently comes to the just more than to the unjust, or more particularly, why it came to Job. But God allows Job to see Him spiritually, and be reconciled to Him in peace, love, and wisdom.

Buber does not regard the conclusion of Job as philosophically satisfactory, or experientially comforting. He regards it as the mysterious truth of God's dealing with His Chosen People. In addition to being steeped in the Hebrew Bible and biblical faith, Buber subsequently lived through the horrific "Job" experience of the Holocaust. In introducing the book of Job as the masterpiece which first fashioned the dilemma of human suffering, Buber notes that the question maintains its same terrible, mysterious power in contemporary life. In living his own life as a Jew in twentieth-century Europe, Buber walked a narrow ridge between faith and philosophy, salvation and the dark night of human suffering. He wrote *The Prophetic Faith* in 1949, just a few years after the most devastating "Job" experience in Jewish history. In the face of what appears to be the ultimate absurdity and meaninglessness of the Holocaust, "we feel a touch as of a hand":

> Jeremiah's historical figure, that of the suffering prophet, apparently inspired the poet to compose his song of the man of suffering, who by his suffering attained the vision of god, and in all his revolt was God's witness on earth, as God was his witness in heaven.[12]

The idea of dialogue is central to Buber's account of human relations, and of the ideal relationship between a person and God. Both his philosophy and his religion take dialogue, or the I–Thou relationship, as the ultimate value. Just as a person must be treated as a Thou, so must God be addressed as the Eternal Thou. The history of religions, however, is similar to the history of interpersonal relations in that the Eternal Thou is typically treated as an "It." As Buber writes:

---

12. Ibid., 197.

> If to believe in God means to be able to talk about Him in the third person, then I do not believe in God. If to believe in Him means to be able to talk to Him, then I believe in God. [13]

This passage, and numerous passages like it, reveal Buber's passionate commitment to a God to whom we can speak and responds to us but not a God who can be turned into an object. Moses knew that the face of God cannot be seen; Buber adds that the idea of God cannot be grasped. To render God as an idea is to reduce relationships with God from the I–Thou to I–It. Unlike the individual Thou which "must disappear into the chrysalis of the It in order to grow wings again," the Eternal Thou is ever Itself: The Eternal Thou is Thou by its very nature; only *our* nature forces us to be drawn into the It-world and It-speech." [14] In Buber's I–Thou philosophy, which is also his theology, true God is the Eternal Thou who remains free of "It-ness," mysterious, imminent yet transcendent, and is the other pole of human dialogue. Philosophers and most religious believers, in Buber's view, are well practiced at reducing the Eternal Thou to an object, a force, a supplier of information and solutions within the "It" world. The Bible also records repeated incidents in which the People of the Lord, the people to whom God responded in an I–Thou way, reduced God—in their eyes—to an "It." In contrast to the idea of God generated by endless philosophic disputes, God of the Hebrew Bible is a Presence, a Person who acts and to whom we can speak.

In his book *Between Man and Man*, Buber attempts to apply what he said in his *I and Thou*, "with particular regard to the needs of our time." [15] The conclusion of *Between Man and Man* also serves as an excellent summary of the philosophy of human nature derived from *I and Thou*:

> This course [of lectures, 1938] shows, in the unfolding of the question about the essence of [humanity], that it is by beginning

---

13. Martin Buber, "Autobiographical Fragments," in Paul Arthur Schilpp and Maurice Friedman, eds., *The Philosophy of Martin Buber*, 24.
14. Martin Buber, *I and Thou*, 148.
15. Martin Buber, *Between Man and Man*, xi.

neither with the individual nor with the collectivity, but only with the reality of the mutual relation between [person to person], that this essence can be grasped.[16]

The key term in this text, and in Buber's overall philosophical position, is *between*. By definition, community takes place whenever the between is an I–Thou relation: "The bright edifice of community . . . is the work of the same force that is alive in the relation between man [a person] and God." [17] Community is a holy achievement because it is the realization of the Eternal Thou between persons. Although ecologist Thomas Berry did not frequently mention Buber's I and Thou, Berry's frequently quoted cosmological statement, "the universe is a community of subjects, not a collection of objects," is a restatement of Buber's ideal.

If we understand the force of Buber's I–Thou philosophy, with its emphasis on hallowing everyday existence, we will appreciate both pairs of contrasts which are essential to the meaning of human life: Community as distinct from collectivity, and person as distinct from an isolated individual. In the face of this increasing prevalence of collectivity over community, and strident individualism over genuine personhood, is it reasonable to hope for the survival of Western civilization? In Buber's address, "Hope for this Hour," which he delivered in Carnegie Hall, New York City, in 1952, Buber answered this pressing question:

> Direct, frank dialogue is becoming ever more difficult and more rare; the abysses between man and man [person and person] threaten evermore pitilessly to become unbridgeable. I began to understand at that time, more than 30 years ago, that this is the central question for the fate of mankind [humankind]. Since then I have continually pointed out that the future of man as man [true humanity] depends upon a rebirth of dialogue.[18]

16. Ibid.
17. Martin Buber, *I and Thou*, 155.
18. Martin Buber, *Pointing the Way*, 222.

After a lifetime of personal struggle, which gave him an informed understanding of human inability to realize the Eternal You in everyday life, Buber is nevertheless not without hope:

> At its core the conflict between mistrust and trust of man conceals the conflict between the mistrust and trust of eternity. If our mouths succeed in genuinely saying "Thou," then, after long silence and stammering, we shall have addressed our eternal "Thou" anew. Reconciliation leads towards reconciliation.[19]

C. G. JUNG: ARCHETYPAL HEALER

Sigmund Freud, the brilliant, courageous explorer of the unconscious, demonstrated that every individual is occasionally (and in some cases more than occasionally) controlled by unconscious complexes. Until Freud, there was very little understanding of the causes of or cures for unconscious compulsions. Jung began his equally brilliant career indebted to Freud for having revealed the extent of the influence of the unconscious on all aspects of human life. The extraordinary friendship between Freud and Jung—and its tragic ending—showed some of the same unconscious forces that the two of them were trying to understand and explain. When they met for the first time in 1907 in Vienna, they talked for thirteen hours straight. The early phase of their friendship was promising not only for each of them, but obviously for psychology and Western thought and culture.

At the start of Jung's career, both Jung and Freud probably assumed that their intense collaboration had only superficial differences—country, ethnicity, and a half generation. In fact, however, the differences were deep and would play out with extreme intensity. The two greatest psychologists of the twentieth century were unable to prevent their personal psychologies from overwhelming the collaboration to which they were initially committed. The end of their friendship in 1913, six years after it began as a great intellectual love affair, has all of the characteristics of a Greek tragedy: Freud needed to function as

---

19. Ibid., 229.

the wise-old-man archetype and needed Jung to function as his adopted son. There were also conflicting myths, symbols, and images at work due to Freud being Jewish in deeply anti-Semitic Vienna, and in an emerging profession heavily populated by Jewish psychologists, whereas Jung appeared to be the very essence of Swiss Christianity.

By carefully reading their lives and thoughts we can foresee that Freud would hold to his revolutionary yet rather materialistic worldview while Jung would venture into the spiritual and symbolic realms and return with original insights thoroughly at odds with Freud's most cherished dogmas. It was this word "dogma" that Freud attached to his formulation of the Oedipal complex that prevented Jung from accepting the mantle that Freud was too willing to bestow upon him. The self that Jung sought to heal is the ordinary conscious self, properly called ego, unable to acknowledge both its personal unconscious and the vast and wise collective unconscious. According to Jung, the purpose, meaning, and task of each human life is to bring the ego into creative relationship with Self, the ideal representation of which is the archetype Christ. Jung used the term *individuation* to refer to this lifelong, profoundly challenging task. He brought to the patient—the typical modern person oblivious to the wisdom of archetypes, myths, symbols, and images—his scholarship and deep reflection on the relation of conscious and unconscious realities.

In *Memories, Dreams, Reflections*, the memoir that Jung dictated in the last year of his life, he explains that his life was "not on the surface to see," almost the exact words used by Sri Aurobindo in response to a prospective biographer. Early in this memoir, Jung explained that in retrospect he detected two personalities throughout his life vying to dominate his attention and commitments: Personality One was intellectual, scientific, and practical, while Personality Two was imaginative, artistic, and amenable to the mysterious.[20] Personality Two sought for an explanation for repression and complexes in deep, mysterious realms, and discovered the reality of archetypes, the foundational psychic struc-

20. Carl Jung, *Memories, Dreams, Reflections*, 147.

tures active in cosmic and human consciousness. Jung functioned as Personality One in choosing medicine, Personality Two when observing occult phenomena with his mother, and then combined the two as a lifelong commitment to be physician and as well as a researcher of occult phenomena and esoteric teachings. Like Jung, Steiner lived in two worlds: similar to Jung's Personality Number One he lived in the ordinary world of family, friends, nature, books, science and technology, and similar to Jung's Personality Number Two, he lived in the spiritual world available to him by native clairvoyance.

Just as Steiner at age seven was visited by the ghost of his aunt who had committed suicide, in Jung's childhood and adolescent years he was visited by dreams and visions. In Jung's middle years, and very definitely with the advent of his research concerning his own unconscious, and myth, Personality Two emerged as a full complement, and then a stronger pole, to Personality One. After his break with Freud at age thirty-eight—one year ahead of Steiner's experience of the Cosmic Christ and the beginning of his esoteric career at the age of thirty-one—Jung undertook "a voyage of discovery to the other pole of the world"[21] and dedicated himself to the service of the psyche. While studying the unconscious both in the experience of his patients and what he called his myth, the patterns of his unconscious life, he observed the ability of the unconscious to reveal its secrets in obscure and ingenious ways. *The Red Book,* a masterpiece of art and psychology, on which Jung worked from 1916 to 1930, contains magnificent paintings which depict Jung's deep exploration into his unconscious. He continued this exploration, which was bewildering and terrifying, until 1918 when he "began to emerge from the darkness."[22]

Jung's career as well as his mode of analysis and his approach to healing led him to observe and ultimately to serve the expression of deep psychic structures called archetypes, including the Self, the Shadow, the Mother (as revealed successively by images of Isis, Sophia, Mary), the Wise Old Man, Death and Rebirth,

---

21. Ibid., 189.
22. Ibid., 194.

the Circle, the Mandala, the Tree, the *puer aeternus* (the "eternal boy" who seems, and perhaps strives, not to develop according to his chronological age), and several others. According to Jung archetypes are not directly knowable but they express themselves through myths, symbols, and images. *Arche* in Greek means beginning, the original structure and primal foundation, as in the first line of Genesis, "In the *beginning* God created..." and also the first line of the Prologue to the Gospel of John, "In the *beginning* was the Word...." "*Arche*" is contained in the words *architecture, archeology,* and *archaic.* In Jung's several decades of research concerning psychic influences on human thinking and action, he found images derived from a variety of archetypes.

According to Jung, images expressive of these archetypes can be observed in all cultures, particularly in arts and religions, and other endeavors in which the unconscious is allowed to express itself. Jung was drawn to Egyptian, Greek, and Chinese scriptures and icons, and other ancient texts that reveal powerful images and symbols. While he was determined to be understood as an empirical scientist, because of his ability to access these depth dimensions he was also a Platonist and an esotericist: He conversed with symbolic realities that are similar to the ideal Forms described by Plato and he researched esoteric disciplines such as alchemy. Although Jung was a physician steeped in the worldview of central European intellectuals, and was particularly influenced by the restriction on knowledge established by Kant at the end of the eighteenth century, he was still determined to show that the universe teems with significance, and to do so empirically, without reliance on belief. In so doing, Jung advanced the worldview known as Romanticism which flowered in the nineteenth century in reaction to the brilliant and supremely efficient worldview— yet supremely limited—of the eighteenth-century Enlightenment.

As Jung showed, the whole of humanity, in all cultures until the scientific revolution of the modern West, experienced the universe as alive and communicative, including the heavenly bodies, and the elements of Earth, air, fire, and water. Beginning in seventeenth-century Europe this enchantment was driven out of the cosmos by a worldview that Max Weber in the nineteenth century called "disenchanted." Anyone living within this atom-istic and alienating worldview, that was generated by Descartes and Newton in the seventeenth century and has been dominant in the West at least since the eighteenth century, does not expect to experience the universe as numinous or revelatory. This disen-chanted worldview is self-fulfilling. In contrast, those who live in an enchanted world, live in conscious relation to the creativity of the unconscious and are open to synchronicities, coincidences that are actually suggestions from the unconscious to the con-scious that essentially says "pay attention to this." To live in an enchanted world gives the opportunity to know and care that wakeful messages are sent from a deep and wise source.

Jung's worldview can be understood as Mahayanist and transpersonal: It is as wide and deep as the universe, a path on which nothing prepersonal or transpersonal is lost. In this view, the crucifixion and resurrection of Christ, for example, happened on both the physical–conscious and the unconscious level of psyche. Such events continue to happen in psyche (through myths, symbols, and images) in ways that affect conscious life. This pro-cess takes place most effectively through religion and art, pre-cisely where numinous images are depicted and venerated. In the great divide between secular and esoteric thinking, Jung would seem to occupy a middle position, determined to present himself as a psychiatrist and empirical scientist while at the same time, especially toward the end of his life, to be a courageous explorer of mysterious unconscious depths. Freud knew his younger col-league well when he cautioned Jung not to disappear into the occult. While Jung did not exactly disappear, he did frequently descend into the occult or esoteric, the usually secret and very confusing depths of the unconscious.

Whereas traditional religious believers, particularly of the Abrahamic faiths, almost always characterize their contact with the spiritual in terms of ascent and transcendence, Jung's jour-ney to the unconscious more typically uses depth metaphors. The famous exchange between Jung and Martin Buber might be thought of as a contest between Jung's depth and Buber's tran-scendence. Because these spatial metaphors are used to refer to the invisible and ineffable, they can be misleading as well as revealing. Similarly, synchronistic revelations from the unconscious can be ignored, can be a source of wonder and enlightenment, or they can also be misinterpreted and misused. *Panpsychism*

It is important to recognize that for Jung matter is also psyche (or psyche is also physical). Within the context of his fascination with synchronicity, Jung wrote insightfully on the way that consciousness, particularly the unconscious, affects physical events: The universe speaks wisely through material signs and events. Psyche—including the visible and invisible, spirit and matter, good and evil forces—uses physical as well as mental instruments in order to reveal itself to persons who pay attention. The universe is alive, active, wise, and influential, all the way down (and up) to a non-ordinary level, to dreams and sacred images, to the *I Ching*, tarot cards, astrological transits, and to synchronicities in seemingly ordinary moments of daily life.

As this book is about varieties of Mahayana, numinous, imaginative, etheric, and some other concepts posited against the dominant paradigm, it is therefore also about Jung's concept of synchronicity, one of the most important concepts—and practices—in the worldview that this book is recommending. As a young person I believed in grace; then, during the early adult years when my version of "Personality Number One" was in charge, news from the other side was not readily expected and if sent not much acknowledged. During the decades that I have been reading and teaching Steiner and practicing Anthroposophy, I have come to be increasingly convinced that the line between the divine and human, spiritual and ordinary, is thinner than is typically admitted even by religious believers. The advantage to Jung's account of synchronicity is simply that it joins theory and experience; it is the fruit of his Personality One and Personality Two working in harmony.

In a similar way, and with great effect, Richard Tarnas, a scholarly and highly intuitive exponent of the Jungian worldview, has fused his own version of the two personalities. Following his masterful *Passion of the Western Mind* (1991), in *Cosmos and Psyche: Intimations of a New Worldview* (2006),

Tarnas explains and supports a cosmology based primarily on Jungian archetypes. Tarnas shows that synchronicity is one of the surest keys to unlock the secrets of Jung's research into the unconscious. Just as it is typical for individuals to experience I–Thou and I–It experiences before having the names for them, it is almost certain that synchronicity names a host of experiences in search of a name and explanation. Jung's writing on synchronicity helps us to understand a host of common experiences, and twelve pages in Richard Tarnas's *Cosmos and Psyche* provide a clear and insightful account of the worldview that both sustains Jung's theory and introduce anyone to a new awareness and a new set of relationships.

As Tarnas shows, to believe in synchronicity is a worldview changer: If one is convinced of Jungian synchronicity, the world really is different from what the dominant paradigm claims. Synchronicity—the meaningful, revelatory, interplay between the unconscious and conscious, between depth and surface, between the universe and one individual—renders the cosmos wise and worthy of a person's attention. A genuine synchronicity—it must be admitted that the line between genuine synchronicity and interesting coincidence is not obvious—requires close attention and integrity. Like contemporary accounts of karma and rebirth, synchronicity lends itself to inflation and nonsense as well as to an enchanted universe. But synchronicities do happen, as when, in the correct state of mind, we consult the *I Ching* or research the intimate analogical relationships between planets and human affairs. We can also think of a synchronicity as the poem or sonata written by the universe, fortunately heard by an awake person. Music and poetry would seem to be obvious examples of this phenomenon: musical and poetic images are "there" to be reached by anyone possessing and developing the capacity to do so.

At the very least, a synchronicity is an "aha," a jump from ordinary to non-ordinary consciousness. A genuine synchronicity warrants a "Wow, thank you for that!" But a person with a disenchanted worldview who notices what appears to be an interesting, even startling coincidence will let this moment, pregnant with meaning, pass without a "wow" or a "thank you." Note Emerson in his "Self Reliance":

> A man [person] should learn to detect and watch that gleam of light which flashes across his mind from within, more than the luster of the firmament of bards and sages. Yet he [or she] dismisses without notice his thought, because it is his.[23]

Of course, Emerson was one of the first to recognize and publicize that the gleam of light that belongs to each of us comes from Light, from the Absolute Mind, universe, and the unconscious. As Owen Barfield, in the conclusion of his own favorite book, *Unancestral Voice*: in contrast to thought from the memory it is possible to have thoughts that are "your substance and your life; so that to perceive them is verily to perceive the spirit within you in the act of creating." [24] "The spirit within you" is what communicates synchronistically. It makes all the difference whether someone is convinced that the universe does in fact communicate insights and meaningful hints, or whether the universe is cold, exclusively material, silent, and disinterested, in which case a synchronicity will not happen, or will happen to no avail.

For Jung, the central source of meaning and wisdom, at least for Western humanity throughout most of its history, has been the archetypal life of Christ. He writes, "What happens in the life of Christ happens always and everywhere. In the Christian archetype all lives of this kind are prefigured."[25] Like Steiner, Jung sees Christ as the archetype of the Self and the exemplar of human development; unlike Steiner, Jung does not focus particularly on Krishna or Buddha, or on archangels. Jung's account of archetypes might seem at first to be luxurious or quaint, perhaps a pastime for introverted intellectuals. Yet he shows that just the opposite is true: Paying attention to archetypes, whether the Self or

---

23. Ralph Waldo Emerson, "Self-reliance," quoted in Gertrude Reif Hughes, "Hearing Steiner's Anthroposophy in Emerson's Prophetic Voice," in Robert McDermott, ed., *American Philosophy and Rudolf Steiner*, 6.

24. Owen Barfield, *Unancestral Voice*, 162.

25. C. G. Jung, *Psychology and Religion*, in *Psychology and Religion: West and East*, para. 146.

Christ, archetypes of unity, or of personal development, is crucial for the healing and development of individuals and culture.

In less than two weeks, following a severe liver illness, Jung wrote *Answer to Job* (1951), an intensely personal essay on the book of Job. As Jung wrote to his friend Henri Corbin, "I felt as if I were listening to a great composition, or rather a concert. The whole thing was an adventure that befell me, and I hurried to write it down."[26] He wrote in order to convince Jewish and Christian theologians to abandon their view that God is all-good while evil is the work of humanity. He wrote as a physician and on behalf of his patients whose suffering seemed to him to be compounded by a theological view he considered psychologically mistaken and harmful. In every respect this book was intended to be an answer to Job's anguished questions to God concerning the suffering that, it seemed, God poured on him particularly, and an answer to why Yahweh/God not only allows but also inflicts suffering on individuals and groups. Writing in 1951 Jung had to be intensely aware of World War II and the Holocaust which ended only six years prior. Similarly, Buber's discussion of Job appears in a chapter aptly titled "The God of the Sufferers" in his book, *The Prophetic Faith* (1949).

After many years of reflection and discussion with Christian colleagues, Jung had concluded that evil, equally with good, is not only derived from God but an essential part of God's nature. Using traditional Jewish and Christian terminology for the personification of evil, Jung argues that Satan is parallel to Christ and as much as Christ, Satan is a son of God. Like Buber, Jung treats the book of Job as though it were telling a true story in which Yahweh actually made a bet with Satan for the loyalty of a virtuous soul. Jung goes beyond Buber in arguing that Job is morally superior to God, and Job needs God, God needs Job and humanity even more. Jung writes: Yahweh "needs Job's loyalty, and it means so much to him that he shrinks at nothing in carrying out his test."[27]

Jung's argument, replete with passion and sarcasm, is aimed primarily against the *privatio boni* theory attributed to St.

26. Carl Jung, quoted in Gerhard Wehr, *Jung: A Biography*, 382.
27. Carl Jung, *Answer to Job*, para. 604.

Augustine that essentially says that God is by definition all good, and so all forms of evil and suffering are necessarily the privation of God and outside of God. St. Augustine was arguing against the worldview of the Manicheans that divided reality, including God, into darkness and light, or evil and good. Jung's position is very close to, and perhaps identical with, the Manichean position that Augustine opposed. Jung essentially says that the God image depicted in the book of Job, and as understood almost uniformly by Jewish and Christian thinkers, leaves the nature of God and the cause of evil unanswered. We have to admit that Buber, despite having intense personal reasons to find a satisfactory answer to suffering and its relation to the destiny of Israel, also left the mystery of Job unsolved. Buber concludes that Job's suffering did lead Job to see God, which is perhaps a sufficient explanation for God's behavior and Job's suffering, but the nature and motives of God remain mysterious. Jung essentially replies that the nature of God is less mysterious once we understand that God includes evil as much as good. We should not be surprised when God condones evil and suffering, both of which issue from God's own nature.

In later sections of his *Answer to Job* Jung suggests that the problem of God's nature that the book of Job leaves unanswered is answered by the incarnation of Christ, who combines both divinity and humanity and offsets Satan. (This solution, of course, would not be attractive to Buber.) By Jung's account, God the Father and the whole of creation is divided between two warring divine beings, Christ and Satan. To some extent Jung builds his case on the writings of Clement of Rome, the first-century Christian theologian:

> Clement of Rome taught that God rules the world with a right and a left hand, the right being Christ, the left Satan. Clement's view is clearly monotheistic, as it unites the opposites in one God. Later Christianity, however, is dualistic, inasmuch as it splits off one half of the opposites, personified in Satan, and he is eternal in his state of damnation.[28]

---

28. Ibid., 357–158.

As is evident in the history of philosophy, there are many dualisms, not all of which can be avoided. Jung has avoided the dualism between God and evil but he has not avoided the dualism inside God, one which is eternal, because God is eternal.

RUDOLF STEINER ON LUCIFER, AHRIMAN, AND CHRIST

Steiner sees Christ as the solution to the double problem of evil and suffering. Christ is the balance between the two tempters Lucifer and Ahriman. Christ evolves, or ascends by means of the struggle against these tempters. According to the New Testament account, Christ was tempted by Satan three times but according to Steiner, the first temptation was by Lucifer, the second was by Ahriman, and the third was by both Lucifer and Ahriman.

Both by his clairvoyance experience and exoteric research, Steiner understood the mysterious function of evil primarily in terms of two tempters in a polar relationship: Lucifer, the tempter on behalf of spiritual presumption, and Ahriman the tempter on behalf of a "nothing but" reductionism. Neither Lucifer nor Ahriman are evil per se; they indirectly serve freedom and love. Steiner states: "The gods who further the progress of evolution surrendered their omnipotence to Lucifer in order that human beings might become free." God "shared wisdom and might with Lucifer and Ahriman." [29] Whereas Ahriman has worked against individualism of any kind, and in favor of inhuman collectivism, Lucifer has worked for individualism, but one that is entirely selfish:

> [Humanity was] in a state of union, then one of separateness as a consequence of the luciferic principle that promotes selfishness and independence. Together with selfishness, evil came into the world. It had to, because without evil humanity could not take hold of the good.[30]

With wars, torture, rape, conquest, and psychological abuse in every dimension of human life, throughout all of human

---

29. Rudolf Steiner, "Universal Religion: The Meaning of Love," in *Religion: An Introductory Reader*, 194.
30. Ibid., 200.

history and perhaps with little prospect of its diminishment, this method of realizing the good certainly appears to be a regrettable arrangement. Is this the best that God and the Hierarchies could devise?

Steiner definitely does not recommend any of the horrible forms of suffering that befall the innocent; he spent his life trying to eradicate suffering. He was convinced, however, that evil and suffering, both as component and means of human destiny, make possible all that is good in human life. For Steiner, the goal of human life, individually and collectively, is love, but love is only possible over against its opposites, fear and hatred. Steiner lectured frequently on obstacles to spiritual striving. One obstacle is presumption to which humanity is led by Lucifer and his legions. Anyone under Lucifer's influence feels he or she needn't show up on time, pay taxes, practice safe sex, visit the sick, bury the dead, care for a child or the elderly, or listen to someone who is boring. We feel ourselves to be among the saved, the enlightened, and need not meet any ordinary responsibilities. The Luciferic temptation leads humanity to think that all is well, and especially I am well, deeply spiritual and therefore free of the need to care for the material world. Because of our assumed special spiritual status by virtue of our religion or spiritual practice, we are led to think that God will care for the suffering; it is for me, educated and chosen, to enjoy and exemplify God's grace landing on my work and my relationships, exactly as it should. By the Luciferic temptation I allow myself to think that if I were God I would have done the same—that God should heap blessings on me and less so on others makes perfect sense, is the kind of good judgment we can expect from God.

Ahriman's influence, almost the exact reverse of Lucifer's and at the present time far more powerful, leads us to think that there is no enlightenment because there is no spirit, no height, no depth, nothing numinous or sacred. There is nothing but the physical: human life is all money, sex, and power. Steiner says many times that as evidenced by its disenchanted cosmology, alienated psychology, nihilistic philosophy, and idolatrous religions, the modern West is deeply under the influence of Ahriman's "nothing but"

perspective. By having given Steiner the task to oppose materialist thinking Steiner's Master set him on a direct confrontation
course with Ahriman. But, of course, Steiner was not alone in
opposing Ahrimanic forces that are operating so powerfully in
the modern world. Billions of Asian and Western religious believers, as well as the ideals and practices of Dorothy Day, Buber,
Tagore, Sri Aurobindo, Teilhard, the Dalai Lama, Amma, Joanna
Macy, and scores of other spiritually striving souls are devoted to
thwarting the power of Ahriman, though they seldom identified
it as such. But more than most spiritual teachers and traditional
religions, Steiner seems to have had a special knowledge of Lucifer and Ahriman and their works.

While the Goetheanum was burning to the ground, the *Representative of Humanity*, Steiner's unfinished thirty-foot wood
sculpture, was housed in a separate building nearby. It depicts
two tempers: on one side, Lucifer luring humanity away from
matter, and thereby away from humanity's fundamental task
to transform matter into spirit; and on the other side, Ahriman,
sclerotic and deadening, leading humanity away from spirit. In
the center is Christ, the Logos, Light Being, holding the balance
between matter and spirit. In Steiner's opinion, Christ entered
human hearts and proved the reality of love. When a centurion
pierced His side and He bled into Earth, Christ performed a
homeopathic, alchemical deed. According to Steiner, for all time
Christ has prevented Lucifer and Ahriman from gaining total
domination over the evolution of human consciousness. Humanity is intended to evolve from bondage to freedom as well as from
lethargy to love, but the Luciferic and Ahrimanic beings have
proven very effective in throwing humanity off course. The self
and the universe are filled with Christ—but they are also under
the influence of Lucifer's unrealism (all is well, no need to strive)
and Ahriman's hyper-realism (there is no reason to strive because
there is no sacred source, guide, or goal; there is no sacred anything). Anthroposophy can be understood as a call to join this
battle on the side of Christ (love and balance) against Lucifer and
Ahriman, the tempters who, while not evil, brilliantly unbalance
individuals and humanity.

Rudolf Steiner's Representative of Humanity

CONCLUSION

This conclusion offers my assessment of the contributions by Martin Buber, C G. Jung, and Rudolf Steiner concerning the concept of God in relation to the reality of evil and suffering. Buber sees the combination of evil and suffering as a mysterious instrument by which an individual can enter into dialogue with God. Jung sees evil at every level, including divinity itself. Steiner sees evil primarily in terms of two tempters, Lucifer and Ahriman who, while incomparably effective in their strategies against human evolution, are nevertheless ultimately subordinate to divinity, specifically, to the Trinity Father (Ground of Being); Son (Logos, Word); Holy Spirit.

Buber counters Jung's conception of psyche with a traditional theism. For Buber, the God of the Hebrew scriptures is real, is the Creator, is absolute, and is all good, to which Jung responds that the God of the Bible is a God-image that needs to be understood in the context of psyche. For Buber, Yahweh is the transcendent ultimate, and therefore the creator of psyche. Psyche was created by God and is certainly not the creator of God. For Jung, psyche is primary, generates and holds archetypes, including the image of God. Buber and Jung considered their respective worldviews to be antidotes to the poverty of Western religious experience and religious thinking. Buber made a case for a God worth worshiping and addressing in dialogue; Jung made a case for psyche within which human experience can deepen and the human person can attain individuation.

But for Buber and for all three Abrahamic religions God did not come to be, least of all through psyche. In a famous filmed interview, Jung exclaimed that he knew that God exists. Later, he explained that he should have said that he knew the God-image exists, an expression of what he understood to be God. The difference between Jung and Buber, or between Jung's position and theism, is that Jung is writing as a depth psychologist, not as a theologian or philosopher. For Buber, and for everyone nurtured on the Abrahamic worldview, there is God and whatever God created—universe, Earth, especially humanity, and a history of relationships between God and people, and between groups and individual people. As Buber focuses on the between—God and His people, Jung also focuses on the between of the conscious and unconscious, between the ego and Self. Jung doesn't deny (or affirm) the Abrahamic worldview but he essentially says (and warns) that it misses most of the great drama that is revealed in religion and art—the infinitely varied world of archetypes that resides in the unconscious and expresses itself through myths, symbols, images, and synchronicities.

The key to unlocking the treasures of Jung's thought, and to avoid fairly common misinterpretations, is to keep in mind that everything, absolutely everything, is or is in psyche. If Jung's concept of psyche were not plural we could say that it is the same as the Hindu Brahman, the Chinese Tao, or the Godhead of the Abrahamic religions. Because Steiner and Jung are both empiricists (strictly adhering to their own experience instead of an abstract system), and phenomenologists (attentive to phenomena, what actually happens), they both focus on specific contents, specific images and ideas. For Steiner, the Trinity (Ground of Being, Logos, and Spirit) is the ultimate ontological reality such that whatever exists does so by virtue of the Trinity. Jung also affirms the Christian Trinity—and he also views psyche as the ultimate ontological category. This might mean that for Jung, psyche, a psychological term, and Trinity, a Christian theological term, are phenomenologially coextensive. Both are "pluralized"—psyche by archetypes, myths, and symbols, Trinity by the Father, Son, and Holy Spirit.

The mature expression of Jung's spiritual insights did not emerge until the 1930s, after Steiner's death in 1925, and Jung did not reveal a full spiritual and esoteric worldview comparable to Steiner's until the 1950s. Jung's exploration of the occult that led to his break with Freud in 1913 should have been sufficient to put him and Steiner in contact. In his practice, Jung reportedly treated many anthroposophic patients. Despite the many important topics and tasks that Steiner and Jung shared, they all but ignored each other. Steiner perhaps did not know of Jung's work on myth and archetypes beginning in 1913 but Jung knew of Steiner's work throughout the last several decades of his life. One of the anthroposophists with whom Jung knew well was his cousin Ernest Fiechter (1875–1948), the architect of Jung's home in Kusnacht, a student of Steiner himself, and in later life a priest of the Christian Community. Nevertheless, in 1935 Jung wrote: "I have already read a few books by Steiner and must confess that I have not found anything in them that would be of any use to me at all."[31] In the same letter he wrote concerning anthroposophists and theosophists:

> I have also become acquainted with very many anthroposophists and theosophists and have always found to my regret that these people imagine all kinds of things and assert all kind of things for which they are incapable of producing any proof at all.[32]

It is not clear what Jung would have counted as proof, but in his own writing he argues against proof required by science in favor of the proof provided by direct spiritual experience. Jung's dismissal of Steiner resembles the dismissal of Jung by many dominant paradigm thinkers who cannot imagine a world beyond the senses, or a wise unconscious teeming with wise messages to be received by the psychologically and spiritually attentive.

Like Jung, Steiner was a healer of modern Western consciousness, but whereas Jung focused on the relationship between the conscious and the unconscious by way of archetypes and their representation in myths, symbols, images, Steiner focused on higher levels of thinking and relationships to exalted beings. While we should avoid taking spatial metaphors literally, it nevertheless can be said that Jung focused on the relationship between surface and depth (the deep unconscious) whereas Steiner focused on the relation between surface and height, as in the reality of the nine Hierarchies, as well as higher beings such as Krishna, Buddha, Christ, Sophia, and the Archangel Michael. The question, "how far up, or how deep, do you want to go?" can be addressed equally to Jung and Steiner. They both offer sage advice to local,

---

31. Gerhard Wehr, *Jung: A Biography*, 466.
32. Quoted in Wehr, 466.

personal, timely problems based on a deep and vast understanding of a numinous and mysterious Universe. They seem to me the largest and deepest thinkers in this book, and among the largest and deepest of the last hundred years—along with, of course, Sri Aurobindo, Teilhard de Chardin, and His Holiness the Dalai Lama. Buber, Jung, and Steiner were trying to lead Western humanity from disenchantment to the life-sustaining noumenal realm which Buber identifies as God, Jung as the unconscious, and Steiner as Trinity, Hierarchies, and many exalted beings.

Mahatma Gandhi; Dorothy Day
Rev. Martin Luther King, Jr.; Archbishop Desmond Tutu

8

SOCIAL JUSTICE

MAHATMA GANDHI AND HIS LEGACY: GANDHI'S EXPERIMENTS WITH TRUTH

In the eighteenth century India was still divided, as it had been for many centuries, by more than a dozen languages and cultures, rather like Europe at the present time. As there was no central Indian government, it was easy for Britain to create the East India Company in several Indian states. Soon after, the British began building roads to transport products, then they protected their trade routes with armed guards, then they established English language schools. By the mid-nineteenth century, during the reign of Queen Victoria, the only government of India was the British government. Like many Indians of middle and upper middle class, in his early twenties, Mohandas Gandhi went (or rather was sent by his uncles) to London to study law. With his newly awarded law degree, he went to South Africa to join an enormous Indian community that had established its socioeconomic and rights status approximately midway between the ruling white minority and the virtually enslaved native black majority. Gandhi, his wife Kasturba, and his four children lived in South Africa for twenty-one years, from 1893 to 1914.

In 1894 Gandhi read Tolstoy's *The Kingdom of God is Within You*, a passionate critique of class privilege (by a person who maintained the extraordinary privileges of his wealth and class). Gandhi advocated particularly on behalf of servants and lower-class workers who were required to clean the human waste of their employers. This experience led Gandhi to begin a campaign for equality in sanitation, which he espoused and practiced for the rest of his life—unlike Tolstoy who simultaneously lamented and indulged his life of luxury. Sanitation reform remained an important part not only of Gandhi's campaign on behalf of the indentured class of Indians in South Africa, but also on behalf of the Untouchables in India.

One of Gandhi's major life-defining experiments (of which he had many) began immediately upon his return to South Africa in 1906. Although he was a lawyer and he had a first-class train ticket on his way from Durban to Johannesburg, he was evicted because the first-class compartments were reserved for "whites only." As he sat in the cold train station through the night, he experienced an example of the discrimination endured daily by large groups of Indians both in South Africa and India. In response to these and countless other abuses that he and the Indian community suffered in a society governed by British and Dutch whites, he developed *satyagraha*, the principles of nonviolence that would govern his thought and behavior for the remainder of his life. *Satya* means truth, as in accuracy, but also the correct way; *agraha* means "enthusiasm" or "positive will."

At the beginning of his experiment, Gandhi used the terms *satyagraha* and *passive resistance* synonymously, but eventually discarded *passive resistance* because he insisted that conflict must lead to reconciliation and even to love. Furthermore, *satyagraha* requires a willingness to suffer for one's opposition. Gandhi launched a strategic campaign on behalf of hundreds of thousands of disenfranchised Indians living in South Africa. Admittedly, he did not work on behalf of the black majority, all of whom were far more oppressed than the Indian South Africans. He founded the Natal Indian Congress and the periodical *Indian Opinion* as a means of informing Indians of his campaign—and of his opinions on a wide range of topics. This was the beginning of Gandhi-led *satyagraha*, which can be summarized as follows:

1. Means and ends are inseparable. Dignity of all persons in a dispute, including one's oppressors, must be respected as a means to a solution and equally to the creation of a cooperative

society. It is not acceptable to say, for example, one must break a few eggs to make an omelet if "eggs" refers to people.

2. Injustices, whether specific deeds or an entire system, can be viewed as evil but one's enemies must be viewed as prospective collaborators. Conversion from opponent to ally happened countless times in Gandhi's career as a *satyagrahi*, including in his relationship with the white government of South Africa and British Government of India.

3. *Satyagraha,* truth force, is not merely a solution to a particular problem; it is a way of life, an approach to all problems and to all relationships.

After developing his philosophy of nonviolence for more than a dozen years in South Africa, Gandhi returned to India and joined the movement for independence from British rule. By the time the West came to know Gandhi on his arrival in India he had been developing his philosophy of *satyagraha* (truth force) with considerable success. It was soon clear to the leaders of the Independence movement as well as to the British rulers of India that Gandhi was a leader of unusual ability. Surely the Indians, and perhaps some of the British, must have seen that this newly returned moral and political leader was a kind of Arjuna, the warrior in the ancient civil war whose depression while on the firing line at the beginning of a civil war elicited profound revelation from the god Krishna. Gandhi was deeply influenced by the Bhagavad Gita, particularly its teaching of selfless action, but unlike Sri Aurobindo, Gandhi did not believe that Krishna actually instructed Arjuna to fight. At the moment of his assassination, the Mahatma cried to Ram, the god who proceeded Krishna in the line of avatars that manifest Vishnu in human history.

The difference between Gandhi and the Arjuna of the Bhagavad Gita, of course, is that we know nothing of Arjuna's biography, not even whether he was historical or fictional, whereas we have information concerning every day of the last thirty-five years of Gandhi's life, from his arrival in India in 1914 until he was assassinated in 1949. In addition to Gandhi's great works, we also know about his foibles and errors of judgment. However tempting it might be for some to focus on the negative aspects of his biography, it is important to remember and learn from his astonishing accomplishments and heroic virtue under fire. It is also important to keep in mind Gandhi's radical attempt to discover all principles of moral action by his own experience. This devotion to his "experiments with truth" (the exact title of his autobiography), is the more remarkable considering his modest and seemingly unpromising early life. Given his early life, it is surely amazing that as an adult he would be admired worldwide as Mahatma, "great soul."

Mohandas Karamchand (M. K.) Gandhi was born in 1869 in Gujarat, in northwest India. His mother was extremely pious, as much a Jain as a Hindu; his father was a government official and already in middle age when Mohandas was born. Gandhi could as accurately (though not as felicitously) have entitled his autobiography "my battles with the white rulers of South Africa, with the British rulers of India, with the enforcers of the caste system, with all instances of entrenched power and injustice"— and perhaps especially "my battles with myself." He won many of the battles he fought, but at least one, his relationship to his own sexuality, he mostly lost. This particular battle began when he was thirteen and married to Kasturba, his wise and saintly wife. On the night his father died, while Mohandas, age thirteen, was responsible for his father's care, he neglected his duty while enjoying sex with Kasturba. Mohandas's extreme moral sensitivity, not to say scrupulosity, took hold and seems not to have left him even in his last years.

It is inviting to argue either for or against a consideration of the failings or inconsistencies of a great figure—and Gandhi, like Tolstoy, is clearly a great figure with conspicuous failings. By contrast, there is very little criticism of Nelson Mandela, Archbishop Tutu, or the Dalai Lama. I have been looking in vain for blind spots and character flaws in Rudolf Steiner. Far more than any of these individuals, some of whom do not recommend their lives at all, Gandhi presented his life as his work with no separation of his thought and behavior, including especially sex. Consequently, it is justified, and perhaps necessary, to attend to his failings in precisely those parts of his life which he presented himself as a model.

Gandhi also seems not to have understood that his immediate family—Kasturba and four sons—needed as well as deserved more attention from him than other members of the ashram of which he was the leader and teacher. By giving his wife scarce attention and considerable ill treatment, and by giving his sons the same amount and quality of attention that he gave to other children, Gandhi proves a painful example of the price sometimes paid by the families of those who devote their lives to large social issues. Further, Gandhi experimented with minimal inherited assumptions, and without the positive influence of his culture and his well-adapted colleagues. Gandhi's inspiring development and continuing importance are due primarily to his resistance to the working assumptions and commitments of virtually everyone around him, British and Indian, mill owners and workers alike, in favor of his own unique thinking and experimentation. Unfortunately, some of his "experiments with truth" show that Gandhi was not very sensible or sensitive. This is regrettable in that he intended his life to be his mission and his message.

A full account of Gandhi's struggles with sex would include his relationship with a male architect, Hermann Kallenbach, with whom he lived for approximately eighteen months. In his careful study, *Great Soul: Mahatma Gandhi and His Struggle with India*, Joseph Lelyveld does not conclude whether Gandhi's relationship with Hermann Kallenbach was sexual but he provides more than ample evidence that it was intensely erotic. Gandhi had taken a vow of celibacy in 1904, as a result of which he and Kasturba began to sleep separately; their four sons were born 1888 to 1900. In 1910 Gandhi and Kallenbach founded Tolstoy farm and began to live together. At the outset of World War I Gandhi sailed for India and Kallenbach, with a German passport, was prevented from entering India. The two men did not meet again until 1937, by which time Kallenbach was a committed Zionist living in Palestine.

Gandhi continued his battle with sexual desires throughout his life. In his sixties he caused his colleagues and followers consternation by arranging for his great-niece Manu to sleep next to him on his mat, both of them in little or no clothing. Gandhi intended that this "experiment," which he did not hide from the countless people around him day and night, would provide him with the challenge of controlling his erotic desires. He was convinced that his success would contribute to his own resolve and that of his followers committed to the chastity vow as part of *satyagraha* discipline. He seems to have had no awareness of the impact of this experiment on Manu or of the extent to which the experiment would detract from his mission.

However regrettable the negative aspects of his biography, Gandhi clearly stands out in the twentieth century as an example, however imperfect, of what Steiner means by an ethical individual, a person who begins a new chain of moral events. Again and again Gandhi alone had the belief, and the courage to act on the belief, that entrenched social, political, and moral thinking and practices could be challenged and replaced. He repeatedly showed that a better way was possible, and worth sacrificing for. He offered many original and just solutions, and offered to suffer the cost of such innovation on behalf of justice. He stayed on the nonviolent firing line throughout his adult life and in the end showed the world that his experiments were largely successful. As we know from the nonviolent leadership of Martin Luther King, Jr., Archbishop Desmond Tutu, His Holiness the Dalai Lama, and Aung San Suu Kyi, Gandhi's life and ideals are clearly worthy of imitation.

Gandhi was not without his opponents and detractors. Not surprisingly, in the 1930s Winston Churchill referred to him as a "half-naked fakir." During World War II at a meeting of the war cabinet Churchill remarked to Jan Christian Smuts, British Lieutenant Governor of South Africa, "You are responsible for all our troubles in India. You had Gandhi for years and did not do away with him." To which Smuts replied, "When I put him in prison he made a pair of slippers for me." When Gandhi went on a hunger strike during World War II, Churchill told the cabinet, "Gandhi should not be released on the account of a mere threat of fasting. We should be rid of a bad man and an enemy of the Empire if he died."[1]

---

1. For Winston Churchill on Gandhi see Louis Fischer, ed., *The Essential Gandhi*, 264–265 and 344.

Sri Aurobindo considered Gandhi to be an insignificant community organizer with neither the knowledge nor the vision to lead India. He considered nonviolence to be unrealistic and counterproductive in response to supernatural evil forces working through susceptible human beings, most particularly the Nazis and their allies who were attempting to control Europe and perhaps the world. Whereas Gandhi focused on the first three chapters of the Bhagavad Gita, the chapters in which Krishna teaches Arjuna the lessons of selfless action, Aurobindo considered selfless action, or *karma yoga*, to be important for civil work but only one of four yogas, along with knowledge, devotion, and meditation. Aurobindo focused particularly on Krishna's revelation in chapters 9 to 11 of his transcendent divinity. It could be said that Gandhi aligned himself with Arjuna while Aurobindo aligned himself with Krishna. Except in their opposition to the British rule of India, Gandhi and Sri Aurbindo, two of the most important Indian spiritual teachers of the first half of the twentieth century, completely failed to appreciate each other.

Among the countless tributes to Gandhi, Einstein's stands out: "Generations to come, it may be, will scarce believe that such a one as this ever in flesh and blood walked upon this earth."[2] But the most important and lasting tribute to Gandhi is the inspiring activists who have led major nonviolent campaigns against repressive governments using Gandhian principles of nonviolence.

DIETRICH BONHOFFER

Dietrich Bonhoeffer (1906–1945), a German Lutheran minister, provides an instructive example of the practice of Christian discernment. In the early 1930s, amidst intense struggle with the rise of Nazism, Bonhoeffer felt increasingly drawn to India. He wrote to Gandhi, asking if he could spend several months sitting at his feet and sharing in his pattern of daily life. Bonhoeffer wanted to form a monastic community in Germany—he believed the future of the German church depended on it—and planned to use Gandhi as his model, including Gandhi's commitment to community

---

2. Albert Einstein in Ibid., 269.

living, ascetic practices, nonviolent resistance, and the ethics of the Sermon on the Mount. In a letter dated 1934, Bonhoeffer describes his eagerness to learn from Gandhi:

> It sometimes seems to me that there's more Christianity in [India's] 'heathenism' than in the whole of our Reich Church. Christianity did in fact come from the East originally, but it has become so Westernised and so permeated by civilized thought that, as we can now see, it is almost lost to us.[3]

In India, Bonhoeffer discerned the work of Christ. And this discernment was simultaneously an experience of judgment. The authentic 'Christianity' of a Hindu community became a mirror in which the Western church could perceive its own profligacy and degradation. Bonhoeffer did not wish to become a Hindu, nor was he interested in anything resembling interfaith dialogue. It is rather his exclusive commitment to Christ that drove him to Gandhi. He discerned Christ's way in Gandhi; while the church crumbled to ruins all around him, Bonhoeffer perceived Jesus Christ living and active in India, and so he resolved to seek Christ there, to learn from the 'heathens' what it would mean to become a disciple of Christ.

DOROTHY DAY

Dorothy Day (1897–1980), a convert to Roman Catholicism, was an American journalist, cofounder of The Catholic Worker, a servant of the poor, and a friend and collaborator of several Catholic pacifists, including Thomas Merton and the Berrigan brothers, Daniel and Philip, both priests. Dorothy Day saw the divine in the poor, the voiceless, the disadvantaged, and in all those controlled or manipulated by the powerful—by which she usually meant the state, the wealthy, and to some extent, the Catholic Church. Dorothy Day and Thomas Merton quoted Gandhi in their opposition to the Vietnam War.

On the recommendation of George Schuster, editor of *Commonweal*, the liberal Catholic weekly magazine, Peter Maurin

---

3.   Dietrich Bonhoeffer, *London, 1933–1935*, 152.

came into Day's life in 1932. At that time, she was thirty-five, a single mother, and living in lower Manhattan. Peter gave her an introductory lecture on economics and the New Testament, particularly Jesus's exemplary love for the poor and marginal. Day had written for *The Masses*, and for several other Communist newspapers and magazines. Within six months she and Peter Maurin founded and edited a newspaper called *The Catholic Worker*.

Maurin and Day learned from Karl Marx that very few people control the resources of the world, and the ways that this imbalance decisively works against the majority. Whereas Hegel thought that consciousness creates and guides institutions, such as political and financial institutions, Marx reversed Hegel: He argued that institutions control people's consciousness or worldview. Through her study, Day, like Gandhi, King, and other social and moral reformers, realized a deep truth: institutions do influence consciousness, but consciousness also influences institutions. Both need to be transformed simultaneously, in concert with the other. Consciousness decisively affects what people consider to be ideal, and possible, and institutions determine what people are able to accomplish.

In her autobiography, *A Harsh and Dreadful Love*, Dorothy Day quotes a passage from Dostoyevsky's *The Brothers Karamazov*: when a woman explains to Father Zozima that she needs gratitude as a repayment for the love she gives, Father Zosima replies: "Just love people. Just give and you will see that you come alive and that you are a person instead of just a possessor," to which the woman replies, "But people are so ungrateful and I could not do it if I did not get some gratitude in return." Father Zosima answers with the words that Dorothy Day repeated many times:

> Love in action is a harsh and dreadful thing compared to love in dreams. Love in dreams is greedy for immediate action, rapidly performed and in the sight of all. People would give their lives if only the ordeal does not last long but is soon over. We are all looking on and applauding as though on the stage. But active love is labor and fortitude and for some

people, too, perhaps a complete science, but I predict that just when you see with horror that in spite of all your efforts you are getting further from your goal instead of nearer to it, at that very moment you will reach and behold clearly the miraculous power of the Lord who has been all the time loving and mysteriously guiding you.[4]

In the case of Dorothy Day, one has the sense that she is being lovingly and mysteriously guided by a divine wisdom. Although her life was full of woe and loneliness, she was capable of deep insight concerning life and love. It is easy to make a similar observation concerning each of the great servants of nonviolence, justice, and peace. While it is difficult to explain how Gandhi evolved from such a little life to one so vast in wisdom and influence, it is also possible to discern a special karmic guidance that made him possible. Similarly, it is surprising that Dorothy Day would evolve from a middle-class professional to a person of deep Catholic faith with an inexhaustible devotion to the poor. It seems that she emerges as a person following a higher, or deeper, self. Dorothy Day's only friends were the poor or suffering, and those committed to serving the poor and suffering. She wrote essays and opinion pieces every week, along with two memoirs, and like Gandhi and King, learned from the push of events what she thought and what to write. Her writings record her lived experiences of injustice and violence, and occasional triumphs over each. Day's *Catholic Worker* was a way of pulling together quotations from Jesus, Tolstoy, Gandhi, Merton, and Emmanuel Mounier the French Catholic Marxist.

Like Gandhi, who spent six years in jail during the forty-five years that he led nonviolent protests, and like King who was jailed many times during the twelve years of his civil rights leadership before he was assassinated at age thirty-nine, Day was also arrested many times during her years of protest against oppression of the poor. Throughout the lives of Gandhi, Day, and King, whether marching, writing, fighting injustice, serving the voiceless, or unjustly jailed, these activists were devoted to practicing

---

4. Dostoyevski in William D. Miller, *A Harsh and Dreadful Love: Dorothy Day and the Catholic Worker Movement,* 9.

the way of nonviolence. They regarded nonviolence as the only convincing way of showing respect for one's seeming enemies who may be one's future friends. They devoted their lives to reducing the effects of injustice and manifesting and improving positive qualities in society.

Rev. Martin Luther King, Jr.

Martin Luther King, Jr. (1929–1968), wrote, "If humanity is to progress, Gandhi is inescapable. ... We may ignore him at our own risk." While he was steeped in the American black church, Martin Luther King, Jr., forced himself to emerge as an individual unbounded by his situation—not by his family, race, religion, or even by his role as a civil rights leader. By patient heroism, and by bold imagination, he emerged as an individual able to inspire other individuals and groups, and eventually vast segments of humanity. He came to embody the ideal that Steiner espoused: a genuine individuality in service of universal values and universal humanity. The Presidential Medal of Freedom posthumously awarded to Rev. Martin Luther King, Jr., accurately summarizes the significance of his mission and achievement:

> Martin Luther King, Jr., was the conscience of his generation. A southerner, a black man, he gazed on the great wall of segregation and saw that the power of love could bring it down. From the pain and exhaustion of his fight to free all people from the bondage of separation and injustice, he wrung his eloquent statement of his dream of what America could be.[5]

One hundred years after Lincoln's Gettysburg Address and his signing of the Emancipation Proclamation, King explained that he could never adjust to segregation or discrimination. He complimented Lincoln on having been similarly "maladjusted" to slavery. In his Gettysburg Address Lincoln summarized his

---

5. Citation of the posthumous award of the Presidential Medal of Freedom, in James M. Washington, *A Testament of Hope: The Essential Writings and Speeches of Martin Luther King., Jr.,* iv.

conviction in a sentence almost as famous as the first sentence of the Declaration of Independence on which it is based:

> Fourscore and seven years ago our fathers brought forth on this continent a new nation, conceived in liberty, and dedicated to the proposition that all men are created equal.

King urged his audiences to be as maladjusted as the prophet Amos who, in the face of injustice, cried out: "Let judgment run down like waters and righteousness like a mighty stream" (5.24). King urged his audience, and through them all Americans, to fight injustices and struggle toward the greater potential of humanity.

> As maladjusted as Abraham Lincoln who had the vision to see that this nation could not exist half slave and half free. As maladjusted as Jefferson, who in the midst of an age amazingly adjusted to slavery could cry out, "All men are created equal and are endowed by their Creator with certain inalienable rights and that among these are life, liberty and the pursuit of happiness." As maladjusted as Jesus of Nazareth who dreamed a dream of the fatherhood of God and the brotherhood of man. God grant that we will be so maladjusted that we will be able to go out and change our world and our civilization. And then we will be able to move from the bleak and desolate midnight of man's inhumanity to man to the bright and glittering daybreak of freedom and justice.[6]

American history reflects a three-phase progress of human rights from the Declaration of Independence to Lincoln's Emancipation Proclamation to the profoundly moving speeches and sermons of Martin Luther King, Jr. This evolution, initially from vote franchise exclusively to white males of European descent, currently franchises all citizens irrespective of race, class, religion, and gender. The liberation movements on behalf of those who do not fit conventional sexual, gender, or family norms (such as lesbians, gays, and transgendered) are experiencing impressive victories, and will be followed by campaigns, already underway,

---

6. Martin Luther King, Jr., "The Power of Nonviolence," in Ibid., 14–15.

for the liberation of animals, and then for the sustainability of the Earth itself.

All of these liberation movements of the twentieth and twenty-first centuries are movements focused on the eradication of prejudice, and at a deeper level they are all essentially movements toward universal respect. They all spring from the eighteenth-century Enlightenment, from the writings of remarkably progressive thinkers such as John Stuart Mill. They are also Gandhian and partly Christian. King's teaching and practice of nonviolence is Gandhian in that it is based on universal respect. King's lifework, like Gandhi's, aims at universal love, including, as taught and exemplified by Jesus, the love of one's enemies.

King, who stated that if he would be called a drum major, he would want to be called a "drum major for righteousness,"[7] represents the fusion of Christian and Gandhian nonviolence, expressed in his own individuality. As he matured, his writings, interviews, lectures, sermons, and courageous actions issued from and served the ideal of nonviolence as a way of life—politically and personally. In an extensive and significant review of Taylor Branch's *At Canaan's End*,[8] Garry Wills recounts the extent of the persecution of King by J. Edgar Hoover, the lifelong director of the FBI:

> One of the marvels of King's life is that he stood up to probably the most intense and sustained of Hoover's campaigns of character assassination. Hoover had King tapped (legally), bugged (illegally), deprived of advisers, vilified in planted stories, left unprotected in danger. He quietly undermined him in every available forum. He had colleges cancel honorary degrees, senators cancel honorary dinners. He tried to block the Ford Foundation from giving his program a grant. To prevent King's receiving the Nobel Prize, he tried

---

7. In the first rendering, this "if" was left off the King monument on the capital mall, thereby giving the mistaken impression that King called himself a "drum major for righteousness."

8. See Branch's magisterial volumes on King's leadership of the Civil Rights Movement: *Parting the Waters: America in the King Years, 1954–63*; *Pillar of Fire: America in the King Years, 1963–65*; *At Canaan's End: America in the King Years, 1965–68*.

to provoke him into committing suicide before leaving for Oslo. He refused to inform King of death threats the FBI knew about, something the organization regularly did for others. Hoover had reached such a berserk extreme that he was hoping for an assassination. King was this crazed Ahab's Great Black Whale. How did King survive all this? He would not have, if he had ever stooped to returning hate for hate with Hoover. That would have tripped him up without fail. King said, "I refuse to hate," and repeatedly told his allies that love was their only real weapon. That is the profound lesson in the power of nonviolence. Hate and violence are self-destructive. Whatever his other faults, fidelity to nonviolence was King's one towering virtue. He frequently expressed disappointment with others—with Johnson, with Hoover, with many of his own followers or putative friends, with the white power structure. But he did not poison himself with enmity. Even his depressions were self-punitive rather than accusatory. That is the astounding record of the man. He lived with constant threats to his life, subject to vicious racist calumnies, ridiculed by former allies, stalked by Hoover's agents, denounced by high government officials—yet he never lashed back with anger or violence.[9]

At the conclusion of a sermon at the National Cathedral in Washington, D.C., on the occasion of the fortieth anniversary of Rev. Martin Luther King, Jr.'s last sermon in the same pulpit, Taylor Branch, the author of the magisterial three-volume history of King's role in the American civil rights era, recounted that after his last sermon King went back to Memphis to stand with the downtrodden, striking workers. Despite death threats both on the way to Memphis and on arrival, King was determined to be with the families of Echol Cole and Robert Walker, the two sanitation workers who, two days before, had been crushed by a malfunction in the back of a sanitation truck.[10] Branch recalled:

---

9. Garry Wills, "An American Iliad: Martin Luther King, Jr. and America Now," *New York Review of Books*, 6 April 2006, 20–26.

10. Memphis city rules forbade black employees to seek shelter from rain anywhere but in the back of their compressor trucks, with the garbage.

You may have seen the placards from the sanitation strike, which read "I Am a Man," meaning not a piece of garbage to be crushed and ignored. For Dr. King, to answer was a patriotic and prophetic calling. He challenges everyone to find a Lazarus somewhere, from our teeming prisons to the bleeding earth. That quest in common becomes the spark of social movements, and is therefore the engine of hope.[11]

The Lazarus in this passage is not the one whom Jesus "raised from the dead" in the Gospel of John, but the lame beggar in the Gospel of Luke (16:19–31) who was denied even the crumbs from the table of a rich man. In the parable, both the rich and poor man died, Lazarus ascending to heaven, the rich man descending to hell. The rich man, in anguish, seeing Lazarus the beggar "in the bosom of Father Abraham," called to Abraham to have Lazarus bring him some water to quench his thirst. Father Abraham replied that during his life of wealth and privilege he had refused crumbs for Lazarus, now fortunes are justly reversed. In his sermon King emphasized that the rich man failed to treat Lazarus as a person; even when requesting water he addresses Abraham, not Lazarus. Branch concludes:

> The lesson beneath any theology is that we must act toward all creation in the spirit of equal souls and equal votes. The alternative is hell, which Dr. King sometimes defined as the pain we inflict on ourselves by refusing God's grace.[12]

A direct line runs from Jesus to Gandhi to King. In a passage from his Nobel Peace Prize Acceptance Speech, December 1964, King states:

> After contemplation, I conclude that this award which I receive on behalf of that movement is a profound recognition that nonviolence is the answer to the crucial political and moral question of our time: the need for man to overcome oppression and violence without resorting to violence and oppression. Civilization and violence are antithetical

---

11. Taylor Branch, quoted in Wills, "An American Iliad."
12. Ibid.

concepts. Negroes of the United States, following the people of India, have demonstrated that nonviolence is not sterile passivity, but a powerful moral force which makes for social transformation. Sooner or later all the people of the world will have to discover a way to live together in peace and thereby transform this pending cosmic elegy into a creative psalm of brotherhood. If this is to be achieved, human beings must evolve for all human conflict a method which rejects revenge, aggression, and retaliation. The foundation of such a method is love.[13]

HIS HOLINESS THE DALAI LAMA

Tenzin Gyatso, the current Dalai Lama (b. 1935), never left the moorings of Tibetan Buddhism, but extended his monastic vocation to the entire world. From his teen years when he escaped to India from his beloved Tibet, His Holiness the Dalai Lama has lived with tens of thousands of Tibetans who are in Dharamsala, guests of the Government and people of India. The history of Tibet, like the history of India, has been characterized by violence, some of it between tribes and most of it domestic violence against women, but the Dalai Lama, following the powerful example of Gandhi, has advanced the cause of nonviolence throughout the entire world—except in the People's Republic of China where even possession of his photograph is punishable by prison.

In the following statement, the Norwegian Nobel Committee offered its reasons for awarding the 1989 Nobel Peace Prize to His Holiness the Dalai Lama:

> The year's Nobel Peace Prize has been awarded to H. H. the Dalai Lama, first and foremost for his consistent resistance to the use of violence in his people's struggle to regain their liberty.... It would be difficult to cite any historical example of a minority's struggle to secure its rights, in which a more conciliatory attitude to the adversary has been adopted than is the case of the Dalai Lama. It would be natural to compare him

---

13. Martin Luther King, Jr., "Nobel Prize Acceptance Speech," in James M. Washington, ed., *A Testament of Hope: The Essential Writings and Speeches of Martin Luther King, Jr.*, 224–225.

with Mahatma Gandhi, one of the century's greatest proponents of peace, and the Dalai Lama likes to consider himself one of Mahatma Gandhi's successors.[14]

In his "Nobel Peace Prize Lecture" His Holiness stated:

> The awarding of the Nobel Prize to me, a simple monk from Tibet, here in Norway, also fills us Tibetans with hope. It means that, despite the fact that we have not drawn attention by means of violence, we have not been forgotten. It also means that the values we cherish, in particular our respect for all forms of life and the belief in the power of truth, are today recognized and encouraged. It is also a tribute to my mentor, Mahatma Gandhi, whose example is an inspiration to so many of us. This year's award is an indication that this sense of universal responsibility is developing.[15]

If I may disagree with His Holiness just this once: He is a monk and he is from Tibet but he is not simple! Like Gandhi and Martin Luther King, Jr., for the Dalai Lama nonviolence is the essential principle that he has practiced consistently throughout his adult life. Nonviolence should be understood as a subset of the Tibetan Buddhist conception of compassion, the fundamental ideal that governs the Dalai Lama's life and teachings as a Buddhist monk. Note his words: "In particular our respect for all forms of life and the belief in the power of truth."

Many Christians like to claim that their ideal is love and consider the ideal of Buddhism to be a heartless law of karma, but it would be difficult to establish a difference between the Christian ideal of love, *agape*, and the ideal of compassion that His Holiness the Dalai Lama has taught and exemplified for the past six decades. Whereas a saint might attain to heaven as a suitable reward for a virtuous life, a *bodhisattva*, if as virtuous as a Christian saint (probably not difficult for a Tibetan), would then forego Nirvana in favor of returning to Earth to help all suffering sentient beings. Here is the bodhisattva vow

---

14. Sidney Piburn, ed., *The Nobel Peace Prize and the Dalai Lama*, 17–18.
15. Ibid., 39–40.

as spoken by His Holiness at the conclusion of his "Nobel Peace Prize Lecture," and on many other occasions:

> For as long as space endures,
> And for as long as living beings remain,
> Until then may I, too, abide
> To dispel the misery of the world.[16]

Nonviolence, which by the Dalai Lama's admission has not positively affected Chinese policy and practice in Tibet, has nonetheless been his strategy for more than fifty years. The core of this nonviolence is respect, affirmation, and even love in the face of hatred and cruelty. Just as Martin Luther King, Jr., incredibly, managed not to be morally shaken by J. Edgar Hoover's illegal torment, nor to strike back at him or the FBI or other malicious detractors, His Holiness the Dalai Lama, even more incredibly, has managed not to be crippled by the Chinese torturers and not to strike back in justifiable rage. In this same tradition, Archbishop Desmond Tutu not only successfully practices nonviolence, but has created a commission for truth and reconciliation, truly one of the most inspiring and promising contributions to the cause of justice, peace, and love.

ARCHBISHOP DESMOND TUTU

Like Rev. Martin Luther King, Jr., and His Holiness the Dalai Lama, Archbishop Desmond Tutu (b. 1931) is a direct moral and spiritual descendent of Mahatma Gandhi, and like them his resemblance to Gandhi is focused primarily on a nonviolence that resonates from a deep and profound understanding of love, a love that goes deeper than nonviolence. Tutu remained dedicated to nonviolence in the face of the oppressive and violent Apartheid enforced by the white government of South Africa. The policy and practice of nonviolence was effective in South Africa against Apartheid, though the picture is rather complex

---

16. The first line has also been translated: "for as long as any sentient beings live," and the fourth line has been translated, "to soothe the sufferings of those who live."

because of the constant threat and frequent outbursts of violence as advocated by others. The collapse of Apartheid, as Tutu has acknowledged repeatedly, was also significantly due to divestments by governments and organizations, including many universities. As Tutu has also repeated often, the white regime had power but not authority. Even though his nonviolent campaign against Apartheid was initially ineffective, and it appeared that the white rulers of South Africa would never grant civil rights to native blacks, Tutu did not descend to violence or hatred.

When Apartheid did finally give way to a free election in 1994, Nelson Mandela, clearly one of the most inspiring individuals of the twentieth- and twenty-first centuries, was elected president, ushering in an era of civil rights for all South Africans. Mandela asked Archbishop Tutu to establish and direct the Truth and Reconciliation Commission, an organization and process intended to purge the country of its painful past. The confessions of the perpetrators of horrific torture and deaths against protestors, all classified as terrorists, make unbearable reading even now years after their telling. Archbishop Tutu explains the foundational idea of the Truth and Reconciliation Commission: "Forgiving means abandoning your right to pay back the perpetrator in his own coin, but it is a loss that liberates the victim." Tutu compares the act of forgiveness to opening the window and drawing curtains in a dark and stuffy room: "Then that light which has always been available will come in and air will enter the room to freshen it up. So it is with forgiveness." Further: "In the act of forgiveness we are declaring our faith in the future."[17]

The South African Truth and Reconciliation Commission is increasingly recognized as a powerful tool for rebuilding societies torn by racial and ethnic strife. Tutu writes:

> To work for reconciliation is to want to realize God's dream for humanity—when we will know that we are indeed members of one family, bound together in a delicate network of interdependence.[18]

17. Archbishop Desmond Tutu, *No Future without Forgiveness*, 272.
18. Ibid., 274.

A significant component of this interdependence is the bond between the past, present, and future. Just as a community, society, or civilization can boast of its contribution, it need also acknowledge the offenses of its past, seek forgiveness for them, and be willing to forgive its offenders. In addition to the evidential physical and psychological benefit of forgiving and being forgiven, there is a spiritual reward that might be initially more difficult to track but that nevertheless is real and in need of further research.

Both Archbishop Tutu in his book *No Future Without Forgiveness* and Sergei O. Prokofieff in his book *The Occult Significance of Forgiveness* discuss the case of Simon Wiesenthal, a concentration camp survivor who refused to respond to a dying SS officer who had begged Wiesenthal for forgiveness. In the widely read anthology, *The Sunflower: On the Possibilities and Limits of Forgiveness*, Wiesenthal tells the story himself of that young SS officer tormented by his participation in setting fire to a house and forcing several hundred Jews to remain inside while it burned. A Jewish family had jumped from the burning house; the SS soldier joined in shooting the family as they landed on the ground. The young officer, dying of grenade wounds, sought the forgiveness of a Jew, saying he could not die in peace without being forgiven. Wiesenthal left him without replying; the officer died the next day.

In later years Wiesenthal defended his decision saying that it would have been improper for him to offer forgiveness in place of another. Archbishop Tutu, who has heard many horrific first-person confessions of torture, disagreed with Wiesenthal's position. Sergei O. Prokofieff, a Russian anthroposophist (and grandson of the composer), who lived through the years of Soviet tyranny and genocide, offers an esoteric understanding of forgiveness. Specifically in reference to the Wiesenthal case, Prokofieff asserts that Wiesenthal's decision not to forgive the dying SS officer "is indeed the central moral problem of our time."[19] Drawing directly on the lectures of Rudolf Steiner after World War I, Prokofieff explains that the act of forgiveness exercises a deep and enduring influence

---

19. Sergei O. Prokofieff, *The Occult Significance of Forgiveness*, 21.

on a person's life after death and also contributes significantly to the possibility of peaceful social life. This is a profound topic, one that can only become more urgent as the worldwide cruelties of the twentieth century spread into the twenty-first century.

Gandhian *satyagraha* has both convincing symbolism and some powerful societal victories to its credit. The nonviolent campaign led by Martin Luther King, Jr., and the generally nonviolent campaign in South Africa led by Archbishop Desmond Tutu, can be considered successful. On the other hand, Gandhi's recommendation to Buber that the Jews engage in nonviolence against the Nazi war machine in central and eastern Europe was naive and presumptuous. Other Gandhian campaigns have been unsuccessful: the Dalai Lama's nonviolent leadership has proven a failure in response to China's violent decimation of the land and culture of Tibet. Yet Gandhi continues to be an enduring source of inspiring statements, the kind that lift consciousness from the pedestrian "business as usual" to a glimpse of a better world. While Gandhian nonviolence has achieved only limited success, it is also possible that if relatively unsuccessful *satyagraha* campaigns had chosen violence over nonviolence, the bloodshed could have been far worse than the mixed results of the nonviolent campaigns.

RUDOLF STEINER'S IDEAL OF A JUST SOCIETY

Although he worked vigorously against the continuance of the horrific and pointless World War I, and wrote an extensive document to that end, Steiner was apparently not devoted to nonviolence. Instead, as a way of preventing violence and war he was in favor of constructing a fair and just society. During and after World War I, Steiner lectured frequently on societal problems, and particularly on threats to individual freedom and communal harmony. His concerns include the nature of national and cultural identity, as well as the ideal functioning of society, law, and economic theory and practice. To each of these topics Steiner brought original esoteric insight, or clear-seeing, concerning the interior life of society and of the individual in ordinary societal relations. Steiner's approach to the social sciences and his level of research hold important implications for these fields.

In his foreword to Rudolf Steiner's *The Boundaries of Natural Science,* Saul Bellow states that we cannot accomplish social renewal until we start to attain knowledge of the spiritual, and raise to consciousness what would otherwise remain unconscious. He recommends Steiner as an initiate whose experience and teaching can help the West to move beyond the boundaries of materialistic thinking to the imaginative and liberating experience of psychic and spiritual forces. Bellow urges the West to develop a closer, truer relation to the external world and the interior self. He writes:

> We cannot even begin to think of social renewal until we have considered these questions. What is reality in the civilized West? "A world of outsides without insides," says Owen Barfield, one of the best interpreters of Steiner. A world of quantities without qualities, of souls devoid of mobility and of communities which are more dead than alive.[20]

By the time Rudolf Steiner began his comprehensive analysis of the social and political ills of his time—a task thrust upon him by the suffering and chaos generated by World War I as well as by his mission as a servant of incarnational thinking and service—he had already spent more than a decade applying his esoteric knowledge of humanity and the universe to a wide range of practical problems. Though politics and economics might seem to be unpromising areas for the application of esoteric research, Steiner is nevertheless as insistent on individual freedom, and development of spiritual depth in the political and economic spheres, as in the cultural.

In addition to drawing on his theory of human nature, Steiner's social philosophy also presupposes his reading of human history, particularly the evolution toward human individuality during the Christian and modern Western epochs. In *The Mission of the Archangel Michael,* for example, he argues for the distinctive combination of freedom and social solidarity which became

20. Saul Bellow, *Boundaries of Natural Science,* foreword, xiii.

possible at the dawn of what he refers to as the Michaelic Age, the time since 1879 that he has identified as a time over which the Archangel Michael exercises dominion—without violating human freedom. Steiner views this age as a time of extraordinary challenge and opportunity. On the side of challenge, the present age has generated new problems and therefore requires new solutions:

> Externally, humanity today approaches serious battles. In regard to these serious battles, which are only at their beginning . . . and which will lead the old impulses of Earth evolution *ad absurdum*, there are no political, economic, or spiritual remedies to be taken from the pharmacy of past historical evolution. For from these past times come the elements of fermentation which, first, have brought Europe to the brink of the abyss, which will array Asia and America against each other, and which are preparing a battle over the whole earth.[21]

Like many of the views expressed in Steiner's lectures, this passage sounds contemporary when in fact it was spoken exactly a century ago.

On the side of opportunity, Steiner maintains that this difficult age makes possible the realization of global community and meaningful interpersonal relationships. Such a realization can overcome, or at least reduce, human chaos, violence, and loss of meaning. To follow the Michaelic path by living at the forefront of a free and profoundly awake contemporary consciousness requires that each person respond to all other persons in terms not only of their physical existence or personality but equally in terms of their suprasensory reality.[22]

Steiner insists that social relations be firmly rooted in the spiritual—but not at a remove from social pressures, violence, and suffering. In strictly secular terms, "suprasensory reality" might best be understood as respect and dignity, or perhaps as the practice of Martin Buber's "I–Thou" relations. Some of the activitsts of the

---

21. Rudolf Steiner, *The Mission of the Archangel Michael,* 53.
22. In *I and Thou* Martin Buber does not use this language but his concept of I–Thou, or I–You (in contrast to I–It), affirms something of the depth and integrity of personal relations to which Steiner is pointing.

twentieth and twenty-first centuries, such as Gandhi and Nelson Mandela, use this secular language and mean precisely that, with very little, if any, reference to a spiritual core. When Martin Luther King, Jr., the Dalai Lama, and Archbishop Tutu use this language—"dignity, respect, human or civil rights"—they intend secular ideals and values, but they also assume a soul or spiritual dimension.

Reference to soul or spirit with respect to His Holiness the Dalai Lama is a difficult topic in that he adheres to the Buddhist doctrine of no-soul while at the same time holding to karma and rebirth. Perhaps we should say that individual karma and not the soul has a suprasensory dimension. By contrast, King and Tutu assume a Christian conception of soul, one that they share in part with Steiner. Whereas most Christians, including King and Tutu, hold to two principles of the human being—a mortal body and an immortal soul—Steiner holds to four principles, the first three of which are mortal: a physical body, an etheric body, and a lifelong soul. The fourth, spirit or "I," is immortal. All of this might be significant theoretically but in practice might not make much difference, depending on whether the believer in question is attempting to gain insight concerning the afterlife, karma, rebirth, or forgiveness.

In secular terms, Michaelic thinking may be understood as the ideal of a universal human community. It is possible that Josiah Royce's ideal of the Beloved Community, later adopted by Martin Luther King, Jr. is precisely this humanistic conception. It seems more likely, however, that both Royce and King (and King's professors at the Boston University School of Theology in the early 1950s who were students of Josiah Royce) were implicitly affirming a spiritual reality, a universal human body similar to the Roman Catholic doctrine of the Mystical Body of Christ. By this conception of a universal human community mysteriously held by the risen Christ, both individuality and social solidarity can be understood and practiced with a saving spiritual reality, which Steiner refers to as suprasensory. The obvious obstacle to Steiner's attempt to combine free individuality and universal fraternity is the nineteenth- and twentieth-century passion for nationalism in economics and politics, and to some extent religion. For certain powerful countries, especially France, England, Japan, Germany, Russia, and the United States, this passion has expressed itself in attempts at economic and military domination. In recent decades China, too, has emerged as a major force in *Realpolitique*.

Steiner's position on nationalism seems to me quite subtle and helpful: he rejects the nationalistic outlook and its constant companion, patriotism, yet he often refers positively to "folk soul" characteristics of each of the European cultures that he analyzes. He both criticizes and recommends the concept of "a people" in the Hebraic sense, and folk culture in the European sense. He offers concrete exercises for overcoming the tendency to view the world narrowly from the vantage point of one's people. Steiner wants each culture to develop its distinctive personality without considering itself to be superior to other cultures. He articulated this subtle two-sided ideal in numerous lectures on social philosophy delivered after World War I. The following passage, from "Specters of the Old Testament in the Nationalism of the Present," delivered on December 7, 1918, well summarizes Steiner's social teaching with respect to individualism and social relations. Steiner's insistence that brotherhood is possible only by affirming other human beings in their irreducible integrity clearly resembles Buber's *I and Thou*:

> For only when we carry the other human being within ourselves can we really speak of human brotherhood, which has appeared thus far only in an abstract word. When we form a picture of the other person, which is implanted as a treasure in our soul, then we carry within the realm of our soul life something from [that person], just as in the case of a bodily brother we carry around something through the common blood. This elective affinity as the basis of the social life must take the place in this concrete way of the mere blood affinity. This is something that really must evolve. It must depend upon the human will to determine how brotherhood shall be awakened within every human being.[23]

23. Rudolf Steiner, *The Challenge of the Times*, "Specters of the Old Testament in the Nationalism of the Present, 176–178.

Steiner's basic statement on the social nature of human life is contained in a book that he wrote in 1919, variously titled in English *The Threefold Commonwealth*, *The Threefold Social Order*, and *Towards Social Renewal: Basic Issues of the Social Question*. According to Steiner, in conformity with human nature, society should consist of three separate but related realms: the economic, the political or rights, and the spiritual–cultural:

1. The rights sphere (legal and political). In this sphere everyone is equal.
2. The economic sphere: This should be the sphere of interdependence but is more typically the sphere of intense competition.
3. The free cultural sphere in which individuals are in fact not equal in capacity. This sphere includes creativity, religion, arts, education, and all endeavors by which one expresses one's individuality. This sphere needs to be protected by the rights sphere and protected from the incursion of the economic sphere (obviously the reverse of the social structure of capitalism).

According to this structure, every member of society belongs to all three realms, but the realms themselves ought not exercise influence beyond their proper sphere. He wrote:

> The point is rather to find how the three members can be brought together, so that they may really work in the social organism with inherent intelligence, just as the nerve and sensory system, the heart and lung system, and the metabolic system, for example, work together in the natural organism of [the human being].[24]

As Stewart Easton points out in *Man and World in the Light of Anthroposophy*, many people in the present age, particularly young people, have an intuitive feeling for this ideal community of free individuals but tend to look for models in the past. One such model is the motto of the French Revolution, "Liberty, Equality, Fraternity" which, according to Easton, is now capable of realization but was not possible when it came to consciousness at the end of the eighteenth century. Easton explains that according to

---

24. Rudolf Steiner, *World Economy*, 134.

Rudolf Steiner, each of the three ideals of the French Revolution is the aim of one of the three domains in the social order: spiritual and cultural, rights and law, and the economy.

> Liberty in the cultural spiritual life, that is, freedom of thought; equality in the life of rights, in which every [human being] has the same rights as every other; and fraternity in the economic life, in which human, economic, and material needs are satisfied through a free exchange of goods throughout the world, unimpeded by national boundaries or other hindrances.... According to Steiner, nations should not as such disappear in the future, but their role becomes much more limited; if it is so limited, it cannot give birth to or foster the growth of nationalism. The Michaelic, Christian principle of universalism [the opposite of the Christian principle of exceptionalism], the overcoming of the bonds of blood, is *required*, according to Steiner, in our age and in the future. The means by which we move toward it is above all through the recognition of the three domains of the Social Order.[25]

Steiner's threefold social order is partially analogous to the tripartite system of government prescribed by the United States Constitution: each of the three branches is necessary and equal, and no one branch should exercise control over either of the other two. Of course, all three branches of the United States government are in the political sphere. Steiner describes the rights, economic, and cultural spheres at length, as well as their proper contributions and limitations, and contends that many of the ills and injustices of modern Western social life are largely attributable to imbalance among them. It is clear at present that all three branches of the United States government are overwhelmed by the economic sphere—exactly the problem that Steiner's threefold organization is intended to solve. Steiner is particularly critical of the economic and political control of education, which rightly belongs exclusively in the spiritual–cultural domain.

---

25. Steward C. Easton, *Man and World in the Light of Anthroposophy*, 330–331.

Steiner first announced his "fundamental social law" in *Anthroposophy and the Social Question,* three essays published in 1906 to 1908:

> In a community of human beings working together, the wellbeing of the community will be the greater the less individuals claim for themselves the proceeds of the work they themselves have done—i.e., the more of these proceeds they give over to their fellow workers, and the more their own requirements are satisfied, not out of their own work done, but out of work done by the others.[26]

Steiner explains his conception of the economic sphere in a cycle of fourteen lectures delivered in 1922, entitled *World Economy: The Formation of a Science of World Economics.* Though many regard pleas for economic reform as idealistic or naïve, Steiner argues that his proposal is not utopian but grounded in human nature. He believes that there is need in society for competition, but it belongs in the cultural rather than in the economic sphere. In the economic realm, the relationship between producers, distributors, and consumers should be one of fraternity and intelligent cooperation. The three parts of the social order require interdependence, balance, and reciprocity. The economic realm cannot be reformed independently—the political and cultural–spiritual. The economic sphere is a useful place to discern the imbalances in all three that have proven disastrous in contemporary social life.

For the economic sphere to function properly and contribute to the overall health of society, it must be governed by a social science that is responsive to the integral working of the entire threefold social order as well as to the inevitable transition from national to world economies. Steiner's lectures on world economy are based on detailed analyses of production and distribution. He offers solutions to economic disharmonies by casting economic processes in the light of a worldwide system. As local economic relationship must ultimately be conceived and reformed in light of a national network, so must each national economy increasingly

---

26. Rudolf Steiner, *Anthroposophy and the Social Question,* 24.

recognize its essential interdependence within the world economic order. Such an expansion of the economic order on a global scale, however, should not lead to an expansion of the economic order into the political or cultural realm.

Like Karl Marx and other political economists, Steiner laments the modern conception of human labor treated as a commodity. But as Stewart Easton points out, Steiner's solution to this problem is quite different from that of most social and economic thinkers. Steiner separates production and remuneration into discreet societal spheres:

> The first problem is how to produce economic goods as efficiently as possible with a minimum of wastefulness; the second is how to remunerate the workers. The first is an economic problem, the second is a question of human rights, and therefore does not belong to the economic domain at all, but rather to the "judicial" or "rights body."[27]

The exact relationship and limitations between the economic and rights spheres ought not be decided in the abstract. In making these distinctions, Steiner repeatedly turns to specific cases such as whether a tailor should purchase his clothing readymade or make his own, and the value of peas for a farmer and for consumers.

To the extent that one is conscious of Steiner's work as a spiritual scientist, particularly the epistemology articulated in *Philosophy of Freedom*, it is possible to appreciate his insistence that economic life requires each transaction to be conceived and executed as part of an economic picture at once detailed and comprehensive. He recommends the following approach to economic life:

> To act rightly in the economic sense, we must make up our minds to enter into the events of production, trade, and consumption with a picture thinking.... Economic judgments cannot be built on theory, they must be built on living association,

---

27. Stewart C. Easton, *Man and World in the Light of Anthroposophy*, 339–340.

where the sensitive judgments of people are real and effective; for it will then be possible to determine out of the association— out of the immediate experiences of those concerned—what the value of any given thing can be.[28]

According to Steiner, an economic association should be properly balanced in itself as well as in harmony with the global network of economic associations. Such harmony in the economic sphere contributes to and in turn is dependent upon balance in the rights sphere. The most distinctive feature of Steiner's theory of the political sphere—and historically the most novel—is its impartiality. As Easton observes, "Obviously, if the State provides education for its citizens, or if it owns or manages industry, it cannot be impartial in relation to either education or industry."[29]

Steiner did not write at length on the rights sphere. He did, however, contend that the administration of justice should limit its task to the administration of police and armed forces, maintaining order in the state, and arbitration. Within this general framework, Steiner examines specific rights such as those affecting ownership, particularly land ownership which he places in the economic sphere. He recommends that the economic sphere be enlarged to a worldwide context without loss of attention to detail. Similarly, the sphere of rights needs to be conceived globally or universally. In the same way that partiality is an enemy of sound economic thinking, it is disastrous in the sphere of rights.

Of the three social spheres, Steiner lectured most frequently on the cultural–spiritual. As the sphere of rights contributes impartiality and objectivity to the threefold social order, the spiritual–cultural sphere contributes the creativity and free thinking of each individual. Consequently, for education to make its necessary and free contributions to the social order, the political sphere must allow schools, teachers, and the learning process to proceed unimpeded by partisan political or undue economic interests. In Steiner's view, all of the creative arts and intellectual pusuits properly belong to the cultural sphere and as such must be free

---

28. Rudolf Steiner, *World Economy*, 131.
29. Steward C. Easton, *Man and World in the Light of Anthroposophy*, 351.

from the domination of either economic or political influence. All of Steiner's writings and lectures on Waldorf education presuppose the kind of freedom—and the Waldorf Schools throughout the world intend such freedom—prescribed in Steiner's threefold social teaching.

This position clearly has theoretical merits but a closer look at the economics of education and industry seems to show that there are problems that are simply too large to be solved without the help of national and state government. Some of Steiner's followers have been emphatically opposed to government involvement in the cultural sphere, particularly education. Fortunately, Steiner insisted that problems be solved concretely, and by imaginative thinking; unfortunately, on these social scientific topics Steiner's ideas appear to be caught in a host of abstract principles and political ideology.

Overall, Steiner's writings show him to have been progressive and insightful concerning the diversity of cultures. His comments on individuality, the universality of the human being, and the development of nations and groups, are very contemporary even three or four generations after they were written. However, from contemporary social and cultural perspectives, it is clear that some of Steiner's lectures on race and what he referred to as "folk soul" characteristics are not free of late nineteenth- and early-twentieth-century biased assumptions and attitudes. These statements—some outright false and some merely unenlightened—comprise approximately a dozen pages out of a total published work of more than 300 volumes, most of which Steiner did not have an opportunity to review or revise. To the extent that these statements become known to the general public, e.g., to parents of children attending Waldorf schools, they will need to be explained and assessed within the historical context in which they were spoken. They should also be accompanied by expressions of apology for whatever offense they might cause contemporary sensibilities.

Ironically, while these unenlightened statements are truly regrettable, they could have the positive effect of helping some of Steiner's followers free themselves from the simplistic, fundamentalist assumption that his words should be taken as unquestioned truths instead of, as Steiner intended, progress reports to be continually checked and improved by subsequent esoteric and exoteric research. In the case of statements that are no longer acceptable, because of politically and morally informed opinion, some of Steiner's statements will need to be replaced.

Steiner researched great spiritual beings such as Krishna, Buddha, and Tibetan masters but he had scant knowledge of the cultures of Asians, Africans, South Americas, Native Americans, or African Americans. He had extensive contacts with people from Europe, Britain, the United States, and Canada, and rightly believed that the English-speaking world played an important role in advancing the evolution of human consciousness. However, his perspective and writings are not as planetary or universal as is needed at present. His view of the evolution of consciousness too closely resembles the overly confident nineteenth-century European, and particularly Germanic–Romantic, view of history—as a straight line from the Greeks through Christendom, to the modern West. In the late twentieth and early twenty-first centuries, however, the great insights as well as the most inspiring biographies and movements have frequently been found outside of Europe among people of color—Gandhi of India, Martin Luther King, Jr., of Black America, His Holiness the Dalai Lama of Tibet, both Nelson Mandela and Archbishop Desmond Tutu of South Africa, and Aun San Suu Kyi of Myanmar.

John Dewey
Maria Montessori
John McDermott

9

EDUCATION

In a book devoted to comparisons between Rudolf Steiner and twentieth-century "kindred spirits," John Dewey's and Maria Montessori's approaches to education automatically present themselves for comparison. Unfortunately, these three great pedagogues, as well as contemporary teachers influenced by them, have missed each other almost entirely. Steiner and Dewey, born two years apart but with Dewey living a full quarter century longer than Steiner, both have roots in German idealist thought, particularly Hegel. Their mature thought, however, settled at opposite ends of a philosophical spectrum. Dewey's and Steiner's intellectual contributions range over many disciplines, including the sciences, social sciences, and arts, along with their approaches to education. Writings on educational philosophies often cite Dewey and Montessori, though not usually comparatively, whereas Steiner's approach is typically ignored even though it is at least as significant as Dewey's and Montessori's.

As the literature comparing Dewey–Montessori–Steiner is either slight or nonexistent, it seems to me a service to all three communities to offer a set of similarities and differences among these three approaches to education. This is especially the case concerning the Waldorf approach, which issues directly from Steiner's anthroposophic insights and consequently is more different from Dewey's and Montessori's approaches than they are from each other. The greatest divide is between Dewey's completely secular, or humanist, orientation aimed at public schools and Steiner's spiritual-esoteric approach as far as possible free from government support and influence. Montessori is in the middle between these two: although she was a lifelong Roman

Catholic with a close association with Theosophists in India during World War II, neither religion nor spirituality is a discernible component of the Montessori approach. Like Steiner she was positive toward religious traditions, like Dewey her approach and method are strictly based on experience and observation.

The approaches of Dewey, Montessori, and Steiner are devoted to the ideal of freedom in a creative relationship with order, and to liberating the child from both chaotic or dispiriting environments. All three, when properly understood, oppose both rigidity and license. All three have influenced several generations of educators throughout the world. If one counts only early childhood schools, Montessori schools would be the largest private school system in the word; if one counts elementary schools, Waldorf would be largest and growing rapidly (including more than 300 early childhood schools in the People's Republic of China created in the past five years[1]).

JOHN DEWEY'S APPROACH TO EDUCATION

My knowledge of Dewey's approach to education is influenced by the writings of and my conversations with my three brothers: John has written extensively on Dewey's philosophy, including his philosophy of education, Ray (R.P.) teaches Dewey in the Stanford University School of Education, and Joe implements Deweyan values through the Coalition for Worker Education in New York City, of which he is the founder and CEO. For the four of us Dewey is a model professor as well as an advocate for democracy and social justice. This is interesting in relation to me, as advocates for Waldorf see it as a comprehensive improvement over Dewey's approach. I hope that anthroposophists reading this book will appreciate the question I often ask of Dewey: are his insights into the way children learn and his trust in the schools of a democratic society sufficient, or is Steiner's spiritual-esoteric knowledge concerning child development, curriculum, methodology, and school structure an essential addition? I offer a double reply: For parents and children for whom a secular approach is

---

1. See Ian Johnson, *The New Yorker*, February 3, 2014.

sufficient, Dewey's approach is valuable and deserves to be cultivated. For parents and children in search of a spiritually based education (and community), the Waldorf approach is positive and deserves to be cultivated.

The son of a grocer and homemaker, John Dewey spent his formative years in Vermont. His philosophy is characterized by social humanism, metaphysical naturalism, and pragmatic intelligence. He was committed to "a common faith," the values that a culture could hold in harmony without claims on behalf of any particular religious tradition. He was primarily a philosopher but also a social activist and educator. Dewey celebrated the wisdom of shared intelligent experience; he appreciated and advanced the ideal of individualism rooted in, deepened by, and in service to an ever-enlarging community. His humanistic religion of democracy stands with Emerson, James, and Royce against a view that holds self and culture in opposition. Dewey did not affirm the transcendent to a degree found in the writings of Emerson, James, and Royce, but this might be less important than his contributions as a critic of the passive and the static and as a servant to many individuals, communities, and ideals.

Dewey's thought is continuous with the Emersonian–Jamesian tradition, but throughout his sixty-year career as a philosopher and public intellectual he was more in touch with the challenges of urban America (Chicago and New York in contrast to the nineteenth-century Concord of Emerson or the Cambridge of James, Royce, and Whitehead). Even more than urban, Dewey's focus is more national and international. In terms of his commitments to community, Dewey is closer to Royce than to James. Dewey's critique of American culture consisted primarily in his contention that America was failing at democracy, particularly with respect to education. Dewey could be included in chapter 8 on social justice which features the Gandhian tradition. But above all, Dewey is secular. His position in this regard is well justified by the vitriolic attacks and distortions generated against him by educators and religious believers, particularly attacks from Roman Catholics for his attempt to introduce democratic and experiential components into education.

Dewey wanted all social sciences—including sociology, politics, psychology, history, and law—to be deepened by philosophy, and for philosophy to learn from, and particularly to affect, social life and thought. Concerning the function of philosophy he wrote:

> Philosophy recovers itself when it ceases to be a device for dealing with the problems of philosophers and becomes a method, cultivated by philosophers, for dealing with the problems of men [humanity].

As a philosopher, public intellectual, educator, and citizen Dewey exposed and opposed privilege and certainty.

Dewey saw religious belief, and particularly a commitment to the eternal with a focus on an afterlife as endangering both fidelity to the present and the spirit of open inquiry. The cause of justice is often served by communities, institutions, movements, and individuals such as John Dewey who stand as exceptions to Royce's (and Steiner's) claim that all human beings, whether consciously or unconsciously, seek the eternal. Dewey did not do so, and his life and work are models of virtue and fidelity to democratic communities. The moral superiority of a person who holds a secular worldview is rather problematic for the pro-religion worldview I espouse. For Dewey, secularism is morally superior to religion because it is more democratic, without claims to superior or exclusive knowledge.[2] I find it difficult to disagree with Dewey here.

In his Terry Lectures at Yale in 1934 Dewey recommended to America "the elements of a religious faith not confined to sect, class, or race." He might well have added "not confined to a religion and based instead on a faith in democracy":

> We who now live are parts of a humanity that extends into the remote past, a humanity that has interacted with nature. The

---

2.   The argument between atheism and faith has been vigorous since the eighteenth-century Enlightenment. For a thoughtful recent entry see Philip Kitcher, *Life After Faith: The Case for Secular Humanism*, and review by Adam Kirsch, "Is Reason Enough," *New York Review of Books* (April 23, 1913), 42–43.

things in civilization we most prize are not of ourselves. They exist by grace of the doings and sufferings of the continuous human community in which we are a link. Ours is the responsibility of conserving, transmitting, rectifying, and expanding the heritage of values we have received that those who come after us may receive it more solid and secure, more widely accessible, and more generously shared than we have received it.[3]

Douglas Sloan, emeritus professor of the philosophy and history of education at Columbia Teachers College, has set out the terms of the positive components and limitations of Dewey's philosophy of education from an anthroposophic and Waldorf perspective. Sloan asks an important question:

Dewey's work on experience and art contains rich resources and radical implications for modern education and culture. Will it be possible to tap and develop them fully, without having to affirm, however implicitly, the last vestiges of the positivism in which they are lodged?[4]

By positivism Sloan means Dewey's reliance on scientific thinking as the proper and in most respects the sole method of thinking.

In John McDermott's case for Dewey, the scientific character of his thinking is mostly ignored in favor of Dewey's emphasis on experience, and particularly its social context. Dewey may not be so much positivist or scientific as he is devoted to discrediting intuition and transcendence. He opposes any intellectual commitments that might work against freedom to experiment and grow, and democratic institutions. Dewey's conviction that all pedagogical experience is necessarily and thoroughly social and institutional separates his approach from any that celebrates an atomistic individualism—of the kind that is mistakenly attributed to Emerson, but is more characteristic of existentialism and American capitalism. Dewey's major text on education is entitled *Democracy and Education*, not the reverse: According to Dewey,

---

3. John Dewey, *A Common Faith*, 55.
4. Douglas Sloan, "John Dewey's Project for 'Saving the Appearances': Exploring Some of Its Implications for Education and Ethics," in Robert McDermott, ed., *Rudolf Steiner and American Philosophy*, 183–224.

education issues from and sustains democracy. In this still important book Dewey sets out the purpose of his educational philosophy in the context of a democratic society:

> The following pages embody an endeavor to detect and state the ideas implied in a democratic society and to apply these ideas to the problems of the enterprise of education. The discussion includes an indication of the constructive aims and methods of public education as seen from this point of view, and a critical estimate of the theories of knowing and moral development which were formulated in earlier social conditions, but which still operate, in societies nominally democratic, to hamper the adequate realization of the democratic ideal. As will appear from the book itself, the philosophy stated in this book connects the growth of democracy with the development of the experimental method in the sciences, evolutionary ideas in the biological sciences, and the industrial reorganization, and is concerned to point to the changes in subject matter and method of education indicated by these developments.[5]

John McDermott offers this summary of Dewey's concept of experience, the key to his philosophy of education:

> The human organism is aggressively self-conscious. This transaction between the human organism and nature is experience. The transaction is ever striated not only with problems, knots, but with the problematic as an ontological condition of being in and of and about the world. To be human is to be constantly, ineluctably, irreducibly faced with the problematic.[6]

The ideal school affirms and practices all of the virtues that Dewey represents and advocates, and then, to the extent possible, adds the virtues that Steiner advocates. It would be ideal if to these democratic values Waldorf could add a curriculum based on the development of the child, including the fullest possible

---

5. John Dewey, *Democracy and Education: An Introduction to the Philosophy of Education*, iii.
6. John McDermott, "The Gamble for Excellence," in Douglas R. Anderson, ed., *The Drama of Possibility: Experience as Philosophy of Culture*, 415.

opportunities to participate in science and art, to learn from teachers committed to the welfare of the school and of every child in it—teachers on a lifelong path of self-development—and to never experience dogmatism and intolerance. Dewey's philosophy and approach to education are significantly different from Steiner's but nevertheless compatible with commitment to a spiritual and esoteric worldview that is by nature undemocratic (simply because Steiner claims to know what very few human beings know, or believe possible). It must be admitted that Waldorf schools are almost entirely populated by middle- and upper-middle-class families. (Charter Waldorf schools do tend to serve a broader parent body.) In terms of social justice, Waldorf schools in general do not contribute to the resolution of the race or class conflicts deeply entrenched in American society—but then it is not at all clear that public schools do.

Maria Montessori's Approach to Education

The following passage from John McDermott's introduction to E. M. Standing, *Maria Montessori: Her Life and Work*,[7] though written in reference to Montessori, is equally applicable to the approaches of Dewey and Steiner:

> Maria Montessori had great hope that ours would be the century of the child. For that hope to be realized one thing above all was necessary, that Western civilization cease viewing the human situation as hierarchical—as a ladder on which our first steps take meaning only from the last. Within such a conceptual framework, the child was required to become an adult as quickly as possible, and the education of children was characterized by the imposition on the child of the needs and frame of reference of the adult world.[8]

---

7. John J. McDermott, "Introduction," in E. M. Standing, *Maria Montessori: Her Life and Work*, xi.
8. John J. McDermott, "Liberty and Order in the Educational Anthropology of Maria Montessori," in Douglas R. Anderson, ed., *The Drama of Possibility: Experience as Philosophy of Culture*, 428.

My relationship to the Montessori approach is slight but with a long history: In addition to my brother John's prominence on behalf of the Montessori movement,[9] in the early 1970s my son attended a Montessori school in Greenwich, Connecticut, founded and directed by Nancy Rambusch, then president of the American Montessori Society.

Maria Montessori (1870–1952)[10] was an Italian physician and biologist, but her fame rests on her original insights concerning child development and early childhood education. In 1896 she became the first female physician in Italy. Despite the typical hostility she faced as a woman in the male-dominated medical profession, she became an expert in pediatric medicine and began her work with children afflicted by various forms of retardation. (Similarly, Rudolf Steiner began his work as an educator by tutoring a child with a hydrocephalic condition.) At age twenty-eight Montessori gave birth to her only child, Mario. The child's father was not married to Maria and soon left her. Knowing that admission of her child out of wedlock would totally block her career, Maria placed Mario in foster care and visited him frequently. One can easily imagine the pain that this separation from her only child must have caused this sensitive observer and advocate for children.[11] When Mario was a teenager, he was united with his mother and became her support throughout her career.

In 1900, at age thirty, Montessori was appointed co-director of an institute for training teachers of children in need of special care. From 1903 to 1908, she conducted anthropological research on such children, and published *Pedagogical Anthropology* in 1910 (in English in 1913). In 1906 she began to direct a house for children (the first Casa dei Bambini), for fifty to sixty

---

9. The summations of Montessori's approach to education are indebted to the writings of my brother John J. McDermott who, while an advocate on behalf of Dewey's approach to education, for a dozen years was president of the American Montessori Society.

10. This biographical information is drawn from the standard biography, Rita Kramer, *Maria Montessori: A Biography.*

11. This separation worked out better for Montessori and her son than the case of Martin Buber whose mother abandoned him to her father-in-law's family. When Buber's mother returned to him as an adult, he described that event as a "miss-meeting."

children ages three to seven. She observed that when children are provided with properly crafted materials able to attract their interest they invariably began to work with these materials in an orderly and disciplined manner. These observations and the materials Montessori introduced became the foundation for the Montessori Method.

Dewey was generally quite tolerant and flexible in his thinking and commitments, but was critical of Montessori in his two references to her method in his major work, *Democracy and Education.* Specifically, Dewey criticized Montessori's dependence on carefully designed materials intended to attract and hold the child's attention. Dewey opposed materials "which express the intellectual distinctions which adults have made." He continues:

> But the first stage of contact with any new material, at whatever age of maturity, must inevitably be of the trial and error sort. An individual must actually try, in play or work, to do something with material in carrying out his [or her] own impulsive activity, and then not the interaction of his energy and that of the material employed.[12]

The first and second decade of the twentieth century saw the publication of Montessori's basic writings, including *The Montessori Method: Scientific Pedagogy as Applied to Child Education in the Children's Houses*, which was translated into many languages and was widely influential. By 1913 there were more than one hundred Montessori schools in the United States. At the time of Montessori's death in 1952 there were more than 4,000 Montessori preschools worldwide, but very few in the United States. In addition to widespread admiration and imitation, there was also opposition, particularly by William Heard Kilpatrick, a follower of John Dewey, perhaps the most influential professor of education of his generation, and author of *The Montessori Method Examined* (1914). Primarily as a result of his criticism and active opposition, the Montessori approach made little progress in the United States in the second quarter of the twentieth century.

---

12. John Dewey, *Democracy and Education*, 154.

The Montessori movement in the United States between the two world wars was also slowed by dissension among Montessori's followers and, it must be admitted, by Montessori herself, who identified herself with the movement in a way that fostered adulation and strict imitation over experimentation and collaboration. It also seems likely that resistance to Montessori in the United States was also likely due to her three unchangeable disadvantages: She was a woman in a field dominated by men at the top (the theoreticians in charge of the schools of mostly women teachers); she was a Catholic in a still predominantly Protestant and secular culture; and she was Italian while Italy was on the opposite side of the United States in both world wars.

Despite resistance on several fronts, Montessori's method, particularly in the last half century, has exercised a profound affect on early childhood education. Like Dewey, Montessori's influence has spread so thoroughly into almost every field concerning child development that many dominant theories and approaches have lost specific connection to her influence. Rita Kramer writes:

> She passes the test for the real innovator—many of her ideas have become part of our common language of discourse about the subject of educating the young. A random list of ideas, techniques, and objects familiar to everyone in the field of childhood education today, all of which go back to Montessori's work at the start of the century, all of which she either invented or used in a new way, might include the following (my paraphrase):
>
> • The child is different from, not a smaller edition of, an adult.
> • Real learning is experiential, not passive reception of knowledge.
> • Children learn through play.
> • Children will establish their own order if given the chance to do so.
> • Schools exist to give children the right to develop their skills.
> • The "open classroom" and "ungraded" class in which children are grouped by interest and ability rather than age.
> • The child is learning from birth, and five or six is too late to begin to attend to the child's education.
> • Early stimulation is significant for later learning.

- A child's learning materials should be interesting to the child.
- Schools must be part of a community that includes participation of parents.[13]

In addition to these contributions it is important to credit Montessori with the establishment of a method that seeks to replace the Cartesian dualistic worldview with one that is rooted in evolution and development, with a rich understanding of the child's need for positive experience. John McDermott convincingly shows the continuity (not the direct textual influence) of Montessori's approach with the empiricism of James and Dewey. He then offers a comprehensive summary of the significance of Montessori's method, including a comparison with Dewey:

> She shares with Dewey an evolutionary and experimental pedagogy, but she is far more willing than he to submit religious and spiritual qualities to the rigorous demands of concrete educational processes. Deeply committed to Catholicism, Montessori nevertheless opposes that type of religiously oriented school which is characterized by an educational theory outmoded in language and insight and negligent of empirical data about the human personality. Montessori demands that the data of anthropology and the natural sciences take their place at the base of educational practices, including those of a religious nature. By comparison, then, with other modern efforts, Montessori's view of the child is perhaps the most comprehensive available.[14]

Of course, if one were to attend to the four dimensions of the child in Steiner's anthropology—physical, etheric (subtle), psychic (soul), and "I" (identity)—not even Montessori's approach would be as comprehensive as Steiner's. The range of Montessori's influence is not as deep or as wide as Steiner's. John McDermott writes: "The most striking feature of Montessori's work is that her method, her teachers, and the learning children in her

---

13. Ibid., 373–374.
14. John McDermott, "Liberty and Order in the Educational Anthropology of Maria Montessori," in Douglas R. Anderson, ed., *The Drama of Possibility: Experience as Philosophy of Culture*, 429.

programs are found throughout the world. No other education has such global influence."[15] Perhaps, but the influence and spread of Waldorf is surely comparable, and Steiner's insights are surely deeper and more comprehensive than those of either Dewey or Montessori.

STEINER'S WALDORF APPROACH TO EDUCATION

For the past thirty-five years I have been variously involved in the Waldorf approach: my wife is a retired Waldorf kindergarten teacher, our daughter attended two Waldorf high schools, and I have lectured more than a dozen times to faculty and parents of Waldorf schools on the relation of Waldorf education to Rudolf Steiner. Our two San Francisco grandchildren attend the San Francisco Waldorf School.

In the years following World War I, the anthroposophic movement took up the challenge of social and political renewal. Steiner believed the insights gained through anthroposophic study could lead the way to a just society. In the years before his untimely death in 1925, he either launched or encouraged initiatives in alternative banking, scientific research, agriculture, medicine, religion, and the arts. Steiner spoke to a wide variety of audiences on the need for a Threefold Commonwealth in which cultural institutions such as schools would be freed of all government influence. Like Dewey and Montessori, Steiner saw education as the foundation for a just and creative society.

In 1919, in response to a plea from Emil Molt, owner of the Waldorf-Astoria Cigarette Factory in Stuttgart, for help in educating the children of his employees, Steiner developed a model educational experiment based on anthroposophic research concerning the inner life and child development. He recruited the teachers and knew each child by name. He also delivered more than a hundred lectures on the Waldorf approach to education. Tragically, Steiner died in 1925, six years after founding the first and only school in his lifetime, the model for the Waldorf School Movement. Waldorf Schools spread throughout Germany, then

---

15. Ibid., 432.

the rest of Europe, and then North America. The first Waldorf School in the United States was founded in New York City in 1926. There are now more than a thousand schools around the world, more than 150 in North America, and in recent years schools have sprung up in the major cities in South America, Israel and other Middle Eastern countries, South Asia, South and East Africa, Russia, China, Taiwan, and Japan.

With good reason, Waldorf teachers are fond of repeating as a mantra Steiner's advice concerning the child:

> Receive the child in reverence,
> educate the child in love,
> and send the child forth in freedom.

A second mantra by Steiner sometimes follows: "A child's reverence for others develops into a reverence for truth and knowledge."

Reverence is one of the two virtues, along with humility, that Steiner recommends in the first chapter of his foundational book, *How to Know Higher Worlds*. Love—and thinking characterized by love—is Steiner's fundamental commitment and the goal that he posits for the evolution of humanity. In Steiner's understanding, freedom is not given to humanity, but rather something to be attained through spiritual effort. The right education can set the child and young adult on this path to freedom. The attainment of freedom is the great task for humanity in the present age, and a precondition for love. These three terms—reverence, love, and freedom—also serve as a reminder that according to Steiner, the child recapitulates the ages of the evolution of consciousness.

In the beginning, humanity was gifted with a reverent relationship to the divine that was slowly lost. This loss, which made possible the attainment of individuality, is characteristic of the Axial Age (eighth to second centuries BCE) or, according to Steiner, the third and fourth cultural periods (eighth millennium BCE to fifteenth century CE). Distance from the divine that humanity experienced during these two millennia led to the possibility of human love and reverence freely given. Freedom is the necessary condition for the full realization of love, understood as the reconnection lost in the devolution/evolution of humanity, from unfree intimacy to a loss of intimacy to recovered intimacy. In creating the Waldorf curriculum Steiner utilized the Recapitulation Theory introduced by Ernst Haeckel, according to which "all humanity has gone through the time of the prehistoric cultures; then came the Greek and Roman cultures, followed by the development of the Middle Ages, and so forth, right up to the present time."[16]

According to Steiner, the young child is a creature of will seeking connection, and is characterized by the exercise of will. As Montessori divides the child's life into six-year periods Steiner holds to the seven-year rhythm. In the first seven-year period, birth to seven, the child typically seeks goodness, and needs to feel that the world is good. In the second seven-year period, ages seven to fourteen, the child is attuned to the beauty of the world. In the third seven-year period the young adult generally seeks truth, and consequently admires worthy individuals and suffers the hypocrisy of adults whose words and deeds suggest untruth.

Crucially, like both Dewey and Montessori, Steiner's Waldorf approach emphasizes the full development of head, heart, and hands, as is often said. However, in all three approaches the three types of learning should be understood in reverse. In the early years, all three educators begin with the body (the hands), and then the emotional life (the heart), and then the thinking life (the head). With the onset of adolescence, the student's thinking is addressed directly along with emotional engagement and will activity Most important, for all three educational approaches, these capacities are to be distinguished but not separated. Children not only think and enjoy with their body, but the body also thinks and enjoys. Waldorf schools in particular are characterized by the attempt to integrate children's feeling, willing, and thinking to maximize their freedom and responsibility for nature, for themselves, and for the global human community. One could summarize the development of the intellect by saying that it expresses itself first in the will (i.e., the limbs, especially the hands) at ages one to seven, in the feeling soul at ages seven to fourteen, and then in thinking at age fourteen and beyond.

---

16. Rudolf Steiner, *The Spirit of the Waldorf School*, 34.

The Waldorf schools are especially significant for reconciling sciences and the arts on the basis of a single source and methodology—namely, active, heartfelt thinking. In this respect, all Waldorf schools are, or should be Emersonian—i.e., devoted to the development of imagination. With Dewey and Montessori, Steiner is devoted to providing a learning environment and pedagogy conducive to the learning of each child. Their differences are also instructive: Dewey is committed to maximizing the opportunity for each child in his or her social context. He is focused on the whole child but as contrasted with Montessori, and in definite contrast with Steiner, he puts little emphasis on the inner life of the child. Steiner never loses sight of the child's spiritual reality, including an awareness of the child's individual destiny. Waldorf teachers often speak of the fascinating ways that children lead their parents to the Waldorf school and immediately find ways of signaling that they are at home there.

One of the best known, and least understood, features of Waldorf education is its reluctance to teach reading—and intellectual thinking, in general—until the children are seven years old, or more accurately until their teeth begin to change. This ideal sharply conflicts with Montessori's attempt to enable children to read as early as possible, by age three or four. Obviously, when considered only superficially, the Waldorf approach lends itself to ridicule: critics and skeptics have no doubt noted that children do not read with their teeth. The change of teeth, which might occur unusually early or late in some children, is not significant in itself, but it signals the important change taking place in the child at this time. Steiner describes in detail how the task of the infant, the toddler, and the kindergartner is to develop his/her physical organism. The energies devoted to forming the inner organs and brain are freed up for "school" learning in the seventh year. The hardening that takes place in the body is manifest most obviously in the teeth. Therefore the onset of the second dentition is one sign that the child is ready for school. Steiner explained:

> Before the change of teeth the child is not yet aware of its
> separate identity and consequently cannot appreciate the

characteristic nature of other persons, whose gestures, man-
ners of speaking, and even sentiments it imitates in an impon-
derable way....With the change of teeth, new soul forces of
feeling, linked to breathing and blood circulation, come into
their own, and the child begins to distance itself from other
people who are not experienced as individual characters.[17]

Steiner discussed from a spiritual perspective all of the seven-
year transitions from the change of teeth at age seven, puberty at
age fourteen,[18] descent of the "I" or spiritual identity at approximately age twenty-one, and on through each seven-year phase
until death. Steiner's discussion of the significance of the change
of teeth at age seven is but one of many examples of his attempt
to explain inner spiritual development by reference to physical
change, and vice versa. Puberty, of course, is another important
example. Steiner also offered important observations concerning
the transformation which takes place approximately between age
twenty and twenty-one—specifically, the emergence of the "I" or
spirit in the individual and the consequent ability to chart one's
free spiritual life. All of these phases, and the appropriate educational processes which ought to accompany them, take place in
a social context that Steiner also reads from the vantage point of
spiritual perception.

Among the many startling statements Steiner made to teachers one concerns daily rhythm and sleep. He claimed that in sleep
we "digest" the day's experience and continue to learn. Tuesday's
lesson builds on Monday's with the expectation that children
understand the material on a deeper level because they have slept
on it. The week, too, has its rhythm, as do the month and the
year. All outer rhythms, whether annual, monthly, or circadian,
inform the shape of lesson plans at a Waldorf school. In essence,
the rhythm of the Waldorf curriculum is breath. The inhalation
is the moment of concentration and contraction; the exhalation

17. Rudolf Steiner, "The First School Years: From Whole to Part," in
    Roberto Trostli, ed., *The Rhythms of Learning*, 140–141.
18. One assumes that Waldorf teachers are aware that their female
    students are beginning puberty much earlier, many at age twelve and an
    increasing number at age ten.

relaxes and expands. As it does to soul and spirit (mind) this applies to the physical body. Waldorf teachers like to speak of the art of teaching as the art of healthy rhythms. Only administrators or bureaucrats with little or no experience of happy children, and certainly not Waldorf teachers, could impose on children expectations devoid of healthy organic rhythms currently in evidence in schools throughout the world.

Immeasurable damage is being done to elementary school children as a result of testing and electronic learning, among other mistaken and misused forms of pedagogy, and even greater damage seems to be in store for children and adolescents whose schools fail to understand, or even to consider, the inner life of the human being from birth to death. Steiner does not lose sight of the image of the adult human being toward which the child is unconsciously moving, and that is mysteriously calling children to the full realization of their destiny as individuals (what Jung refers to as individuation). In this great evolution, both teachers and parents exercise decisive influence. The key ingredient in that influence must be love.

The concept of love in the Waldorf approach to education is intended not as a vague ideal, or a sentiment, but a deep and truthful relationality. Love for the children should motivate all aspects of the their education, including curriculum, pedagogy, recreation, artistic expression, conversation, and especially nurturing of the inner life. The silent thoughts of teachers must be loving so that all teaching arises from an inner, living experience of love. The task of teachers is to love their students regardless of how they present themselves. Both the intellectually gifted and the socially awkward, the artistic genius and children who rarely experience success, are to be loved equally in the Waldorf classrooms.

Although the academic subjects remain the "bread and butter" for all teachers, Waldorf teachers see their task in a greater context. Social development, emotional maturity, and self-confidence in practical life are all essential in the Waldorf classroom. The Waldorf attitude towards the spiritual aspect of existence is summarized by Steiner:

As teachers, we must aim at turning our young human beings into social beings by the time of puberty. We must also try to cultivate in them religious feelings, not in a bigoted or sectarian way, but in the sense that they acquire the seriousness necessary to recognize that the physical world is everywhere permeated by spirit. They should not feel inwardly satisfied with merely observing the outer sense world but should be able to perceive the spiritual foundations of the world everywhere.[19]

Teachers of children under the age of seven have the challenging task of helping children to stay as long as possible in the world of healthy images—not images created to sell products or instill fear. Teachers are expected to provide children with attitudes and actions worthy of imitation by them. As Steiner explains, "During the first seven years, children's activities mirror and imitate their surroundings—above all through gestures, including the subtle inner gestures that live in speech."[20]

Class teachers need to be worthy of the trust that children will naturally invest in the teacher's authority. A major change in method is required during early adolescence. Waldorf elementary teachers are expected to remain and advance with their class for eight years. This continuity enables teachers to establish a deep relationship with each child. Then, increasingly in the years following the onset of puberty, "Children enter the time of life when they can form their own judgments on matters concerning the world at large." By the eighth grade, and often beginning in the sixth and seventh, children tend to pull away from their class teacher. There is a necessary "cooling down" and a more matter-of-fact atmosphere in the classroom. As with adolescents pulling away from their parents, within a few years the affection and esteem for their teacher almost always returns in full force.

One of the most prominent characteristics of Waldorf education is artistic activity. Steiner stated that "Everything must be taught in mobile and colorful pictures, not in dead static

---

19. Rudolf Steiner, *The Fundamental of Waldorf Education*, 132.
20. Ibid.

concepts."[21] Waldorf teachers typically have spent two years in art courses, such as singing, flute, speech, eurythmy, sculpture, painting, and drama. Although Waldorf schools have specialty art teachers, elementary and high school teachers are expected to be able to integrate the arts with all other subjects. The main lesson books that students create in elementary grades, and sometimes in high school, are usually works of great care that Waldorf alumni cherish for a lifetime.

The Waldorf curriculum is informed by evolution, cultural as well as biological, and also includes a close attention to the patterns of history. The high school curriculum emphasizes awareness of global events, what Steiner referred to, and recommended, by the term *symptomatology,* the signs of the time playing out as the child is awakening to the historical world. Waldorf curriculum includes the study of the world religions in a sequence that is thought to be in harmony with the children's development, and with the evolution of cultures. Waldorf pedagogy seeks to include in all lessons a respect for Earth and sustainable lifestyles. Each Waldorf school, even those in crowded buildings in urban areas, typically has a garden that students tend throughout the year. Waldorf schools set a high standard with their concern for ecology. Remarkably, this started in the 1920s!

Waldorf school teachers take their vocation seriously. Waldorf faculties are known for their dedication to every child in the school; the faculty study the children who present certain challenges to their teachers. Thursday evening meetings fail to end as scheduled because faculty continue to discuss matters of deep concern to the life of the school. Administrators are elected by the faculty. All of the Waldorf teachers—early childhood, elementary and high school, and specialty teachers (music, arts, eurythmy, crafts)—speak to the parents about Waldorf pedagogy. Of course, the teachers also meet regularly with parents concerning the progress of each child in their care. To be a Waldorf teacher is to be devoted to a more than full-time job. For most, though, it is an immeasurably rewarding task.

---

21. Ibid., 179.

Perhaps the best summation of the spirit of a Waldorf school would be to quote the verse that Steiner gave to the students in the very first one. In grades five through eight Waldorf students recite this verse at the start of each school day:

I gaze into the world
In which the sun is shining,
In which the stars are sparkling,
In which the stones repose,
Where living plants are growing,
Where sentient beasts are living,
Where human souls on Earth
Give dwelling to the Spirit.

I gaze into my soul
That lives within my being,
The world Creator moves
In sun light and in soul light,
In wide world space there without,
In soul depths here within.

To thee, Creator Spirit,
I will now turn my heart
To ask that strength and blessing
To learn and for work may grow
Within my inmost being.

Rabindranath Tagore

ART AND AESTHETICS

RABINDRANATH TAGORE: SPIRIT IN ART

In the same way that Sri Aurobindo and C. G. Jung insisted that their truest lives were not visible for a usual biography, the life of Rabindranath Tagore (1861–1941) is most fully expressed in the astonishing range of artistic works that he produced from age eight to eighty. As one of his biographers, Dhurjati Prasad Mukerji comments, "Tagore's life history is mainly the biography of ideas and artistic creations." He continues:

> Tagore's crises are all subjective, begotten by this spirit, even if nursed by the objective situation....This does not mean that he did not share in the tragedies of his country and the world. That he did, but his actions remained essentially personal, spiritual."[1]

The resistance of deep thinkers to having their biographies written has not at all discouraged biographers: There are lengthy biographies of all three of these thinkers, as well as of other thinkers treated in this book, including the three American philosophers, Teilhard, Montessori, Carson, Gandhi, and the Dalai Lama. A life lived in interior depths, it appears, can nonetheless be a life of great influence. On the occasion of Tagore's seventieth birthday, Jawaharlal Nehru, who became the first prime minister of India, wrote:

---

1. Dhurjati Prasad Mukerji, *Tagore—A Study*, 15, quoted in Amiya Chakravarty, ed., *A Tagore Reader*, 380–381.

Rabindranath Tagore has given to our nationalism the outlook of internationalism and has enriched it with art and
music and the magic of his words, so that it has become a
full-blooded emblem of India's awakened spirit.[2]

Tagore was born the grandson of Prince Dwarkanath Tagore,
the head of an enormous, wealthy, highly cultured Bengali family and a close collaborator of Ram Mohan Roy (1772–1833),
regarded as the father of modern India and the primary reformer
of modern Hinduism. Tagore's father, Maharishi Debendranath,
was a follower of Roy and one of the foremost opponents of
village Hinduism; his mother, Sharada Devi, gave birth to nine
sons and six daughters, of whom Rabindranath was the youngest. Tagore's distant relationship with his mother was similar
to Aurobindo's relationship to his mother, who was probably
schizophrenic. In his *Reminiscences* (1912), Tagore recounts his
memory of his mother's death:

> When my mother died I was quite a child. She had been ailing
> for a long time, and we did not even know when her mal-
> ady had taken a fatal turn.... On the night she died we were
> asleep in our room downstairs.... When in the morning, we
> were told of her death, I could not realize all that it meant
> for me.... As the day wore on, and we returned from the
> cremation, we turned into our lane and I looked up toward
> my father's room on the third floor. He was still in the front
> verandah sitting motionless in prayer.[3]

Tagore responded more profoundly to the suicide at age
twenty-five of his sister-in-law, Kadambari Devi. Kadambari,
who had come to the Tagore estate as the bride of one of Tagore's
brothers, was an accomplished writer who had strongly encouraged Rabindranath's poetry. Kadambari's note prior to her suicide was destroyed by the Tagore family, but Rabindranath's
response has survived as literature as well as biography:

---

2. Jawaharlal Nehru, *The Golden Book of Tagore,* quoted in Ibid., 386.
3. Rabindranath Tagore, quoted in *Reminiscences,* 93.

When death suddenly came, and in the moment tore a gaping rent in life's seamless fabric, I was utterly bewildered. All around, the trees, the soil, the water, the sun, the moon, the stars, remained as immovably true as before, and yet the person who was as truly there, who, through a thousand points of contact with life, mind, and heart, was so very more true for me, had vanished in an instant like a dream. What a perplexing contradiction! How was I ever to reconcile what remained with that which had gone? [4]

Tagore appears to have recovered through insight that proved characteristic of his later thought and expression. In the same passage he wrote:

The all-pervading pressure of worldly existence is compensated by death, and thus it does not crush us. The terrible weight of eternal life does not have to be endured by man—this truth came over me that day as a wonderful revelation. [5]

Tagore began publishing poetry at age eight. Strangely, when Tagore was eighteen his father arranged for him to marry a ten-year-old illiterate girl who worked on the Tagore estate, whom Rabindranath did not know, and with whom he seemed to have had little in common. His wife, Mrinalini died, in 1902, age thirty-two; Tagore did not remarry and died at age eighty. Sri Aurobindo also had an arranged marriage to a young woman similar to Tagore's wife, and also named Mrinalini. Aurobindo's marriage would have resembled Tagore's had Aurobindo's Mrilalini not died of tuberculosis before she spent even a night with her much older husband. Gandhi married his wife Kasturba when they were both thirteen, but Kasturba proved to be an ideal lifelong partner, very powerful and in many respects as admirable as her husband. Nonetheless, Tagore did not allow his unfulfilling and sometimes tragic personal life to impede his artistic growth and expression.

---

4. Rabindranath Tagore, quoted in Krishna Dutta and Andrew Robinson, *Rabindranath Tagore: The Myriad-Minded Man*, 89.
5. Ibid.

When Tagore was awarded the Nobel Prize for Literature in 1913, his work was not well known in the West but his *Gitanjali* was known to W. B. Yeats who had recommended Tagore for the Nobel Prize. In India Tagore was regarded as the country's foremost artist and esthetician. He wrote hundreds of Bengali songs (including songs that were adopted as the national anthems of India and Bangladesh), created hundreds of paintings, and wrote dozens of books on aesthetics, education, and politics. In a letter to Tagore, Albert Schweitzer referred to him as being as important to India as Goethe was to Europe. Except perhaps Schweitzer (physician in the Congo, musician, scripture scholar, cultural historian), Steiner is the only other European comparable to either Goethe or Tagore. Emerson if probably the only American artist–philosopher comparable to Goethe, Tagore, Schweitzer, or Steiner. India boasts two such artist–philosophers, Tagore and Sri Aurobindo, who were both spiritual geniuses as well.

Sri Aurobindo, steeped in the Upanishads (as well as in Hegel and Nietzsche), and author of *Savitri*, one of the longest poems in the English language, had a deep affinity for the poetry of his fellow Bengali. In his *Future Poetry,* Aurobindo refers to Tagore as a *rishi*, a spiritual teacher such as those who first chanted the Upanishads. (In passing, Sri Aurobindo typically includes a negative reference to the Buddhist ideal of Nirvana.)

> The idea of the poet who is also the Rishi has made again its appearance....
>
> To find our self and the self of things is not to go through a rarefied ether of thought into Nirvana, but to discover the whole greatest integral power of our complete existence.
>
> This need is the sufficient reason for attaching the greatest importance to those poets in whom there is the double seeking of this twofold power, the truth and reality of the eternal self and spirit in man and things and the insistence of life.... The poetry of Tagore owes its sudden and universal success to this advantage that he gives us more of this discovery and fusion for which the mind of our age is in quest than any other creative writer of the time. His work is a constant music of the overpassing of the borders, a chant-filled realm

in which the subtle sounds and lights of the truth of the spirit give new meanings to the finer subtleties of life.[6]

In the West, the term *Renaissance* refers to the brilliant fifteenth- and sixteenth-century thinkers and artists who transformed European thought and culture, including Nicholas of Cusa, Leonardo da Vinci, Marselio Ficino, Nicholas Copernicus, Pico della Mirandola, Michaelangelo, and Raphael. This Renaissance celebrated the interpenetration of the physical and spiritual, particularly through the arts. Another "Renaissance" of comparable genius occurred in India from the first half of the nineteenth century to the midle of the twentieth, primarily in Bengal. Led by Maharishi Debendranath Tagore and Keshab Chandra Sen, the distinguished followers of Ram Mohan Roy, this renaissance transformed India and Hinduism. Its next generation of descendants included both Rabindranath Tagore and Sri Aurobindo, both Bengalis, though Tagore lived his entire life in Bengal whereas Sri Aurobindo spent age seven to twenty-one in England. Unlike the European Renaissance, the Bengal Renaissance was not followed by a philosophical and scientific revolution, such as the one led by Galileo, Bacon, Descartes and Newton, that effectively separated the physical and spiritual, and subsequently led to denial of the spiritual. The Bengal Renaissance celebrated the artistic and the spiritual and the essential harmony between them. It also fostered harmony among worldviews.

When Swami Vivekananda, the disciple of the great remarkable saint, Swami Ramakrishna, who had deeply absorbed Ram Mohan Roy's passionate, scholarly, visionary writings on the harmony of religions and was a great scholar and teacher in his own right, made his celebrated speeches at the first World Parliament of Religions in Chicago, 1893, he was completely comfortable speaking extemporaneously on the ideal of religious unity. Roy was steeped in Islam and Christianity as well as in Hindu scriptures, especially Upanishads and the Bhagavad Gita. He was a scholar of Arabic, Persian, Hebrew, Greek, and Latin. In 1828 he founded Brahmo Samaj, a movement for the reestablishment of

---

6. Sri Aurobindo, *The Future Poetry*, 321–323.

Hinduism based on the Universal Brahman. Roy had two truly great followers, Debendranath Tagore (father of Rabindranath) and Keshab Chandra Sen (a scholar of Carlyle and Emerson). Roy can be considered the first scholar of comparative religion as well as the inspiration of Vivekananda, Tagore, and Sri Aurobindo.

Debendranath Tagore and Keshab Chandra Sen turned Brahmo Samaj into a national movement for the renewal of classical Hinduism and for religious unity. The Samaj movement declined toward the end of the nineteenth century but the ideas that Roy was the first to express and that Debendranath Tagore and Sen preached throughout India proved directly influential on Rabindranath Tagore as well as partly on Sri Aurobindo, and indirectly on Gandhi who learned from the Brahmo Samaj movement both the harmony of religions and the inseparability of religion and social justice.

By 1930, at age seventy, when Tagore delivered the Hibbert Lectures at Oxford, he was in correspondence or conversation with the major Western thinkers and artists of his generation, including W. B. Yeats, Robert Frost, G. B. Shaw, H. G. Wells, and Albert Einstein. In India he has two equals: Sri Aurobindo, revolutionary, mystic, poet, philosopher, and cultural historian; and Gandhi whom Tagore both admired and criticized. Because Tagore and Aurobindo were both Bengali poets as well as mystics and cultural historians, Tagore is more similar to Aurobindo, but because Gandhi and Tagore were so well known in the West (whereas Aurobindo was not, and still is not), the latter two were invariably paired. As V. S. Naravane writes in the first sentence of his authoritative essay on Tagore:

> Gandhi and Tagore are the two eyes of modern India's soul. They are the two banks that have determined the course and current of Indian thought in our age. Like Plato and Aristotle, they completed each other in the very process of contradicting each other.[7]

This statement about Gandhi and Tagore is exactly the kind of statement that one finds throughout Tagore's writings: What is

---

7. V. S. Naravane, *Modern Indian Thought: A Philosophical Survey*, 111.

thought to be opposite can be shown to be complementary, and in fact, in harmony. This is also the kind of statement one finds throughout V. S. Naravane's *Modern Indian Thought*, a masterful study of Ram Mohan Roy, Swami Ramakrishna, Swami Vivekananda, Rabindranath Tagore, M. K. Gandhi, Sri Aurobindo, S. Radhakrishnan, and Ananda Coomaraswamy—a cluster of genius and creativity on a par with classical Athens and the Italian Renaissance.

Continuing the pairing of Gandhi and Tagore, Amiya Chakravarti, Tagore's secretary and editor of *A Tagore Reader*, writes the following:

> To the world outside India, Tagore and Gandhi were the two great personalities who represented the spiritual genius of India. In 1931 Gandhi wrote of Tagore: "In common with thousands of his countrymen I owe much to one who by his poetic genius and singular purity of life has raised India in the estimation of the world."[8]

For Tagore—poet, short story writer, song composer, novelist, playwright, essayist, and painter—*rasa yoga* (the discipline of art and beauty) is the primary instrument for the expression of Brahman. Tagore offers a contemporary Upanishadic aesthetics: Brahman contains the artist and the artist reveals Brahman in relation to contemporary thought and culture. Tagore was concerned with truth and justice in every contemporary situation. Unlike Gandhi and similar to Aurobindo, Tagore studied and wrote Indian and Western philosophy. Like Gandhi he was deeply engaged in Indian and international politics. As Gandhi practiced *karma yoga*, Tagore practiced *rasa yoga*. As V. S. Naravane explains the difference:

> For Tagore, the Real is Beautiful; for Gandhi it is Good....They were both humanists. Gandhi's humanism had a moral–social basis while Tagore's was colored by his aesthetic–mystical experience.[9]

---

8. Amiya Chakravarty, ed., *A Tagore Reader*, 390.
9. V. S. Naravane, *Modern Indian Thought*, 112.

Tagore was a great traveler. Whereas Aurobindo did not leave Pondicherry for the last forty years of his life, having previously journeyed only to England, and Gandhi lived only in India, England and South Africa, Tagore made extensive visits to Japan, United States, England, Burma, Hong Kong, and Indonesia. Partly because of his travels his letters comprise twelve volumes. In addition to his lifelong work as an artist, Tagore was an informed participant in international politics. Ever the reconciler, he was equally sympathetic to and critical of India and the West. In 1915, for example, he wrote to C. F. Andrews, a devoted friend of both Gandhi and Tagore, with one of his typical assessments of the British colonization of India. Subsequent to this assessment, India remained under the rule for the next thirty years, until 1947, six years after Tagore's death, one year before the assassination of Gandhi, and three years before the death of Sri Aurobindo. Tagore wrote in language that was later used by Gandhi (who arrived in India from South Africa one year after this letter), and by Martin Luther King, Jr. in his assessment of the white privilege and power structure of the United States:

> In India, when the upper classes ruled over the lower, they forged their own chains. Europe is closely following Brahmin India, when she looks upon Asia and Africa as her legitimate fields for exploitation.... Thus Europe, gradually and imperceptibly, is losing faith in her own ideals and weakening her own moral supports.... It is a moral duty for every race to cultivate strength, so as to be able to help the world's balance of power to remain even. We are doing England the greatest disservice possible by making it easy for her to despise us and yet to rule; to feel very little sympathy for us and yet to judge us.[10]

Immediately following the 1931 Salt March led by Gandhi that was brutally suppressed by the British Government of India, it was Tagore who announced to the English-language media in India and England that by its brutality the West (in this case England) had forfeited any claims to moral superiority over India.

---

10. Rabindranath Tagore to C.F. Andrews, Calcutta, July 11, 1915, in Amiya Chakravarty, ed., *A Tagore Reader*, 24–25.

Unfortunately, immediately following its independence from England in 1947, India experienced its own internal brutality: nine million Hindus and Muslims crossed between India and Pakistan resulting in the slaughter of one million civilians, mostly by face-to-face killing.

Before turning to Tagore's aesthetics it would be worth savoring the summary of his life and work offered by V. S. Naravane:

> He never stopped growing. The universe remained for him perennially interesting. He savored every stimulus with undiminished joy.
>
> That is why the story of Tagore's life is so full of surprises. Superficially regarded, his appears to be a sheltered, uneventful life, free from want or structure. But closer observation reveals eddies and whirlpools under the apparently calm surface. And again the world discovered with a start that Tagore could not be taken for granted. His ideas could not be docketed, nor his actions predicted, nor his art labeled. From a deeply meditative existence he often jumped into the fray of social and political controversy. At sixty he emerged as a painter; at seventy he startled his readers with new experiments in style and diction; at eighty he worked out a youthful philosophy of life in which the mystery of death was beautifully accommodated. For all his mysticism he would unexpectedly come forward as a practical realist, a champion of science, democracy, and economic planning.[11]

It would be unlikely for anyone with even a slim knowledge of Rabindranath Tagore not to have come upon Einstein's concluding response in a dialogue with Tagore in New York in 1930. As this dialogue is between the greatest scientist of the twentieth century and one of the greatest artists of the twentieth century, their every word warrants our attention.

Throughout the dialogue, Einstein had been defending his view that while beauty is subjective and dependent on the human mind, certain truths about the cosmos are objective and independent of human thought. In response, Tagore stated: "If there is some truth which has no sensuous or rational relations to the

---

11. V. S. Naravane, *Modern Indian Thought*, 114.

human mind it will ever remain as nothing so long as we remain human beings." In the next to the last sentence in the dialogue Einstein exclaimed, "Then I am more religious than you are!" In response to Einstein, Tagore ignored any reference as to which of them might be "more religious" and instead ended the dialogue by repeating his religious position: "My religion is in the reconciliation of the super-personal man, the universal human spirit, in my own individual being."[12] Tagore referred to his statement as a summation of his Hibbert Lectures published as *The Religion of Man*, that he had delivered earlier that year. In this summary Tagore affirms the ideal relationship between the transcendent and the human, as well as between two modes of expression, the passionate and the serene. His basic philosophical position, including his metaphysics, epistemology, ethics, and aesthetics, is steeped in the Upanishads, the philosophical–mystical texts chanted and memorized by Hindu teachers beginning in approximately eighth century BCE. In the Upanishads, Brahman—or in Tagore's terms, the "super-personal"—expresses itself through the human. Tagore's family recited the Upanishads as some Christian families read and quote the Bible and most Muslim families read and quote the Qur'an. One of his biographers claims that "Rabindranath's entire life is only an evolution and a development of his Upanshadic education."[13]

Einstein was able to say that he was more religious than Tagore because he was assuming as a criterion of religion a theistic concept of God. But Tagore's concept of the divine is more monistic than theistic. He sees the human realizing its unity with the divine not through an avatar such as Krishna or a god-man such as Christ but through art. The unity is there beneath the surface—always was and always will be—but mysticism and art are needed to realize the unity. If art were to be accepted as the mediator between human and divine, as Tagore asserts, he could have proclaimed himself "more religious." Tagore could have agreed with Einstein: There are cosmic and physical realities,

---

12. Rabindranath Tagore, *The Religion of Man*, 225.
13. Prabhat Mukerji, *Rabindra Jivani*, vol. 1, 32, quoted in V. S. Naravane, *Modern Indian Thought*, 117.

ontologically given. But he could have gone on to insist that these realities are interpreted by human beings, and most effectively by artistic, creative minds. As Goethe explained, and Einstein would have had to agree, all facts are theory-laden. All realities, no matter how ancient, vast, or solid, are interpreted. The physical world may be independent of the human mind for its existence but not for its description. Tagore could have agreed and then added that the same is true of spiritual reality—i.e., Brahman, a position that he holds throughout his writings. Tagore could have added that as Einstein was practicing science as *jnana yoga* (thinking yoga), he was practicing both *rasa yoga* based on *jnana yoga* (art that assumes spiritual knowledge), and that he and Einstein were coming to the same position even though in that remarkable dialogue they appeared to disagree.

As the Cosmos spoke to Einstein, Brahman or Infinite Spirit spoke to Tagore. We might consider Einstein a Upanishadic scientist. The major difference between their perspectives is Tagore's insistence that the universe is personal, not in the anthropomorphic sense affirmed by the Abrahamic religions, but in the philosophical, Upanishadic sense that it contains the same qualities as the human. The universe and the human person are joined soul to soul. Tagore wrote, "In art the person in us is sending its answers to the Supreme Person."[14] He artistically balances the two aspects of Brahman: *nirguna*, or Brahman without qualities—i.e., without the time and space of the created world—and *saguna*, or Brahman that creates, sustains, and transforms the created world by truth, love, and art. *Nirguna* and *saguna* are held together by art and by love. "Love has *nirguna* at one end and *saguna* at the other."[15] For Einstein, physics is the link; for Tagore, art is the link.

As Tagore can be called a Upanishadic artist, he can also be called Mahayanist. He subscribes to the wide path: all arts are ways to reconcile the human and divine. His art partakes of an infinite and enduring spiritual realm but is not removed from

---

14. Rabindranath Tagore, *Personality*, 38.
15. *Shantiniketan,* I Series: *Samanjasya,* quoted in V. S. Naravane, *Modern Indian Thought,* 129.

Earth or humanity. His art is profoundly humanist but always with an eye on oneness and transcendence. The themes of all his artistic endeavors—and they are remarkably many—is reconciling, harmonizing, joining, and balancing. The creative activity of Brahman (in its *saguna* phase) is carried out by the warmth and affection celebrated by the Vaishnava (devoted to Vishnu) poets of Bengal. Ever the skillful sustainer of opposites, Tagore's vision balances Upanishadic mysticism with Vaishnava passion. As V. S. Naravane notes:

> Tagore took what was the most positive in both traditions. To him the most satisfying worldview was that in which there was room for the warmth and exuberance of the Vaishnava poets as well as the ethical idealism and mystic intuition of the Upanishadic sages.[16]

Tagore's poem *Dui Nari* ("Two Women") depicts the reconciliation of two artistic forces, Urvashi, the Dionysian, and Lakshmi, the Apollonian:

> At some unprecedented moment, when the waters of the primeval ocean were churned, two divine forms arose from the endless deep. One was beautiful Urvashi, queen of the passions, temptress of the gods. The other was Lakshmi, maternal and pure, benefactress of all that lives and breathes.[17]

This harmony of opposites is one of the strongest characteristics of Tagore's art and aesthetics. Perhaps the reconciliation most important for Tagore's life and work is that between religion and art, two pathways between human and divine:

> My religion is essentially a poet's religion. Its touch comes to me through the same unseen and trackless channels as does the inspiration of my music. My religious life has followed the same mysterious lines of growth as my poetic life. Somehow they are wedded to each other.[18]

---

16. Ibid., 118–119.
17. Ibid., 161–162.
18. Rabindranath Tagore, quoted in Ibid., 123.

One of the secrets of Tagore's "double line of growth" is simply his attempt to embrace the finite as an expression of the infinite. There are many statements by Tagore that refer to imagination as a dynamic process, a subtle force or energy, that could be expressed without distortion by Steiner's term "etheric," the realm between the physical and the soul, or between nature and spirit. The poem *Gitanjali*, which Tagore wrote in English, provides an example of the similarity between the cosmic rhythm and Steiner's concept of the etheric:

> The same stream of life that runs through my veins night and day runs through the world and dances in rhythmic measures.
> It is the same life that shoots in joy through the dust of the earth in numberless blades of grass and breaks into tumultuous waves of leaves and flowers.
> It is the same life that is rocked in the ocean cradle of birth and death, in ebb and flow.
> I feel my limbs are made glorious by the touch of this world of life. And my pride is from the life throb of ages dancing in my blood this moment.[19]

Tagore identifies this cosmic rhythm with Shiva, most commonly shown as Nataraja, the exquisitely calm god surrounded by flame, his arms beating the rhythmic transformation of the cosmos. Naravane explains:

> The dance of the seasons finds its response in human actions. By one foot of the Nataraja the outer world of form is stirred, and by his other foot the inner world of human spirit is set in motion. And the poet says: "O Nataraja! I am your artist-disciple. I shall accept your mantram of universal rhythm."[20]

By referring to the creative, rhythmic power of nature and the human, Tagore in effect deifies the power behind all phenomena. "Tagore's *Jivan-devata* is nothing but the spirit of life in nature

---

19. Ibid., 141–142.
20. Ibid., 142.

and man."[21] Naravane could have written that the *jivan-devata* is the etheric. While it is still accurate to say, as I did above, that Tagore is a Upanishadic artist and esthetician, it would be more true to call him an etheric artist. The etheric expresses itself in rhythms and patterns. Waldorf teachers develop their etheric bodies in order to facilitate the development of their students' etheric bodies. Farmers spread biodynamic formulas on their soil in order to enhance its etheric forces. The anthroposophic sculptor works with clay in order to enhance and express its etheric quality, in order for it to breathe. The Christian Eucharist, perhaps, joins spirit and matter by bringing about a change at the etheric level. Similarly, Tagore concludes:

> This world, whose soul seems to be aching for expression in its endless rhythm of lines and colors, music and movements, hints and whispers, and all suggestion of the inexpressible, finds its harmony in the ceaseless longing of the human heart to make the Person manifest in its own creations.[22]

STEINER ON ART AS SPIRITUAL ACTIVITY

The previous chapters have treated Steiner as a philosopher (chapter 3), as an esoteric researcher of evolution of consciousness (chapter 4) and in chapters 4, 5, and 6, of exalted beings (Krishna, Buddha, Christ, Sophia), and in chapter 7 as a healer of the individual and the world. Chapters 8 to 10 treat him as the creator of the Waldorf approach to education, as a social theorist, and as an early ecologist. Steiner also worked very creatively and influentially at several arts. Histories of early twentieth-century art acknowledge that artists such as Wassily Kandinsky was deeply influenced by Theosophy, as taught in the first decades of the twentieth century, but they fail to mention that the teacher of Theosophy in the German-speaking world during those decades was Rudolf Steiner. One of the major conflicts between Steiner and Annie Besant, head of the Theosophical Society, concerned Steiner's determination to introduce arts at the international

---

21. Ibid., 143.
22. Rabindranath Tagore, *Personality*, 32–33.

Theosophical Society meeting of 1907. All his life Steiner answered requests for advice from sculptors, painters, poets, and musicians, and on his own he designed very significant buildings, including the double-cupola building, the Goetheanum.

Anthroposophical artists are fond of quoting Steiner's reply, when asked at the end of his life whether there was anything that he wished he had done differently, he said that he would have worked more on art. This is noteworthy because he did spend a tremendous amount of his time in artistic activity and lecturing on various arts. He spent ten years designing and overseeing the construction of the Goetheanum, a magnificent wooden structure on top of a commanding hill near Basil, Switzerland. Steiner believed people from disenchanted cultures would benefit from seeing the presence of spiritually inspired forms in this building. It was a great tragedy for Steiner, Anthroposophy, and more generally for the spiritual aspirations of people in the West that the Goetheanum was burned to the ground within months of its completion.

Because Steiner was also a philosopher, an esoteric researcher of exalted beings, and an expert on farming and medicine, he did not say, as Tagore did, that art is the primary link between the spiritual and physical, or infinite and finite. But he did think that art is one of the best links, and an especially effective way for Western humanity to experience spirit. He agreed with Tagore's conception of art as non-utilitarian, and added an emphasis on art as spiritually therapeutic. He sought to show how each art has the power to strengthen and heal the various parts of the human being, as follows:

> Etheric body: Architecture, sculpture, eurythmy
> Astral body: painting
> "I": music, poetry

This assignment of relationships between various arts and corresponding parts of the human person is approximate and a good start on the way to observing and developing the therapeutic function of each art, but it is only an approximation, and in fact an oversimplification. Each of the parts of the human being, particularly the etheric and astral, has its own specific parts, or levels, and they are also closely connected to the other parts.[23] The import of this information derived from hundreds of lectures that Steiner developed for practicing artists is not so much to make exact or exclusive correlations as to encourage observation and practice.

Art, which essentially means the disciplined exercise of imagination, is an essential activity for individuals and civilization. Like Tagore, Steiner insists that art is essentially non-utilitarian— and therefore paradoxically useful, in fact essential, for artists and their audience, the culture. According to Steiner the artistic process is a free initiative, one that must not be controlled by external practical pressure. This freedom is equally true of an ethical deed, a true ("I–Thou) social relationship, and the composition of a line of poetry or a watercolor painting. Aim and discipline require freedom and mutuality to create: the lines that come to a poem and the color that comes to a painting express free spiritual relationship.

Both Tagore and Steiner emphasize the positive influence of sensory life as the first half of the creative process, and individual imagination as the second half. If deprived of immediate access to the sensuous, the mind (i.e., the thinking, feeling, and willing individual artist, whether or not so professed) will nevertheless create. During the crackdown by the military dictatorship in Myanmar, Ma Thanegi, a Burmese artist, was imprisoned in 1988 for assisting Aun Sang Suu Kyi. As a journalist reports, "Worrying that she might lose her touch as a painter, she painted in her mind, and by the time she emerged from prison she had also completed two novels and committed them to memory."[24] This unremitting drive of the creative spirit demands itself to be honored in each individual.

---

23. See Hermann Poppelbaum, "The Concept and Action of the Etheric Body," in Jochen Bockemühl, et. al., *Toward a Phenomenology of the Etheric World*, 217.

24. Caroline Moorehead, "A New Start in Mandalay," *New York Review of Books*, June 5, 2014, 55.

In his lecture "Impressionism and Expressionism," Steiner remarks that he considers there to be "two original sins having to do with artistic creation and appreciation":

> Copying is certainly one of them—that is, to merely imitate, or reproduce, an object of the senses. The other original sin seems to me to be the attempt to express, or represent, the suprasensory through art.…A sign of a soul life run wild, so to speak, is a contentedness with the mere illustration, or imitation, or whatever is provided exclusively by the world of the senses. On the other hand, demanding that art embody an idea, something purely spiritual, is a sign of being possessed, in a sense by one's own understanding and reason.[25]

Steiner does not say so in this lecture but the two artistic "sins" just cited are examples of the two temptations that Steiner frequently warns against. The first is the Ahrimanic, which seduces the human to lazily settle for the immediately evident as though it were the whole of reality, the view that appearance is all there is and no more, in short, copying. The second temptation, the Luciferic, suggests that we can go directly to the spiritual without regard to the material and sensuous. The middle way advocated by Steiner can be seen in between these extremes. Steiner's indications for watercolor, for example, calls for attendance to the light shining through the colors, and what each color is trying to say in relation to the others in the emergence of form. One has to obey the colors. To paint an angel or Christ or Mary Magdalen requires collaboration with color on the way to form. Steiner's aesthetics call for sensory–suprasensory, creativity, not merely (Ahrimanic) sensible nor presumptuously (Luciferic) suprasensory.

Lines of poetry and colors on wet cardboard are alive with possibilities waiting for the exercise of free imagination. The process of art is purposive but not controlling. Ideally, the poet and painter are realizing Buber's "I–Thou" relationship. The writer of a poem and painter of watercolor invite words and color to emerge through their imaginations. The crucial characteristic of

---

25. Rudolf Steiner, quoted in Michael Howard, ed., *Art as Spiritual Activity: Rudolf Steiner's Contribution to the Visual Arts*, 197.

all art is free initiative, free expression, in relationship. In the second half of his *Philosophy of Freedom* Steiner advocates for free deeds, decisions and actions that break the chain of received thinking. Similarly, and in accord with Emerson's plea for all to have "an original relation to the universe," Steiner wants the artist to make an original relation to the universe through light and color, form, rhythm, function, and sound. Most importantly, he wants social structures and processes—organizations and relationships, including economic—to be artistic, to be creative, and of course to be free.

To Steiner, art is essential for spiritual beings (angels, archangels, and the entire hierarchy), for the human realization of love and freedom, and for the overcoming of utilitarian thinking and behavior. Goethe revised the first line of the Prologue to the Gospel of St. John, "In the beginning was the Word" to "In the beginning was the deed." Steiner's aesthetics says the same, that in the beginning is a free deed, "an original relation." Anthroposophy is a path to lead the spiritual in the individual to the spiritual in the universe: The usual way to express this relationship is free, loving, spiritual thinking, and an equally valid way is art.

Half of the courses in the curriculum of Waldorf teacher training are devoted to the arts, not to make art teachers but to make future teachers artistic, to enable them to instill in themselves artistic patterns, rhythms, perceptions, and observations. As an artist, esthetician, and teacher of both artists and teachers, Steiner was trying to teach an imaginative way of life that puts one effectively in relation with the universe—with family members, organizations, babies and students, colors, myths, stories, historical events, numbers, seeds, cells, chemical formulas, farms and gardens, planets and galaxies. Art, like other spiritual practices, is a full-time commitment.

All arts require disciplined effort. This is especially so of eurythmy, the art that Steiner created as an antidote to purely physical dance. Performance of eurythmy is intended to be *etheric,* an expression of the inner life. Steiner created eurythmy in response to the mother of Lori Smits who asked Steiner if he would work with her daughter, who wished to be a dancer.

Steiner taught the young dancer several dozen gestures by which to express the inner qualities of sound. As poetry and music participate in the spiritual world, and create through the agency of the poet and musician, eurythmic gestures enable the eurythmist to manifest artistically the inner reality of sound.

It is the ultimate insult for a group of eurythmists to judge another eurythmist to have lapsed into dance—i.e., dropped from etheric to physical movement. Excellent dance (whether ballet, modern, or some other style) is thrilling and fabulously artistic, but it is on a different level than eurythmy, the difference being the expression and appreciation of the physical body as distinct (but not separate) from the etheric. The intimate relation of sound and gesture fulfills Steiner's conception of Anthroposophy: Eurythmy links the spiritual in the individual (specifically the etheric body of the eurythmist) to the inner reality of the universe (specifically poetic images or musical expression).

Steiner created eurythmy, and eurythmists practice and teach eurythmy, very consciously aware of the task of the time: The need to connect, actively and with some difficulty, spirit and matter. Given the evolution of consciousness, and the accelerating speed of the loss of what Barfield calls participation, we might consider Anthroposophy to be a discipline of re-participation in spirit and divinity. According to Steiner, the curse of the time is automatic unconsciousness, the failure of free thinking, willing, and loving. Steiner created the Goetheanum, among other reasons, in order to stage eurythmy performances and his four mystery dramas. Unlike Tagore's plays, Steiner's four dramas are esoteric, essentially the dramatic presentation of characters who recur in four historical periods working on the same continuing karmic challenges and relationships.

In addition to the Goetheanum building by which Steiner sought to bring the etheric into expression through wooden forms, stained glass windows, and painted ceilings, Steiner worked on an enormous statue that he titled *The Representative of Humanity*. Fortunately, when the Goetheanum burned the statue was safely in the carpentry shop next to the Goetheanum where Steiner lived during the last nine months of his life. This statue shows Lucifer on one side representing the spiritual separated from earthly life, and Ahriman on the other side representing the material in its most mechanistic and sclerotic manifestation. In the center the image of Christ strives to hold the material and spiritual in balance. Tagore, who had a deep understanding of Christianity, would have appreciated this artistic balance of spirit and matter in one harmonious artistic expression.

As Tagore's art and aesthetics can be regarded as Upanishadic, Steiner's art and aesthetics are best understood as Western esoteric and Christo-centric. Steiner refers to his sculpture as the "representative of humanity," or *anthropos*, the ideal of humanity, yet this figure is *also* clearly Christ. Steiner considered Christ, a divine being fully incarnated into the fully human life of Jesus of Nazareth, to be the ideal reconciler of spirit and matter—the balance between the out-of-balance Lucifer and out-of-balance Ahriman.

While Lucifer and Ahriman are not standard icons in orthodox Christianity, Christ clearly belongs to Christianity and is not, or at least not yet, a figure that is readily available to non-Christians, who of course constitute the majority of humanity. Consequently, it would seem that Steiner's art, understood as the reconciliation of spirit and matter, and ideally symbolized by Christ, must be understood as Christian in some sense. But in what sense? One understanding among many is found appropriately in an introduction to Steiner's lectures on Goethe's *Faust*. The following passage by Frederick Amrine, an internationally known Goethe scholar, deserves to be quoted at length, particularly in a discussion of Steiner's art and aesthetics, which must include Goethe, and especially *Faust*, to which Steiner devoted two enormous volumes of lectures:

> Nobody would mistake Mahler for an orthodox Christian....
> Nor should anyone mistake Goethe for a conventional Christian, but the end of *Faust* seems at first glance to be invoking a thoroughly orthodox vision of the afterlife. My contention is that these three difficult cases—Goethe, Mahler, and Steiner—are mutually illuminating....

I submit that the parallels between Mahler's interpretation of *Faust* and Steiner's are uncanny, and that Mahler is a welcome guide in helping us to understand Steiner rightly. Like Mahler and Goethe before him, Steiner invokes the language of religion as a means of transcending religious orthodoxy. All three are heralds of free spirituality.[26]

Without at all qualifying Amrine's deep understanding of Goethe and Steiner, I need to reconcile his understanding with my own understanding that Steiner's art is in some sense Christian. "The reconciliation of spirit and matter, and ideally symbolized by Christ, must be understood as Christian in some sense." Steiner assumes and affirms freedom. Amrine's reference to Goethe, Mahler, and Steiner, as "heralds of free spirituality" does not negate Steiner's conviction that Christ—and not merely the term *Christ*—is the reconciler of spirit and matter as well as of humanity and divinity. As art is the realm of freedom, I believe that Steiner leaves the interpretation of Goethe's and his own Christian symbolism to be both art and spiritual reality, or to use the title of his first lectures on Christianity, a matter of "mystical fact."

Each chapter in this book asks the reader "how far do you want to go?" Amrine's analysis leaves us free to experience and to respond to these artists with ever deeper questions, such as: Is Steiner's "Representative of Humanity" a depiction of the ideal human being or a depiction of Christ, the Second Person of the Christian Trinity, incarnated in Jesus of Nazareth? It would seem both. Does Steiner expect this figure to be experienced as the Christ of the New Testament? Christ as the reconciler of spirit and matter includes an actual deed in time and space. As Amrine notes, "Steiner uses the language of religion as a means of transcending religious orthodoxy," but Steiner also works as an artist and teacher of artists in such a way as to leave artist and audience free to go as far as they wish to go, and are able to go, on a karmically informed journey from religious language to "mystical fact,"

---

26. Frederick Amrine, "Introduction: Rudolf Steiner's *Faust*," in Rudolf Steiner, *Anthroposophy in the Light of Goethe's Faust: Writings and Lectures from mid-1880s to 1916*, xxiii–xxvi.

from the image of Christ in art to the ontological reality of Christ who is the source of art.

For Steiner true art never violates freedom; it is always "a herald of free spirituality." Consequently, Steiner would almost certainly agree with Amrine's analysis, and he would surely be pleased to be grouped with Goethe and Mahler. But if he were lecturing not to artists but to Lutheran priests or New Testament scholars, Steiner might well refer to Christ very differently—not inconsistently or exclusively, but from a different perspective. When speaking of art and aesthetics, he would leave the reader or the audience free to fill in, extend, or deepen his Christian terminology and iconography, but in a Christian context he would also affirm the ontological meaning of Christian terms. For Steiner as for Tagore, the arts are pointers, rather like the Zen distinction of the finger and the moon, except that in addition to speaking and writing on the process of pointing—the arts—Steiner occasionally, as in his lectures on the events in the New Testament, tries to describe the moon.

According to Steiner's understanding of various arts, all true arts enable the artist and the observer or listener to get a glimpse of spirit, such that serious students of one or another art can glimpse further and deeper, just as a student of the Upanishads, the Bhagavad Gita, or John's Gospel, can see further and more accurately. The plant reaches to the sun and becomes more sun-like; the soul reaches toward spirit and becomes more divine. Artists such as Bach, Mozart, Beethoven, and Mahler, like Dante, Shakespeare, Goethe, and Rilke, all enable us, if we make the effort to learn to glimpse spirit, to overcome the alienation that is the inheritance of the modern Western humanity. It is necessary in this time to reconcile matter and spirit, human and divine. In aesthetics, this is the function of art; in theological terms this is the function of the incarnation and resurrection of Christ.

The burning of the first Goetheanum caused intense suffering for Steiner. He was convinced that the design of the building, the arrangement of the columns, the stained glass, the stage for eurythmy, and his mystery dramas would have provided modern Western observers a successful observation of spirit in matter, or matter expressing spirit. It was widely reported that while Steiner was watching the Goetheanum burn through the night he witnessed the etheric body of the building go up in flames—its wood from all over Europe and north America, the loving devotion of its workers during the previous ten years. Steiner was convinced that Western humanity, caught between denial of spirit and, in Amrine's term, "religious orthodoxy," might have been able to glimpse spirit in wood, spirit in willing work, spirit in love. The loss of the Goetheanum led Steiner to start again, designing a new building, and to broaden his work in education and agriculture, among many other activities.

Thomas Berry, Rachel Carson,
John Grim and Mary Evelyn Tucker, Sean Kelly,
Brian Thomas Swimme, Elizabeth Allison

11

On Behalf of Gaia

I came to ecology after four decades of studying, teaching, and writing about philosophies, religions, and spiritual teachings. When I finally focused on ecology I did so rather reluctantly. I felt that this ecological crisis—mind that it was destroying Earth and all species for all future generations—was interfering with my work and intruding on interesting conversations. I have been asked, sometimes with a hint of bewilderment, what was wrong with me, how could I have missed the most important challenge facing humanity for the foreseeable future, the one challenge that trumps all others? I have several explanations, none of them adequate alone, but they perhaps approach plausibility when taken together: My appreciation of nature is entirely aesthetic and contemplative, not at all scientific; my healthy-minded temperament (in the phrase of William James) was a sufficient shield against acknowledgement of the impending catastrophe; and the environmental advocates were annoying (no less so because they were correct), and not infrequently depressed and dogmatic. Now, of course, all other concerns must be a second priority to the environmental crisis. There is no "out," no place to hide, no more time, and no excuse.

Although I am now convinced that Steiner's esoteric research on nature should be brought to bear on the ecological crisis, in the 1980s and 1990s I did not have an eye for his contribution to ecology. *The Essential Steiner* (1984), for example, completely neglects Steiner's ideas on nature. Once I joined Philosophy, Cosmology, and Consciousness (PCC) program after nine years as California Institute of Integral Studies (CIIS) president, I was influenced by PCC faculty: Richard Tarnas, Brian Thomas

325

Swimme, Sean Kelly, and Elizabeth Allison. I have also been influenced by colleagues who have taught in PCC or in other CIIS programs: Matthew Fox, Ralph Metzner, Sam Mickey, Elizabeth Sahtouris, Charlene Spretnak, William Irwin Thompson, and David Ulansey. Elizabeth McAnally, a PCC doctoral student, is editor of the Forum on Religion and Ecology (FORE) website, hosted at Yale. Mary Evelyn Tucker and John Grim, the wife and husband team who created and direct the field of Religion and Ecology, are close friends of Brian Thomas Swimme and me. They taught a course on religion and ecology in PCC in the early 2000s. Because Tucker and Grim carry the mantle of Teilhard de Chardin and Thomas Berry they are discussed in the second section of this chapter, "Teilhard and Thomas Berry."

My friend and colleague Sean Kelly teaches in and directs a concentration in Integral Ecologies in our university with "Integral" in its name: California Institute of Integral Studies (CIIS), so named because integral is the name of the yoga philosophy of Sri Aurobindo and his follower, Dr. Haridas Chaudhuri, who founded CIIS in 1968. (Ken Wilber's use of the term *integral* for his thought and various initiatives issues from the same source, the integral philosophy of Sri Aurobindo.) As I was active in the Sri Aurobindo community in the 1970s, and was a friend of Dr. Chaudhuri before I served as president of CIIS in the 1990s, it follows that my approach to ecology would be Integral. My approach also strives to be as esoteric and as plural as the approach of Rudolf Steiner.

The primary purpose of this chapter is to attempt to answer whether there might be advantages to adding a spiritual or esoteric dimension to secular humanist approaches to ecological issues. What is gained, for example, by including the vision and approach of the pre-ecological mystical scientist, Teilhard de Chardin, whose major work, *The Phenomenon of Man,* was published in 1959,[1] three years prior to Rachel Carson's *Silent Spring*? Steiner's esoteric research concerning the fate of Earth was published more than a generation earlier. Might Teilhard's

---

1. See an improved translation by Sarah Appleton-Weber, *The Human Phenomenon.*

and Steiner's perspectives nevertheless be relevant for the ecological crisis as it intensifies? The first section of this chapter discusses the five principles of integral ecology developed by Sean Kelly:[2] evolutionary, planetary, transdisciplinary, (re)enchanted, and engaged. The second section explores the Teilhard–Thomas Berry tradition; and the final section recommends the esoteric ecology of Rudolf Steiner

Sean Kelly's Integral Ecology Principles

1. Evolutionary

Kelly's first principle asserts that "we now stand at a singular and in many ways unparalleled moment...the early though quickly accelerating phase of the sixth mass extinction of species, and in the process bringing to an end the 65-million-year geological period called the Cenozoic."[3] Perhaps the most prominent lineage for evolutionary ecology that embraces the numinous worldview is traceable to Teilhard de Chardin and Thomas Berry and has been subsequently developed by Matthew Fox, Brian Thomas Swimme, Mary Evelyn Tucker and John Grim, James Conlon, and Drew Dellinger. The works of Duane Elgin, an evolutionist, ecologist, and exponent of Big History, are also important in this category.

2. Planetary

Kelly's second principle is also concerned with cosmology, the cosmos as a whole system, or as the most inclusive ecosystem, but with a focus on Earth as a living planet called Gaia. While some ecologists focus on a narrow, though of course important and perhaps urgent, area of the total ecosystem, some others, like those in the Teilhard–Berry lineage, Joanna Macy, and Duane Elgin focus on the parts in relation to the whole.

---

2. Sean Kelly, "Five Principles of Integral Ecology," in Sam Mickey, Adam Robbert, Sean Kelly, eds., *The Variety of Integral Ecologies: Nature, Culture, and Knowledge in the Planetary Era* (unpublished ms.).

3. See www.speciesalliance.org and its major project to date: a full-length documentary, *The Call of Life: Facing the Mass Extinction*.

3. Transdisciplinary

Transdisciplinarity "concerns what is at once *between* the disciplines, *across* the different disciplines, and *beyond* all discipline[s]." Instead of being limited to multidisciplines (biology, chemistry, history, etc.), with their respective limitations and boundaries, a transdisciplinary ecology strives to view the total ecosystem in such a way that contains and transcends the relevant disciplines. The model for this approach is the work of Sean Esbjörn-Hargens and Michael Zimmerman (2009), as well as the work of Sean Kelly, Adam Robberts, and Sam Mickey.

4. Engaged

If we count teaching, writing, lecturing, and meditating on ecology, as we should, as engaged action then every name in this chapter would be considered engaged. To learn the names of prominent activists and activist organizations, the single best source is Paul Hawken's *Blessed Unrest* (2007), which lists thousands of books, organizations, and movements devoted to ecological research and activism. Any consideration of ecology faces an overwhelming number and variety of approaches, experts, and activists. Deep and extensive ecological thinkers as well as committed activists are in evidence; it is the fossil fuel industries and their lobbies that are preventing the work of enlightened researchers from effecting the necessary change.

5. (Re)enchantment

The "re" in this principle refers to recovery of the experience of spiritual meaning deep in the cosmos and Earth. Kelly refers to a sequence of numinous influential paradigms which are quite different from each other but can be joined together in opposition to the dominant disenchanted, materialistic, secular paradigm of most ecologists. Re-enchantment is especially important in this chapter because it is an essential characteristic of the worldview offered by Teilhard, Thomas Berry, and Rudolf Steiner. As Sean Kelly and I have been influenced by German idealism, Romanticism, Jung, and evolution of consciousness, our approach to ecology is naturally focused on (re)enchantment in response to the natural world. Here is a passage by Kelly that expresses my own evolutionary-philosophical perspective:

> For the ancients as well as for Medieval and most Renaissance practitioners of "natural philosophy," the cosmos was seen as pervaded with spiritual meaning. The Platonic notion of the World Soul (*anima mundi*); the Stoic idea of the cosmic Logos; Saint Paul's view of the world in labor with the cosmic Christ; Saint Francis's relationship to animals and to "brother Sun and sister Moon;" the magical correspondences between minerals, plants, animals, stars, and other heavenly beings of the alchemists; the two parallel revelations of the theologians (the book of scripture and the book of nature): These and other related notions all manifest the essential quality of what Owen Barfield calls "original participation," by which he means a mode of being and of consciousness which involves the idea that there exists "behind the phenomena, *and on the other side of them from me*, a represented which is of the same nature as me. Whether it is called 'mana' or by the names of many gods and demons, or God the Father, or the spirit world, it is of the same nature as the perceiving self, inasmuch as it is not mechanical or accidental, but psychic and voluntary."[4]

Although not to the same extent as the Teilhard-Berry lineage or the esoteric ecology of Steiner, Nature writers such as Thoreau, John Muir, Aldo Leopold, René Dubos, and Loren Eisley express the numinous quality of the natural world. Rachel Carson's careful, scientific writing was also inspired by and carries a sure current of numinous wonder.

I am convinced that the human community and Earth need all of the thinker-activists mentioned in this section. In the United States civil rights movement, Martin Luther King, Jr. and Malcolm X were both necessary. John Herman Randall, Jr., the Columbia University philosopher in the tradition of John Dewey, opened his wise book, *The Role of Knowledge in Western Religion*, by arguing that not every individual needs a religion (like Dewey, Randall

---

4. Sean Kelly, in Mickey, et.al., *The Variety of Integral Ecologies* (unpublished ms.).; quotation from O. Barfield, *Saving the Appearances*, 42.

did not) but every culture does.[5] Extending this same claim, not everyone reading this chapter will want to embrace a worldview similar to Teilhard's, or the Dalai Lama's, or Aurobindo's, or Jung's—Steiner's. I do claim some of us need to because a culture, and its approach to ecology, especially in a time of undeniable disasters, needs to include spiritual and esoteric insights.

Some children and students of atheist professors (which seems to include most professors) in a predominantly post-religious culture (not numerically but among the intellectual and cultural elite) will continue to look for a more spiritual version of evolution and a more substantial version of a re-enchanted cosmos. In my opinion—and I have written this book primarily in support of this opinion—it is important that spiritual and esoteric approaches be available to anyone seeking them, openly with their diverse advantages and limitations. The thinkers highlighted in this book represent very different claims and commitments—to Krishna, to Buddha, to Christ, to Sophia, to the Upanishads, to archetypes of the collective unconscious. Yet most of them agree on the existence and efficacy of one or more spiritual realities, forces, or beings that are the real, ontological sources of the numinous and (re)enchantment.

This chapter asks the question, "Where do I want to live and work on this spectrum?" At the secular noncontroversial end (because it claims relatively little concerning the deeper process of evolution or the source of (re)enchantment) we might miss the truth of the big picture; at the other end (Teilhard's Christian spirituality or Steiner's esoteric research) we might sign on to a worldview that is too vast for local concern and engagement. If we embrace a vision such as Teilhard's or Steiner's, its affirmation of divine source, guidance, and goal might offer simplistic confidence. We might assume that irrespective of whether ecological catastrophe is on the way to the entire Earth, the cosmos is nevertheless heading toward a happy ending in the long run, and so there is no need to get anxious about global warming or species extinction.

As the planetary ecological crisis is the single most profound, inescapable challenge of our time, and no doubt for centuries to come, it is critically important to find the most effective insights

---

5. John Herman Randall, *The Role of Knowledge in Western Religion*, 5.

concerning the nature of this threat and its possible solutions. Except perhaps for books on religion, on the American Founders, or on World War II, no other topic has been the subject of more volumes from more diverse perspectives than the continuing ecological catastrophe. Hence the question: Do you want to stay with one of the secular, scientific approaches or consider, *in addition*, aesthetics, ethics, or a numinous dimension, whether religious or spiritual? Do you want to consider *as well* an esoteric approach? The italics in the previous two sentences are meant to signal my conviction that the ecological crisis requires all positive perspectives and commitments, from the many secular humanist replies to the mystical vision of Teilhard and esoteric research of Steiner. In a similar way, the champions of social justice such as Martin Luther King, Jr. and Archbishop Desmond Tutu marched as well as prayed. The Indian independence movement needed both the *satyagraha* of Gandhi and the Integral Yoga of Sri Aurobindo.

If there are spiritual beings devoted to Earth and human evolution, they should be addressed initially by individuals good at such addressing and listening. As many of us as are willing should join their effort—again, in addition to all of the thousands of secular perspectives and contributions, presumably all important. This plural approach is similar to my wanting (as expressed in chapter 9) an educational approach large enough for public schools (ideally with Deweyan values and practices) and private schools (including Montessori and parochial)—and also Waldorf, without which no one would be researching biography and child development relative to curriculum, temperament, the positive relationship of science and art, and the possibility of a spiritual approach without crossing the line into specific religious teachings and practices. Diversity in approach in both education and ecology is necessary for the magnitude in shift that is required.

Rachel Carson was a scientist, trained in biology and precise in her analyses and critiques. Nothing less would have been effective against politicians and corporate interests. It is possible that if Carson had included in *Silent Spring* an enthusiastic account of the reality of spirit in relation to the fate of the Connecticut River or the farms on Long Island, the ecological movement would not have immediately followed the publication of her book. An ecologist such as Rachel Carson, whose *New Yorker* essays and subsequent *Silent Spring* launched the environmental movement in 1962, or Elizabeth Kolbert, whose essays in the *New Yorker* a half century later and two volumes, *Fieldnotes from a Catastrophe* (2006) and *Sixth Extinction* (2014), have alerted readers to the latest stage of the ecological crisis, represent secular ecological thinking at its foundational core and serve as impressive examples of activist engagement.

TEILHARD DE CHARDIN AND THOMAS BERRY

Many contemporary ecologists excel at several of Kelly's five principles, in most cases more thoroughly, or more currently than Teilhard or Steiner, but Teilhard and Steiner excel at all five, although it should be acknowledged that their engagement was primarily subtle or on the level of consciousness. Readers committed to secular humanism might find it difficult to appreciate the significance for ecology of Teilhard's Roman Catholic mysticism or Steiner's Christian esotericism. Thomas Berry offers an especially interesting perspective for this chapter because he knew and was committed to all five characteristics very deeply, and in his determination to gain the attention and commitment of non-Christians and Christians alike, he carefully redefined Earth in terms of numinosity and sacredness but without explicit references to God, Christ, or even ontological affirmation of spirit. In effect, he moved away from Teilhard (he had never gone near Steiner) and closer to the positions of Rachel Carson, Aldo Leopold, Loren Eisley, Wingari Maathai, and Confucianism. Hence the question of this chapter: What are the advantages and disadvantages in Berry's position over the positions of Teilhard or Steiner—or Sri Aurobindo, or His Holiness the Dalai Lama? At another level, which of these positions is not only most effective at this time (essential though that consideration clearly is), but also at the deepest and highest level true with respect to cosmos, nature, humanity, and Earth, and not to be ignored, with spiritual beings?

Beginning in the 1950s, when I was a high school student working on weekends at a retreat house where Thomas Berry served as priest, I became one of his unofficial students and then his friend. In 1964 he officiated at the wedding of my wife Ellen and myself and subsequently baptized our children, the first of whom is named Darren Thomas after Thomas Berry. Beginning in 1964, while I was finishing a doctorate in philosophy at Boston University and teaching at Manhattanville College, I attended Berry's courses on Hinduism, Buddhism, and Chinese thought that he taught first at St. John's University and then at Fordham University where I also studied Sanskrit with him. In 1975 he arranged for me to take his place on a Fulbright to the Open University. In response to powerful critiques, alarming reports, and failed conferences concerning the fate of Earth, Thomas decided to subordinate his career as a scholar of Asian religions to the battle against ecological devastation.

Throughout the 1980s and early 1990s, while I was deeply involved in the study of Steiner and the work of various administrative positions, I paid very little attention to the thought of Teilhard or Thomas Berry. Fortunately, in the mid-1990s, thanks to my friendship with Brian Thomas Swimme, Mary Evelyn Tucker, and John Grim, I returned to both Teilhard and Berry. As I discovered while jointly teaching a course with Brian Swimme entitled "Teilhard and Thomas," and again in writing this book, my five-decade friendship with Thomas notwithstanding, my thinking, no doubt due to the influence of Steiner, is more enthusiastic in response to Teilhard. As in every chapter of this book, I found my sympathies closer to Teilhard, from first to last a "Mahayanist," than to Berry, who was in the last decades of his life, at least in his writings, a Confucian and "Theravada" humanist. Of course, my admiration for Thomas Berry's life and thought, my gratitude for his inspiring influence, and the privilege of his friendship are truly beyond measure.[6]

---

6. See three letters to Thomas Berry in Herman Green, ed., *The Ecozoic: A Tribute to Thomas Berry*, No. 2 (2009), 172–177, and CIIS.PCC.Faculty.RobertMcDermott.Publications.

As was true of Teilhard, Berry's most remarkable quality was his unfailing kindness. He was as compassionate as he was learned. He was also in some important sense a saint: A selfless servant of humanity and Earth. It is important to see Berry's life work, again like that of Teilhard, as seamless: His passion for the sacred dimension of every moment, his love for every true word and every tree, are all inseparable from his passion for the cosmos. While cosmic, Berry's vision for the Earth does not at all sacrifice the particularity of multiple civilizations with their varied ways of thought and expression. His vision includes the history and fate of humanity and of individual persons, the continuing miracle of animals and plants, and the wisdom and complexity of the physical world. His cosmologically based ecology includes the field of lilies in which he saw divinity, and the great oak overshadowing the Riverdale Center for Religious Research on the edge of the Hudson.

Thomas Berry (1914–2009) spent his youth and the last two decades of his life in Greensboro, North Carolina, and most of his adult life in New York City. Berry's thinking may be said to have spanned three phases, all at the forefront of important developments: first, a Christian appreciation of Asian religious traditions, second, an evolutionary vision informed and inspired by Teilhard de Chardin, and third, a post-Christian (and significantly Confucian) humanist ecology. Berry discovered Teilhard's writing in the early 1960s while he was deep in the study of Asian religions. Teilhard had written his volumes relevant for ecology throughout the first half of the twentieth century, and they were published in English beginning in 1959. In addition to Teilhard, Berry's studies and writings were influenced by Giambattista Vico (the eighteenth-century philosopher of history, and the subject of Berry's 1949 doctoral dissertation), and by Eric Voegelin and Christopher Dawson, all three cultural historians. Berry was also schooled in Plato and Aristotle, Augustine and Aquinas, and Dante. Throughout the 1950s and 1960s he studied the scriptures of Asian religious traditions in their original languages, including Sanskrit, Chinese, and Tibetan. Beginning in the 1960s, and for the rest of his life, he studied and lectured on C. G. Jung and Mircea Eliade;

Native/First Americans; Aldo Leopold's *Sand County Almanac* and "Land Ethic"; indigenous wisdom; the writings of naturalists (especially Henry David Thoreau, John Muir, and Loren Eiseley); feminist spirituality; and contemporary cosmology, especially in collaboration with Brian Thomas Swimme.

From age fourteen, and for the remainder of his life, he was a member of the Passionist Fathers, a Roman Catholic order of monks devoted to the passion of Jesus Christ. When Berry turned his genius to ecology, his commitment would become quite the reverse of his order—instead of a focus on Christ's passion and death as an act of salvation he emphasized creation spirituality and Christ's compassion. It was due to these and other allegedly heretical ideas that his superiors forbad the seminarians in his order to seek his spiritual counsel.[7] Berry's opposition to core Christian teachings was not easy for his relationship with the superiors of his religious order or with his Jesuit colleagues in the Fordham University Theology Department where he taught comparative religion. His devotion to the sacredness of the Earth often led him to stand against those with whom he shared other beliefs and commitments.

Once he turned to ecology Berry seemed distinctly disinterested in Christian scriptures, theology, and philosophy—except to the extent that they seemed to him either helpful or harmful to ecology. It seems to me that by the time Thomas wrote "Contemporary Spirituality" in 1975, at age sixty, his thinking was no longer concerned with Catholic (or even Christian) orthodoxy. He also exhibited no interest in esoteric writings, whether theosophical or anthroposophic. In certain other respects, however, Berry's thought remained Teilhardian, though implicitly: With Teilhard, Berry's thought is emphatically evolutionary (with respect to Earth) and historical (with respect to humanity). With

---

7.   As I was not a seminarian, but rather a fourteen-year-old high school student, after waiting tables at the Passionist Fathers Retreat House near where Thomas was assigned the job of answering the door, I was privileged to attend his informal weekly seminar on Dante. Of course, I understood little or nothing, but I did observe, invaluably, a teacher who loved and embodied the profound and saving power of deep thoughts beautifully expressed.

Teilhard, Berry loved the physical Earth, its materiality as well as its beauty. In the last three decades of his ninety years, he referred to himself as a geologian, or "Earth knower." He was also known as the visionary of "The New Story" of evolution, as well as the formulator and advocate of what he termed "The Great Work," both of which emerge from and advocated a historical perspective, one that emphasizes humanity's urgent ecological task.

At the same time, Berry's historical and moral sense were deeply influenced by a Christian vision and Christian ideals—though extended to include the whole of humanity with no trace of Christian dogmatism or exclusivity. He expanded his understanding of the Christian revelation to include the fullest possible range of religious experience and traditions. His sense of revelation, of the divine-human drama, and the sacred dimension of nature, are to be found in the Christian texts and teachers on whom he focused, particularly those of Thomas Aquinas and Teilhard de Chardin. The triadic view of heaven–Earth–humanity so characteristic of his writings throughout the second half of his life would seem to be increasingly Chinese, both Confucian and Taoist. It is likely that Berry did not emphasize the Christian content of his thought because some characteristically Christian dogmas and beliefs are distinctly negative with respect to ecology. His emphatic and consistent defense of the rights of nature, which had not been historically a Christian concern, was influenced by Aldo Leopold's "Land Ethic." Berry's thought is synchretistic, universal, and incorporates multiple traditions. The essential core, or root metaphor, would seem to be aptly expressed by his account of a mystical experience at age nine in the field of lilies near his home in Greensboro: The Earth is alive, myriad, and filled with mystery and divinity.

With increasing moral authority and an oracular mode of expression, Berry produced a powerful critique of contemporary Western civilization. My colleague Jacob Sherman referred to Berry's mode of expression as "present prophetic." Although Berry did not want to be regarded as a prophet, his style of pronouncement certainly resembles the warnings of an Isaiah or Jeremiah. *Dream of the Earth*, the first volume in the Sierra Club series on Nature and Natural Philosophy, established Berry's reputation as a deep ecological thinker; he then published *The Universe Story*, which he coauthored with Brian Swimme, who was initially his student and subsequently his colleague and friend. This was followed by *The Great Work*, which constitutes a *cri de coeur* in response to the devastating impact on Earth of the modern globalized extractive economy. With unmistakable desperation (though not despair), he argued against the modern Western worldview—and for a "New Story" intended to help humanity at least to slow, and ideally to reverse, the current advance toward ecological collapse.

For Berry, history tells the story of the divinity of Earth and of human consciousness. One wonders whether, in his view, the incarnation of Christ was necessary for the evolution of humanity. His primary concern was not theological but ecological: He favors only those philosophical and theological claims that promote the sacredness of Earth. He did not approve a view of the incarnation of Christ that presupposes a fallen Earth or fallen humanity, as in the myth of the Garden of Eden in Genesis. In this respect, he opposed the Augustinian dualistic strand in Christianity in favor of the tradition of Thomas Aquinas, Francis of Assisi and Saint Bonaventure, and especially followed the evolutionary vision of Teilhard de Chardin. Berry was devoted to two great tasks simultaneously: A critique of the modern Western worldview that is partly responsible for the destruction of Earth, and the articulation of a new vision, "A New Story." Berry says that in order for the modern West to extract itself from its pathological alienation from Earth, it needs a new cosmogenic myth, a new story of the universe.

The decade from 1968 to 1978 witnessed a series of historically, scientifically, and culturally transformative events. From the first photos of Earth from space in 1968 to the Clear Water Act of 1977, the Western world began to respond to the fact of impending devastation of the entire Earth biosystem. In response, in 1978 Berry published "The New Story," a brief but powerful essay on behalf of the revelation of the universe through human consciousness.[8] In writing, lecturing, and discussing his cosmol-

---

8. First published as the first volume of *Teilhard Studies*, and reprinted in Arthur Fabel and Donald St. John, eds., *Teilhard in the 21st Century: The Emerging Spirit of Earth*, 77–88.

ogy, and specifically in telling the new story,[9] Berry does not refer to his perspective as a worldview or paradigm but rather as a story, as an historical narrative. His use of story resembles the Sanskrit *lila*, which means the tale or drama of the universe. "The New Story" refers to the evolution of consciousness from the primal wisdom traditions through the great civilizations, to modern Western science, and now to a great transitional phase. In Berry's telling, the new story includes the previous three wisdoms (indigenous, Axial,[10] and modern Western) while moving toward the wisdom of a new Earth community.

The means to this transformation is the Universe Story itself. Berry is urging a reconnection with all species and the entire cosmos, not as things external to our consciousness, but as subjective beings. In the second chapter of *The Great Work*, "The Meadow across the Creek," in which Berry recounts his mystical experience of the field of lilies at age nine, he introduces the sentence that he will repeat many times in subsequent writings and that will become a mantra associated with his life work: "The difficulty is that with the rise of modern sciences we began to think of the universe as a collection of objects rather than as a communion of subjects."[11] Although Berry does not use Martin Buber's I–Thou terminology,[12] he does show that for humans the natural world has typically become an "it" rather than a "thou."

---

9. "The New Story" refers both to the essay and to the concept.

10. The concept of Axial Age was introduced by Karl Jaspers, *The Origin and Goal of History*, 1–21. Berry's close friends believe that he introduced the concept of a Second Axial Age to refer to the radical transformations characteristic of the twentieth century, but he did not develop it in print. Instead, it was developed by his friend Ewert Cousins in his *Christ in the 21st Century*, 7. Although not by the exact term "Second Axial Age," in his *Way to Wisdom* (1951), Jaspers refers to a comparable phenomenon: "Perhaps mankind will pass through these gigantic organizations to a new axial age, still remote, invisible, and inconceivable, an axial age of authentic human upsurge," 103.

11. Thomas Berry, *The Great Work*, 16.

12. Buber's classic volume focuses almost exclusively on person-to-person relations, but the first of three realms in which relations arise is "life with nature;" the second is the human, and the third is the spiritual. Buber refers to I–Thou relationships with animals and with a tree.

For Berry, the new story will restore the unity of divinity, cosmos, Earth and humanity. In his own journey, and in his emphasis on the journey metaphor, Berry was Augustinian, while in his attempt to establish the continuity of divinity and nature, he more closely resembles Thomas Aquinas (the Thomas whose name he chose when he was ordained a priest). And again like Aquinas, he was a Christian trying to move from Platonism toward Aristotelianism. While he appreciated Platonic Ideas he cautioned that they can divert one's attention from the Earth and human experience, blinding one to the value of the natural, the immediate, and the particular. Berry's most substantial achievement, and presumably his most lasting, was his passionate expression of a complex and comprehensive worldview that aims to restore the intimacy and complementary creativity of cosmos, Earth, and humanity. His life work has been expertly summarized in *Evening Thoughts* by his devoted friend and exponent, Mary Evelyn Tucker.[13] In her "Editor's Afterword: An Intellectual Biography of Thomas Berry" she writes:

> From the Latin texts of the Church fathers, to the Sanskrit texts of Hinduism and Buddhism, to the Chinese classics of Confucianism and Taoism, Berry's search for an understanding of the guiding forces in the human journey was intense, persistent, and rare. He sought grounding in the past as a means of reading the demands of the present and anticipating the needs of the future.... He anticipated by several decades the need to understand other cultures and religions, and he foresaw the environmental crisis before it loomed in public consciousness.[14]

Whereas Teilhard views humanity and Earth as complementary, Berry affirms Gaia as the source of humanity, not as its counterpart. Simultaneous with writing "The New Story," Berry articulated a trenchant critique of the destructive mindset of the modern West, and particularly all that has been lost by its

---

13. Mary Evelyn Tucker has a joint appointment with her husband John Grim as professors in the School of Divinity as well as the School of Forestry and Environmental Studies, at Yale. For additional information on Mary Evelyn and John, see the next section.

14. Mary Evelyn Tucker, "Editor's Afterword," *Evening Thoughts*, 151.

presumptuous rejection and perversion of traditional sources of wisdom. While deeply rooted in the West, and particularly important as an antidote to the materialism, capitalism, and consumerism characteristic of the Western culture over the past two centuries, and also increasingly of Asia, Berry's "New Story" is global in its sources and audience. "The New Story" assumes a Christian perspective on time and history but rejects the Christian emphasis on sin and salvation. Berry incorporated teachers, texts, and traditions of diverse cultures (particularly classical Chinese) according to whether they seemed to him to help the cause of ecological sustainability.

Berry considered both the Christian and the secular worldviews to be in a pathological rage against Earth. In his view, the Christian church continus to violate humanity by regarding it as fallen and in need of a divine rescue, while post-Christian secularity violates Earth by regarding it as a dead resource waiting to be exploited for commercial gain. In some of his ecological references he seems to have been influenced by the controversial essay by Lynn White, Jr., "The Historical Roots of Our Ecologic Crisis" that blamed Christianity for the ecological crisis.[15] Berry's New Story is intended to restore the sacred to both humanity and Earth. Just as Teilhard wrote *The Human Phenomenon* in order to help his readers to *see*,[16] Berry told the New Story in order to help his students, audiences, and readers to *hear* the universe revealing a new consciousness through humanity. Some of Berry's pronouncements suggest the influence of the Siberian trapper, Derzu Uzala. "Seeing" would seem to be aligned with science whereas "hearing" would seem more aligned with story. The New Story includes many new stories, all indicating that a new collaboration between the wisdom of the universe and the creativity of the human community is underway. Berry's New Story is the story that the universe has been telling to an increasing number of individuals since the beginning of global consciousness and the emergence of evolutionary cosmological science. Rather than the story's creator, Berry considered himself to have been an early

---

15. *Science* 155: 1203–1207 (March 10, 1957).
16. Teilhard de Chardin, *The Human Phenomenon*, 3.

hearer of this story—though he obviously was also a creator in that he gave this story its dramatic thrust and primary metaphors.

If, as Berry was convinced, the new story is comprehensive of all other true stories, it might be especially urgent for the present age of transition when the West seems not to have a universally agreed-upon story—and certainly not to have a story adequate to address the ecological devastation that threatens Earth. The New Story as Berry tells it is particularly significant because he is someone who listened widely and deeply and relayed the story with insight and passion. His "New Story" is particularly convincing because it clearly issues from its author's personal qualities: Reverence and humility, serious scholarship, active poetic imagination, openness to new ideas, enthusiasm for the passions and insights of others, and abiding love for Earth. For the last thirty years of his life, from approximately 1975 to 2005, the New Story was the central, defining motif of Berry's writing, lecturing, and influence. He considered the New Story to be the single best hope for the transformation of consciousness, from ignorant disregard for and destruction of Earth to ethical and creative sustainability.

The Dream of the Earth, a collection of wide-ranging essays, established Berry's reputation as an ecological visionary both in the tradition of and perhaps at the level of Aldo Leopold. The book contains fascinating and highly original essays on technology, economics, education, Christianity, the American experience, patriarchy, bioregions, and Native Americans. The last two essays, "The Dream of the Earth" and "The Cosmology of Peace," are signature essays for the book and for the remainder of Berry's life work. They signal his decisive turn to a terminology accessible to diverse religious and non-religious perspectives. Berry recasts the English translation of the Greek *Logos* of the Prologue to St. John's Gospel "In the beginning was the Word" to "In the beginning was the dream"(196–197).[17] The following passage attributes to Earth the powers that Christian theology attributes to Christ/the Logos: "The Earth acts in all that acts

---

17. References to *The Dream of the Earth* are in parentheses. Compare Goethe's revision of this text: "In the beginning was the deed."

upon the Earth. The Earth is acting in us whenever we act. In and through the Earth, spiritual energy is present."[18] In this and many similar passages, Berry means the immanent Earth as Tao, Earth in its capacity to reveal itself by numinous images and sacred symbols expressed through the arts and in sacred dreams. He took great pleasure, for example, in talking about the dreams of Black Elk.

Because he was eager to appeal to non-Christians and Christians alike, and because he wanted to lead his audience away from cultural assumptions, Berry's language tends to be cosmic rather than limited to any one tradition, whether religious or cultural: "Our cultural resources have lost their integrity. They cannot be trusted. What is needed is not transcendence but 'incendence,' not the brain but the gene"(208). This preference for the gene over the brain represents a critique and proposal. Berry urges the human community to return to its cosmic mooring, away from the values of a cultural coding that is imperiling Earth: "The present situation is so extreme that we need to get beyond our existing cultural formation, back to primary tendencies of our nature itself, as expressed in the spontaneities of our being" (209). Berry considers "those basic humanistic ideals that have directed our cultural traditions over the past millennia" to be the cause of the disasters presently befalling Earth. Consequently, he urges that "we must reach far back into the genetic foundations of our cultural formation for a healing and a restructuring at the most basic level." These quotations suggest a definite shift from the theism that Berry inherited from Catholic theology and philosophy to an affirmation of Jungian archetypes as well as Mircea Eliade's patterns and the mythic concepts of historical religions. His is also a shift from transcendence to immanence.

Berry introduced a Jungian conception of psyche and Eliade's conception of the numinous as a way of restoring a more intimate relationship between humanity and Earth. He also focused increasingly on a Confucian triad: Tao, Earth, and Humanity. He presents this triad with the conviction that it is currently, urgently revealing itself to and through Earth and human

---

18. Thomas Berry, *The Sacred Universe*, 71.

consciousness. "Dream" in this sense is a very special, active, more-than-rational numinous agency: Earth is dreaming itself in the alert, imaginative, intuitive human person and human community. This "Dream" is deeper than the ideas of contemporary culture. Current cultural coding must now be replaced by cosmic coding, the symbols, images, and dreams of the universe as experienced through the intimate relationship between Earth and humanity:

> Our genetic coding, through the ecological movement and through the bioregional vision, is providing us with a new archetypal world. The Universe is revealing itself to us in a special manner just now. Also the planet Earth and the life communities of the earth are speaking to us through the deepest elements of our nature, through our genetic coding. (215)

Berry is calling for an end to what he calls an "autism" that has characterized human consciousness during the past several centuries (215). The universe is calling to humanity "to renew our human participation in the grand liturgy of the universe" (215).

The title of Berry's second ecological book, *The Great Work: Our Way into the Future* (1999), gave its name to the movement for which he is the primary inspiring source. The book is a powerful righteous, indictment of four dominant institutions of the West: governments, corporations, Abrahamic religions, and academia. Berry asserts that faulty human consciousness has led to the "terminal phase of the Cenozoic Era," i.e., the end of the arc of Earth evolution that is gradually (or, alas, not gradually!) succeeding the era that began with the fifth mass extinction 65 million years ago. This era of Earth evolution appears to be coming to a tragic end because the human species acts as though it has rights over all other species:

> The deepest cause of the present devastation is found in a mode of consciousness that has established a radical discontinuity between the human and other modes of being and the bestowal of all rights on the humans. The other-than-human modes of being are seen as having no rights. They have reality and value only through their use by the human. In this context the other

than human becomes totally vulnerable to exploitation by the human, an attitude that is shared by all four of the fundamental establishments that control the human realm: governments, corporations, universities, and religions—the political, economic, intellectual, and religious establishments. All four are committed consciously or unconsciously to a radical discontinuity between the human and the nonhuman. (4)

With an eye on these four fundamental institutions, and no doubt writing with an active awareness of Aldo Leopold's "Land Ethic," Berry emphatically affirms the rights of trees, rivers, mountains, and all other components of the natural world:

> All rights are limited and relative. So, too, with humans. We have human rights. We have rights to the nourishment and shelter we need. We have rights to habitat. But we have no rights to deprive other species of their proper habitat.... We have no rights to disturb the basic functioning of the biosystems of the planet. We cannot own the Earth or any part of the Earth in any absolute manner. Consequently, the human community must give up the assumption of those rights which violate the other-than-human world, and must begin to understand its rights entirely in the context of the Universe and Earth, and no longer in the context of Enlightenment humanistic values. The historical mission of our times is to reinvent the human—at the species level, with critical reflection, within the community of life systems, in a time-developmental context, by means of story and shared dream experience. (5)

In another well known chapter, "The Fourfold Wisdom," Berry recommends the wisdom of indigenous peoples, of women, of the classical civilizations (despite their disregard of the indigenous and the feminine), and modern Western science (despite its tendency to disenchant the cosmos in the process of explaining its origin and evolution). Berry interprets these sources of wisdom available to contemporary humanity in the context of their respective times and places of development, and with respect to their contributions to the evolution of consciousness. Each of these four sources of wisdom, along with others, have contributed to

"The Great Work." It is now time for humanity, in concert with all species, the entire Earth, and the cosmos to contribute in ways appropriate for its capacities.

Because human behavior increasingly affects the natural order (e.g., by unsupportable population growth and an exploitive economy), it is crucial for the survival of Earth that every person hold, and act on, the truest understanding of the Earth–human relationship. An essential characteristic of what Berry refers to as "The Great Work" of this age is the replacement of the modern Western mindset[19] with an Earth-sustaining relationship. For this to happen, the dominant worldview must be decisively discredited and a sustaining myth or story established in its place. As Berry was a scholar, deep original thinker, and servant of the Earth, he was well equipped for this task, and he served it faithfully. However, as he well knew, more work is needed to bring into focus the power of an intimate relationship between humanity and Earth.

From the late 1970s through the 1990s Thomas Berry was probably Teilhard's foremost exponent in North America, as president of the American Teilhard Association.[20] Berry built upon Teilhard's attempt to enable humanity to see Earth anew, to see its spiritual dimension, to see it as the most advanced expression of divinity. In some respects the Teilhardian vision remained deep in Berry's thought. The choice between "Teilhard and Thomas" seems to me crucial as well as intriguing. Is the ecological situation so disastrous and so urgent that we need to side with Berry where he separates his thought from Teilhard's? Or, would we be wise to add Teilhard's profound affirmation of Christ in every aspect of the evolution of Earth and humanity? Although my thinking has evolved to be more resonant with Teilhard than with Berry, I do not urge students or audiences, or readers of this book, to prefer one over the other. Both are positive and necessary.

---

19. For the "postmodern mindset," see Huston Smith, *Beyond the Post-Modern Mind*.
20. See Winifred McCullough, *A Short History of The American Teilhard Association*.

The case for Berry's humanistic perspective is easy to make; the case for Teilhard, as for Steiner, is more difficult, though perhaps as important. In *Dream of the Earth* (1988) and *The Great Work* (1999), Berry referred to Teilhard only in passing. He continued to write essays about Christianity, and particularly Roman Catholicism, in an effort to rouse that tradition to the fate of the Earth. For that purpose he largely ignored Teilhard's Christian vision and references to Christ, and regarded much of the Christian tradition, particularly its emphasis on sin and salvation over creation and revelation, as distinctly negative relative to ecology. Teilhard and Berry seemed to live about equally in nature and in the mind. They loved every detail of the natural world, yet were equally devoted to the world of books and ideas.[21] They were careful, imaginative, and indefatigable readers, thinkers, authors, and lecturers. In their lives and writings, Teilhard and Berry advanced the Thomist affirmation of the continuity between the human and divine, the natural and supernatural. They were both at odds with Augustinian Manicheism, and its later reformulations by Reformation Protestantism (particularly Luther, Calvin, and New England Puritanism). All of their thought, interests, and writings are characterized by what William James called "healthy-mindedness" (the opposite of which James refers to as "sick souls," exemplified by Augustine, Kierkegaard, Tolstoy, and others).[22]

So far from being divided souls, Teilhard and Berry held spirit and matter, humanity and divinity, in a single vision. Mary Evelyn Tucker has located three themes in the vision of Teilhard that exercised a profound effect on Berry's thinking.[23] The first is developmental time: Like Teilhard, Berry came to see the universe as "an unfolding cosmogenesis." Berry completely accepted Teilhard's claim that evolution, far from being a mere hypothesis, is "a condition of all experience." Berry's every claim presupposes radical

---

21. Thomas knew his audience. Brian Swimme and I recently discovered that, when I visited Thomas in Riverdale, he typically showed me some newly purchased books, or an essay he had just finished; when Brian visited him, he typically showed Brian his favorite trees.

22. William James, *The Varieties of Religious Experience.*

23. Mary Evelyn Tucker, "An Intellectual Biography of Thomas Berry," in Thomas Berry, *Evening Thoughts*, p. 162–165.

temporality and the irreducible influence of evolutionary phases. His critique of Christian teachings, such as the Fall as depicted in Genesis and the exclusivity of the biblical revelation, is based on his conviction that many teachings that were adequate (and thought to be true and unchanging) in a previous historical and cultural context are simply no longer adequate for the present time.

Second, Berry derived from Teilhard "an understanding of the psychic–physical character of the unfolding universe."[24] Both Teilhard and Berry subscribed to a panpsychist understanding of matter—i.e., the belief that matter is conscious all the way down to the seemingly least significant components of the universe. In the web of cosmic and earthly relations, no component is insignificant. As Tucker notes, "Matter, for both Teilhard and Berry, is not simply dead or inert but is a numinous reality consisting of both a physical and spiritual dimension." In this respect, Teilhard and Berry are in the great Romantic tradition that has struggled to establish the unity of matter and spirit. This tradition, which includes particularly Goethe, Emerson, and Steiner stands against, on the one side, theists who typically see the Creator and creation as separate, and on the other side, naturalists, which include many modern Western scientific and social scientific atheists from Feuerbach to Hawking and Dennett, who deny the reality of a Creator altogether.

Third, Berry also incorporated into his own thought the law of complexity-consciousness first formulated by Teilhard. Tucker provides a clear summary of this Teilhard–Berry conviction: "As things evolve from simpler to more complex organisms, consciousness also increases." The most profound increase in consciousness, of course, is the evolution of humanity—and the myriad ways that humans continue, exponentially, to increase evolution of consciousness and complexity. Although obviously recent in the great arc of the evolution of consciousness, humans now threaten the balance of Earth's systems. Whereas Teilhard considers the human influence on the evolutionary process to be essentially positive, Berry considered this influence to be increasingly disastrous, and during the last thirty of his life sought to

---

24. Ibid.

find ways to expose and reduce the negative impact of humanity on all life forms. At this time the assumptions of technological progress and of unlimited resources necessary for capitalism have both proven to be Faustian: We have gained more knowledge (of a certain limited kind) and more power (to control physical and economic life), but at the cost of a sustainable relationship between humanity and Earth. Berry was influenced by Teilhard's radical historical/evolutionary sense, but he broke with Teilhard's optimistic trust in modern Western science and technology.

It must be acknowledged that in several important respects Berry found Teilhard's thought disappointing and counterproductive. In Berry's "Teilhard in the Ecological Age,"[25] his only writing on Teilhard, Berry discusses several topics concerning which he has a mixture of agreement and disagreement with Teilhard. First, he extends Teilhard's interpretation of the evolutionary process. Berry considers Teilhard's position to have left Earth and humanity too separate. Berry is eager to show the intimacy and continuity, and perhaps congruent identity, of Earth and humanity: "The human might better think of itself as a mode of being of the Earth rather than simply as a separate being on the Earth" (66). Berry agrees with Teilhard's critique of the Catholic Church for its lack of passion for the human as such and for human inquiry, "two basic elements of modern thought" (68), but he finds that Teilhard was merely trying to turn the attention of the Church to the human sciences and to the technological controls over the natural world: "He was not really turning Christian thought to the created world in its natural splendor" (68). Berry agrees with Teilhard's desire to replace the existentialist angst characteristic of twentieth-century European thought with an emphasis on human psychic energy, but then renders a severe criticism of Teilhard's failure to see what might be called the shadow side of human energy.

Berry agrees with Teilhard's "appreciation for the mystical quality of the scientific endeavor," but he criticizes Teilhard's

---

25. Thomas Berry, "Teilhard in the Ecological Age," in Fabel and St. John, *Teilhard in the 21st Century*. The remaining references in this chapter to this essay are in parentheses.

failure to recognize the extent to which it is also a "conquest and domination over the spontaneities of the natural world" (71). Berry then gives an important summary criticism of Teilhard that is simultaneously a summation of Berry's own position:

> Neither Teilhard nor his opponents seem to have realized that the greatest challenge to his work would derive from the planetary disturbance consequent on the ideas of progress that were then being proposed throughout Western society. They could not see that the glory of the human was becoming the desolation of the Earth or that the desolation of the Earth was becoming the destiny of the human. (73)

I think it is important to add another disagreement between these two great lovers of nature, both loyal, compassionate priests: Berry considered it dangerous to posit a final goal for Earth and humanity. More specifically, he resisted Teilhard's claims for the Omega Point, a teleological future which, in Teilhard's view, is guaranteed by the incarnation and suffering of Christ. For Berry, the goal is the present moment, made possible in combination with the past and in service to an ideal future, but without the comfort of a divine rescue. In his view the future is radically undetermined, perhaps unfortunately dependent on human wisdom and will.

Fortunately for Berry and for the causes he served, he has been blessed in his younger collaborators. Matthew Fox has published more than twenty volumes which forcefully advance Berry's vision. Mary Evelyn Tucker and John Grim have organized eight conferences on ecology and each of the world's religious traditions, each of which has led to the publication of a significant volume: Judaism, Christianity, Islam, Hinduism, Buddhism, Confucianism, Taoism, and Indigenous wisdom. Brian Swimme collaborated with Berry on *The Universe is a Green Dragon* and *The Universe Story*. Tucker and Grim have produced, and Swimme has written and narrated *The Journey of the Universe*, a handsome, convincing fifty-minute documentary that essentially depicts Berry's vision of the evolution of the cosmos from the primordial flaring forth to the present ecological crisis. Most recently, Grim and Tucker have published an important summation of the academic field that they have created and continue to guide: *Ecology and Religion.* In Sophia, the program that James Conlon chairs at Holy Names University (Oakland, CA), and by his five slim volumes, he has introduced students to Berry's vision. Drew Dellinger has enthralled audiences with poetry inspired by the cosmic vision of Thomas Berry.

STEINER'S ESOTERIC ECOLOGY

From his earliest years in southern Austria surrounded by natural beauty and spirit beings to which he had access, Steiner lived in an enchanted world. As the student of Felix Kogutsky, a shaman and herbalist, Steiner was able to work with the healing power of herbs. As the editor of Goethe's natural scientific writings he steeped himself in the natural-scientific research of the greatest naturalist of the early nineteenth century. Steiner was also deeply influenced by the entire circle of post-Kantian Romantic thinkers, especially Schelling, whose nature philosophy enabled Steiner to bridge his deep inner experience as an "I" influenced by the subjective idealist philosophy of Fichte with the world of nature to which he was devoted from childhood, and which he deepened by his study of Goethe.

The term *ecology,* or *oekologie,* was defined by the German biologist Ernst Haeckel in 1866, as "the comprehensive science of the relationship of the organism to the environment." Steiner was thoroughly familiar with Haeckel's thought, and particularly embraced the insight that Haeckel contributed to biology—namely his "law of recapitulation": That Ontology recapitulates phylogeny. This is a formulaic expression for the idea that as living bodies develop, as they come to be what they are essentially or ontologically, they mysteriously but lawfully reenact the evolutionary development of all nature. The agreement and disagreement between Steiner and Haeckel in the last quarter of the nineteenth century can be seen as the core alternative between naturalistic and spiritual approaches to nature, and thereafter, to ecology. Steiner expressed gratitude to Haeckel for his profound contributions to biology and philosophy of nature but then added that Haeckel's work was incomplete because it ignore the role of spirit in nature.

During Steiner's lifetime an ecological movement had not emerged as a necessary response to nature. Steiner's lectures on nature preceded by two generations Carson's *Silent Spring* and the first Earth Day (April 1970). However, many lectures that he delivered almost a century ago provide a solid foundation for what might be called an esoteric ecology. Ever prescient, Steiner lectured on the eventual collapse of bee colonies, on the state of the soil, and on the fate of Earth. His entire worldview emphasizes Earth as a living being, as Gaia, a complex physical reality permeated by etheric (life-giving) forces. In his view humanity consists of a combination, at one level, of soul and spirit, and at another, of physical and etheric realities. Because he affirms the deep interdependence of all organisms and a vast array of cosmic forces and cosmic beings we can regard Steiner's esoteric research as a foundation for ecology and a corrective worldview for recovery from ecological destruction.

As is well known to students of the history of philosophy, Descartes, in his attempt to force philosophy to conform to mathematical certainty, created a dualism that split reality into mind and matter, internal and external. In particular, he described the human being in terms of two substances, *res cogitans* and *res extensa*—a thinking thing (mind) and an extended thing (matter). Thereafter both philosophy and science focused on matter as the primary reality, effectively reducing mind to matter. Mind came to be synonymous with brain, and spirit, which had been the source and foundation of mind, fell out (or rather was driven out) of this conception of the human being. Mind also increasingly fell out of the conception of reality, which came to be regarded as material.

The same process of increasing materialism at the expense of spirit and transcendence characterized the post-seventeenth-century concept of the order of nature as the result of chance, and more importantly, and rather dogmatically, as not the result of a divine creation. This view led to the generally accepted belief that divinity itself was, and is, a dispensable myth, a fiction. Creation just is; it was not created and is not guided. In the nineteenth century, particularly as a result of the publication of Darwin's *Origin of Species* in 1859, science and philosophy were increasingly in general agreement that nature evolved on its own, from mineral to plant to animal to human. In the process, mind was reduced to matter, and the link between the interior and exterior of nature was lost. This link that Steiner calls the etheric, the life principle, or the subtle body, is the layer between the human mind and material world, as well as between spirit and matter throughout the whole of nature. The loss of the etheric led to an increasingly unquestioned dominance of the role of the external world and to the diminishment of the inner world.

It seems curious that Western practitioners of *taichi* or *chigung* do not resist references to *ch'i*, but references to an etheric or subtle realm seem to cause unease. While *ch'i* and the etheric might or might not be two terms for the same reality, it is clear that they are experientially very similar. The etheric is the life principle of the physical, whether plant, animal, or human. When the etheric departs the body of the deceased person, that lifeless body (the body without its etheric) is entirely different from the body, perhaps one minute prior, that was physically enlivened by its etheric principle. Steiner paid close attention to the etheric in all living bodies and prescribed medicines and artistic activities (described in chapter 10, "Art and Aesthetics") for strengthening the human etheric.

The concept of the etheric as Steiner explains it is also responsible for many otherwise mysterious experiences: images of the recently deceased, the discipline of homeopathy, the inner quality of sound expressed by eurythmy, and presumably, what Jung refers to as Earth's memories. The early phases of Earth, as well as the early phases of human history, are stored and can be retrieved from the etheric of Earth and the etheric of the human being. Jung worked on the retrieval of such memories but he did not have the concept of the etheric; instead he simply referred to all mid-level realities as psychic.

Steiner would agree with Thomas Berry's statement that the violation of Earth is both biocide (killing life), but also deicide (killing divinity). I myself assume that the goddesses of the Jumna and Ganga rivers in north India must be essentially etheric beings currently suffering a slow death—victims of deicide as well as biocide—due to chemical pollution. Unlike some theistic theologies according to which there are two essential partners, God and humanity (or Creator and creation), in Steiner's view divinity consists of many levels, all active in relation to the meaningful evolution of humanity on many planets and through many stages of consciousness. Such a picture is probably too vast and too complex for contemporary thinking, but if its major components were to be taken seriously Earth and life forms would probably have a better chance of survival.

Steiner recounts the entwined history of Earth and humanity, emphasizing their current challenging relationship. He views this relationship as analogous to the young person who must separate from his or her parents in order to establish a mature adult-to-adult relationship. In this sense, it is appropriate that humanity should experience itself rather homeless, as though merely living on Earth, rather than, as in the past, from, in, through, and of Earth. For Steiner, humanity and Earth have a mutually dependent *telos* (purpose and goal). The double goal of humanity is freedom and love; the goal of Earth is to be transformed by human love freely given to Earth.

Steiner's philosophy of nature is completely and emphatically evolutionary; in his view, humanity issues from Earth, unlike most evolutionary philosophies of nature. Steiner also sees Earth issuing from humanity, specifically from the ideal conception of the human, *Anthropos*, the human as archetype. From the beginning of creation/evolution, or to use Brian Swimme's phrase, from the primordial flaring forth, the archetypal human has been a reality in the mind of the Creator, the Father/Mother God, the Ground of Being. With respect to creation, however, Steiner does not so much speak of a Creator as he does of the Logos of the Prologue to John's Gospel, "through Whom all things came to be." The Earth evolved with the ideal of the human as its inner reality, its presupposition and goal.

The ideal human, or cosmic "I" both precedes and follows the early stages of Earth evolution. Earth is not an object at the end of a long umbilical cord connected to a distant Creator; it is the manifestation of the Creator (or Logos) from the beginning and forever after. To see, to think, to love Earth is to see, think and love the divine expressing itself. According to Steiner, whose cosmology is properly called panentheist, there is divinity before creation, but there is no creation without divinity, more specifically without Logos and Sophia. The separation of Earth and humanity is necessary for the present time but it also needs to be overcome. It is a task, not a situation to be accepted passively. It is essential for each person to oppose the karmically driven separation of humanity and Earth. Alienation is to be transformed by love. It follows from Steiner's affirmation of the spiritual reality of Earth that every individual human being needs to reconnect with Earth, not as an external object but as one's living body. In this respect Steiner and Berry are in accord. An intense and necessary form of love has emerged as an antidote to the human as child and Earth/Gaia as parent. We humans have been led to separate from Gaia in order to return to Gaia as a full partner.

Earth is permeated and sustained by spirit—more precisely by Sophia, the divine feminine, the mother of all mothers, and therefore of all bodies. As a result of the objectification and alienation characteristic of modern Western consciousness, the human body has come to be alien to the human soul and mind. As humanity has splintered into parts, each part of the human person has become alien to all the other parts, and all parts alien to the whole, resulting in an alienation of each person from Earth and cosmos. Steiner writes: "The world around us is filled everywhere with the glory of God, but we have to experience the divine in our own souls before we can find it in our surroundings."[26] The urgent task at present is for each individual to activate his or her own spiritual self in order to see the cosmos and Earth as spiritual selves—exactly what Steiner intends by Anthroposophy: "a path of knowledge to lead the spiritual in the individual to the spiritual in the universe."

Anthroposophists are fond of quoting Goethe's statement, "Matter is never without spirit, spirit is never without matter," but this statement does not accurately summarize Steiner's position— nor Teilhard's, nor Aurobindo's. It expresses a pantheist rather

---

26. Rudolf Steiner, *How to Know Higher Worlds,* p. 23.

than a panentheist position. For these three latter spiritual thinkers, matter is never without spirit but spirit *can* be without matter, as when the divine existed prior to creation, and presumably will exist after creation. This conception of spirit independent of matter does run the risk of diminishing the importance of matter. It is certainly easier and less controversial to omit any reference to spirit without matter but if less metaphysically and epistemologically adequate, and by implication also less adequate ecologically.

As I have asked in all of the previous chapters of this book, "How far do you want to go?" Each of us can go as far as a humanist, or deep ecologist, or spiritual ecologist, or we can at least try to go in the direction of an esoteric ecology such as offered by Steiner. One of the crucial differences between Steiner's ecology and other's is the reality of the etheric. Of course, the etheric is philosophically more than can be affirmed by a humanist or deep ecological perspective, but because the etheric concerns the interplay of physical and invisible realms, believing in it makes a crucial difference in one's understanding of the material world.

Steiner's cosmology, and particularly his account of the living Earth now called Gaia, deepens our understanding of the human–Earth relationship. From myriad angles, and at several levels, he celebrates the wise and creative Earth, including rocks, minerals, chemicals, plants, animals, and humanity, as well as the creative spirit that drives these to their maximum collaborative expression. When Steiner looks at bees (on which he delivered nine lectures in 1923), or the eye, or human blood, he simultaneously sees their exterior by sense perception, and their interior by intuition. His appreciation for Earth includes his detailed esoteric knowledge of the influence of the Nine Hierarchies, from cherubim to angels,[27] and heavenly bodies, including the evolution of the solar system. He sees the continuing guidance of angels and archangels,

---

27. This is a reference to the nine hierarchies referenced throughout Hebrew and Christian scriptures and Western esoteric traditions. The hierarchies were first systematically delineated by Dionysius the Aeropagyte in the sixth century CE. In his *Outline of Esoteric Science*, and in lectures, Steiner introduces his own terms for these nine levels of spiritual beings. See Robert McDermott, "Introduction," *The New Essential Steiner*, 68, and Edward Raugh Smith, *The Burning Bush*, 15.

of Buddha and *bodhisattvas,* and of Christ and Sophia. Perhaps most significantly, he sees Christ surrounding the Earth, permeating its etheric envelope. Steiner's contribution to ecology issues from a higher knowledge and focuses on the sources of, as well as possible solutions for, the current threat to the health and survival of Earth.

In his series of lectures *The Occult Significance of the Bhagavad Gita,* Steiner lists three steps in spiritual development: instruction in the ordinary concepts of our thinking, the path of yoga (essentially the transformation of thinking, feeling, and willing), and the expansion of one's vision of the cosmos. Similar to the spiritual-scientific vision of Teilhard,[28] Steiner offers a vision of Earth suffused with Christ. This union of Christ and Earth is so thorough that actions against Earth, which of course characterize human behavior at present, should rightly be considered deicide, an essential idea developed by Thomas Berry. Ita Wegman, MD, the colleague with whom Steiner stated that he had collaborated in previous lives, explains Steiner's intent:

> The Christianization of the teaching consists in recognizing that the destiny of the Earth is included in the destiny of a human being. ... [Hu]mankind now living will feel itself increasingly responsible for the destiny of the planet Earth itself.[29]

Steiner's devotion to the Earth and to the cosmos is apparent in many series of lectures, each given in response to a request for help. Answering the plea of farmers, Steiner lectured extensively on a method of agriculture based on his suprasensible knowledge of the etheric forces operative in soil, plants, and animals. This method of farming, called biodynamic, is an increasingly important agricultural alternative to the chemically dominated farming now prevalent on the entire surface of Earth.[30]

---

28. See Pierre Teilhard de Chardin, "The Mass of the Earth," in *The Heart of Matter.*
29. Ita Wegman, "The Mystery of the Earth," 97 (Thanks to Adrian Hofstatter, O.P.).
30. This discussion of biodynamic farming is indebted to Jeremy Strawn, former BD farmer, Waldorf high school science teacher, and MA student in Philosophy, Cosmology, and Consciousness.

In the previous section of this chapter I explained that Thomas Berry seemed to me uninterested in Steiner. Now, at a distance of several decades, I realize that the problem might not have been Steiner's ideas but my presentation of them to Berry: instead of telling him about Steiner's Christology, and karma and rebirth, I should have told him about Steiner's lectures on biodynamic farming and agriculture, but in the 1970s I was deliberately ignorant about biodynamic agriculture. Throughout the 1980s, while president of the Rudolf Steiner Institute in Maine, I knew Marjorie Spock, Will Brinton, and Herbert Koepf, all internationally known biodynamic farmers, in whose farms I had no interest. The job of telling Thomas Berry about Steiner's biodynamic agriculture fell to his friend Sr. Adrian Hofstetter, OP.[31] In 2007 Sr. Adrian sent to Richard Tarnas (whose *Passion of the Western Mind* had influenced her own research on Aristotle and Aquinas), two paragraphs that Thomas Berry had sent her for one of her many writing projects. This endorsement by Berry of biodynamic agriculture is worthy of a wider circulation:

> In these early years of the twenty-first century we become increasingly aware that this century must bring a healing to the destructive influence of the twentieth-century on the life systems of Earth. The urgency of this issue had already become obvious during the late years of the last century. Searching for guidance in responding to this situation, we meet with a long list of helpful personalities from all fields of human–Earth concerns. Yet few offer such guidance as Rudolph Steiner (1861–1925) in his writings on biodynamic gardening.
>
> Already during Steiner's lifetime in the late nineteenth and early twentieth centuries the destructive influence of modern economics had become clear, although exaggerated confidence in modern developments prevented any adequate response. It became clear to Steiner that a more comprehensive understanding of Earth economy, as well as a more effective style of cultivating the land, was needed. This insight led to his remarkable series of eight agricultural lectures, given in Silesia, Germany, in 1924, and their rapid dissemination throughout the world

---

31. See Adrian Hofstetter, OP, *Earth-Friendly: Re-visioning Science and Spirituality through Aristotle, Thomas Aquinas, and Rudolf Steiner.*

as a guide to biodynamic gardening, a new agricultural development. While this teaching of Steiner already inspires many American projects, it needs to be more widely appreciated.[32]

Steiner delivered the agriculture lectures in response to the request of a number of farmers (who were also members of the Anthroposophical Society) who had observed decline in the health of their livestock and crops. These farmers formed an "experimental circle" in which they applied and refined, over the next several years, the suggestions Steiner made during his agriculture course.[33] By the end of the twentieth century, the biodynamic method of agriculture had been taken up by farmers and gardeners throughout the world. Biodynamics is enjoying ever-increasing popularity today, as many turn toward more sustainable, less impactful means of growing food.

Although the volume of lectures is usually referred to simply as "The Agriculture Course," the full title is revealing: "Spiritual Foundations for the Renewal of Agriculture." All of Steiner's practical works—economics, medicine, education, and many others—should have this same title, "spiritual foundations for renewal." With respect to agriculture, Steiner conducted and communicated spiritual-scientific research in order to share with farmers a conception of the ideal farm, one that would be a "self-contained organism." In such an organism the various elements of the farm landscape, the cultivated fields, the animals, and even the marsh, woodland, or wild spaces, should all function as parts of an organic whole. It is the task of the farmers to bring each component into dynamic balance. In order to provide fertile soil it is necessary to continuously raise crops. The right kind and number of animals need to be present to provide the manure that can be returned to the soil. These animals, in turn, require grazing land, or feed, and these, too, should be grown within the boundaries of each farm.

---

32. Correspondence from Thomas Berry to Adrian Hofstetter, 2007. Reprinted with permission.
33. See Rudolf Steiner, *Spiritual Foundations for the Renewal of Agriculture.*

Of course it is nearly impossible to provide from within one farm all of the requisite components for a farm's fertility, but this is nonetheless the ideal that should be striven for. By cycling the material and forces generated by the farm within the farm itself (as opposed to importing manure from elsewhere), the farm becomes individualized, and is thus able to develop increased vitality. This harmonizing and concentrating of vital support, accomplished through the willed activity of a farmer, serves to heal the Earth by providing subtle or etheric forces as well as physical nutrition. Steiner's all-encompassing ecological vision shows the farm to be embedded in a context larger than that imagined by any other approach. A biodynamic farm, in contrast to an organic or permaculture farm, is seen to be fed not only by terrestrial factors such as its soil type, topography, and weather patterns, but by the entire cosmos. The rhythmic movements of sun, moon, and planets, as well as fixed stars, influence plant and animal growth through a play of cosmic forces. Such planetary forces are just as essential to the wellbeing of a farm organism as the physical forces of each particular location. Biodynamic farmers must plant and harvest in harmony with these subtle patterns.

Since agriculture is inevitably a disruption of the naturally occurring interplay of natural forces in a location, it is important to impart to the soil (and the plants and animals that live off the soil) an increased sensitivity and receptivity to the cosmic forces affecting Earth from above, and through reflection in the Earth, from below. The biodynamic method for enhancement of soil is accomplished by inserting "preparation" into the compost which is spread directly on the land. These preparations, made by combining herbs into certain animal "sheaths" at specific times in the yearly cycle, are also applied to the land at cosmically attuned times, and serve to awaken the soil to cosmic forces, and to bring Earth into concert with the heavens. In addition to providing this view of the farm organism and the cosmic ecology in which the farm is placed, Steiner encouraged farmers to develop their capacity of observation, or sensitivity, to the interplay of these earthly and cosmic forces, and to the spiritual beings that are active in guiding the elements. It would be amiss to think Steiner gave a method, or recipe, which one could simply follow.

According to Steiner, the dynamic web of relationships on the farm, even animals and plants, is mediated by suprasensible or etheric forces. By orchestrating these forces in harmony with the natural cosmic rhythms, a farm is transformed alchemically from a quantifiable operation of inputs and outputs to a wellspring of vitality and healing of both Earth and the humans who participate in the farm. Ultimately, it is the conscious awareness of cosmic forces, and the intention to harmonize and cultivate plants and animals in relation to the widest reach of the cosmos, that distinguishes biodynamics from other ecological endeavors.

The deepest component of Steiner's ecological worldview is Goetheanism, his use of the natural philosophy of Johann Wolfgang von Goethe. Spiritual or meditative thinking applied to nature finds its fullest expression, prior to Steiner, in the writings of Goethe. He developed what he referred to as a "gentle empiricism," especially as applied to his pioneering observation of the metamorphosis of plant forms. Goethe conducted thousands of investigations into the world of plants by imaginative thinking. He entered so deeply and sympathetically into the life of the plants he observed that he was able to see/think the plants' essential or formative ideas—i.e., their etheric bodies. Goethe's highly conscious receptivity to the inner reality of what he termed the *Urpflanze*, or fundamental creating principle of the plant, is an example of what Steiner means by a path of knowing "to guide the spiritual in the individual to the spiritual in the universe."

For Steiner, the human development of intuition leads to an intimate knowing of the world, including the physical and archetypal Gaia. A knowing of the forces inside Gaia will lead the knower to recognize his or her capacity for knowing through a higher dimension of self. Not only is there no conflict between spiritual development and a cognitive relation to Earth, they reinforce each other. Steiner states:

> We would have good reason to avoid spiritual study if it took away the meaning of all the beauty that flows into our souls when we observe the wonderful world of flowering plants and

fruiting trees or any other aspect of the natural realm, such as the starry heavens and so on, and if, as a result, we were advised to abandon all this in favor of spiritual contemplation. But this is not at all how it is.[34]

For the past several centuries, a large segment of humanity, particularly in the West, has experienced this separation of spirituality from love of the natural world. For Steiner, spirituality is necessarily cosmic and Gaian. Steiner frequently notes that ancient texts, such as the Bhagavad Gita, retain some sense of the ways in which spiritual beings built up Earth and still guide the human being between death and rebirth. From contemporary scientific cosmology as well as by esoteric research Steiner was aware of how a modern person could feel insignificant relative to the unfathomable vastness of the universe. He also frequently emphasized, however, that the human being is not adrift in a meaningless cosmos but is a carefully attended resident of the universe guided by beings of infinite wisdom. The "starry worlds" are alive in the human being during his or her life on Earth, and active in every human being between death and rebirth. Steiner once again emphasizes the advantage of spiritual or esoteric knowledge, in this case with respect to Earth:

> Along with the Earth, one remembers those ancient days when the Earth was united with the other planets in our solar system. One recalls ages when the Earth had not yet separated, because it had not yet condensed and become firm within as it is today. One recalls a time when the whole solar system was an ensouled, living organism, and human beings lived within it in a very different form. Thus, the metallic veins in the Earth lead us to the Earth's own memories. When we have this inner experience, we can understand very clearly why we are sent to Earth by the divine spiritual beings who guide the universal order. Living in Earth's memories like this causes us to gain a real sense of our own thinking for the first time. Because we have comprehended Earth's memories, we feel how our thinking is connected with Earth itself.[35]

---

34. Rudolf Steiner, *At Home in the Universe*, 89.
35. Ibid., 95.

Steiner describes the role of the hierarchies in the formation and continual guidance of the Earth, and in the formation and guidance of humanity. If he were alive today he would of course urge his audiences to focus on possible ecological catastrophes such as global warming and species extinction. He would also urge, as he did in his lectures during the last five years of his life, that humanity needs to restore its relation to the inner life of Earth—particularly to Earth as a living expression of the inner life of the cosmos and the nine spiritual hierarchies. This restoration is what it means for humanity, in Steiner's phrase, to be "at home in the universe." Steiner recounts that the angels, archangels, and archai participate in cosmic creation. They whisper to human beings who are listening ("those who have ears to hear"): "We are the creative beings of the cosmos, and we look down in Earth existence upon the earthly forms shaped by the quartz rock and its relatives."[36] Steiner also explains that as a result of this revelation by the angels, archangels, and archai, human beings in the spiritual world after death recognize that they must return to Earth because that is the only way for humanity to perceive the activities of the hierarchies on Earth. Steiner concludes:

> To understand the human being, we must reach into all the mysteries involved in the being of nature as well as in the spirit of the cosmos. Ultimately, human beings are intimately connected with all the mysteries of nature and universal spirit. The human being is in fact a universe in miniature.[37]

Steiner's emphasis on the loving-thinking relationship between humanity and Earth can well serve as the catalyst for contemporary ecological thinking and activism. Further, it provides the esoteric foundation necessary for the restoration of Earth to its rightful place as the nurturer of humanity and the rightful object of human gratitude.

In many lectures dating from 1913, Steiner insisted that increasingly throughout the twentieth century and thereafter the etheric body of the Sun Being, the Cosmic Christ, would begin to

---

36. Ibid., 96.
37. Ibid., 104.

envelop Earth. If true, this is the most dramatic of Steiner's ideas concerning ecology, and particularly the fate of the Earth at this time. It is worth considering whether Christ in His (or Its) etheric is enveloping the etheric of Earth as a counter to the damage to the physical Earth caused by human misdeeds. This is a picture to be contemplated: the etheric, life-giving and life-sustaining body of Christ surrounding Earth, nurturing and sustaining it against the devastation inflicted on it by the poison generated by human consumption. If this is true, it is a sublime instance of divine atonement as well as an inestimable failure by humanity, one that will presumably continue to function karmically in the spiritual world forever after. In Steiner's view, a great battle is underway, perhaps resembling the "harrowing of hell," Christ's descent into hell on the day between His crucifixion and resurrection.

At this perilous time, Christ in the etheric appears to be once again in a battle against Lucifer and Ahriman, the powerful tempters working against the evolution of humanity. It might be that the great ecological struggle underway between those who are trying to change human behavior and those committed to business as usual are unwittingly participating in an even greater battle. We might picture Christ and His allies, the archangel Michael and the divine Sophia, in battle against Ahriman who pushes humanity deeper into materialism along with Lucifer who convinces human beings that they are already spiritual, that all will be well without effort. As in the great statue that Steiner carved, *The Representative of Humanity,* Christ strives to hold matter and spirit in an ideal balance of mutual enhancement. The key to this balance is the etheric, the life force at risk in human consciousness and nature at the present time.

Teilhard was also convinced of the close relationship between Christ and Earth, but did not have the concept of the etheric by which to experience and explain this relationship. Yet, Teilhard's "Mass of the World" might be best understood as his sense that the living Earth is spiritually related to Christ. Steiner's account of Christ between His resurrection and ascension points to His continuing in the etheric realm, or as an etheric being. It seems appropriate to think of Christ in the etheric as the resurrected body that, according to the New Testament, appeared to Mary Magdalene at the tomb and to the disciples on the road to Emmaus. This is all profoundly mysterious. If true, the entire ecological crisis might somehow, also mysteriously, be transformed, elevated, rendered spiritual.

In his *Philosophy of Freedom* Steiner emphasized the spiritual significance of free deeds, such as those that seem intuitively right, are costly, and might seem ineffectual in the push and pull of daily life. In his view, such deeds, karmically right and in service to divine beings, will live and work spiritually if not immediately and visibly. In a similar way, Josiah Royce argued for the efficacy of the lost cause. An inspiring example of Steiner's counsel on the importance of a free moral deed (and by extension Royce's case for the lost cause) was the deed of Marjorie Spock, a eurythmist, farmer, translator, Waldorf high school teacher, and a deep anthroposophist. At age eighteen Spock, who was the daughter of a physician and younger sister of Benjamin Spock, MD, left Barnard College to study eurythmy with Rudolf Steiner in Dornach. She saw the Goethanum burn in 1922. In the mid-1950s she and her partner, Polly Richards, owned a farm on Long Island. I know some parts of this story from Marjorie and other parts from Marjorie's friends: When New York State began to spray Long Island farms with DDT, Marjorie and Polly committed a true moral deed, at great financial expense, and in legal terms almost certainly in vain. Armed with months of research, in a Garden City courtroom Marjorie argued against the right of New York State to poison Long Island farms.

In the months prior to Marjorie's doomed case against New York State, Rachel Carson asked her socially prominent friends in Connecticut to write an essay in an important periodical in order to expose the pollution of the Connecticut River by corporations. None of her friends, including writers, scientists, and lawyers, were able or willing to do so, but one friend told her of the case being argued in Garden City in which two women were suing New York State—hopelessly, of course. Rachel Carson moved to Garden City, sat in the courtroom day after day, befriended Marjorie and Polly, and set about writing a series of essays for the *New Yorker* which were then published to extraordinary effect. She expanded those essays into a full-length book, *Silent Spring*, which is widely credited with launching the ecological movement. Marjorie's Spock's spiritually right deed proved efficacious indeed.[38]

---

38. This story is also told in Robert Musil, *Rachel Carson and her Colleagues*, 111–116.

12

SPIRITUAL PRACTICE

This chapter offers a personal account of my spiritual commitments as well as the spiritual inspiration and teachings available from Sri Aurobindo, His Holiness the Dalai Lama, Teilhard de Chardin, and Rudolf Steiner. All four of these spiritual teachers exhibit special abilities and offer special contributions. As I explained in chapters four and five, Sri Aurobindo was a poet, a scholar of Indian thought and culture, and most importantly, an expert practitioner and teacher of Integral Yoga. The Dalai Lama is a scholar of Tibetan Buddhism (its philosophy and spiritual practice), as well as a teacher and exemplar of nonviolence and forgiveness. Teilhard de Chardin was a world-class paleontologist as well as a Roman Catholic priest and mystic. In my view, none of these teachers has a serious deficit: None has been guilty of a scandal, or possessed an embarrassing blind spot or character deformation. Each exemplifies all four yogas—knowledge, action, love, and contemplation—important for serving effectively as a spiritual teacher.

This chapter articulates how each of these spiritual teachers might guide one in cultivating greater wisdom and compassion (or insight and love). The spiritual attainment of each of these teachers is the source and the guarantee of their advice. While it is possible that flawed spiritual teachers could communicate important general insights concerning spiritual practice, the virtuous lives of these four individuals stand behind their teachings. The virtuous character and self-knowledge of a spiritual teacher is a crucial factor in determining whether their teaching and practices are worthy to be followed. With so many excellent teachers, there is surely no need to settle for a spiritual teacher of questionable character. Because of my fifty-year career as a professor of philosophy of religion, I consider religious and spiritual thinkers primarily in terms of *jnana yoga* (spiritual thinking and knowledge). But, of course, I have my eye on the ways and extent to which their *jnana yoga* practice, the spiritual quality of their thinking and writing, can benefit the world. Because ideas are powerful influences on individual lives and on culture, it seems obvious that I should teach only the best thinkers and exemplars I can find.

Similarly, I befriend colleagues whose thinking, behavior, and influence can be trusted, by whom I am inspired, and for whose lives and ideas I am grateful. Because I am an anthroposophist with a personal, academic, and spiritual relationship to many colleagues and friends with the same core commitment as myself, I could name many anthroposophic friends whom I admire and whose influence I welcome. Similarly, it follows from my practice of Anthroposophy that I am committed to understanding and relating to practitioners of other spiritual paths; this list would include many more individuals I admire. The teachers to whom I return faithfully, or never leave, are the four I have chosen for this chapter: Sri Aurobindo (my first spiritual teacher after I read myself out of my Roman Catholic upbringing during college), His Holiness the Dalai Lama (whom I take to be the most inspiring spiritual exemplar and teacher alive), Teilhard de Chardin (from whom I have learned the spirituality of Earth), and of course Rudolf Steiner, the sole spiritual teacher to whom I am joined by all three jewels: He is my teacher, his worldview and practices are my *dharma*, and anthroposophic institutions and individuals worldwide are my *sangha* (community).

I am beholden to teachers in Hindu, Buddhist, and Christian traditions, but I belong to only two spiritual communities, Anthroposophy (including the School of Spiritual Science and the Christian Community of San Francisco) and Grace Cathedral, the Episcopal cathedral of the San Francisco diocese. Participation in a *sangha* is typically an influential component of one's spiritual striving. Grace Cathedral does not affirm Steiner's vast esoteric research concerning the events depicted in the New Testament, but it offers instead a beautiful and inspiring setting for the celebration of the Eucharist, and enlightened sermons. I also attend the Christian Community's Act of Consecration of Man (which was first spoken by Rudolf Steiner) in order to experience the Christian sacraments in light of Steiner's esoteric research. My wife and I celebrated our fiftieth anniversary at both Grace Cathedral and the San Francisco Christian Community.

I agree with His Holiness the Dalai Lama that in general it is better for spiritual seekers to stay in their own tradition. In the 1960s my wife and I were unable to find a Roman Catholic Church in which I could participate without objection. From age twenty-eight to thirty-five I participated in various Aurobindo communities, but I had a sense that my *karma* placed me in relation to Christianity and the West. When I discovered Rudolf Steiner's writings in 1975 (at age 35) and various anthroposophic *sanghas* immediately thereafter, I felt that I had found my *dharma*. Steiner uses the term *Michaelic souls* to describe individuals who inwardly ask the questions that lead them into spiritual lives. One can recognize them by their work toward transforming the world and themselves for the sake of the evolution of humanity, Earth, and the cosmos. Prime examples of Michaelic souls are those discussed in this chapter: Sri Aurobindo, His Holiness the Dalai Lama, and Teilhard de Chardin, but I am not a member of a sangha devoted to them or their works. I have not been tempted to think of myself, for example, as an "Aurobindo anthroposophist." Similarly, I was overwhelmed by the experience of meeting His Holiness but I have not been tempted to join a Tibetan Buddhist community. Bob Thurman and I taught a course on Gandhi and H.H. the Dalai Lama at CIIS in the early 1990s, and I have since read more than a dozen books by and about His Holiness, but I have not become a Buddhist anthroposophist. Because Teilhard focused attention on Christ, and not at all on himself, I have found that to be devoted to the science and Catholic spirituality of Teilhard is to be led past Teilhard to Christ.

According to Steiner, Anthroposophy is compatible with all religious traditions, but I find this claim to have both theoretical and practical limitations. While I have found it complementary to participate fully in the community and sacramental life of Grace Cathedral, it would be more difficult to hold Steiner's esoteric teachings together with traditions such as Aurobindo's Integral Yoga or the H.H. Dalai Lama's Tibetan Buddhism. Aurobindo does not admit the divinity and saving power of Jesus Christ, and the Dalai Lama does not acknowledge the evolution of consciousness. Joining Integral Yoga or Tibetan Buddhism to the practice of Anthroposophy would prove so complicated that, I would expect, either Anthroposophy or the other tradition and practice would eventually give way. Many of my friends who are both Jewish and anthroposophists no longer practice Judaism. I am speaking in general; there are surely individuals with unusual, and entirely admirable, karmic destinies that include more than one tradition. My friends Arthur Zajonc and Will Keepin, two impressive individuals, seem to me to belong to more than one *sangha*—one hundred percent each.

INTEGRAL YOGA OF SRI AUROBINDO

Sri Aurobindo's Integral Yoga is based significantly on the Bhagavad Gita. As I described in chapter 5, "Krishna, Buddha, and Christ," the Bhagavad Gita primarily teaches three yogas: knowledge, action, and love (or devotion). As *jnana yoga* it teaches knowledge of Brahman and Krishna. As *karma yoga* it teaches that Arjuna should fight without regard to the outcome. As *bhakti yoga* it teaches that Krishna loves Arjuna and through him loves the whole of creation. The Gita also teaches contemplation, a fourth yoga that is easy to miss because it is woven throughout the text, supporting each of the other yogas. Both the Gita and Sri Aurobindo give brilliant, effective spiritual teaching: They explain that a person should practice the transformation of knowledge, action, and love because it will lead to love from and for Krishna, a divine consciousness full of bliss. Furthermore, the yogas teach gratitude that the god Krishna who is one with Brahman, so cares about errant humanity that He comes into a human situation, if not human form, to teach correct *dharma*. The Gita teaches that even in the most horrible situations such as hand to hand combat that will leave almost everyone dead, it is possible and efficacious to remain Krishna-conscious. To do so is to experience Krishna's love. Unfortunately, because of its determinism and affirmation of war, I find that the Bhagavad Gita does not immediately fill me with thoughts of love. Like the Stoics, the Bhagavad Gita teaches *amor fati*, love of fate. The human situation that Krishna teaches is so totally determined that He tells Arjuna five times to go and fight the civil war without regard to who will be killed because "they are already dead."

Perhaps the best way to appreciate the teaching of the Gita is to consider its positive effects on those great spiritual figures who have effectively integrated its yogas. Sri Aurobindo himself is an impressive example of an integrated yogi: He displays fabulous knowledge, deep love of the divine, and informed action in service of humanity—particularly concerning India and warring nations. Similarly, His Holiness the Dalai Lama is an exquisite embodiment of knowledge (e.g., he defended his PhD dissertation in Tibetan philosophy quoting Tibetan scriptures in front of 2,000 learned monks). He shows deep love for Tibetans and all oppressed peoples, and ceaseless activity on behalf of peace. Teilhard—scientist; digger in the soil; lover of Christ and Earth; loyal servant of the Church, the Jesuit Order, his friends, and his profession—serves as another inspiring example of integral spirituality. Steiner is a knower beyond comparison, an active worker for human transformation, a profound lover of divinity and humanity, and a great practitioner of prayer and meditation. It should be noted that the three yogas taught in the Gita—knowledge, action, and love—are the same as thinking, feeling, and willing, the three disciplines that Steiner teaches.

Among those whose practice of one yoga seems to have left others undeveloped we might suggest that on some important topics Gandhi would have benefitted by more knowledge, and Aurobindo by a deeper understanding of Buddha and Buddhism as well as of Christ and Christianity. While the Catholic hierarchy has never been a promising place to look for love or selfless action, Christianity along with all other fully formed religious traditions includes individuals who are impressive examples of the integration of knowledge, action, and love. Thomas Aquinas and Thomas Merton would seem to be such examples. In the Hindu tradition, I especially recommend Tagore, and in the Buddhist tradition, in addition to His Holiness the Dalai Lama and Thich Nhat Hanh, I recommend both Joanna Macy who is a systems theorist, Buddhist practitioner, and warrior activist serving many human and other Gaian communities oppressed and in danger of extinction, and Jack Kornfield, who is creator of the Spirit Rock Meditation center, a meditation teacher, and author.

Consistent with Aurobindo's commitment to the evolution of consciousness, he acknowledges that the Bhagavad Gita is limited to its time. As with all Axial-age texts (those between eighth and second centuries BCE), the Gita shows no awareness of the need for a new civilization or a new consciousness: In response to the *adharma* that led to the civil war, Krishna recommends a return to traditional society, not an evolution to a new one. Whether by virtue of Aurobindo's having absorbed Hegelian philosophy at Cambridge, or by his original genius, he tried to find evidence for evolution of consciousness in the Upanishads and the Gita. In his *Synthesis of Yoga* and his other major works, *Life Divine* and *Savitri*, he provides a full account, called *purna* (or Integral) Yoga, of knowledge, action, and love in service of a new, definitely advanced humanity made possible by the descent of Supermind.

Until her death in 1973, the Mother of the Sri Aurobindo Ashram reportedly continued to work with the Supramental Manifestation through her physical and psychic being. In this chapter on spiritual practice the question naturally arises: How are we to relate to the Mother's attempt to transform the cells of her body by the spiritual power (reportedly) made available by the descent of the Supermind? More fundamentally, how am I to relate to the Supermind in my daily life? I doubt that I know an answer to this obvious and difficult question, but as I have been thinking about possible replies I will offer the following: We might not find what we seek but we will even more certainly not find what we do not seek. Of course, we might seek something that is not there: Krishna the avatar, buddha nature, the incarnation of Christ in the etheric, Teilhard's concept of Omega Point, and the Supermind concept of Sri Aurobindo and the Mother might not exist. Even if one or more of these do exist, they might not be accessible by my ability. But if there is any chance at all of my reaching one or more of these transcendent realities, it will be possible only by effort. Because I assume that at the highest levels, spiritual beings, powers, and ideals are at least compatible and probably overlapping, I also assume that if we would advance even a little closer to any one of these transcendent realities, that closeness would likely bring us closer to another, and perhaps to all.

It seems to me that the effort to experience Supermind is itself transformative. Whatever else Supermind (or Krishna's avatar appearance, or Buddha's Enlightenment, or the incarnation of Christ) might be, it is characterized by love, or they would not be worth our attention. We can understand Supermind as love by thinking of the divine manifesting itself ever more forcefully, creatively, and sacrificially. As the divine would seem by definition to be sufficient unto itself, any descent, whether as Krishna, Buddha, or Christ, and any goal, such as Omega Point or Beloved Community, is perhaps best understood as the divine luring humanity back home. As Augustine exclaimed: "My heart is restless until it rests in Thee."

In response to the Mother's attempt to transform the cells of her body—which, had she completely succeeded, would presumably have allowed her body to live indefinitely—it seems appropriate for us, along with Sri Aurobindo and the Mother, to view the human body as an instrument of future evolution, as an opportunity—even perhaps obligation—to purify and spiritualize it and all matter. One way to understand Auroville, the utopian city first envisioned by the Mother, and now built on the coast of the Bay of Bengal five miles north of the Sri Aurobindo Ashram, is to see it as an experiment in transformation of physical life, including architecture, transportation, sex, and money. For the Mother, "purify and spiritualize" does not mean to avoid; it means self-transformation and selfless work toward a new humanity able to create a more peaceful civilization worthy of Sri Aurobindo's vision of The Life Divine on Earth.

HIS HOLINESS THE DALAI LAMA

Principally because of the positive reports of his intensely observed life and extensive teachings—not to mention his infectious joy—His Holiness the Dalai Lama might be the foremost spiritual teacher on the planet at the present time. (As of this writing, it is too early to predict whether Pope Francis will continue to evolve and actually transform the Catholic Church.) The Dalai Lama's worldwide fame and admiration issue from his dedication to the practice and advocacy of compassion as a solution to all human conflicts. His devotion to compassion is confirmed by his response toward the Chinese government and Han Chinese troops who, during the past fifty years, have murdered perhaps one million Tibetans, have destroyed thousands of Tibetan Buddhist monasteries, and are succeeding in their attempt to obliterate Tibetan language, culture, and religion. Perhaps more than any other individual, and surely more than any other head of state (as he was until recently), His Holiness has the credibility to speak truth to power, always with the same message: compassion.

The essential meaning of the Dalai Lama's life and teaching is to spend as many lifetimes as it takes to overcome suffering by replacing selfishness with compassion, and should he succeed, to help all other sentient beings down to the last cockroach to do the same. Deep thinkers on love and compassion have long noted that love (and compassion) requires wisdom. While a loving motivation is certainly positive, without adequate knowledge appropriate to the situation (whether a moment or lifetime), a loving response can miss the essential task, the singular opportunity. It is most fortunate, then, that His Holiness the Dalai Lama is a highly accomplished scholar in Buddhist philosophy and science, a scholar of world religions, and increasingly an expert on contemporary Western physics and psychology (again, not the "simple monk" he claims to be). More importantly, the Dalai Lama has disciplined himself to learn from every meeting, every moment, every conversation, and every hour spent in meditation. What has he learned? In myriad ways he has gained the wisdom of love through learning non-attachment.

According to the core teaching of the Dalai Lama, as well as of the Buddha, there are no real substances, only phantom-like processes and relations.[1] All Buddhist schools agree that attachment is based on illusion, and that it obscures wisdom and compassion and causes suffering. The mantra at the end of the *Prajnaparamita Hrdaya Sutra,* a singularly important Mahayana text, extols the wisdom that is *gate, paragate,* "gone beyond, beyond." For the Dalai Lama, in theory and practice, this means non-attachment even to Tibet—even to the Tibetan land, monasteries and language, all systematically being driven to extinction by the People's Republic of China. It means non-attachment even to the thousands of monks tortured and killed, the nuns imprisoned and raped. On the ladder to truth and peace, wisdom and compassion, the Dalai Lama daily exposes the cruelty of the Chinese occupation, but only in a way that leaves the Chinese free to see their own error and to develop the compassion that would enable them to abandon their commitment to genocide.

A person who is serious about spiritual practice should spend all waking hours attempting to reduce his or her inveterate grip on the illusory self, the belief that he or she is a discreet entity and of lasting value. This illusion is at the source of all *dukkha,* of discontent and suffering. Because I fear that I will not endure, I cling to objects and pleasures that support the illusion of my self, my ego, as a value unto itself. The world around me may be dying but I will live! The Dalai Lama reminds his listeners and readers that "religious practice is a twenty-four-hour occupation." Anything less will not lead to the realization that everything to which I am attached does not exist in the way that I automatically assume. Because I cannot or will not rid myself of these attachments, I suffer when I lose what I want to keep and gain what I should not want. This teaching is simple and direct, and at the same time entirely too profound to sustain except by ceaseless effort. Nothing less will lead to the kind of wisdom and compassion for which Buddha and His Holiness are revered.

---

1. The metaphysics of Buddhism is similar to that of William James and A. N. Whitehead, though without the spiritual practices that are the core of Buddhism.

In 1994 His Holiness joined a group of Catholic monks and nuns at the John Main Seminar in order to explore similarities and differences in their respective spiritual practices. Father Lawrence Freeman explained the meaning and practice of meditation in the Christian context, and Thupten Jinpa, the translator for His Holiness, explained the Buddhist worldview and practice. His Holiness agreed to interpret from his Tibetan spiritual perspective eight passages from the New Testament. Hearing his responses to these passages is rather like observing signals from one mountain top to another. The New Testament passages spoke to His Holiness because his meditation practice (at least four hours a day) had given him "ears to hear." He heard the spiritual truths behind the Christian words and images. In the process of speaking about these texts, the Dalai Lama also explained the method and value of Tibetan spiritual practice, particularly meditation, karma and rebirth, letting go of self, and the practice of compassion.[2]

In order to practice effectively, it is important to serve all three jewels—Buddha, *dharma* (teaching and practice), and *sangha*. With respect to karma and rebirth, *dharma* teaching and practice are inseparable: If one tries to follow the line of great spiritual teachers and practitioners from Buddha to His Holiness the Dalai Lama, one is encouraged to accept the relative truth of cognitive and emotional states as the field of transformation. If transformation or enlightenment are ever to be accomplished, one's grasping at the self (once thought to be enduring), must be replaced by realizing the absolute truth of Emptiness. In this state, all entities, including Buddha, are recognized as Empty. Emptiness is the category that breaks reason, that does not allow conceptual resolution. Resting in this irresolvable, paradoxical, enlightenment-generating relative–absolute truth is at the core of Buddhist practice, especially Madhyamika. As the self is not enduring, and escapes even our conceptualization, so does Emptiness escape our intellectual grasp. As most of us are not attempting to follow the Dalai Lama to this extent, we might ask, just how far I should go with this paradox? The Dalai Lama seems to answer, as far as

2. References for this discussion of karma and rebirth: The Dalai Lama, *The Good Heart: A Buddhist Perspective on the Teachings of Jesus*

you can, for each step will bring you closer to wisdom and compassion, and further from *dukkha*.

One of the most difficult subjects for a Buddhist teacher to explain, and for his or her audience and readers to understand, is the double topic of karma and rebirth, particularly the endurance of karma and the non-endurance of the self. A straightforward summary statement is possible: The self is illusory but karma continues from life to life.

To begin to work with the reality of karma is to approach equanimity as a habit. It is our habits that are reborn; "I" endure as my karma. His Holiness has stated: "What is reborn from life to life is that in us which identifies with objects blindly" (85). To the extent that I identify with the idea of myself—that I am the center, important, enduring—I continue to suffer. To the extent that I replace self-concern with compassion for others, including my enemies (e.g., the Chinese government, the enemy of Tibet), I suffer proportionately less. His Holiness, an exquisite practitioner of compassion, teaches: "If you do not practice compassion toward your enemy then toward whom can you practice it?" (48). He adds: "Even one's enemies must be seen to be suffering, and so in need of compassion" (68–69). Taking us one step further, His Holiness teaches that once one achieves single-pointed meditation concerning compassion, so that it has been interiorized, "there is no longer a meditating mind and meditated object. Instead, your mind is generated in the form of compassion" (47).

The *bodhisattva*, the ultimate expression of compassion, of selflessness in action, is the person who attains liberation, yet refuses the ultimate transcendence that follows this attainment, and chooses to stay on Earth to aid sentient beings who continue to suffer. His Holiness defines the Bodhisattva as "one with a heroic aspiration toward enlightenment...though capable of ultimate personal liberation, chooses to take upon their shoulders the task of freeing others from suffering" (169). At the conclusion of his speech after being awarded the Nobel Peace Prize, His Holiness recited the bodhisattva vow: "As long as space abides, and as long as sentient beings remain, may I, too, abide and dispel the suffering of beings" (70).

In his tireless work on behalf of world peace, His Holiness gathers (and inevitably leads) groups of leaders of the world's religious traditions. He discourages individuals from leaving one religious tradition for another and considers it beneficial for "the major religions to maintain their uniqueness, their distinctive beliefs, visions, and practices" (73). He also does not advocate seeking a universal religion. He is convinced that even when two religious traditions "diverge at the level of metaphysics," as in the case of Buddhism and Christianity, "these differences need not divide us" (82). His Holiness recommends five ways to foster harmony among religious traditions: public and private meetings, pilgrimages, and meditation. He especially recommends meditation practice that joins intellect and heart, and thereby leads to compassion.

Christian Spirituality: The Mass

When Pope Francis celebrated Mass in Manila in January 2015, nine million people attended. Hundreds of millions of Christians attend the celebration of Mass every week, often at considerable sacrifice. During times of anti-Christian persecution, Christians have risked their lives to attend Mass. In Europe and North America, millions regularly attend Mass quite possibly without a settled opinion on what happens during this familiar yet mysterious ritual. One has to wonder what the people in the pews are thinking when a priest, at the high point of the mass, says the words that Christ reportedly said at His Last Supper with his disciples the night before he was crucified: "This is my body, this is my blood. Do this in remembrance of Me." In light of sophisticated theological teachings since the Protestant Reformation it is unclear how many modern Western Christians believe that the words of the consecration literally announce the "real presence" of the physical body of Christ in ordinary bread and wine.

For a certain percentage of Christians, and certainly a high percentage of former Christians, it strains credulity to think that Christ's physical body is either in the host or in heaven. It seems more likely that modern Christians believe Christ exists only in a spiritual world. This same problem affects three other mysteries at the core of Christian teaching: the bodily Resurrection of Christ on Easter Sunday, the bodily Ascension of Christ forty days after Easter, and the bodily Assumption of the Virgin Mary at the end of her life on Earth. Yet, at the end of Jung's *Answer to Job* he states that the pope's declaration in 1950 of the physical Assumption of Mary into heaven as a doctrine of faith is the most important religious event in the West of the last five centuries![3]

The Roman Catholic Church, Eastern Orthodox Church, and a few Protestant denominations all agree that the Eucharist is a sacrament—i.e., that with the help of prescribed words and deeds—a divine action is initiated and a spiritual transformation is realized. More than even the most compelling sermon, the loftiest prayers, or most inspiring music, the Eucharist, or the Mass, is generally understood to signify that something miraculous happens. Some kind of spiritual change, perhaps best understood as symbolic, takes place during the consecration of the Mass, and this miracle is at the core of Christian spiritual life. Perhaps the significance of this presumed miracle depends exactly on the extent of a person's or community's ability to ascribe meaning to symbolic words and actions.

Emerson's Disavowal

Despite the teachings of the Christian churches, and his own vocation as a Unitarian minister, Ralph Waldo Emerson delivered a life-defining lecture in 1842 (at age 39) in which he argued that the New Testament gives little support to the claim that bread and wine are somehow spiritually changed during the Eucharist. He also argued that there is not evidence supporting the idea that Jesus intended this ritual to be performed for centuries, and in all cultures. After quoting Matthew 26:26–30 and noting the omission of the Last Supper ritual in the Gospel of John, Emerson writes:

> Two of the Evangelists, namely Matthew and John, were of the twelve disciples, and were present on that occasion. Neither of

---

3. Jung, *Answer to Job*, para. 752.

them drops the slightest intimation of any intention on the part of Jesus to set up anything permanent.[4]

At the conclusion of this lecture Emerson announces that he cannot in good conscience continue to administer the Eucharist and offers this disavowal as the primary reason for vacating his ministry:

> As it is the prevailing opinion and feeling in our religious community that it is an indispensable part of the pastoral office to administer this ordinance, I am about to resign into your hands that office which you have confided to me.[5]

Although Emerson's life-changing sermon is apparently little known (standard biographies and studies scarcely mention it), it was a radical statement for both Emerson himself and for the Unitarian denomination of which he was an important representative.

JUNG'S PSYCHOLOGICAL ANALYSIS

Curiously, even though Jung's conclusions on ritual are at the very center of the Christian religion, and his insights compelling, his one-hundred-page essay "The Transformation Symbolism in the Mass" is generally ignored in books about him. Jung analyzed some of the same texts and history as Emerson but, as he does characteristically, he looks to the psychological and specifically symbolic factors at work. For him, the most relevant evidence on behalf of the Eucharist is not the gospels of Matthew, Luke, or John, or the Epistles of Paul, but what seems to him to be the experiences of the priest and congregation in the moment, but not at all focused on his experience of the Mass.

Emerson had to forego ministering the Eucharist because both his scholarship and personal experience did not permit him to continue. Jung wrote an extensive essay on the Eucharist but does not speak of his relationship to it. I have not found any biographies of Jung that refer to his attending Mass. Teilhard's

---

4.   "The Last Supper," in *The Works of Ralph Waldo Emerson*, 419.

5.   Ibid., 432.

experience is the reverse of both Emerson and Jung: He both studied the Mass in its historical and theological context and wrote with poetic passion about his ministering the Mass. Steiner represents an unusual fourth case: he did not minister the Mass but in response to a request from Lutheran priests, he intuited a version of the Mass (including the words and gestures) that he then gave to them.

It seems likely that very few of the thinkers discussed in this book believe in Christian sacraments, and even fewer believe that a transformation happens when the Eucharist is enacted. Of the American philosophers, only Royce and Whitehead would have admitted to being Christian, and of these two only Whitehead attended church. It is notable, then, that Jung, essentially a Gnostic psychiatrist who did not identify as Christian, affirms that in the enactment of the Eucharist a real symbolic or psychic transformation takes place. In Jung's view, the divine really does act, or as he says, "intervenes," in response to the prescribed words and actions of the consecration of the Mass.

It would probably encourage a positive view of the Eucharist if we were to know that Jesus said the words attributed to him, and further that Jesus intended for this ritual to be performed indefinitely and worldwide. Yet it might also be the case that doubting these two factors is not a bar to a positive response such as Jung's. A later understanding could be more profound than the original. Rather than focusing on the deed of Jesus or his purported reflection on it, what does (or doesn't) happen now would seem more crucial: What, if anything, do I and others experience during Mass? If we think that nothing happens, because nothing could, then surely we are unlikely ever to experience a transformation of any kind during the Eucharist ritual. But if we believe that a transformation is possible, and does happen, then as James, Peirce, and Royce would agree, this belief is the first necessary condition for an experience of precisely such a transformation.

Jung's learned essay on the Mass draws on his earlier research on unconscious symbolism and on the process of individuation (the fulfillment of each human life). In his essay, which he delivered as a lecture at the Eranos Conference of 1940/1941, Jung emphasizes that the Mass joins the priest and the congregation to Christ:

> The ritual act commemorates and represents the Last Supper which our Lord took with his disciples, the whole incarnation, Passion, death, and resurrection of Christ. But from the divine point of view, this anthropomorphic action is only the outer shell or husk in which what is really happening is not a human action at all but a divine event. For an instant the life of Christ, eternally existent outside time, becomes visible and is unfolded in temporal succession, but in condensed form, in the sacred action: Christ incarnates as a man under the aspect of the offered substances, he suffers, is killed, is laid in the sepulcher, breaks the power of the underworld, and rises again in glory. In the utterance of the words of consecration the Godhead intervenes, Itself acting and truly present, and thus proclaims that the central event of the Mass is Its act of grace, in which the priest has only the significance of a minister.... It is God Himself as a sacrifice in the substances, in the priest, and in the congregation, and who in the form of the Son offers himself as an atonement to the Father.[6]

Jung's statement that God in the person of the Son intervenes in the Mass, while no doubt surprising to many readers, is perhaps not far from his conviction that archetypal symbols and images regularly intervene in human consciousness, foremost among them the God-image and the image of Christ. Synchronicities are precisely such interventions. In this respect, Jung is close to Steiner and Teilhard: All three, panentheists rather than theists, see the divine permeating the material world, and therefore easily affirm the idea of Christ permeating the bread and wine. This permeation does not require a physical miracle; it requires a symbolic deed, one that activates the deepest, and therefore most permeable, dimension of divinity and Earth, namely Christ in the bread and wine.

---

6. C. G. Jung, "Transformation Symbolism in the Mass," in *Psychology and Western Religion*, para. 378.

Teilhard's "Mass on the World"

Teilhard's "Mass on the World" must surely represent one of the most ecstatic accounts of the celebration of the Roman Catholic Mass. In his essay, first written in 1918, while he was on the French front during World War I, Teilhard's mystical love of Earth and Christ fuse in his act of consecration of Earth and human suffering in the place of an altar, bread, and wine. "Mass on the World" is a work on which he continued to reflect throughout his life. In 1923 he wrote to his friend Abbe Breuil:

> It seems to me that in a sense the true substance to be consecrated each day is the world's development during that day—the bread symbolizing appropriately what creation succeeds in producing, the wine (blood) what creation causes to be lost in exhaustion and suffering in the course of its effort.[7]

Thirty years later, in forced exile in New York after his painful farewell to his family home and friends in Paris, Teilhard wrote essentially the same message in his final essay, "The Christic." In a section entitled "Introduction: the Amorization of the Universe," he affirms his "double perception, intellectual and emotional," of a "Cosmic Convergence" and a "Christic Emergence" that, each in its own way, fill my whole horizon." He continues:

> I saw the Universe becoming amorized and personalized in the very dynamism of its own evolution. It is already a long time since, in response to these new ways of seeing things, still barely defined in my mind, I tried, in *The Mass on the World* and *Le Milieu Divin*, to give distinct expression to my sense of wonder and amazement.[8]

Teilhard's wonder and amazement was focused on a "third nature" of Christ: In addition to man and God, Teilhard believed Christ should be conceived and adored in his theandric being (i.e., combined humanity and divinity) "who is very much greater even than we used to think." This is the Christ of the third phase

---

7. Teilhard de Chardin, "Mass on the World," in *The Heart of Matter*, 119.
8. Teilhard de Chardin, *The Heart of Matter*, 83.

of evolution: Biogenesis, Noogenesis, and then Christogenesis. He continues:

> And then there appears to the dazzled eyes of the believer the Eucharistic mystery itself, extended infinitely into a veritable universal transubstantiation, in which the words of the Consecration are applied not only to the sacrificial bread and wine but, mark you, to the whole mass of joys and sufferings produced by the Convergence of the World as it progresses.
>
> And it is then, too, that there follow in consequence the possibilities of a universal Communion.[9]

Teilhard de Chardin was devoted to Christ and to the divine feminine and also to Earth but it is not clear (at least to me) whether, or to what extent, he sought to bring them together. Two of his most effective interpreters, however, have made explicit what Teilhard seems to have intended but did not bring to resolution simply because when he was writing in the first half of the twentieth century ecological devastation was not in full view. In addition to *Spirit of Fire*, a vivid biography of Teilhard, Ursula King has written important books on this topic: *The Spirit of One Earth, Christ in All Things: Exploring Spirituality with Teilhard de Chardin,* and *The Search for Spirituality: Our Global Quest for a Spiritual Life.* Ilia Delio has written *Christ in Evolution* and edited *From Teilhard to Omega: Co-creating an Unfinished Universe.* In my view these books represent the ideal fusion of Christianity and ecology, joining spirit and matter, theory and practice, mind and heart.

STEINER'S GIFT, THE ACT OF CONSECRATION OF MAN

In 1921, a group of Lutheran priests and seminarians, led by Frederick Rittlemeyer, pastor of the Lutheran Cathedral in Berlin, complained to Rudolf Steiner that in their experience the sacraments, particularly the celebration of the Eucharist had lost its spiritual efficacy. In response, Rudolf Steiner gave the group a renewed version of the standard seven sacraments of

---

9. Ibid., 94.

the Christian Church: baptism, confirmation, marriage, The Act of Consecration of Man (the Mass), ordination of priests, consultation (confession), and last anointing. This section on Steiner's contribution to Christian spirituality (somewhat independent of Anthroposophy), focuses on the Act of Consecration of Man. The first topic, inevitably, is the name: Steiner used the German word *mensch*, which means a person who is honorable and admirable. Unfortunately, "man," the English translation of *mensch*, implies the male, exclusive of females. As Steiner created the priesthood of the Christian Community to include women priests, it was clearly not his intention to create a sacrament that would privilege males.

The Act of Consecration of Man (in respect I always say the full title, just as I always say The Christian Community, not an abbreviation) consists of four parts, the first of which is a reading of the Gospel for the week, and the Creed. The priest speaks without his vestment in order to indicate that he is speaking as an individual. In the Christian Community, no dogma is required; each individual thinks his or her own thoughts. For the second part, the priest offers water and wine to the Father God who is the Ground of the World, and then in prayer to Christ. The priest then surrounds the altar with incense. The third part is the Consecration or Transubstantiation: "The bread and wine are offered, to become by the power of the Father God, the body and blood of the Son. Thereby, the Divine Spirit works into the earthly substance." Evelyn Francis Capel, who was a Christian Community priest, explains: "And yet this substance has already with it the seed of Christ's life, as a consequence of what was done on Golgotha." In the fourth and final part, "the celebrant and members of the congregation receive the Christ-filled bread and wine in His name, and thereafter His blessing of peace."[10]

In giving this sacrament, along with the other six, Steiner explicitly indicated that these sacraments, and the community of priests which administer them, are intended for individuals seeking a religious life either apart from Anthroposophy or as a

---

10. Evelyn Francis Capel, *Seven Sacraments in The Christian Community*, 47–48.

complement. Because Steiner held that Anthroposophy is not a religion and does not privilege any one religion (even though it clearly does privilege Christianity), Steiner did not consider the Christian Community or the sacraments it administers to be an essential part of Anthroposophy.

RUDOLF STEINER AND ANTHROPOSOPHY[11]

The last section of this chapter is about what I, one lone anthroposophist writing with no particular authority, have concluded about ideas and practices that follow from taking Steiner seriously, reading his books and lectures, attending anthroposophic lectures, meetings, and workshops, and reflecting to myself about coming closer to Steiner and Anthroposophy. I hope that after reading this half of the chapter on spiritual practice anyone will be able to understand what it might mean to become a student of Anthroposophy, and what one's attempt at anthroposophic practice means in the life of an anthroposophist who is also a husband, parent, and grandparent, as well as a relative, friend, professor and colleague of scores of individuals who have no relationship to Steiner or Anthroposophy. As I have explained in two memoir essays on my department website,[12] I have been married for fifty years, have lived in two cities (New York and San Francisco), and have worked for three academic institutions (Manhattanville College, Baruch College, CUNY, and California Institute of Integral Studies; as president, 1990 to 1999, and professor, 1999 to the present). All of these experiences have influenced my relationship to Anthroposophy, and Anthroposophy has influenced all of these relationships.

What does it mean to *be* an anthroposophist—or more accurately and modestly, an anthroposopher? This book is full of ideas that Steiner wrote or spoke, but how do we, a century later, work with these ideas and actually *do* what he recommends? Which are the core ideas and core practices? I am often asked, "Does a person have to believe in Christ to be anthroposophist?" And,

---

11. This section is indebted to Bob and Louise Hill.
12. CIIS.PCC.faculty.robertmcdermott.publications.

"Does a person have to believe in karma and rebirth?" Because of the negative components of the history of Christianity, the question about Christ is more controversial than the one about karma and rebirth. In the Christian Middle Ages torture and death did not follow the "wrong" answer concerning karma and rebirth, whereas from Constantine in the third century until at least the nineteenth century, Christians of different denominations regularly killed each other. They also extensively killed non-Christians, especially Jews. There are at least three groups that have serious difficulties with the close relation between Anthroposophy and Christianity, and particularly with Steiner's conception of Christ: Secularists, believers in other religions, and Christians who hold ideas about Jesus and Christ different from Steiner's.

Turning to the question of what is core, what (if anything) needs to be believed and what (if anything) is not allowed, I would suggest that Anthroposophy is about the transformation of one's person and holds no absolute requirements or prohibitions. Above all, Anthroposophy requires freedom of aspiration and expression. There are not, and should not be, creedal statements or required practices. I have heard Arthur Zajonc quote Rudolf Steiner as follows: "It should not be said, 'We as anthroposophists believe...[one or another particular idea].'" By writing about my understanding of, and attempt to implement a very small portion of the spiritual practices that Steiner recommended, I am only providing one example. I am essentially saying: "Here is what I understand and here is what I have been trying to do." I am not suggesting that my combination is the best, and it is certainly not the most advanced. I suspect that my way of integrating Anthroposophy into my busy family and professional life might be too much for some readers, not enough for others, and perhaps simply not relevant for some. But I hope that some of my reflections on the working of Anthroposophy in my life will be interesting for some readers in some ways.

To continue to answer the question about "the core of Anthroposophy," the one-word answer to Steiner's core teaching and core practice is "transformation": evil to good, imbalance to balance, alienation to relation, and foremost, hatred to love. Steiner described Anthroposophy as a path of knowing (including affect and will) to lead the spiritual in the self (the entire person—"I," soul, etheric, and physical bodies) to the spiritual in the Universe (from sand and cells to exalted beings). The process of transforming the self will help to transform the universe, which according to Steiner, is increasingly dependent on humanity to provide the love toward which the universe has been strtiving but cannot attain without the free cooperation of individual human beings.

Reading Steiner thoroughly can take a lifetime, at the end of which we will have forgotten much of what we read. This amnesia can be a source of frustration, especially for those who are accustomed to read such texts from a scholarly perspective. Steiner spoke and wrote in such a way that we as readers must become inwardly active, initiating an engagement with the text that is warmed by genuine interest and an unbiased, open heart and mind. One meets thereby the living ideas of the text—of Anthroposophy—as formative forces that can work in one's own being in a transformative way. One participates (in a Barfieldian sense) in the ideas through a knowing process that Steiner calls living thinking, thereby entering into a relationship with the text as teacher. Steiner eschewed the role of a master or guru for students of Anthroposophy because he recognized that the individual must be left free to meet the ideas he presented without persuasion. He wrote in such a way—admittedly, some find it dry or hard to penetrate—that is intended to leave the reader free of such persuasion, but which leaves the door open for readers to participate in bringing the text to life within themselves. Steiner would say that this kind of reading of his lectures and books provides an opportunity for one to enter into a relationship with Anthroposophy, not just as a body of wisdom, but as *Anthroposophia,* a representative of divine Sophia.

Whereas most religious traditions, especially the Abrahamic religions, are characterized by revealed dogmas which followers are required to believe, Anthroposophy, as Steiner insisted, ideally eschews belief in favor of knowledge about both the spiritual world and spirit in the physical world. Anthroposophy is intended to be a spiritual science such that its spiritual knowledge can be verified by other researchers—natural scientists, Waldorf educators, biodynamic farmers, anthroposophic physicians, Christian Community priests. Ideally, to be an anthroposophist is to be a researcher on a daily and permanent basis, not to be a believer or follower.

If we put some of Steiner's ideas into action, if we warm his ideas and make them our own, we won't need to remember them for ourselves—though it is useful to remember them for others. They will be in our etheric or life body, where mind, will, and heart work in unison. As Teilhard recommends, we will *see* into the Earth, and we will see Christ; with Aurobindo we will see the coming transformation of the physical world; with His Holiness the Dalai Lama we will forego possession in favor of compassion; and with Steiner we will think, feel, and will in ways that activate a loving relationship between our souls and the soul of the world. As advocates for the reality of Sophia we will see the truth and necessity of feminist, relational thinking. An individual's relationship to Anthroposophia/Sophia is the medium through which the creative, transformative force of love can become active in his or her thinking. A living relationship between the world and oneself is made possible by Christ, the primary unifier of spirit and matter and the ultimate transformer of evil into good.

Because Steiner exhibited vast and deep knowledge and insights, it might be a challenge for some who look to him to see the love that propels his research, teaching, and practical works. Instead of recalling some of the serious photographs of Rudolf Steiner (typical of that time) it might be more edifying to picture him teaching the construction workers at the Goetheanum, riding cold drafty trains through the night to another set of lectures in another city, and writing hundreds, perhaps thousands, of sympathy notes to parents of sons killed in World War I. As much as the work of His Holiness the Dalai Lama, the work of Rudolf Steiner was compassion, and to follow Rudolf Steiner as an anthroposophist is to practice compassion, including knowing and willing, without which compassion can be sentimental and unhelpful. If any one of these three aspects of compassion—knowledge, love, and action—are absent, the other two are likely to be distorted. More importantly, in direct opposition to dominant Western thinking, especially in the academy, feeling—the active principle of love—must take up residence in thinking and willing.

Clearly modeled on the forgiveness of his executioners that Jesus spoke while nailed to the cross, Martin Luther King, Jr. and Archbishop Desmond Tutu did not return in kind the hatred addressed in them. Followers of the Mahayana Buddhist tradition affirms Buddha's *dharmakaya*, an infinite and eternal body that is the very essence of compassion. This body, like the body of the resurrected Christ, absorbs and transforms suffering to forgiveness. Whereas the Buddhist and Roman Catholic system of symbols initially seem at odds in "Mass of the World," Teilhard offered suffering humanity to Christ as an act of compassion in the same spirit as Buddhist compassion. Steiner, too, saw human suffering in union with the suffering of Christ and the sacrifices of exalted beings on behalf of Earth and humanity.

For Steiner, acts of suffering and forgiveness are never lost; they follow the soul to the afterlife and to the next life. Such deeds, in fact all deeds, are gathered and rendered efficacious by Christ and higher beings. All loving thoughts and deeds are part of Christ—or, perhaps simultaneously, part of Buddha—and contribute to the mission of Christ against an unloving individualism fostered by Lucifer and unloving focus on the material realm fostered by Ahriman. For Steiner, love is the ultimate reality, pure divinity, and the sole purpose of human life. It is important to strive for good over evil precisely because that victory leads the spiritual warrior to love. He or she transforms the discipline of thinking, feeling, and willing as the way to love. Social life is the battlefield, the *kurukshetra*, of the Bhagavad Gita, that sets the terms for each individual and each group striving for knowledge of right action and devotion, all on the way to unconditional love, lifetime after lifetime. Steiner describes love in several places as a spiritual *substance* that is the most powerful transformative agent working in the world, but that only can be accessed through selfless intention in full, conscious freedom, the kind that Steiner describes in *The Philosophy of Freedom*.

Steiner's *dharma*—his teaching and practice—can be summarized by three interrelated disciplines: living or heart thinking, feeling, and willing, not insignificantly the rough equivalent of the yogas of thinking, love, and action, similar to the yogas taught in the Bhagavad Gita. It is worth bringing to this similarity Steiner's extraordinary esoteric claim that the soul of Krishna was reborn as the soul of Jesus of Nazareth as described in the Gospel of Luke. Before the soul and the "I" of Jesus was joined by the "I" of Zarathustra, the great civilization builder, the Jesus child of the Luke Gospel was inhabited by the soul of Krishna, and therefore by the yogas He taught in the Gita. The soul of Krishna remained part of Jesus, the human vessel who received Christ at His baptism. When Christ, after His resurrection, called to Saul, who was on the road to Damascus to persecute Jews who had become followers of the risen Christ, the light that Saul experienced was the light of Krishna. If true, it is surely astonishing and worthy of meditation that the yogas that Krishna embodied and taught entered Jesus of Nazareth at His birth, and thereby continued as part of the risen Christ, and then from Christ into Paul, and thereby into the very foundation of Christianity.

Steiner's Six Exercises, sometimes misleadingly referred to as "supplementary," offer an excellent set of practices for the development of one's thinking, feeling, and willing. These six exercises, which Steiner describes in *An Outline of Esoteric Science* and which Christopher Bamford thoroughly explains in the collection of Steiner's spiritual practices, *Start Now!*[13] are recommended as a beginning of anthroposophic practice and should ideally remain part of one's daily spiritual work. Although they do not take any special knowledge or skill, they are not as easy as they might appear. The first involves five minutes a day set aside for a concentration exercise: Select a simple object (the simpler the better—for example, a paperclip) and think one thought after another about that object. One of the important parts of this exercise is the experience of deliberately creating a thought, and then another, in a series, all connected—without losing track and without, as Georg Kühlewind often said, "finding oneself in

---

13. Rudolf Steiner, *Start Now! A Book of Soul and Spiritual Exercises.*

Greenland." I don't often land in Greenland but it usually takes only a couple of minutes for me to begin tracking my next task, whether phone call, e-mail, or text. This is as much an exercise for the will as for thinking. It is a good idea to continue this exercise while beginning to practice the second, or to leave the first exercise and focus exclusively on the second.

The second exercise involves only the will. It calls for one to remember to perform a simple task at the same time every day without a reminder (i.e., no alarm and not the last minute before turning out the lights at night). Try to remember, for example, to turn your ring or touch your ear at the same time every day, perhaps midmorning or mid-afternoon. While one's resolve is recent, and the exercise still novel, you might be successful for the first few days, but sometime in the first week a lapse is likely. That is fine, and not unusual; simply start again, and again. If this exercise becomes so automatic that you can remember for a full month, it is time to move on to the third exercise. You can continue this exercise and the first, or leave one or both behind.

The third exercise calls for one to stay steady in his or her reactions to both pleasant and unpleasant situations. Steady should not be understood as indifferent, but rather deeply observant, understanding, and caring, but without excessive or self-indulgent reaction. Krishna is a model of this equanimity and teaches this virtue to Arjuna in steps throughout the Gita: Krishna sees what is about to happen and manages to stay calm but not unloving. As every sculpture of Buddha shows, Buddha remained a model of serenity throughout his forty-five-year ministry. Christ seems to be the prototype of equanimity throughout his life as described in the New Testament, especially during his excruciating passion and crucifixion, as he even forgave his torturers. For twentieth-century examples of equanimity it would be hard to match Teilhard's letters from the trenches during World War I, the compassionate response to the Chinese government by His Holiness the Dalai Lama, Steiner's experience and response to the burning of the Goetheanum, and the Truth and Reconciliation Commission led by Archbishop Desmond Tutu.

The fourth exercise calls for the habit of positivity even (or especially) in the face of whatever we experience as bad or ugly. By being positive we don't deny the negative but rather strive to perceive a positive part of every circumstance that would not have been noticed without special effort. This exercise, and perhaps all of them, are will exercises. It takes significant effort to find something positive in a war, a famine, a premature death, a neurological disease, a burnt home, unemployment, HIV/AIDS, ALS, or depression. Steiner repeats a story about Jesus who passed a decaying dog. While his disciples were understandably repulsed, Jesus remarked on the dog's beautiful teeth.

The fifth exercise recommends the practice of openness to new ideas, new experiences, and new possibilities. I often urge students to consider the "far out" ideas of Aurobindo or Steiner, without, of course, lapsing into gullibility and indiscriminate acceptance of false claims. I think it should also cut the other way: It would be excellent if the followers of Sri Aurobindo and anthroposophists would be open to an idea probably foreign to them, namely, that one of their teacher's ideas might be mistaken. A spiritual exercise for a passionately convinced student of Steiner would be to consider that there was no Atlantean civilization; that the choir at the nativity of Jesus were angels, not Buddha's subtle body; there weren't two Jesus children; souls and etheric bodies of one individual do not enter another individual; and there was no continuity between Elijah, John the Baptist, Raphael, and Novalis. While anthroposophists should regularly question all such ideas, after familiarity with Steiner's writings built up over decades some anthroposophists find it difficult to doubt Steiner's ideas, no matter how implausible they seem to non-anthroposophists.

The sixth exercise is simply stated yet difficult to do: it calls for one to harmonize all five of the previous exercises so that they will characterize one's thinking, feeling, and willing. This probably means returning to one or another of these exercises and starting over. It probably also means making some progress on one or another of the first five but losing track of one or more of the others. That's the bad news; the good news is that these exercises will have a slow but discernible effect on our behavior in unpredictable situations. He or she will be able to take a breath, slow down, be receptive, and check patterns of thinking, feeling, and willing. A person will react calmly when previously he or she would have had a meltdown.

Steiner recognized that the widespread inability to experience another's thinking, feeling, and willing is at the root of racial, gender, and generational misunderstandings and violence. In response, he offered disciplines by which to overcome the alienation afflicting modern Western thinking and culture. Steiner acknowledged a full range of evil, from a single fleeting thought or passing gesture all the way to the work of the tempters, Lucifer and Ahriman. He saw Buddha, Christ, the Archangel Michael, and the goddess Sophia deeply involved in these struggles for the fate of humanity—and at this time, also the fate of Earth, with which Christ has united His etheric body. I think it is exciting to observe Rudolf Steiner, researcher of the two Jesus children, Buddha in the sphere of Mars sacrificing himself for humanity, and other profound esoteric ideas, offering useful, simple, and challenging exercises, appropriate for beginners as well as practiced meditators.

The goal of Steiner's six exercises is to expand the flexibility of one's thinking sufficiently to think new thoughts and new kinds of thoughts, and to do so in a way that engages one's active imagination and will. Such a discipline, if practiced well, can also enable a practitioner to experience more directly the great events of the past, such as Moses's experience of Yahweh or Homer's experience of Athena, Plato's experience of the Forms, or Christ Jesus's experience of the Father, as well as defining breakthroughs of the recent past and present, such as Gandhi's *satyagraha*, the Dalai Lama's compassion, Thomas Berry's insights on the human–earth community, Joanna Macy's into the perils of nuclear waste, or Wangari Maathai's about the intimate relationship between trees, water, and democracy.

As a spiritual path that results in spiritual knowledge rather than mystical union or religious belief, the practice of Anthroposophy should lead to direct knowing, either in the form of

sensorial imagination, or formative, living thinking as opposed
to an abstract intellectual knowing. In such thinking one experiences, and then breaks through, the limit of ordinary, sensory-
based thinking. Steiner's followers typically separate Anthroposophy from both mysticism and religious belief. Yet, given
Steiner's intimate relationship with spirit and divinity, Anthroposophy is in some important sense mystical. And given that
some anthroposophists believe much of what Steiner reported,
for them Anthroposophy may look a lot like a set of religious
beliefs, though Steiner insisted that anthroposophic research
will lead to reliable knowledge, more than belief. Anthroposophists are invited to embrace freedom and love, not dependence
on Steiner's ideas. This term "belief" is complicated in that a
Christian could justifiably reply that religious belief is not a
set of blind loyalties but rather conviction informed by faith,
a general orientation that illumines experience. Teilhard de
Chardin is not an esoteric Christian, but neither are his Christian beliefs in the Trinity, Incarnation, or Resurrection "mere"
beliefs; they are the result of a life of prayer, meditation, study,
and insight, all supported by faith. Students of Rudolf Steiner
and Anthroposophy who dismiss religious belief as inferior to
Anthroposophy might in this respect be disingenuous, because
they typically believe a long list of Steiner's ideas on the basis
of faith in Rudolf Steiner.

Steiner's teaching and path invite all individuals to develop
the capacity for sense-free, will-filled, loving thinking. Anthroposophical thinking is non-ordinary thinking because it is
characterized by love; it is different from mystical experience
because it is characterized by will. Just as Sri Aurobindo wrote
that "all life is a secret yoga," and his Holiness the Dalai Lama
that "spiritual practice is an all-day commitment," Rudolf
Steiner encourages students of Anthroposophy to work toward
the transformation of all their thinking, feeling, and willing,
and to do so with reverence and humility, recognizing that
exalted beings continue to support their efforts. Steiner distinguishes between thinking as we ordinarily practice it—i.e.,
intellectual or brain-bound thinking—and what he calls living

thinking, which moves the thinking process from the head into the heart, and ultimately into the etheric body where one can directly participate in the reality of thought as living process. An example of such living thinking would be Goethe's perception of the archetypal plant, which Schiller referred to as an idea, prompting the response from Goethe, "Then I am seeing an idea."

By this mode of thinking one can deeply comprehend Krishna, Buddha, Christ, and Sophia with the potential to directly know them—though, presumably not so intimately as Steiner did. Similarly, the evolution of consciousness, three-part societal forms, Waldorf education, and spiritually based art can be comprehended anew by thinking that is suffused with heart and will. Two prerequisites for such thinking are reverence and humility, the two criteria that Steiner introduces in the first chapter of his important book *How to Know Higher Worlds*. Spiritual secrets are not disclosed to anyone who seeks them with an irreverent or arrogant attitude. In his chapter, "In Search of a Deeper Order," in *Cosmos and Psyche*, Richard Tarnas tells a parable of two suitors approaching "a deep-souled, subtly mysterious cosmos of great spiritual beauty and creative intelligence."[14] Is a mechanistic, flatland thinker likely to discern and receive the secrets of the universe, or would such secrets more likely be communicated to a person who consciously shares in the mystery and intelligence of the universe?

It is also important to keep in mind Steiner's philosophical argument in support of realism—and the need to experience ideas and spiritual beings as existentially *real*. They have names and should not be considered mere abstractions: They exist and are knowable through their natures and effects. It takes a concerted effort of consciousness—of thinking, feeling, and willing—to experience Krishna, Buddha, Christ, Sophia, Michael the Archangel as real beings actively influencing individuals, civilizations, and Earth. The same is true for virtues and ideals: In contemporary Western culture Platonic ideals—love, truth, beauty, and justice—are not treated as entities with substantive being, as

---

14. Richard Tarnas, "Two Suitors: A Parable," *Cosmos and Psyche*, 39–42.

existentially real. Contrary to Plato's conception, however, Steiner was convinced that ideals evolve. It is also essential to experience Lucifer and Ahriman as existentially real; they are beings with legions of followers working ultimately and indirectly to destroy humanity and Earth.

Because Steiner was convinced that the suffering of humanity was caused primarily by faulty worldviews, he dedicated his life to improving contemporary Western habits of thinking, and eradicating the illusory thoughts they produce. He sought to discover and communicate true ideas on many diverse subjects, including the individual; human nature and human culture; spirit and matter; the past, present, and future; and countless other significant topics. He urged his listeners and readers to give up passive, dead, or abstract thinking for affectionate, lively, and respectful thinking—very similar to the kind of thinking recommended by Goethe and Emerson. His proposal for a new kind of thinking is different from recommending mystical experience in that he warns against the kind of experience that is so unitive it loses relationality. Of all of the topics Steiner wished his audiences and readers to consider throughout life and to think on intuitively and meditatively, he especially recommended karma and rebirth.

In fidelity to the task given him by his Master to return the concepts of karma and rebirth to the Christian worldview, in the last year of his life Steiner gave more than eighty lectures on the working of karma in the lives of influential individuals. His account of rebirth and karma is non-mechanistic, esoterically subtle, and capable of changing a person's relationship toward life, death, and the afterlife, as well as one's relationship to those who have died. Steiner had the ability from childhood— which he consciously developed—to research and disclose the workings of karma in the former lives of many individuals, particularly those who exercised a significant influence on the course of human evolution, as well as those who played a prominent role in the anthroposophic movement.

In his book *Theosophy*, Steiner explains that sleep is an apt image for death because while one sleeps, events pursue their own course independently of one's conscious life. The human personality incarnates anew every morning in the world of action. During the middle hours of sleep, the "I" and the astral body return to the spiritual world. while leaving the physical and etheric bodies asleep. Since waking consciousness consists of the interaction between the astral and etheric bodies, the departure of the astral body to a separate state of being leaves the etheric body free to repair the damage to the physical body incurred during its daytime activities.

The biography of the sleeping self is important in another respect: After death, the sleep biography of each person is relived in reverse order to that of the person's earthly life. Steiner's account of this phenomenon, which reads like a fascinating blend of Dante's *Purgatorio*[15] and *The Tibetan Book of Living and Dying*, can best be grasped by recounting the sequence of events that constitute one's death. The death of the physical body is immediate and irremediable, but the etheric, astral, and spirit bodies survive the death of the physical body for various periods of time. The etheric body, which has recorded all of the experiences of one's lifetime, remains attached to the astral body for approximately three days in order to present, in a vast, instantaneous panorama, the entire life that has just ended. As is now well known as a result of the phenomenon that has been studied as "Near Death Experience," many individuals who have nearly died, for example by drowning or from heart attack, recount similar experiences of a life summary when restored to consciousness.[16]

Having absorbed the panoramic images of one's life from the etheric body, the astral body remains in existence for

---

15. The essential fact of the three levels of Dante's *Divine Comedy* (Inferno, Purgatorio, and Paradiso) is that each deceased person wants to be in the exact level or ring to which he or she has been assigned. This is also the case according to the *Tibetan Book of Living and Dying*.

16. The prominent, reliable first-wave exponents of Near Death Experience are Raymond Moody, Elizabeth Kubler-Ross, and Kenneth Ring. Subsequent to these volumes, see Robert Gottlieb, "To Heaven and Back," *The New York Review of Books*, Oct. 23, 2014; and ibid., "Back from Heaven: The Science," Nov. 6, 2014.

approximately one-third the duration of a person's lifetime. This is where sleep plays its significant and intriguing role. In this phase of the soul's history, the "I" passes through a period called *kamaloca* in which there are two major experiences. During the first, the astral body (soul), which contains one's desires and emotions, continues to seek the kinds of satisfaction it enjoyed on Earth, but to the extent that it continues to seek physical satisfaction, it can only be frustrated. By living through this frustration, one's astral body is gradually purified of the attachment to physical life and is eventually dissolved. It is worth wondering whether the Roman Catholic doctrine of purgatory, so vividly depicted in Dante's *Purgatorio*, might be a version of this same state of consciousness, enduring as long as the astral or soul body is involved in transmitting its experience to the immortal "I."

In the second *kamaloca* experience, the "I" relives its entire past life backwards—from death to birth. All of the deceased person's past actions are now reexperienced, but with a painfully appropriate karmic twist: at this point, the "I" experiences the consequences of its earthly actions as they were experienced by the recipients of those actions. Steiner describes this purgatorial experience in *Theosophy* as well as in one of his last works, *Anthroposophy and the Inner Life: An Esoteric Introduction*, which despite the title is quite advanced:

> We now see that, after a few days, we must begin to experience what we have left unexperienced; and this holds for every single deed we have done to other human beings in the world. The last deeds done before death are the first to come before us, and so backwards through life. We first become aware of what our last evil or good deeds signify for the world. Our experience of them while on earth is now eliminated; what we now experience is their significance for the world. And then we go farther back, experiencing our life again, but backwards. We know that while doing this we are still connected with the Earth, for it is only the other side of our deeds that we experience now.[17]

---

17. Rudolf Steiner, *Anthroposophy and the Inner Life*, 116–117.

In one of his dozens of lectures on karma and rebirth, Steiner refers to two of Ralph Waldo Emerson's previous lives, one as Tacitus, the Roman historian, and Mathilde, daughter of the Countess Beatrix, owner of the Castle of Canossa in the eleventh century.[18] Steiner explains that as a reincarnating spirit does not carry specific thoughts from one incarnation to another, it would be vain to look for continuity of ideas from Tacitus to Mathilde to Emerson, but in our attempt to grasp the mystery of a great thinker such as Emerson it would not be vain to contemplate a soul pattern, orientation, and proclivities, as well as what is new in such a personality. The following is an example of Steiner's research on rebirth, the more interesting because it involves Emerson:

> In the first century AD, about a hundred years after the founding of Christianity, we have an exceedingly significant Roman writer in the person of Tacitus. In all his work, and very particularly in his *Germanica*, Tacitus proves himself a master of a concise, clear-cut style; he arrays the facts of history and geographical details in wonderfully rounded sentences with a genuinely epigrammatic ring. We may also remember how he, a man of wide culture, who knew everything considered worth knowing at that time—a hundred years after the founding of Christianity—makes no more than a passing allusion to Christ, mentioning Him as someone whom the Jews crucified but saying that this was of no great importance. Yet in point of fact, Tacitus is one of the greatest Romans.[19]

Steiner does not say so but we might want to notice that Emerson, while deeply spiritual, spent his life trying to disengage from the influence of Christ and Christianity.

Steiner traced many multiple lives in a similar way, perhaps the most dramatic of which was the four incarnations known as Elijah (the Hebrew prophet), John the Baptist (the precursor of Christ), Raphael (the Italian Renaissance painter), and Novalis (the nineteenth-century scientist, philosopher, and poet). In

---

18. Rudolf Steiner, *Karmic Relationships*, II, 52–56.
19. Ibid., 51–52,

Rudolf Steiner's Core Mission: The Birth and Development of Spiritual-Scientific Karma Research, Thomas Meyer recounts many instances of Steiner's progressing from a seemingly ordinary perception to an extraordinary insight concerning his own previous lives or the previous lives of his colleagues. Steiner himself wrote the results of such instances in letters to Ita Wegman, M.D., probably his closest collaborator, and according to these letters, a person with whom he shared many previous lives. By a series of seemingly insignificant disclosures, perhaps best to be understood as synchronicities, Steiner came to understand that his two previous incarnations were as Aristotle and Thomas Aquinas. As we know from Steiner's mystery dramas, his four plays in which a group of individualities are reborn together in four successive periods of history,[20] significant souls are not reborn in isolation, but rather with a cluster of individuals who share a larger destiny.

One of the aims of karma research is to discern with whom one is karmically intended to work. These are the relationships by which a person is best able to hallow life and to heal past failures. By his conscientious karma research, over two decades until his death in 1925, Steiner located the two colleagues who worked with him in the thirteenth century, during his incarnation as the preeminent Catholic philosopher–theologian Thomas Aquinas. When Steiner and his wife Marie visited the sarcophagus of Albertus Magnus in Cologne where Albertus and his student Thomas had taught, Steiner referred to his wife as his former teacher—i.e., as Albertus Magnus. In the last decade of his life Thomas Aquinas had a cell mate who cared for him and who, along with Albertus, was the only person to know of Thomas's mystical visions at night. This remarkable young monk, Reginald of Pepino, according to Steiner was reborn as Ita Wegman, the physician who cared for Rudolf Steiner in his last year and served his mission faithfully until her death in 1943.

A reaction to Steiner's disclosures concerning previous lives of anthroposophists might reasonably be "How can Steiner know these past lives?" I tend to reply that as Steiner seems to be right,

---

20. Rudolf Steiner, *Four Mystery Plays.*

even amazingly right, on so many other topics, it is at least possible and worth considering—meditatively, intuitively—whether these, too, might turn out to be both right and important. Perhaps these disclosures might be worth holding, lightly, to see if in time they are proved to be a transformative insight into one of the great mysteries of human life.

In New Age subculture the idea of rebirth has been ill served by the embarrassing phenomenon of perfectly ordinary individuals who confidently announce their conviction that they have experienced their previous life, or lives, as royalty, as a world leader, or as a world-class artist. Because Steiner is so far from ordinary, his claim to have lived as Aristotle and Aquinas would seem to support the otherwise implausibility of his astonishing abilities and productivity: Like Aristotle and Aquinas, Steiner absorbed, reorganized, and advanced vast amounts of the knowledge of his time. One of the most forceful obstacles to approaching Steiner is precisely that he knew so much. As Owen Barfield asks rhetorically, "Why should anyone believe that someone could know so much?" Is it possible that this question would be easier to answer if Steiner had previously lived as Aristotle and Aquinas? Could there have been a better start to his task than to have been, successively, these two astonishing knowers—and, in the case of Aquinas, a genuinely holy person? As all of Steiner's capacities and accomplishments are beyond the usual credibility threshold, perhaps the idea of his having lived as Aristotle and Aquinas can be added to his many other implausible, yet possibly true, discoveries.

Steiner's spiritual insights and practical suggestions explain and work with all four parts of the human being. Specifically, he explains the relationship between the Universe and the human "I," the soul, the etheric, and the physical bodies. The weakening of the physical can be cured by strengthening the etheric, the principle that gives and sustains the life of plants, animals, and humans. The primary agency for the etheric is art, especially eurythmy, sculpture, pottery, and painting, but any rhythmic activity and sympathetic relationship with anything living will help to strengthen the etheric. The astral body (or human soul) is connected to the universe through sound; the wonders of music and artful speech help to activate the soul. It is also important to understand and work with one's temperaments—sanguine, choleric, phlegmatic, and melancholic—as a way of balancing one's relationship to all dimensions of the universe. At death, the soul communicates its life experience to the higher "I," the immortal self. A lifetime of experience is preserved in the "I," and returns to Earth for another lifetime, ideally to contribute more to the universe than one will take. The "I" is who I have been, am now, and will be, all by the mysterious mutual interpenetration of myself and the world. Paying close attention to one's multi-lived history is one of the disciplines that Steiner especially recommends for modern Western individuals.

According to Steiner, each human being comes to Earth to engage opportunities for transformation. In ancient times it was far more possible to know one's previous life or lives. Using Barfield's terminology, the loss of participation is the gradual distance between humanity, particularly modern Western humanity, from the divine realm, which includes exalted beings, spirit beings such as angels, and the realm of the dead. According to this picture, the human soul repeatedly journeys to Earth from the spiritual realm seeking experiences, especially thinking, feeling, and willing, that are possible only on Earth. Individuals, nowhere more so than in the modern West, have lost access to their previous lives as well as to the universe, but Steiner contends that it is possible to gain access if we pay attention. In a way quite similar to Jung's description of synchronicity, Steiner offers examples from his own life of times when he was able to glimpse a previous life. We might reasonably respond, "Yes, but that's Steiner." Exactly, but just because these glimpses are not frequent and not infallible should not lead us to denial or discouragement.

Steiner devoted many lectures on karma and rebirth to the process as he had learned of it, but his primary recommendation was for each person to practice paying attention, to come to know the intent of one's higher, essential self beginning at birth, or conception, or even earlier. Discerning the primary intent of one's life—what relationships, what career, what accomplishments, what capacities—is one of the most important parts of anthroposophic spiritual practice. Steiner gave countless examples of the karma of particular individuals over a series of lifetimes in order to encourage his followers to investigate their own multi-lives, and to do so with reverence and humility, without thinking mechanically.

Anyone who wishes to experience Steiner's compassion might want to turn to his verses and meditations. Consider, for example, the verse that he gave to Ralph Courtney in the 1920s for the Threefold Group in New York City. The group was trying to understand and implement to the extent possible Steiner's ideas on the ideal threefold organization of society. But notice that the verse Steiner composed for the group is all about feeling, hearts, striving, and love:

> May feelings penetrate into the center of our hearts
> And seek in love to unite itself with human beings of like goal,
> With spirit beings, full of grace, who, upon our earnest heart-
>   felt striving,
> Strengthening us from regions of light and making luminous
>   our love, are bestowing their attention. [tr. John Beck]

Never losing sight of the need to integrate all three disciplines, Steiner urged that the feelings in the center of our hearts should be permeated by free living thinking and free willing—as in the subtitle of Arthur Zajonc's beautiful book on meditation, "When Knowledge Becomes Love."

At Christmas 1923, Steiner reformed the Anthroposophical Society with himself at its head, not just as its teacher (which he had been since the first founding in 1912) but now responsible for its continuity. On each of the nights between Christmas and New Year's Day Steiner spoke a mantra called The Foundation Stone Meditation that affirmed the reality and asked for the blessing of the Ground of Being, the Logos, and the Spirit, and then in a fourth verse, entirely different from the first three, spoke of the Incarnation of Christ.

At the turning point of time,
The Spirit light of the World
Entered the stream of Earth evolution.
Darkness of night
Had held its sway;
Day-radiant Light
Poured into the souls of human beings:
Light that gave warmth
To simple shepherds' hearts,
Light that enlightened
The wise heads of kings.
O Light Divine!
O Sun of Christ!
Warm our hearts,
Enlighten our heads,
That good may become
What from our hearts we would found
And from our heads direct
With single purpose.[21]

Throughout the twenty-five years of his esoteric mission, Steiner in effect led anthroposophists to ask for the warm hearts of the shepherds that attended the nativity of the Jesus in the Luke gospel, and the wise heads of the magi who visited the nativity of the Jesus in the Matthew gospel, as well as to ask for well-informed wills to lead us to the nativity that is intended for all human hearts and minds. The Christ invoked in this verse transcends Christianity, is cosmic and global, in fact surrounding the Earth, and possibly now burning with the Earth as chemicals have burned the Ganges and Yumna rivers. We know from Steiner's other lectures and verses that his experience of the reality of Christ includes Sophia.

Steiner's vision of Christ includes the yogas of Krishna and the compassion of Buddha. It includes Christ's initiation of Lazarus/John, His crucifixion and resurrection, and His appearance as an etheric body to Mary Magdalen who had etheric eyes to see Him. It includes the history of the West and Christianity, of

---

21. In Rudolf Steiner, *The Christmas Conference* (tr. George Adams), 291.

forces working for and against the evolution of humanity and Earth. Finally, Steiner's vision includes a plea that those of us with ears to hear and eyes to see join in the effort to express through our lives the aspiration of the divine, particularly the love raying out from the incarnate Christ, the inspiration raying from the Holy Spirit, the compassion exuded by Sophia, and the tireless effort of various angelic beings committed to the inherent possibilities of this present time.

Works Cited and Recommended

Allen, Paul Marshall, and Joan DeRis Allen, *The Time Is at Hand! The Rosicrucian Nature of Goethe's Fairy Tale of the Green Snake and the Beautiful Lily and the Mystery Dramas of Rudolf Steiner*. Great Barrington, MA: Anthroposophic Press, 1995.

Anonymous. *Meditations on the Tarot: A Journey into Christian Hermeticism*. Tr. Robert Powell. New York: Jeremy P. Tarcher / Putnam, 1985.

Ashe, Geoffrey. *Atlantis: Lost Lands, Ancient Wisdom*. London: Thames and Hudson, 1992.

Aurobindo. *Bhagavad Gita and Its Message*. Ed. Anilbaran Roy. Twin Lakes, WI: Lotus Press, 1995.

———. *Essays on the Gita*. Puducherry, India: Sri Aurobindo Ashram, 1972.

———. *The Future Poetry and Letters on Poetry, Literature and Art*. Puducherry, India: Sri Aurobindo Ashram, 1972.

———. *The Problem of Rebirth*. Puducherry, India: Sri Aurobindo Ashram, 1999.

Bache, Christopher M. *The Living Classroom: Teaching and Collective Consciousness*. Albany, NY: State University of New York Press, 2008.

Bamford, Christopher. *An Endless Trace: The Passionate Pursuit of Wisdom in the West*. New Paltz, NY: Codhill Press, 2003.

Banerji, Debashish. *Seven Quartets of Becoming: A Transformative Yoga Psychology Based on the Diaries of Sri Aurobindo*. Los Angeles: Nalanda, 2012.

Barfield, Owen. "Introducing Rudolf Steiner." In Robert McDermott, ed. *The New Essential Steiner: An Introduction to Rudolf Steiner for the 21st Century*. Great Barrington, MA: Lindisfarne Books, 2009.

———. *Romanticism Comes of Age*. London: Rudolf Steiner Press, 1966.

———. *Saving the Appearances: A Study in Idolatry*. London: Faber and Faber, 1957.

———. *Unancestral Voice*. Middletown, CT: Wesleyan University Press, 1965.

Baring, Anne, and Jules Cashford, *The Myth of the Goddess: Evolution of an Image*. New York: Arkana / Penguin Books, 1991.

Barnes, Henry. *A Life for the Spirit: Rudolf Steiner in the Crosscurrents of Our Time*. Hudson, NY: Anthroposophic Press, 1997.

Being Human. A quarterly publication edited by John Beck. Anthroposophical Society in America.

Bergson, Henri. *Creative Evolution.* Tr. Arthur Mitchell. New York: Random House, 1944.

———. *The Two Sources of Morality and Religion.* Tr. R. Ashley Audra and Cloudesley Brereton. Garden City, NY: Doubleday Anchor, 1935.

Berry, Thomas. *The Christian Future and the Fate of the Earth.* Ed. Mary Evelyn Tucker and John Grim. Maryknoll, NY: Orbis Books, 2009.

———. *The Dream of the Earth.* San Francisco: Sierra Club, 1988.

———. *Evening Thoughts: Reflecting on Earth as a Sacred Community.* Ed. Mary Evelyn Tucker. San Francisco: Sierra Club, 2006.

———. *The Great Work: Our Way into the Future.* New York: Bell Tower, 1999.

———. *The Sacred Universe: Earth Spirituality, and Religion in the Twenty-first Century.* Ed. Mary Evelyn Tucker. New York: Columbia University Press, 2009.

———. *Thomas Berry: Selected Writings on the Earth Community.* Eds. M. E. Tucker and J. Grim. Maryknoll, NY: Orbis, 2014.

Blofeld, John. *Bodhisattva of Compassion: The Mystical Tradition of Kuan Yin.* Boston: Shambhala, 1988.

Bock, Emil. *The Life and Times of Rudolf Steiner. Vol. 1: People and Places.* Edinburgh: Floris Books, 2008.

Bonhoeffer, Dietrich. *London, 1933–1935.* Dietrich Bonhoeffer Works, vol. 13. Ed. Keith Clements. Minneapolis, MN: Fortress Press, 2007.

Brady, Ronald. "Goethe's Natural Science: Some Non-Cartesian Meditations," in Karl Schaefer *et. al., A New Image of Man in Men: Toward a Man-Centered Medical Science.* Vol. 1. Leander, TX: Futura, 1977.

Buber, Martin. *Between Man and Man.* New York: Macmillan, 1947.

———. *Hasidism and Modern Man.* Edited and translated by Maurice Friedman. New York: Horizon Press, 1958.

———. *I and Thou.* Tr. Walter Kaufman. New York: Charles Scribner's Sons, 1970.

———. *Israel and the World: Essays in a Time of Crisis.* New York: Schocken Books, 1963.

———. *The Knowledge of Man: A Philosophy of the Interhuman.* Ed. Maurice Friedman. Tr. Maurice Friedman and Ronald Gregor Smith. New York: Harper Torchbooks, 1965.

————. *Pointing the Way: Collected Essays.* Ed. and tr. Maurice Friedman. New York: Schocken Books, 1957.

————. *The Prophetic Faith.* Tr. Carlyle Witton-Davies. New York: Harper Torchbooks, 1949.

Bulgakov, Sergei. *Sophia the Wisdom of God: An Outline of Sophiology.* Tr. Patrick Thompson, O. Fielding Clarke, and Xenia Braikevitc. 1937. Rev. ed., Hudson, NY: Lindisfarne Press, 1993.

Campbell, James, and Richard E. Hart, eds. *Experience as Philosophy: On the Work of John J. McDermott.* New York: Fordham University Press, 2006.

Capel, Evelyn. *Seven Sacraments in The Christian Community.* Ed. Tom Ravetz. Edinburgh: Floris Books, 1999.

Carroll, James. *Constantine's Sword: The Church and the Jews, a History.* Boston: Houghton Mifflin, 2001.

Carson, Clayborne, ed. *The Autobiography of Martin Luther King, Jr.* New York: Warner Books, 1998.

Center for Ecozoic Studies. *The Ecozoic: Reflections on Life in an Ecological Age: A Tribute to Thomas Berry* (No. 2). Chapel Hill, NC: Center for Ecozoic Studies, 2009.

Chakravarty, Amiya, ed. *A Tagore Reader.* Boston: Beacon Press, 1961.

Chaudhuri, Haridas. *Sri Aurobindo: Prophet of Life Divine.* 1951. San Francisco: Cultural Integration Fellowship, 1973.

Chaudhuri, Haridas, and Robert McDermott, eds. *International Philosophical Quarterly.* Vol. XII, No. 2: Special Centenary Symposium on the Thought of Sri Aurobindo (1872-1950). New York: Fordham University Press, June 1972.

Combs, Allan. *The Radiance of Being: Complexity, Chaos, and the Evolution of Consciousness.* Edinburgh: Floris Books, 1995.

Cousins, Ewert. *Christ of the 21st Century.* New York: Continuum, 1998.

Cranston, Sylvia. *H.P.B: The Extraordinary Life and Influence of Helena Blavatsky, Founder of the Modern Theosophical Movement.* New York: Tarcher, 1993.

Crockett, William R. *Eucharist: Symbol of Transformation.* New York: Pueblo Publishing, 1989.

Dalai Lama. *The Flash of Lightning in the Dark of Night: A Guide to the Bodhisattva's Way of Life.* Boston: Shambhala, 1994.

————. *The Good Heart: A Buddhist Perspective on the Teachings of Jesus.* Ed. Robert Kiely. Tr. Geshe Thupten Jinpa. Boston: Wisdom Publications, 1996.

———. *Practicing Wisdom: The Perfection of Shantideva's Bodhisattva Way.* Tr. and ed. Geshe Thupten Jinpa. Boston: Wisdom, 2005.

Day, Dorothy. *The Long Loneliness: An Autobiography.* New York: Harper and Row, 1952.

Debus, Michael. *Mary and Sophia: The Feminine Element in the Spiritual Evolution of Humanity.* Edinburgh: Floris Books, 2013.

Delio, Ilia. *Christ in Evolution.* Maryknoll, NY: Orbis Books, 2008.

Delio, Ilia, ed. *From Teilhard to Omega: Co-Creating an Unfinished Universe.* Maryknoll, NY: Orbis Books, 2014.

Dewey, John. *A Common Faith.* New Haven, CT: Yale University Press, 1960.

———. *Democracy and Education.* New York: Macmillan Co., 1961.

Dunne, Claire. *Carl Jung: Wounded Healer of the Soul.* London: Watkins Publishing, 2012.

Dutta, Krishna, and Andrew Robinson. *Rabindranath Tagore: The Myriad-Minded Man.* 1995.

Dutta, Krishna, and Andrew Robinson, eds. *Rabindranath Tagore: An Anthology.* New York: St. Martin's Press, 1997.

Easton, Stewart C. *The Evolution of Human Thinking from Aristotle to Rudolf Steiner.* Private printing.

———. *Man and World in the Light of Anthroposophy.* Spring Valley, NY: Anthroposophic Press, 1975.

Elgin, Duane. *The Living Universe: Where Are We? Who Are We? Where Are We Going?* San Francisco: Berrett-Koehler Publishers, 2009.

Emerson, Ralph Waldo. *The Works of Ralph Waldo Emerson: Four Volumes in One.* New York: Tudor Publishing Co., n.d.

Fabel, Arthur, and Donald St. John, eds., *Teilhard in the 21st Century: The Emerging Spirit of Earth.* Maryknoll, NY: Orbis Books, 2004.

Fischer, Louis, ed. *The Essential Ghandi: An Anthology of His Writings on His Life, Work, and Ideas.* New York: Vintage Books, 1962.

Gardner, John. *The Poverty of a Rich Society.* Great Barrington, MA: Myrin Institute, 1976.

Glatzer, Nahum N., and Paul Mendes-Flohr, eds. *The Letters of Martin Buber: A Life of Dialogue.* Tr. Richard and Clara Winston and Harry Zohn. New York: Schocken Books, 1991.

Goethe, Johann Wolfgang von. *The Green Snake and the Beautiful Lily: A Fairy Tale.* Tr. Julius E. Heuscher. IL. Hermann Linde. Great Barrington, MA: SteinerBooks, 2006.

Gore, Al. *An Inconvenient Truth: The Planetary Emergency of Global Warming and What We Can Do About It.* Emmaus, PA: Rodale, 2006.

Grim, John, and Mary Evelyn Tucker. *Ecology and Religion.* Washington, DC: Island Press, 2014.

Grof, Stanislav. *When the Impossible Happens: Adventures in Non-Ordinary Realities.* Boulder, CO: Sounds True, 2006.

Harrison, Vernon. *H. P. Blavatsky and the SPR: An Examination of the Hodgson Report of 1885.* Pasadena, CA: Theosophical University Press, 1997.

Hawken, Paul. *Blessed Unrest: How the Largest Movement in the World Came into Being and Why No One Saw It Coming.* New York: Viking, 2007.

Heehs, Peter. *The Lives of Sri Aurobindo.* New York: Columbia University Press, 2008.

Heehs, Peter, ed. *Situating Sri Aurobindo: A Reader.* Oxford: Oxford University Press, 2013.

Hegel, G. W. F. *Reason in History: A General Introduction to the Philosophy of History.* Translated by Robert S. Hartman. Indianapolis, NY: Bobbs-Merrill, 1953.

Herberg, Will, ed. *The Writings of Martin Buber.* New York: Meridian, 1956.

Hillman, James. *The Soul's Code: In Search of Character and Calling.* New York: Warner Books, 1996.

Howard, Michael, ed. *Art as Spiritual Activity: Rudolf Steiner's Contribution to the Visual Arts.* Hudson, NY: Anthroposophic Press, 1998.

Hughes, Gertrude Reif. *Emerson's Demanding Optimism.* Baton Rouge: Louisiana State University Press, 1984.

———. *More Radiant than the Sun: A Handbook for Working with Steiner's Meditations and Exercises.* Great Barrington, MA: SteinerBooks, 2013.

James, William. *Essays in Psychical Research.* Ed. Frederick Burkhardt and Fredson Bowers. Cambridge, MA: Harvard University Press, 1986.

———. *The Varieties of Religious Experience.* Cambridge, MA: Harvard University Press, 1985.

Jaspers, Karl. *The Origin and Goal of History.* Tr. Michael Bullock. New Haven, CT: Yale University Press, 1953.

Johnson, Elizabeth A. *She Who Is: The Mystery of God in Feminist Theological Discourse.* New York: Crossroad Publishing, 1992.

Jung, Carl. *Memories, Dreams, Reflections.* Ed. Aniela Jaffe. Tr. Richard and Clara Winston. New York: Pantheon, 1963.

————. *Psychology and Religion: West and East.* Tr. R. F. C. Hull. Vol. 11, *The Collected Works of C.G. Jung.* New York: Pantheon, 1958.

Keepin, William. *Divine Duality: The Power of Reconciliation Between Women and Men.* Prescott, AZ: Hohm Press, 2007.

Kelly, Sean. *Coming Home: The Birth and Transformation of the Planetary Era.* Great Barrington, MA: Lindisfarne Books, 2010.

————. *Individuation and the Absolute: Hegel, Jung, and the Path Toward Wholeness.* New York: Paulist Press, 1993.

King, Ursula. *Christ in All Things: Exploring Spirituality with Teilhard de Chardin.* London: SCM Press, 1997.

————. *The Search for Spirituality: Our Global Quest for a Spiritual Life.* New York: Bluebridge, 2008.

————. *Teilhard de Chardin and Eastern Religions: Spirituality and Mysticism in an Evolutionary World.* New York: Paulist Press, 2011.

Kolbert, Elizabeth. *Field Notes from a Catastrophe: Man, Nature, and Climate Change.* New York: Bloomsbury, 2006.

————. *The Sixth Extinction: An Unnatural History.* New York: Henry Holt, 2014.

Kramer, Rita. *Maria Montessori.* New York: G. P. Putnam's Sons, 1976.

Lachman, Gary. *Revolutionaries of the Soul: Reflections on Magicians, Philosophers, and Occultists.* Wheaton, IL: Quest, 2014.

Laszlo, Ervin. *Science and the Akashic Field: An Integral Theory of Everything.* Rochester, VT: Inner Traditions, 2004.

Lelyveld, Joseph. *Great Soul: Mahatma Gandhi and His Struggle with India.* New York: Knopf, 2011.

Lievegoed, Bernard. *Battle for the Soul.* Stroud, Gloucestershire, UK: Hawthorn Press, 1996.

Lindenberg, Christoph. *Rudolf Steiner: A Biography.* Great Barrington, MA: SteinerBooks, 2012.

Lovel, Hugh. *A Biodynamic Farm: For Growing Wholesome Food.* Austin, TX: Acres U.S.A, 2000.

Macy, Joanna. *Widening Circles: A Memoir.* Gabriola Island, BC, Canada: New Society Publishers, 2000.

————. *World as Lover, World as Self.* Berkeley, CA: Parallax Press, 1991.

Macy, Joanna, and Chris Johnstone. *Active Hope: How to Face the Mess We're in Without Going Crazy.* Novato, CA: New World Library, 2012.

McDermott, John J. *The Drama of Possibility: Experience as Philosophy of Culture.* Ed. Douglas R. Anderson. New York: Fordham University Press, 2007.

McDermott, John J., ed. *The Basic Writings of Josiah Royce.* 2 vols. Chicago: University of Chicago Press, 1969.

———. *The Philosophy of John Dewey: The Lived Experience.* 2 vols. New York: Capricorn Books, 1973.

———. *The Writings of William James.* New York: Random House, 1967.

McDermott, Robert. "Wisdom in Western Philosophy." In *The World's Great Wisdom: Timeless Teachings from Religions and Philosophies.* Ed. Roger Walsh. Albany, NY: SUNY, 2014.

McDermott, Robert, ed. *American Philosophy and Rudolf Steiner.* Great Barrington, MA: Lindisfarne Books, 2012.

———. *The Essential Aurobindo.* Great Barrington, MA: Lindisfarne Press, 1987.

———. *The New Essential Steiner.* Great Barrington, MA: SteinerBooks, 2009.

———. *Six Pillars: Introductions to the Works of Sri Aurobindo.* Great Barrington, MA: Lindisfarne Books, 2012.

———. and V.S. Naravane, eds. *The Spirit of Modern India: Writings in Philosophy, Religion, and Culture.* Great Barrington, MA: Lindisfarne Books, 2010.

McGuire, William, ed. *The Freud/Jung Letters: The Correspondence Between Sigmund Freud and C.G. Jung.* Tr. Ralph Manheim and R. F. C. Hull. Princeton: Princeton University Press, 1974.

McKibben, Bill, ed. *American Earth: Environmental Writing Since Thoreau.* New York: Library of America, 2008.

Mead, G.R.S. *Fragments of a Faith Forgotten: A Contribution to the Study of the Origins of Christianity.* New Hyde Park, NY: University Books, 1960.

Merchant, Carolyn. *The Death of Nature: Women, Ecology, and the Scientific Revolution.* San Francisco: HarperSanFrancisco, 1980.

Meyer, T. H. *Rudolf Steiner's Core Mission: The Birth and Development of Spiritual-Scientific Karma Research.* London: Temple Lodge, 2010.

Miller, William D. *A Harsh and Dreadful Love: Dorothy Day and the Catholic Worker Movement.* New York: Liveright, 1973.

Montessori, Maria. *The Discovery of the Child.* Tr. Mary A. Johnstone. Thiruvanmiyur, India: Kalakshetra Publications, 1966.

Mullin, Glen H. *The Fourteen Dalai Lamas: A Sacred Legacy of Reincarnation*. Santa Fe, NM: Clear Light, 2001.

Musil, Robert K. *Rachel Carson and Her Sisters: Extraordinary Women Who Have Shaped America's Environment*. New Brunswick, NJ: Rutgers University Press, 2014.

Nagel, Thomas. *Mind and Cosmos: Why the Materialist Neo-Darwinian Conception of Nature Is Almost Certainly False*. Oxford: Oxford University Press, 2012.

Naravane, V.S. *Modern Indian Thought: A Philosophical Survey*. Bombay, India: Asia Publishing House, 1964.

Neumann, Erich. *The Great Mother: An Analysis of the Archetype*. Tr. Ralph Manheim. Princeton: Princeton University Press, 1963.

———. *The Origins and History of Consciousness*. Translated by R. F. C. Hull. Princeton: Princeton University Press, 1954.

Otto, Rudolf. *The Idea of the Holy: An Inquiry into the Non-Rational Factor in the Idea of the Divine and Its Relation to the Rational*. Tr. John W. Harvey. New York: Oxford University Press, 1958.

Piburn, Sidney, ed. *The Nobel Peace Prize and the Dalai Lama*. Ithaca, NY: Snow Lion, 1990.

Pramuk, Christopher. *Sophia: The Hidden Christ of Thomas Merton*. Collegeville, MN: Liturgical Press, 2009.

Prokofieff, Sergei O. *The Heavenly Sophia and the Being Anthroposophia*. Tr. Simon Blaxland-de-Lange. London: Temple Lodge, 1996.

———. *The Occult Significance of Forgiveness*. Tr. Simon Blaxland-de-Lange. London: Temple Lodge, 1991.

———. *Rudolf Steiner and the Founding of the New Mysteries*. Tr. Paul King. London: Temple Lodge, 1994.

Ramakrishna. *The Gospel of Sri Ramakrishna*. New York: Ramakrishna-Vivekananda Center, 2000.

Rambusch, Nancy McCormick. *Learning How to Learn: An American Approach to Montessori*. Santa Rosa, CA: Parent Child Press, 1962.

Randall, Jr., John Herman. *The Role of Knowledge in Western Religion*. Boston: Beacon Press, 1958.

Royce, Josiah. *The Sources of Religious Insight*. New York: Octagon Books, 1977.

Schilpp, Paul Arthur, and Maurice Friedman, eds., *The Philosophy of Martin Buber*. La Salle, IL: Open Court Publishing Co., 1967.

Schipflinger, Thomas. *Sophia-Maria: A Holistic Vision of Creation*. Tr. James Morgante. York Beach, ME: Samuel Weiser, 1998.

Sherman, Jacob Holsinger. *Partakers of the Divine: Contemplation and the Practice of Philosophy*. Minneapolis, MN: Fortress Press, 2014.

Spretnak, Charlene. *Missing Mary: The Queen of Heaven and Her Re-Emergence in the Modern Church*. New York: Palgrave Macmilan, 2004.

Standing, E. M. *Maria Montessori: Her Life and Work*. New York: New American Library, 1962.

Stedall, Jonathan. *Where on Earth is Heaven?* Stroud, Gloucestershire, UK: Hawthorn Press, 2009.

Steiner, Rudolf. *According to Luke: The Gospel of Compassion and Love Revealed*. Ed. Robert McDermott. Tr. Catherine E. Creeger. Great Barrington, MA: Anthroposophic Press, 2001.

———. *Anthroposophical Leading Thoughts: Anthroposophy as a Path of Knowledge: The Michael Mystery*. London: Rudolf Steiner Press, 1973.

———. *Anthroposophy and the Inner Life: An Esoteric Introduction*. Ed. Owen Barfield. London: Rudolf Steiner Press, 1994.

———. *Anthroposophy in the Light of Goethe's Faust: Writings and Lectures from mid-1880s to 1916*. Tr. Burley Channer. Great Barrington, MA: SteinerBooks, 2014.

———. *The Archangel Michael: His Mission and Ours*. Ed. Christopher Bamford. Hudson, NY: Anthroposophic Press, 1994.

———. *At Home in the Universe: Exploring Our Suprasensory Nature*. Tr. H. Collison. Hudson, NY: Anthroposophic Press, 2000.

———. *Atlantis: The Fate of a Lost Land and Its Secret Knowledge*. Ed. Andrew Welburn. London: Sophia Books, 2001.

———. *Autobiography: Chapters in the Course of My Life, 1861-1907*. Tr. Rita Stebbing. Great Barrington, MA: SteinerBooks, 2006.

———. *Bees*. Tr. Thomas Braatz. Hudson, NY: Anthroposophic Press, 1998.

———. *The Bhagavad Gita and the West: The Esoteric Significance of the Bhagavad Gita and Its Relation to the Epistles of Paul*. Ed. Robert McDermott. Great Barrington, MA: SteinerBooks, 2009.

———. *The Boundaries of Natural Science*. Spring Valley, NY: Anthroposophic Press, 1983.

———. *The Challenge of the Times*. Spring Valley, NY: The Anthroposophic Press, 1941.

———. *Christianity as Mystical Fact*. Tr. Andrew Welburn. Hudson, NY: Anthroposophic Press, 1997.

——. *The Christmas Conference: For the Foundation of the General Anthroposophical Society 1923/1924.* Tr. Johanna Collis. Hudson, NY: Anthroposophic Press, 1990.

——. *Cosmic Memory: Prehistory of Earth and Man.* Tr. Karl E. Zimmer. Englewood, NJ: Rudolf Steiner Publications, 1959.

——. *Esoteric Christianity and The Mission of Christian Rosenkreutz.* Tr. Pauline Wehrle. London: Rudolf Steiner Press, 1984.

——. *Evil: Selected Lectures.* Tr. Matthew Barton. London: Rudolf Steiner Press, 1997.

——. *First Steps in Christian Religious Renewal: Preparing the Ground for the Christian Community.* Great Barrington, MA: SteinerBooks, 2010.

——. *The Foundation Stone Meditation.* London: Rudolf Steiner Press, 2005.

——. *The Foundations of Human Experience.* Tr. Robert F. Lathe and Nancy Parsons Whittaker (previous translation *Study of Man*). Hudson, NY: Anthroposophic Press, 1996.

——. *Four Mystery Dramas,* 2nd ed. Tr. Ruth and Hans Pusch. Great Barrington, MA: SteinerBooks, 2014.

——. *Freedom of Thought and Societal Forces: Implementing the Demands of Modern Society.* Tr. Catherine E. Creeger. Great Barrington, MA: SteinerBooks, 2008.

——. *Freud, Jung, and Spiritual Psychology.* Tr. May Laird-Brown. Great Barrington, MA: Anthroposophic Press, 2001.

——. *Friedrich Nietzsche: Fighter for Freedom.* Tr. Margaret Ingram deRis. Blauvelt, NY: Spiritual Science Library, 1985.

——. *From Buddha to Christ.* Revised by Gilbert Church. Spring Valley, NY: Anthroposophic Press, 1978.

——. *From the History and Contents of the First Section of the Esoteric School 1904–1914: Letters, Documents, and Lectures.* Ed. Hella Wiesberger. Tr. John Wood. Great Barrington, MA: SteinerBooks, 2009.

——. *The Gospel of St. John.* Tr. Maud B. Monges. Spring Valley, NY: Anthroposophic Press, 1962.

——. *How to Know Higher Worlds: A Modern Path of Initiation.* Tr. Christopher Bamford. Hudson, NY: Anthroposophic Press, 1994.

——. *Intuitive Thinking as a Spiritual Path: A Philosophy of Freedom.* Tr. Michael Lipson. Hudson, NY: Anthroposophic Press, 1995.

——. *Isis Mary Sophia: Her Mission and Ours.* Ed. Christopher Bamford. Great Barrington, MA: SteinerBooks, 2003.

———. *Karmic Relationships: Esoteric Studies.* 8 vols. Tr. George Adams. London: Rudolf Steiner Press, 1974.

———. *An Outline of Esoteric Science.* Tr. Catherine E. Creeger. Hudson, NY: Anthroposophic Press, 1997.

———. *Practical Advice to Teachers.* Tr. Johanna Collis. London: Rudolf Steiner Press, 1976.

———. *A Psychology of Body, Soul & Spirit: Anthroposophy, Psychosophy, Pneumatosophy.* Hudson, NY: Anthroposophic Press, 1999.

———. *Religion: An Introductory Reader.* Tr. rev. Matthew Barton. Ed. Andrew Welburn. London: Rudolf Steiner Press, 2003.

———. *Rosicrucianism Renewed: The Unity of Art, Science, and Religion.* Tr. Marsha Post. Great Barrington, MA: SteinerBooks, 2007.

———. *The Secret Stream: Christian Rosenkreutz and Rosicrucianism.* Ed. Christopher Bamford. Great Barrington, MA: Anthroposophic Press, 2000.

———. *The Spiritual Foundation of Morality: Francis of Assisi and the Christ Impulse.* Tr. Malcolm Gardner. Hudson, NY: Anthroposophic Press, 1995.

———. *The Spiritual Guidance of the Individual and Humanity: Some Results of Spiritual-Scientific Research into Human History and Development.* Tr. Samuel Desch. Hudson, NY: Anthroposophic Press, 1992.

———. *Spiritualism, Madame Blavatsky, and Theosophy: An Eyewitness View of Occult History.* Ed. Christopher Bamford. Great Barrington, MA: Anthroposophic Press, 2001.

———. *Start Now! A Book of Soul and Spiritual Exercises.* Ed. Christopher Bamford. Great Barrington, MA: SteinerBooks, 2004.

———. *Staying Connected: How to Continue Your Relationships with Those Who Have Died.* Ed. Christopher Bamford. Great Barrington, MA: Anthroposophic Press, 1999.

———. *Theosophy: An Introduction to the Spiritual Processes in Human Life and in the Cosmos.* Tr. Catherine E. Creeger. Hudson, NY: Anthroposophic Press, 1994.

———. *Towards Social Renewal: Rethinking the Basis of Society.* London: Rudolf Steiner Press, 1994.

———. *Truth and Knowledge: Introduction to "Philosophy of Spiritual Activity."* Tr. Rita Stebbing. Blauvelt, NY: SteinerBooks, 1981.

———. *A Western Approach to Reincarnation and Karma: Selected Lectures and Writings.* Ed. René Querido. Hudson, NY: Anthroposophic Press, 1997.

———. *World Economy: The Formation of a Science of World Economics.* London: Rudolf Steiner Press, 1972.

Swimme, Brian, and Mary Evelyn Tucker. *Journey of the Universe.* New Haven, CT: Yale University Press, 2011.

Swimme, Brian, and Thomas Berry. *The Universe Story: From the Primordial Flaring Forth to the Ecozoic Era—A Celebration of the Unfolding of the Cosmos.* San Francisco: HarperSanFrancisco, 1992.

Tagore, Rabindranath. *Personality: Lectures Delivered in America.* London: Macmillan, 1921.

———. *The Religion of Man.* Boston: Beacon Press, 1930.

Tarnas, Richard. *Cosmos and Psyche: Intimations of a New Worldview.* New York: Viking, 2006.

———. *The Passion of the Western Mind: Understanding the Ideas that Have Shaped Our Worldview.* New York: Harmony Books, 1991.

Teilhard de Chardin, Pierre. *Christianity and Evolution.* Tr. René Hague. New York: Harcourt Brace and Co., 1969.

———. *The Heart of Matter.* Tr. René Hague. New York: Harcourt Brace, 1976.

———. *The Human Phenomenon.* Tr. Sarah Appleton-Weber. East Sussex: Sussex Academic, 2003.

———. *The Phenomenon of Man.* Tr. Bernard Wall. New York: Harper Torchbooks, 1959.

———. *Science and Christ.* Tr. René Hague. New York: Harper and Row, 1965.

———. *Writings in Time of War.* Tr. René Hague. New York: Harper and Row, 1968.

Tomberg, Valentin. *Christ and Sophia: Anthroposophic Meditations on the Old Testament, New Testament, and Apocalypse.* Great Barrington, MA: SteinerBooks, 2006.

———. *The Four Sacrifices of Christ and the Appearance of Christ in the Etheric.* Spring Valley, NY: Candeur Manuscripts, 1983.

Trostli, Roberto, ed. *Rhythms of Learning: What Waldorf Education Offers Children, Parents, and Teacher—Selected Lectures by Rudolf Steiner.* Hudson, NY: Anthroposophic Press, 1998.

Tutu, Desmond. *No Future without Forgiveness.* New York: Doubleday, 1999.

Van Cromphout, Gustaaf. *Emerson's Modernity and the Example of Goethe.* Columbia, MO: University of Missouri Press, 1990.

Varenne, Herve, and Ray McDermott. *Successful Failure: The School America Builds*. Boulder, CO: Westview Press, 1998.

Walsh, Roger. *Essential Spirituality: The Seven Central Practices to Awaken Heart and Mind*. New York: John Wiley and Sons, 1999.

Washington, James M., ed. *A Testament of Hope: The Essential Writings and Speeches of Martin Luther King., Jr.* San Francisco: HarperSanFrancisco, 1986.

Wehr, Demaris S. *Jung and Feminism*. Boston: Beacon Press, 1987.

Wehr, Gerhard. *Jung: A Biography*. Tr. David M. Weeks. Boston: Shambhala, 1987.

———. *Jung and Steiner: The Birth of a New Psychology*. Tr. Magdalene Jaeckel. Great Barrington, MA: Anthroposophic Press, 2002.

Wilbur, Ken. *Sex, Ecology, Spirituality: The Spirit of Evolution*. Boston: Shambhala, 1995.

Zajonc, Arthur. *Catching the Light: The Entwined History of Light and Mind*. Oxford: Oxford University Press, 1993.

INDEX OF INDIVIDUALS AND CONCEPTS

Topics treated throughout an entire chapter are not listed